Reveal Your Detroit

Bradford Frost

Reveal Your Detroit

AN INTIMATE LOOK AT A GREAT AMERICAN CITY

A Community Engagement Project Led by the Detroit Institute of Arts

DETROIT

Manufactured in Canada.

17 16 15 14 13 5 4 3 2 1

Library of Congress Cataloging-in-Publication Data

Reveal your Detroit : an intimate look at a great American city / [compiled by] Bradford Frost ;
a community engagement project led by the Detroit Institute of Arts.
pages cm
ISBN 978-0-8143-3963-3 (pbk. : alk. paper)—ISBN 978-0-8143-3964-0 (ebook)
1. Detroit (Mich.)—Pictorial works. 2. Photography—Michigan—Detroit—Exhibitions.
3. Photography—Michigan—Detroit—Catalogs. I. Frost, Bradford, editor. II. Detroit Institute of Arts, sponsoring body.

F574.D42R48 2013
977.4'34—dc23

2013006171

Designed and typeset by Somberg Design, Ann Arbor, Michigan
Composed in Rockwell Standard Light, Rockwell Regular, Rockwell Bold and Sabon Italic

TO DANA

My Detroit wasn't complete until you joined the picture

TO DETROITERS EVERYWHERE

However you frame it, we'll only rise together

Contents

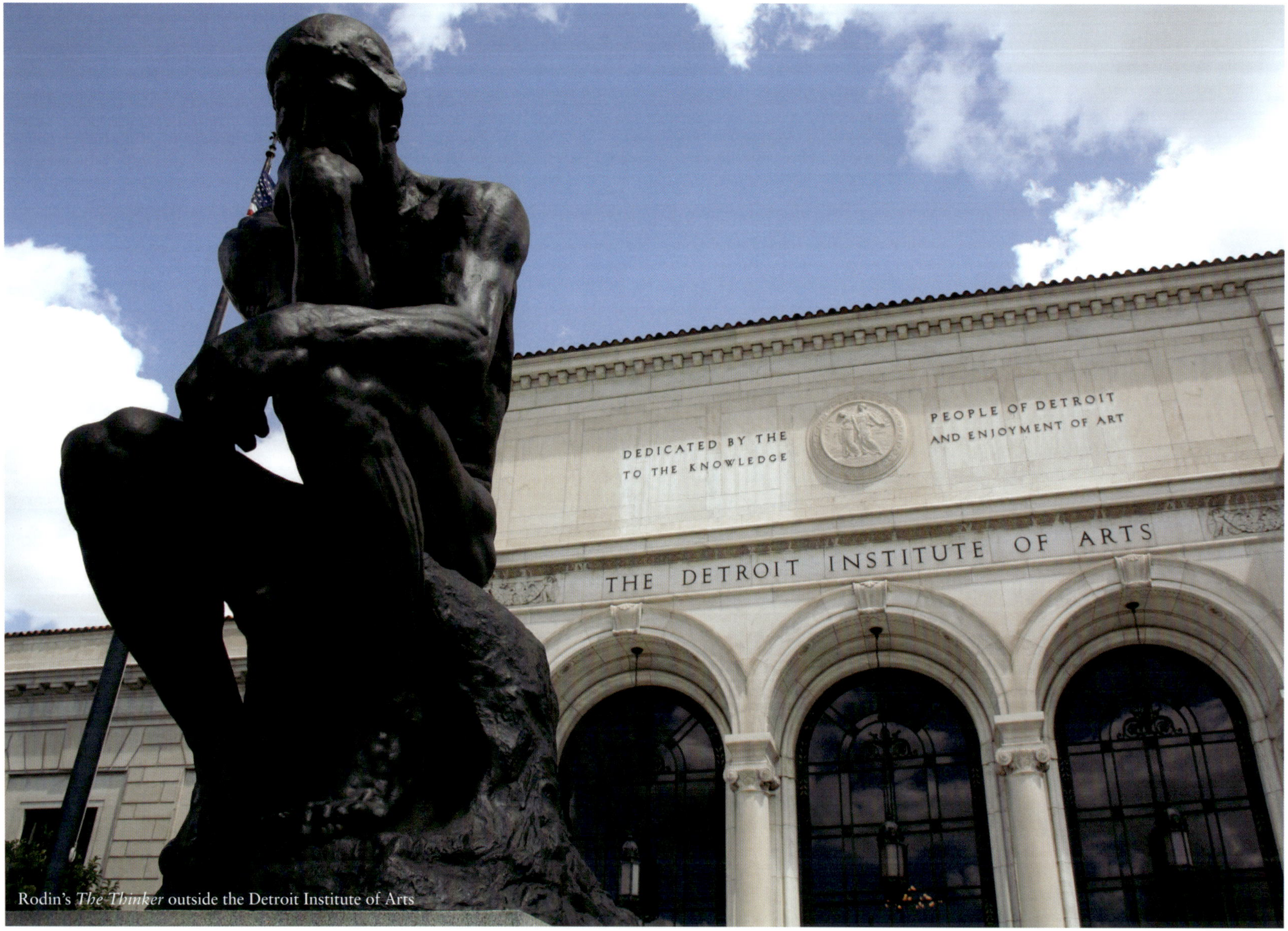

Rodin's *The Thinker* outside the Detroit Institute of Arts

Reveal Your DIA

Annmarie Erickson

Today we are town square!

MUSEUMS AND ARTISTS. They're like yin and yang. It's not always an easy relationship, but it's an enduring one that frequently creates sparks of brilliance. *Detroit Revealed* was one such sparkler. The exhibition was organized by DIA associate curator Nancy Barr and a group of local and national artists and photographers all inspired by Detroit. From Michelle Andonian documenting the reinvention of Ford's Rouge plant to Dawoud Bey interviewing and photographing students at Detroit's now defunct Chadsey High to the neighborhood views of Carlos Diaz to Andrew Moore, perhaps the most well known of the group, photographing Detroit's "spectacular" decline in luscious, large-scale pictures. These visions of Detroit are individual and indelible.

Detroit Revealed featured more than fifty works created from 2000 to 2010. Detroit was revealed in its sturdy neighborhoods, urban prairies, concrete paths, and sagging ruins. The exhibition captured a diverse Detroit, facing the challenges of deindustrialization and urban blight, recording the dignity, despair, and delight of Detroit's people. In many ways, the exhibition was a strong response to the "ruin-porn" narrative that has defined Detroit through a proliferation of online images from artists, journalists, and amateurs over the course of the first decade of this century. Indeed, Andrew Moore has been charged with exploiting Detroit's tragedy in his photographs. Yet from another perspective he is exploring Detroit's urban architecture as it moves through history, looking for the convergence of past and present and recording it. In many ways his work is situated in one of the significant challenges facing Detroit today: what can we reclaim from our past to strengthen the present and build for the future? Detroit Revealed presented a multifaceted view of our city, exposing the fault lines in any single view, particularly the prevailing narrative of failure and decay. In presenting this exhibition, the museum also recognized an opportunity to extend conversation and collaboration beyond its galleries by engaging community-based organizations working to solve Detroit's most pressing issues—through the Reveal Your Detroit project.

In another century, museums were founded as populist enterprises, a way to share the treasures of the world with the public. Time passed and museums became professionalized, developing an expert staff that was frequently better at speaking to other experts than to the public. As for engagement and inviting a creative response with the public? Not likely. More time passed and today's museum visitors are most definitely finding their voices. Museums are not oracles. They are opportunities to discuss issues, identify challenges, and inspire solutions all within a safe, social community. Yesterday we were temple. Today we are town square!

Reveal Your Detroit

We are working to expand our reach into the community while encouraging residents to see the museum as an important extension of civic life.

The Reveal Your Detroit project was a dialogue between the museum, established artists, and community organizations on these questions: What does your Detroit look like? How do you want others to see it? Forty-five community groups accepted the challenge, along with a how-to tool kit containing disposable cameras. First they visited *Detroit Revealed* to find inspiration, awe, or anger in the vision of established photographers. There were lively conversations among the group's participants and with museum staff members about the intent of an artist, the composition of a picture, and the messages it communicated about Detroit. From there, our community partners took to their streets with their cameras to respond to the museum exhibition in visual language. They met the same challenge as the established artists. Show us your Detroit—the Detroit you want the world to see. Empowered by their cameras and the promise of a parallel exhibition that would feature their work, our community partners found their voices and committed them to film—an amazing array of images emerged comprising very personal stories about life in Detroit.

The DIA first encouraged community dialogue several years ago as part of its plan to create a truly visitor-centered museum. We envisioned a place that would be welcoming and accessible to all. We were renovating the building and rehanging the collection, and we turned to the community to help us get it right. Visitor panels—groups of people recruited using diverse criteria who were willing to commit time to the project—critiqued concepts designed to engage them with art. They commented on everything from gallery colors to the use of technology to notions of beauty. They helped create what one newspaper called "the most visitor-friendly museum in the United States." And we are still listening. Whether we are talking to Jews and Muslims about Jesus for a recent Rembrandt exhibition or to teachers on how best to integrate art into the social studies curriculum, our visitors are critical to our understanding of a community that changes daily.

With Reveal Your Detroit and Inside/Out—a project that brings reproductions of museum masterpieces to city streets—the DIA explored another approach to community engagement. We are working to expand our reach into the community while encouraging residents to see the museum as an important extension of civic life. We are developing partnerships with local arts organizations that highlight the importance of local voices in concert with that of a major museum.

Technology is changing our engagements almost daily. We regularly hear from our friends on Facebook and Twitter. Reveal Your Detroit was informed by earlier online projects and was connected

Looking across Woodward from the DIA to Reveal Your Detroit at the Detroit Public Library.

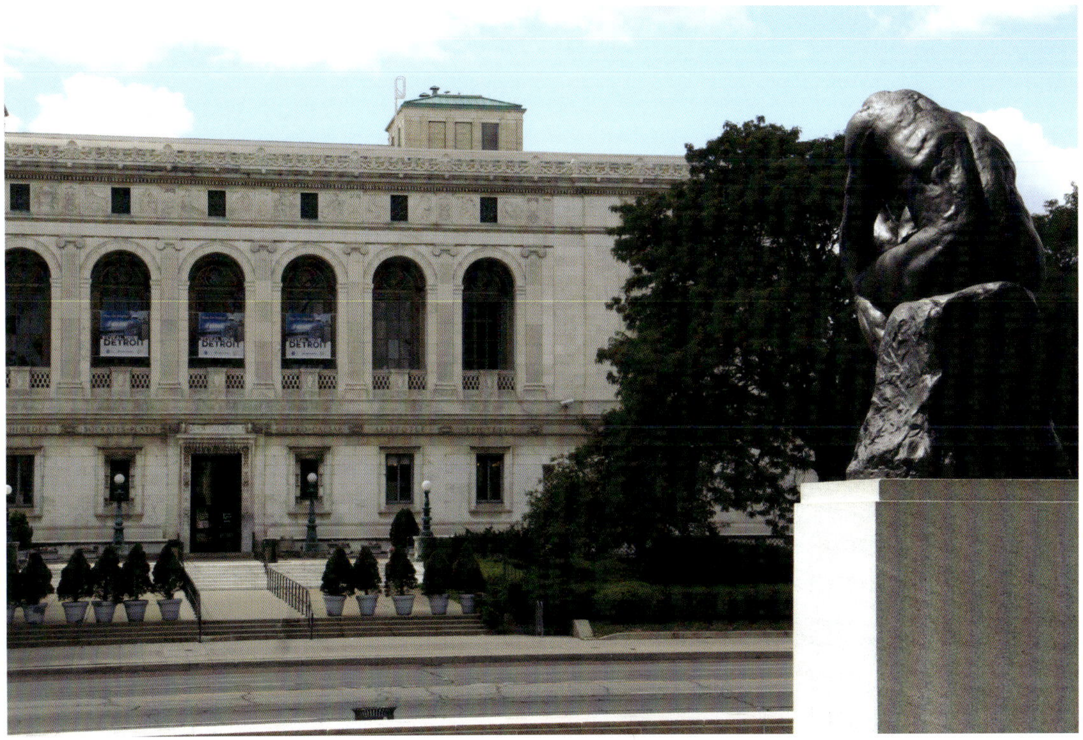

to a larger online collaboration between the DIA and the *Detroit Free Press.* We are all experiencing a generation raised with technology their grandparents could barely imagine, and we know they will continue to move museums, schools, and governments toward even greater transparency, access, and engagement.

Community engagement is an evolving concept, but it stands firmly on the idea that museums and visitors are partners in a grand project, encouraging creative responses to the challenges of daily life. Every gallery presents an example of how someone once answered a question, completed a task, or negotiated a common understanding. Every work of art was contemporary in its time, and many of the challenges issued and answered by artists remain valid today. The DIA believes strongly in the community connections we're creating together, and we predict they will be as vibrant and changeable as a zigzag tour through the museum. We may sometimes feel like yin to the artistic or community yang, but that's part of the challenge and the fun. We talk about how to engage with our audiences every day. We generate ideas and trash them. We work some of them until they come to fruition.

Why bother? Because a museum without a community is a beautiful warehouse. You create energy that fuels the DIA. We're so glad we invited you to reveal your Detroit to your DIA, and to each other.

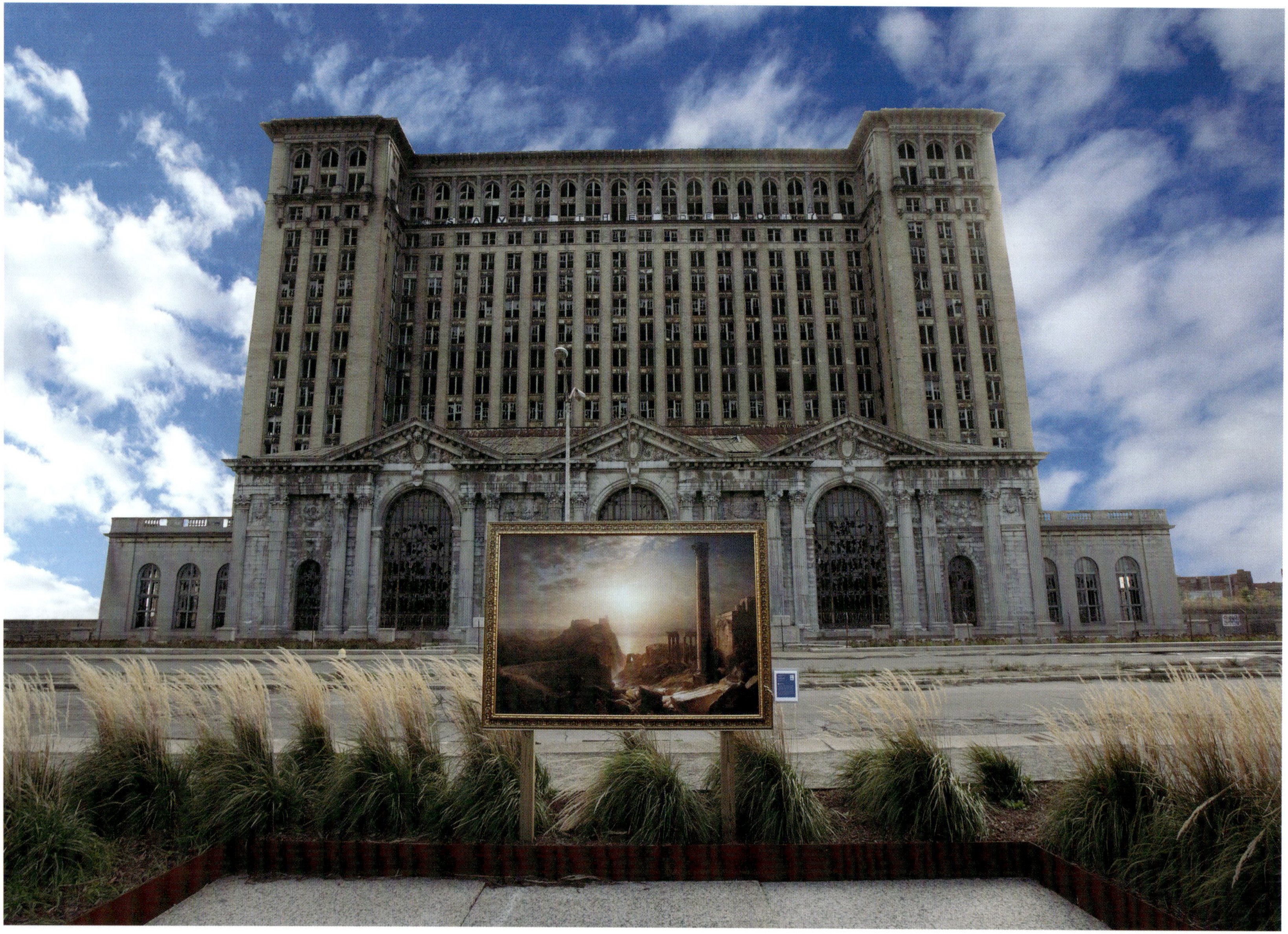

Acknowledgments

REVEAL YOUR DETROIT was made possible with the generous support of the John S. and Lames L. Knight Foundation. In addition to the grant that gave life to the Reveal Your Detroit project and ultimately this book, the Knight Foundation made a historic endowment gift in support of a broad spectrum of community engagement efforts at the Detroit Institute of Arts in late 2012.

As a tribute to the Knight Foundation's generous support and willingness to fund innovative community engagement strategies, we thought it fitting to designate all proceeds from the Reveal Your Detroit book toward future DIA community engagement efforts across Detroit and Southeast Michigan.

A project like this must also acknowledge the significant leap of faith the DIA team took in expanding its partnership efforts to empower residents to creatively respond to a contemporary professional art exhibition. During my tenure as a Detroit Revitalization Fellow at the DIA, I had the privilege of working with an incredible museum team. Special thanks are due to Nancy Barr, Associate Curator of Prints, Drawings and Photographs. Without Nancy's leadership behind the *Detroit Revealed: Photographs 2000–2010* exhibition, which was the sole inspiration for designing a community photography project, Reveal Your Detroit would never have come to fruition.

Many at the museum played critical roles in the development and execution of the project. Special thanks go especially to Cory Joyrich, Julie Burtch, and Christine Kloostra for their early and ongoing support designing and sponsoring the project, Lara Zade for savvy social media promotions, Rachel Westegren and Tim Burns for helping manage the unusual purchases, logistics, and documentation of the participants, Ken Morris for the thoughtful evaluation, and Judy Garvey and other museum docents for steadfastly joining as many community groups as possible during their museum visits. Many others played key roles and I hope they all know how extremely grateful I am for their willingness to pilot innovative community engagement efforts at the museum. I look forward to seeing how the DIA will continue to forge

Knight Foundation

Informed & Engaged Communities

Opposite: *Detroit's Michigan Central Railroad Station played host to Inside/Out, one of the museum's signature community engagement strategies to bring reproductions of masterpieces from the DIA's collection to the streets and parks of metro Detroit.*

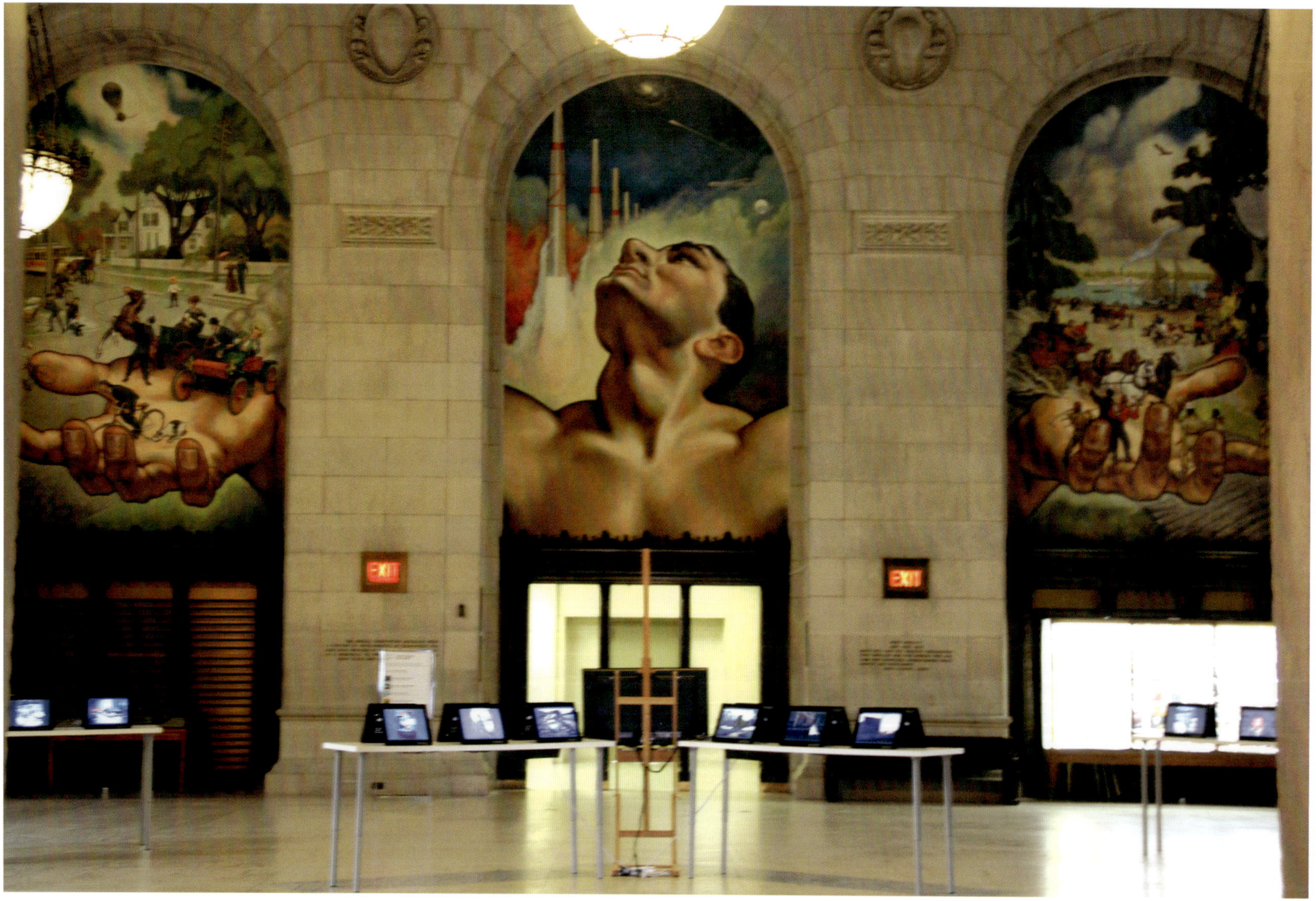

Reveal Your Detroit was first displayed at the Detroit Public Library's Strohm Hall.

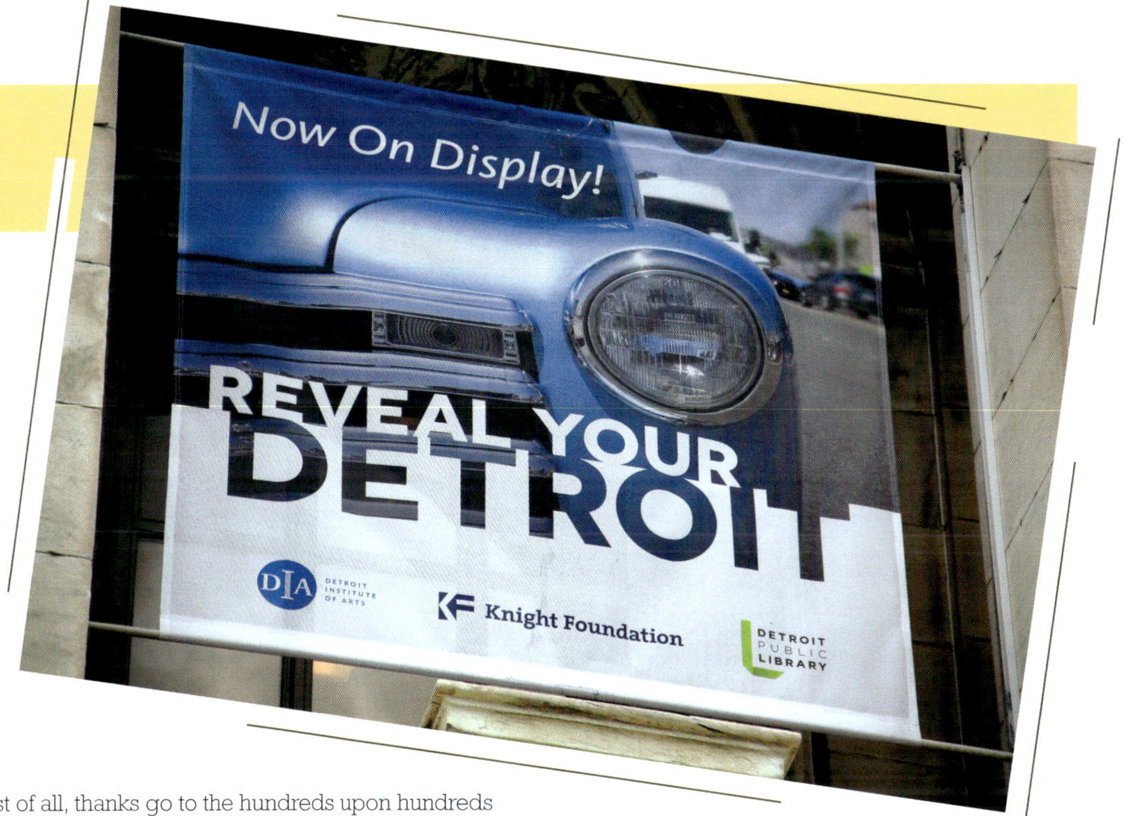

new pathways that align the transformative power of the arts and a visitor-centered mission with Detroit's revitalization imperatives.

I must also thank all of our community group leaders who put tremendous passion into the opportunity to partner with the DIA during the Reveal Your Detroit experience. Mostly volunteers, these leaders are the backbone of community development efforts across Detroit's vastly diverse landscape. It is through their boundless devotion and the truly good work they do that we can all have faith that Detroit's future will emerge brighter despite its significant challenges.

Kudos as well go to the Detroit Public Library for their willingness to host the display exhibition in the historic Strohm Hall from June to August 2012. Many people made that exhibition possible, from the Velocity Cow documentary production team to the DIA's own expert collections management group. It was a truly beautiful show that would not have been possible without the craftsmanship, grit, and ingenuity of Davin Brainard and Zachary Roberts. You both truly made the installation shine.

Most of all, thanks go to the hundreds upon hundreds of residents who accepted the Reveal Your Detroit challenge. Who knew what a stunning collection we would secure when we put those little blue disposable cameras into your hands? We are profoundly grateful for and deeply moved by your creative voice.

To our participants and anyone who dares to dream upon our city's wide canvas, know that your passion for Detroit is palpable. It is also worthy of celebration.

In my own small way, in the pages that follow, I hope to have honored that passion.

—Bradford Frost

Reveal Your Detroit

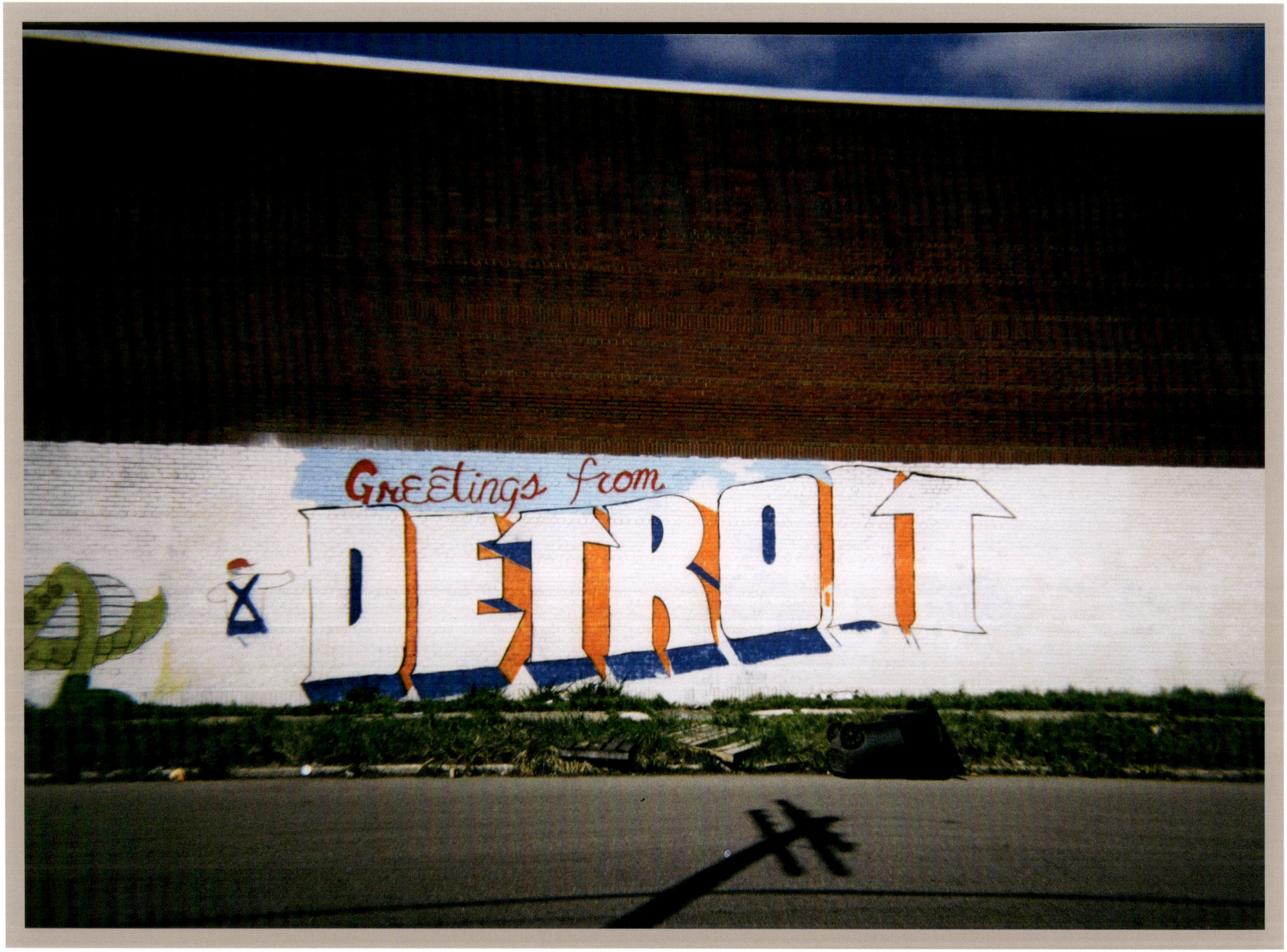
Greetings from
DETROIT

Reveal Your Detroit

IMAGINE: What if you were asked to capture your life in Detroit in just twenty-seven photographs?

What would you share?

Sure, we've long since moved on from the idea of a limited number of images we can capture. With cell phones, digital cameras, and Facebook's unending bandwidth, what's stopping us? But by slowing down and thinking about that prospect—just twenty-seven images—one can really start to catalogue the people, places, intimate details, momentous occasions, and vital moments that give real texture and meaning to our lives.

Twenty-seven images.

What would you reveal?

This was the essence of the Detroit Institute of Arts' (DIA) Reveal Your Detroit project.

Reveal Your Detroit was a community photography project that represented a unique collaboration between the DIA and hundreds of Detroit residents by empowering them to creatively respond to the museum's contemporary photography exhibition *Detroit Revealed: Photographs 2000–2010*. Reveal Your Detroit was designed to help the DIA forge fresh partnerships with its surrounding community, to leverage the museum's heralded collection, and to deepen the connections between the museum and the multitude of community revitalization efforts under way in Detroit.

For the internationally renowned museum, which was then preparing for its tri-county campaign for public support (in a region that has had an uneven track record when it comes to funding regional cultural institutions), this was as local a project as one could design.

For a place like the DIA, with its standards of artistic excellence, Reveal Your Detroit was risky, too.

Opposite: *"Greetings from Detroit," Detroit's Northend neighborhood.*

—Vanguard Community Development Corporation

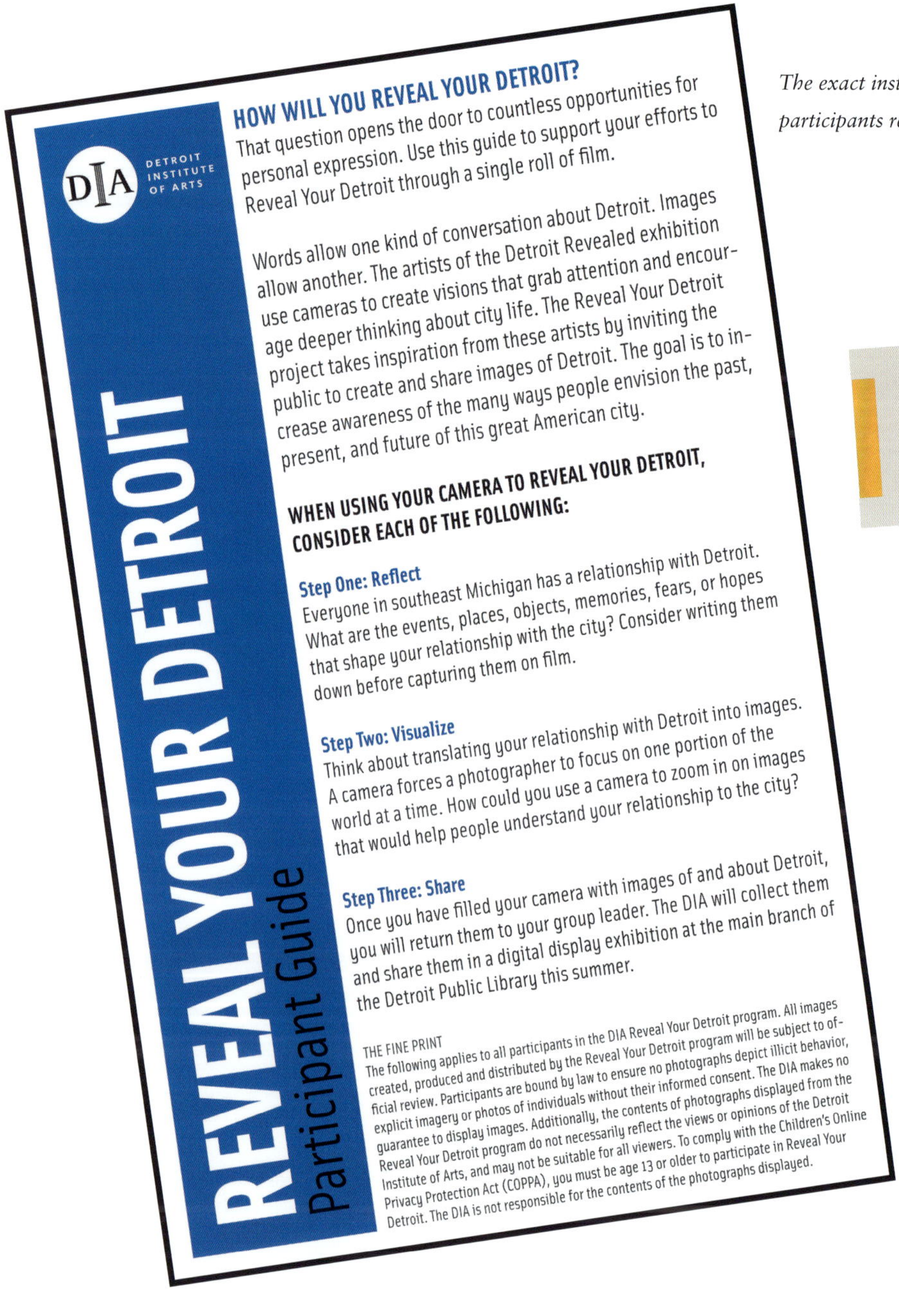

REVEAL YOUR DETROIT

Participant Guide

DETROIT INSTITUTE OF ARTS

HOW WILL YOU REVEAL YOUR DETROIT?

That question opens the door to countless opportunities for personal expression. Use this guide to support your efforts to Reveal Your Detroit through a single roll of film.

Words allow one kind of conversation about Detroit. Images allow another. The artists of the Detroit Revealed exhibition use cameras to create visions that grab attention and encourage deeper thinking about city life. The Reveal Your Detroit project takes inspiration from these artists by inviting the public to create and share images of Detroit. The goal is to increase awareness of the many ways people envision the past, present, and future of this great American city.

WHEN USING YOUR CAMERA TO REVEAL YOUR DETROIT, CONSIDER EACH OF THE FOLLOWING:

Step One: Reflect

Everyone in southeast Michigan has a relationship with Detroit. What are the events, places, objects, memories, fears, or hopes that shape your relationship with the city? Consider writing them down before capturing them on film.

Step Two: Visualize

Think about translating your relationship with Detroit into images. A camera forces a photographer to focus on one portion of the world at a time. How could you use a camera to zoom in on images that would help people understand your relationship to the city?

Step Three: Share

Once you have filled your camera with images of and about Detroit, you will return them to your group leader. The DIA will collect them and share them in a digital display exhibition at the main branch of the Detroit Public Library this summer.

THE FINE PRINT

The following applies to all participants in the DIA Reveal Your Detroit program. All images created, produced and distributed by the Reveal Your Detroit program will be subject to official review. Participants are bound by law to ensure no photographs depict illicit behavior, explicit imagery or photos of individuals without their informed consent. The DIA makes no guarantee to display images. Additionally, the contents of photographs displayed from the Reveal Your Detroit program do not necessarily reflect the views or opinions of the Detroit Institute of Arts, and may not be suitable for all viewers. To comply with the Children's Online Privacy Protection Act (COPPA), you must be age 13 or older to participate in Reveal Your Detroit. The DIA is not responsible for the contents of the photographs displayed.

The exact instructions all Reveal Your Detroit participants received, including the fine print.

Reveal

The museum invited residents and community groups into the *Detroit Revealed: Photographs 2000–2010* exhibition and then sent each visitor off with a disposable camera, committing to a public display of some of the images—a commitment made before a single picture had been taken.

All of this was unprecedented.

Reveal Your Detroit challenged residents to reflect on their lives and to capture twenty-seven images that were important to their Detroit experience. Residents then shared those images with the museum and the broader public. We asked each participant to do the following as they went out the museum's doors:

Reflect.

Visualize.

Share.

Those were the steps our resident photographers took as they clicked through their single roll of film.

The results were extraordinary.

Your Detroit

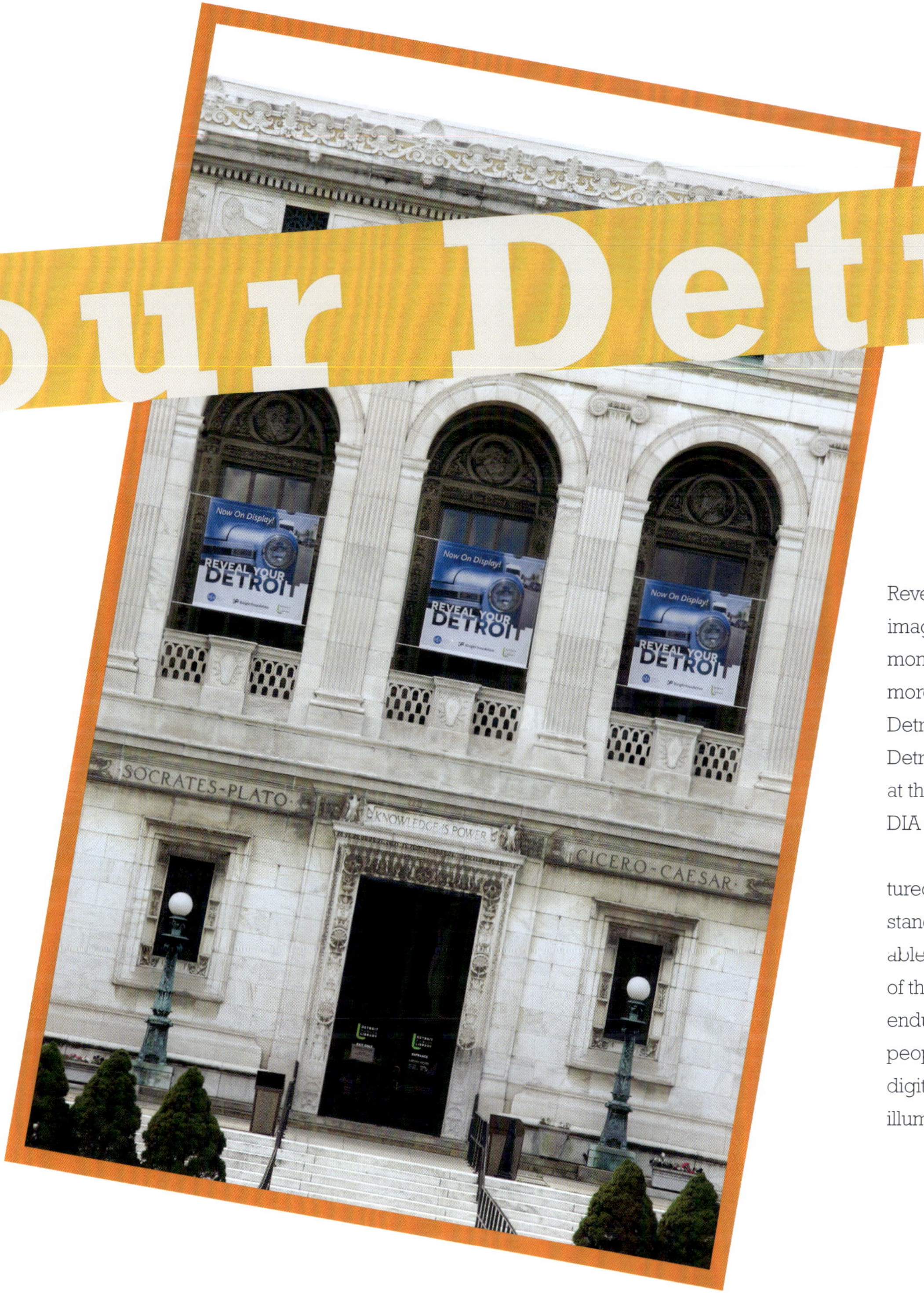

Announced to the public in March 2012, the Reveal Your Detroit project received over 10,000 images via disposable cameras in less than three months. By June, over 1,700 of those pictures, and 600 more submitted online through the DIA's Reveal Your Detroit Flickr page and from the Detroit Free Press Detroit Self-Portrait site, went on display for two months at the Detroit Public Library across the street from the DIA on Woodward Avenue.

From the gritty to the sublime, the images captured a slice of time in Detroit's history. By professional standards most of the shots were good but unremarkable. In a way, however, that was precisely the source of their power. Each picture in the show spoke to the enduring presence and powerful voice of Detroit's people. As they scrolled one by one over the sixty digital photo frames in the Library's Strohm Hall, they illuminated Detroit's durability and evoked the raw

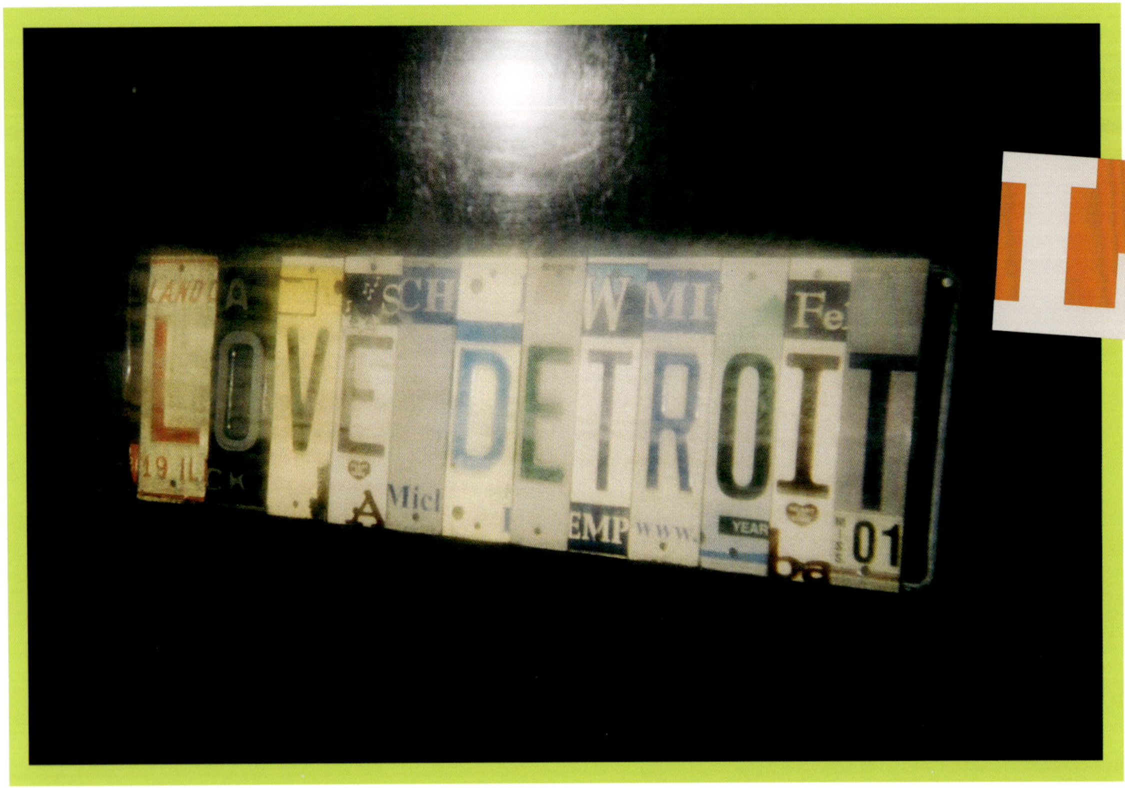

Love

Detroit Love, with the obvious glare from the disposable camera flash. For the digital display exhibition, we included lots of shots for the "love" they showed Detroit despite minor photographic flaws.
—Westminster Kenilworth Association

passion its people feel for the city despite its significant and seemingly relentless challenges.

As the community curator of the Reveal Your Detroit project, I selected photographs for the show with a substantial bias toward inclusion. Every photographer who submitted one of the DIA's disposable cameras ended up with an image in the show along with others from their host group. In some cases, this meant putting up a fuzzy shot; in others it meant a small finger poked through one corner of the frame. In every case, it meant combing through all twenty-seven pictures to try to find the one that best represented the intent of the photographer. Some cameras, for example, came in with five or more shots of the same thing. That signaled the object's overall importance to the photographer. The DIA team aimed to ensure that the best possible image(s) representing the intent of the participant made it into the public display. These "good enough" shots added texture and nuance, ultimately giving the display raw depth and validation as a true community show. Rough edges aside, each picture chosen was significant in its own way.

As you page through this book, remember that these images were taken with disposable cameras

Detroit

by local residents. Not professional or even hobbyist photographers for the most part, but just regular folks.

How This Book Is Organized

Throughout the book, you'll be introduced to each of the forty-five partner groups that completed the whole Reveal Your Detroit experience. Group leader and participant quotes are included to showcase our partners' perspectives. Each group's basic information, or partner profile, explains how many people they guided through the experience and, whenever possible, where you can learn more about them online. In compiling this book, we reached out to all the groups again, asking them to reflect on what they took away from the Reveal Your Detroit experience. We are pleased to share their voices. While every group has at least one image in the book, some have several. Generally, whenever a group's first photo appears, we present their profile.

A handful of shots were also linked to specific photographers. Adding their voices offered us a great opportunity to bring life to the pictures that we weren't able to showcase during the digital photo frame exhibit. You'll find these reflections linked to just some of the wonderful shots in this compilation.

Finally, although some groups may seem to overlap—for example, BE Culturally Exposed could be mistaken for BE EXPOSED: DETROIT—they are distinct. Some groups have images represented in both of the main photo essays that follow. When you see those images and what may appear to be similar group names, know that the differences, while subtle in name, are important to the residents who took part in the project.

It is our hope that, taken together, these partner profiles, photographer takes, and the image captions make for clear reading and happy viewing.

James Feagin was one of the group leaders who partnered with the DIA as part of his Imagine Detroit Together project. We highlight James's group first to show how the project worked for many of our partners and to illustrate how these many voices and groups will be featured in the book.

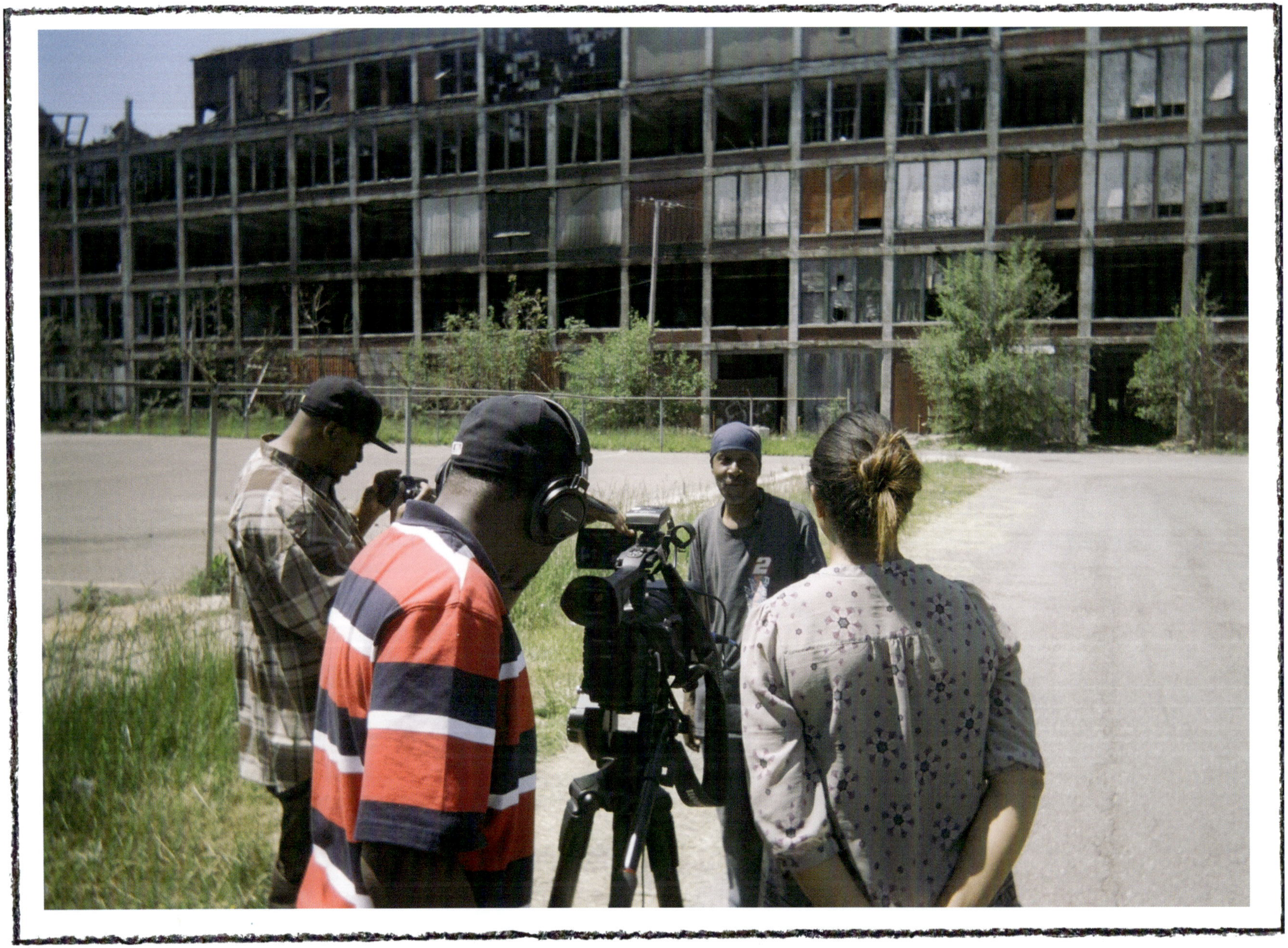

IMAGINE DETROIT TOGETHER

Leader: James Feagin

Participants: 4

www.ImagineDetroitTogether.org

AS AN ENTREPRENEUR who has had many positive male role models throughout my life, I know firsthand how important it is for young men to have someone who is accessible and encourages them to realize their potential.

To see my mentee enjoy his photos being observed and his story being valued was a tremendous experience for both of us. We need more opportunities for people to realize that their stories and creations have value.

Opposite: *The Velocity Cow production crew produced a stunning documentary of the DIA's community engagement project, which can still be seen on YouTube if you search for Reveal Your Detroit.*

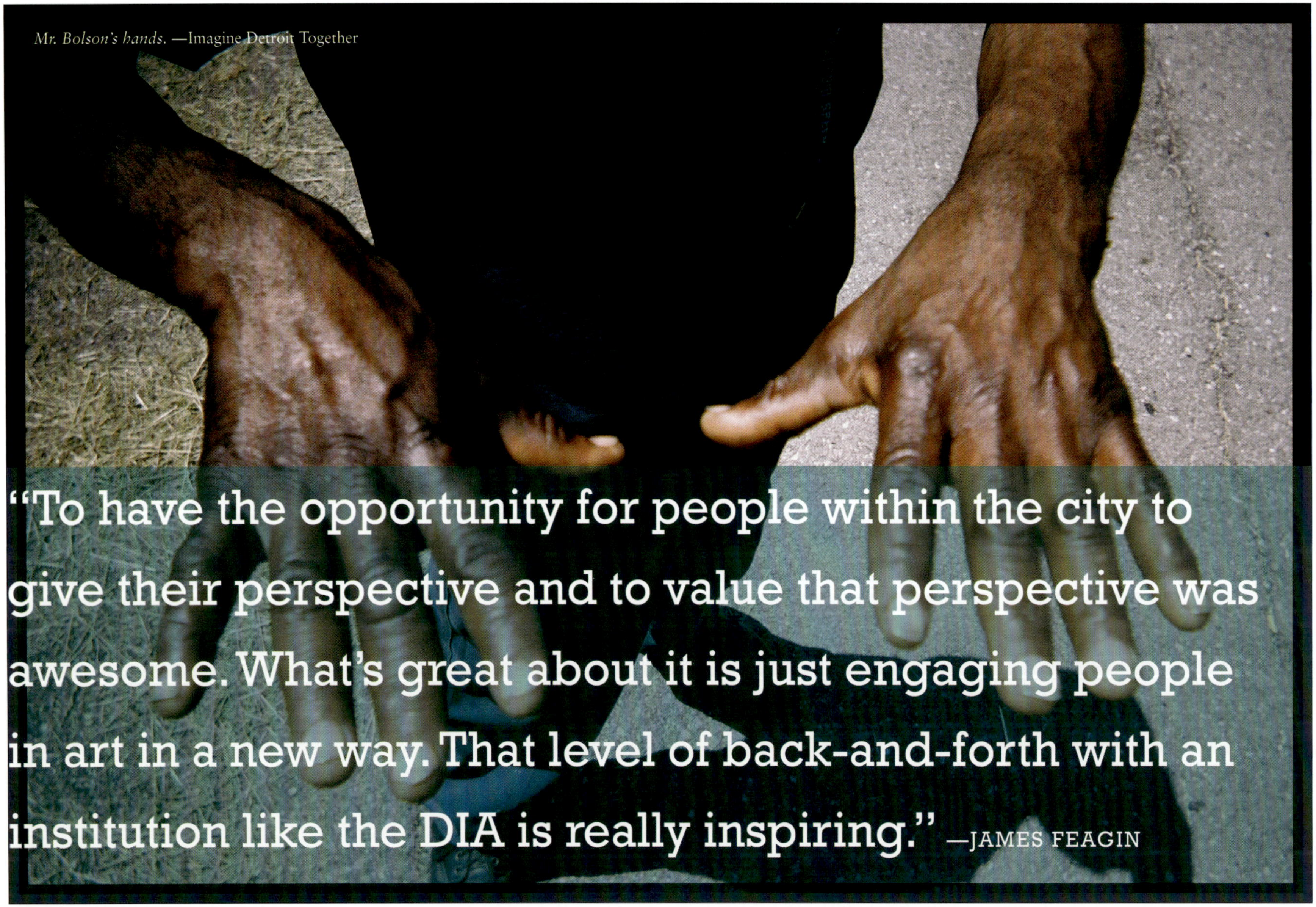

Mr. Bolson's hands. —Imagine Detroit Together

"To have the opportunity for people within the city to give their perspective and to value that perspective was awesome. What's great about it is just engaging people in art in a new way. That level of back-and-forth with an institution like the DIA is really inspiring." —JAMES FEAGIN

James and one of the young men he coaches took their cameras to the historic Packard plant along with a Reveal Your Detroit documentary film crew. They also had a chance to link up with a local resident during their shoot. Check out these shots from Imagine Detroit Together.

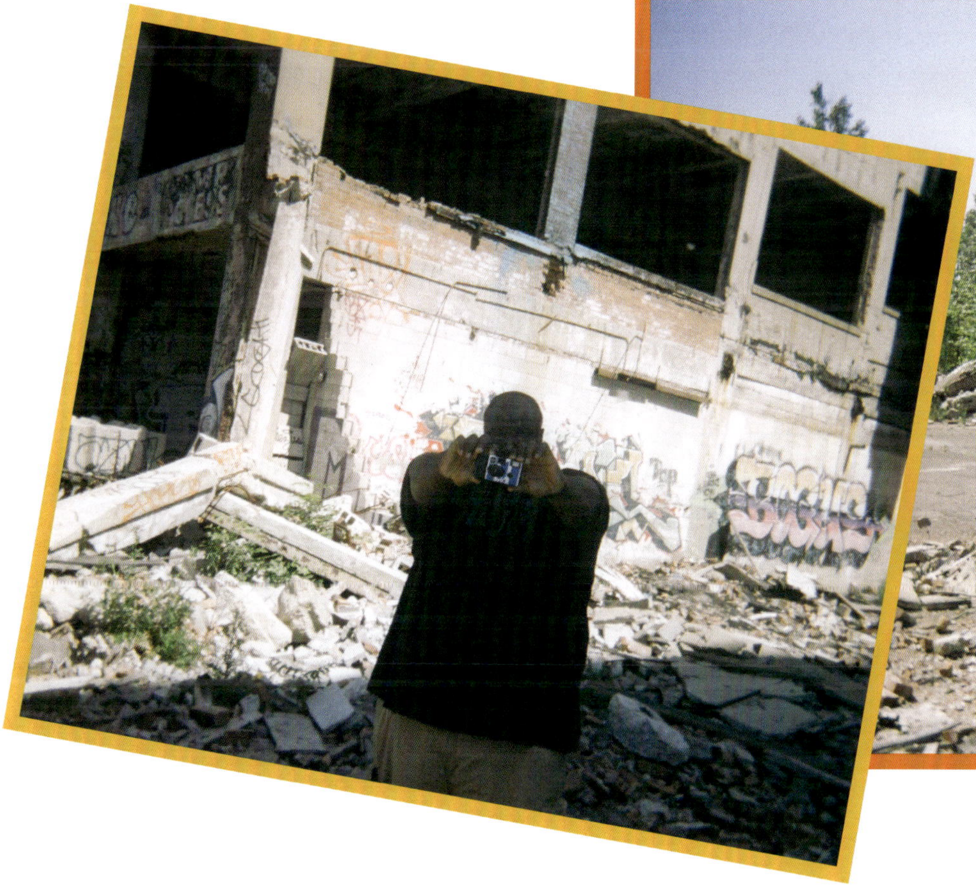

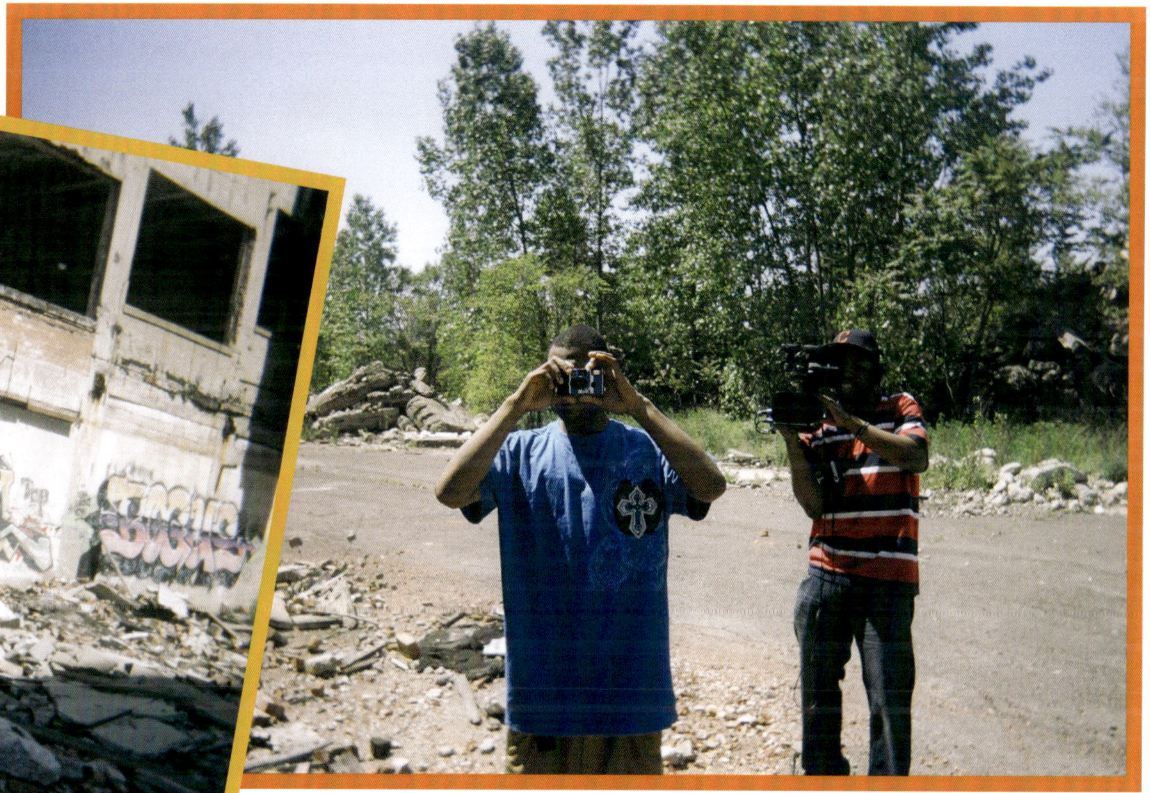

James and his mentee took shots of each other at the same time using the DIA's blue disposable cameras.
—Imagine Detroit Together

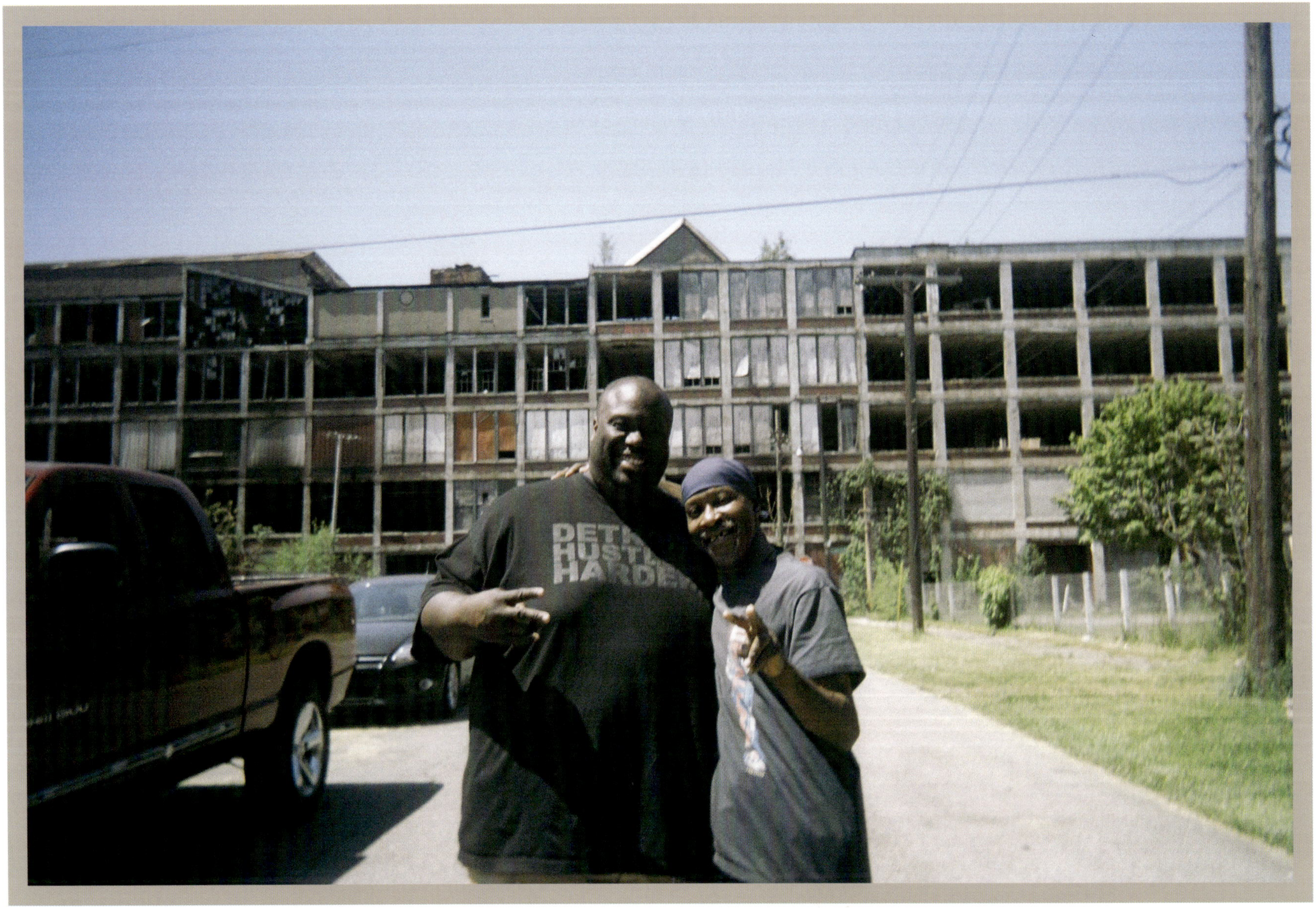

James and the crew made friends with Ronnie Bolson Sr., who has lived near the Packard plant for over fifty years. —Imagine Detroit Together

This was the experience for our groups: come see a professional art exhibition. Go out and capture your life on a single roll of film. Then share the results with the DIA.

As those 2,300 selected images rotated every five seconds on sixty digital frames, every shot took on an important dimension to the Reveal Your Detroit show. The more I looked, the more I began to see their intrinsic beauty.

The simple fact remained: these were pictures taken by folks who live here in Detroit.

And the hunger to show their side of the city was palpable.

Reveal Your Detroit let residents uncover the intimate side of living life in Detroit. It makes for a stunning portrait. It's all the more remarkable because of the larger narrative that engulfed the city at the time. Despite years of negative press and the fact that in 2012 Detroit was in danger of being taken over by a state-appointed emergency manager, residents were eager to take advantage of a museum experience that would encourage them to claim Detroit on their own terms and show their side of the city through film.

Detroit is a city so proud and so full of passion that almost a thousand residents from all walks of life took on the Reveal Your Detroit challenge to use photography as a constructive tool to document what needed to change in the city and show what was right with it, too.

When a Reveal Your Detroit book was suggested, it seemed an obvious way to celebrate this unique community-wide experience. It posed a major challenge, too: how could we pare down the best images from over ten thousand? What story did these images tell? And what was unique about the relationship between the DIA and the community development organizations that took advantage of the opportunity?

We first committed to staying inclusive. But this time, instead of representing every photographer, we decided to include at least one image from every Reveal Your Detroit partner organization.

The next obvious criterion was quality. What were the best images from the show? And what made them "the best"?

A few things.

Reveal Your Detroit let residents uncover the intimate side of living in Detroit. It makes for a stunning portrait.

DETROIT IS A
AND SO FULL OF

First, we wanted to highlight the unique partnerships that were forged through this project. Reveal Your Detroit was a critical learning opportunity and a special way to pilot meaningful Detroit-based partnerships for the museum with civic groups, block clubs, and social service agencies without abandoning its core role as a world-class art institution.

The book highlights the powerful ways these outside organizations fused themselves to the museum's mission to provide visitors a meaningful experience with art while accelerating their group's own goals and objectives. Through the voices of our partners, the results of that mutual leap of faith during Reveal Your Detroit may encourage further collaboration between seemingly disparate groups in the city. It may also serve as a model for cultural organizations that seek to meaningfully collaborate with local community development efforts.

Ultimately, the feedback from our partners celebrates the constructive role the DIA can play in Detroit's revitalization efforts to make our community stronger and more vibrant. It also suggests an ongoing opportunity to design new ways to engage Detroiters with the transformative power of the arts.

What we now know for sure is that the process starts by simply inviting people to try.

Project leaders leveraged Reveal Your Detroit in significant ways. One group turned Reveal Your Detroit into a launching pad for their fund-raising, awareness building, and participatory outreach. Others made it an integral part of their programming activities. A local radio station took advantage of the project to promote regional dialogue.

CITY SO PROUD, PASSION . . .

Throughout the book we zero in on these perspectives and what inspired our groups to tap into the museum's invitation to partner.

Second, we chose images based on sheer quality and overall composition. We selected those that conveyed the overall story of a community-wide photography project. Our intent was to uniquely reflect Detroit from its do-it-yourself spirit to the raw pride residents have for their city.

And, candidly, these images just spoke to me. They are especially strong representations of life here in Detroit. They capture the love this city evokes. With bursts of light and shots of the curious and iconic, a portrait of Detroit unlike any other emerges in these pages.

This is the authentic city.

Our resident photographers never avoided Detroit's challenges. But in many ways, by capturing the simplest details of living here—from Eastern Market days to kids playing on the playground—these images conveyed the project's core strengths. Reveal Your Detroit empowered residents to own their Detroit story—to show that, in the words of one participant, "Detroit is more than abandoned houses and crime; it's a city of families and children and neighborhoods."

Just as Reveal Your Detroit encouraged residents to see their city with different eyes, the project encourages all of us to widen our perspective on Detroit at the same time. Can we see Detroit anew for its profound potential? Can we perhaps soften the rigid lenses we have on this city and entrust actual residents without any particular agenda to give a fuller picture of life in Detroit?

Our resident photographers never avoided Detroit's challenges.

Reveal Your Detroit is also a celebration of Detroit's transformative possibilities and how we must take on that imperative together as residents, institutions, and professionals devoted to strengthening Detroit for generations to come.

This is Detroit's vital transformation.

The rest of the book aims to capture those themes and, through these pages, the story emerges in two parts. First up is "Detroit: The Authentic City." Then, it's "Detroit's Vital Transformation." These two "frames" will no doubt resonate with the people and groups that took part in the project, but the truth is that they bleed through the pictures.

Reveal Your Detroit is a compilation of an authentic community, eclectically diverse and distinctively proud. It's a collection of images that shines a spot light on organizations working to solve problems and promote a strong Detroit future. It's a peek at the shared spaces that give us a collective identity; knowing readers will quickly see that these images could have been taken nowhere else but Detroit.

It's also an insider's take on the city's transformation challenge. From downtown to the city's diverse neighborhoods, these images go deep into Detroit's nooks and crannies. The book documents the enthusiasm and seriousness with which visitors accepted the DIA's invitation to "be the artist," and serves as proof that residents can be empowered to give artistic voice on our shared Detroit canvas.

In short, Reveal Your Detroit represents a true community-wide lens on Detroit from the perspective that matters most: its people.

This is Reveal Your Detroit: an intimate look at a great American city.

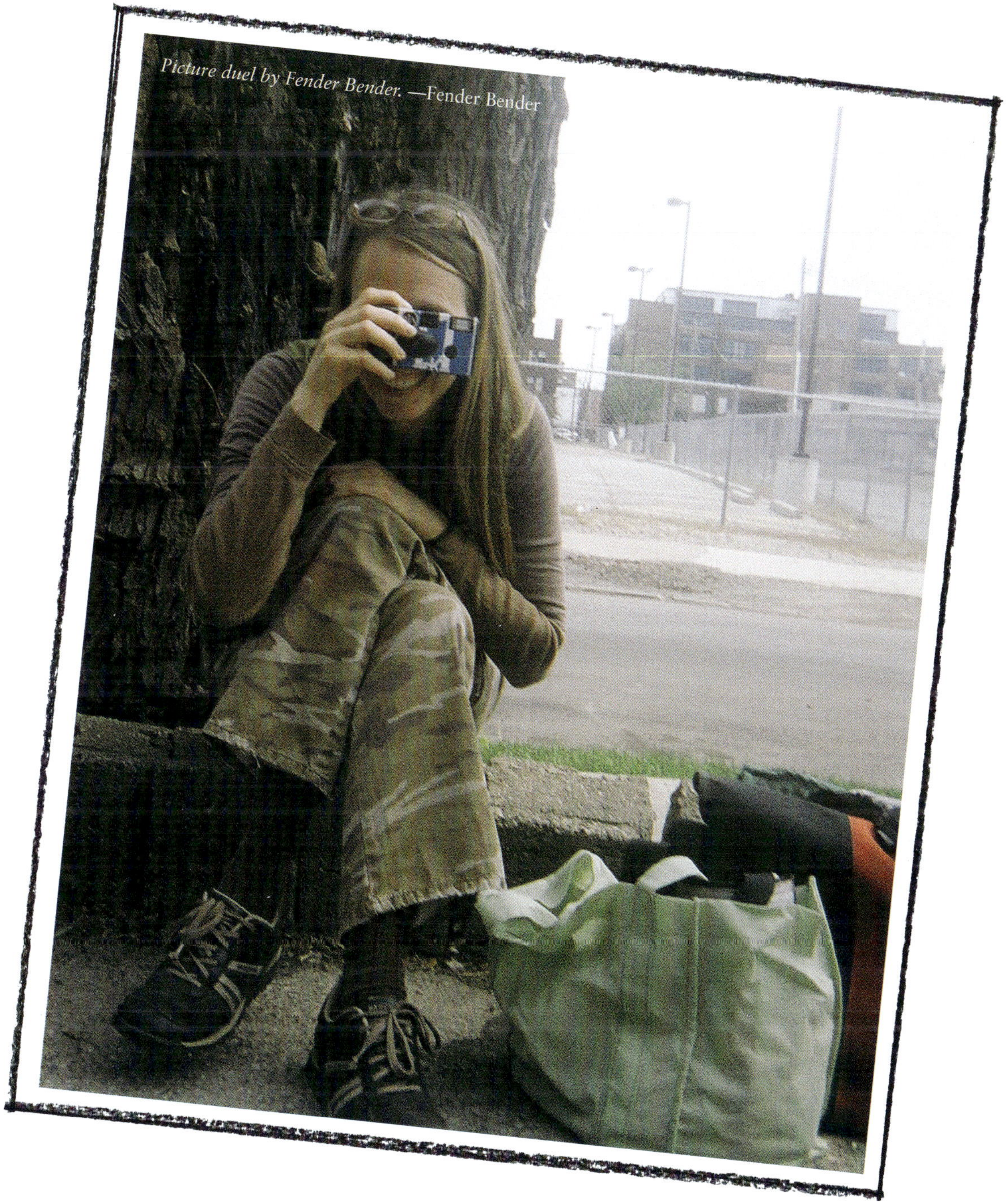

Picture duel by Fender Bender. —Fender Bender

Reveal Your Detroit is a compilation of an authentic community, eclectically diverse and distinctively proud.

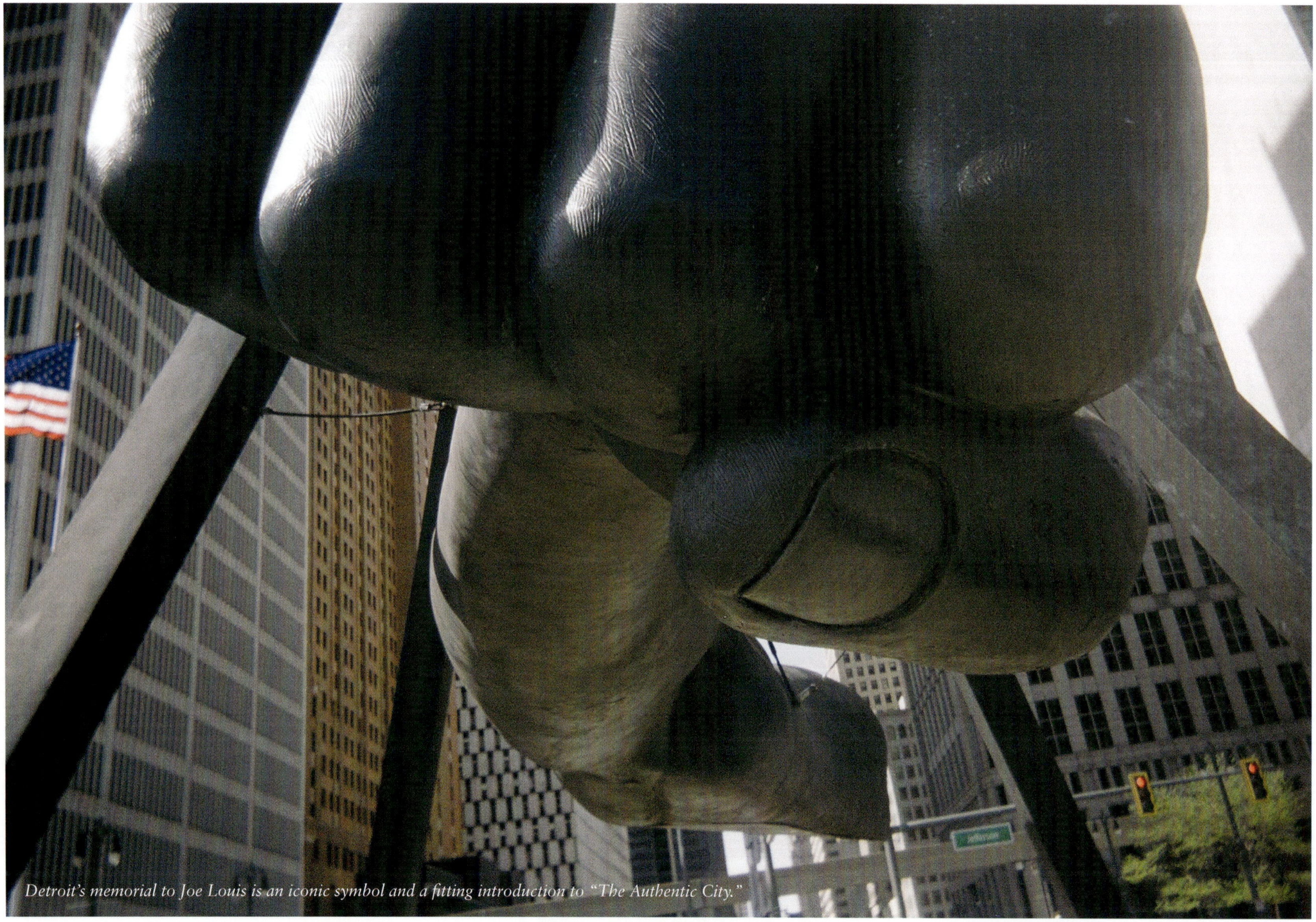

Detroit's memorial to Joe Louis is an iconic symbol and a fitting introduction to "The Authentic City."

The Authentic City

I took this photograph because the Joe Louis fist symbolizes the power and strength that many Detroiters need to have daily. Reveal Your Detroit linked the views of each participant together and showed how much they care for and love the city of Detroit.

TALISE YATARA REED

FROM HISTORIC LANDMARKS to shots of the Renaissance Center from "The Mound," residents captured stunning angles of Detroit's icons. The usual places that pepper national newsreels of the city took on a more intimate feel in the hands of residents using disposable cameras.

Then there were the neighborhoods. Most of Detroit's geography was covered in the ten thousand images that were submitted. But it was clear that certain groups made it a point to highlight Detroit's neighborhood assets. It's been said that every Detroit neighborhood has a future; whatever shape or form that future may take, many of these images speak to those enduring aspirations.

From the lower eastside to Boston Edison to southwest Detroit. From the Northend to the Grandmont Rosedale communities, proud neighborhood associations, block clubs, and youth empowerment groups encouraged active documentation of boulevard streets, distinctive Detroit homes, and curious neighborhood treasures.

Our partners took on Detroit from personal angles, capturing vivid dimensions of daily life in the city. They documented Detroit's many nooks and crannies. The images show Detroit's gritty side. They show Detroit's bright side, too. This section lets the images and group leaders and a handful of photographers really speak for themselves.

See them all here. These images make up Detroit: The Authentic City.

AWESOME NEWS TASKFORCE DETROIT

Leader: Marshalle Montgomery

Participants: 10

www.awesomefoundation.org

Opposite: *A blue-collar town works.*
—Awesome News Taskforce

THE AWESOME NEWS TASKFORCE is the thirtieth chapter of the worldwide Awesome Foundation. The Detroit chapter awards metro Detroiters $1,000 micro-grants for innovative journalism and civic media projects that create ripples of inspiration and engagement throughout the city. The purpose is to assist citizens, organizations, and community leaders who are inventive and willing to give a voice to untold stories about metro Detroit.

Our team participated in Reveal Your Detroit by announcing our April micro-grantee, "Strong and Beautiful," at the Detroit Revealed exhibit. We explored the exhibit and used it as an inspiration for the young people involved to learn and see the impact of telling stories from a personal perspective.

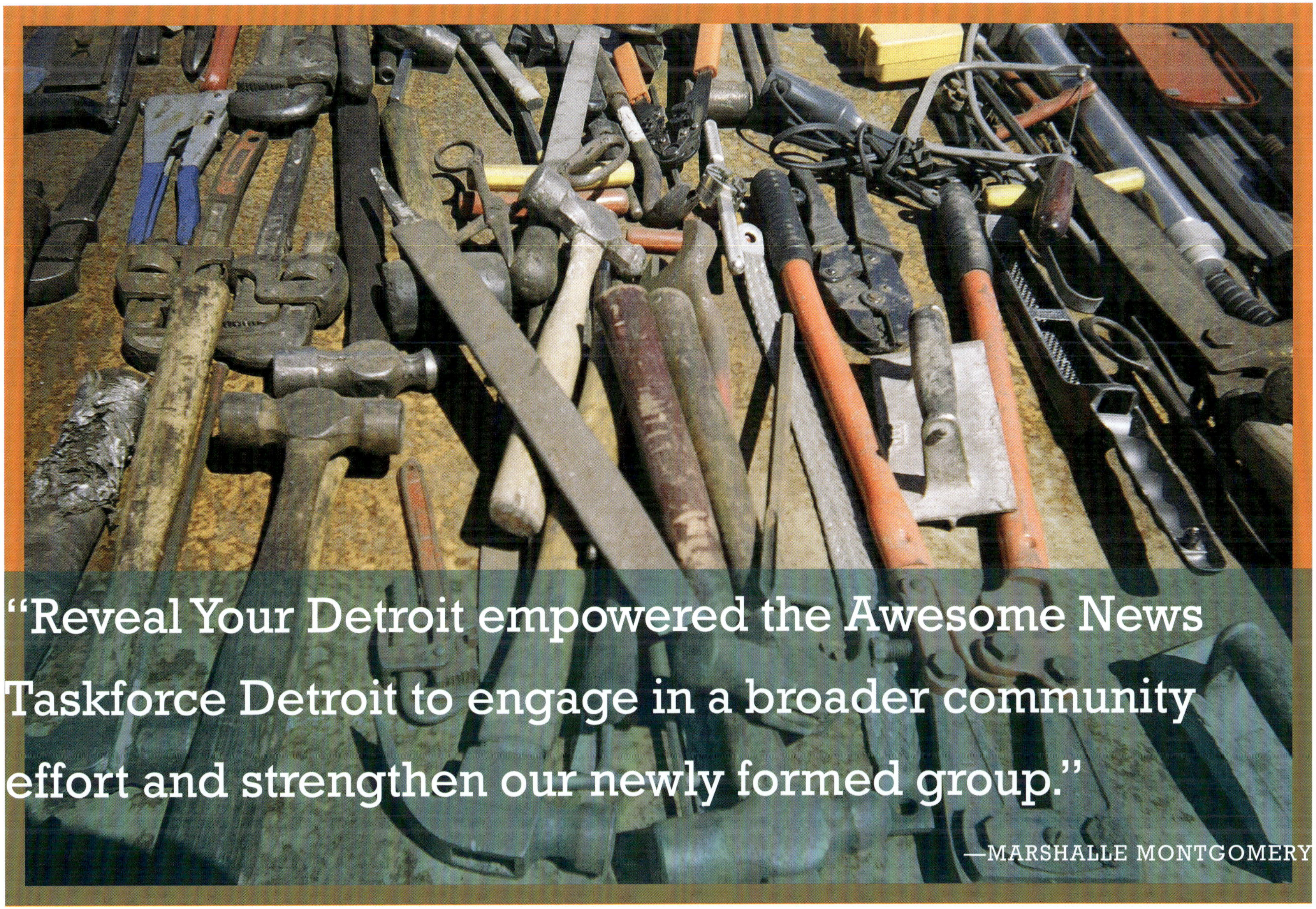

"Reveal Your Detroit empowered the Awesome News Taskforce Detroit to engage in a broader community effort and strengthen our newly formed group."

—MARSHALLE MONTGOMERY

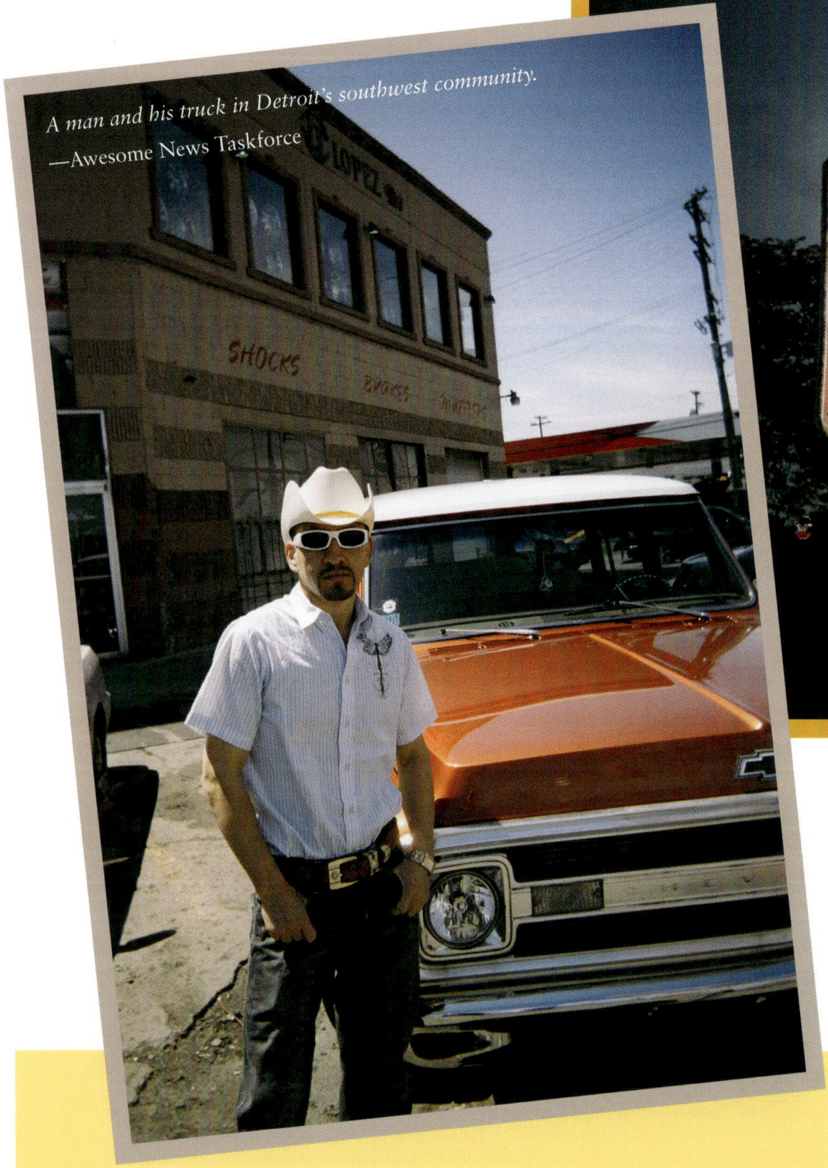

A man and his truck in Detroit's southwest community.
—Awesome News Taskforce

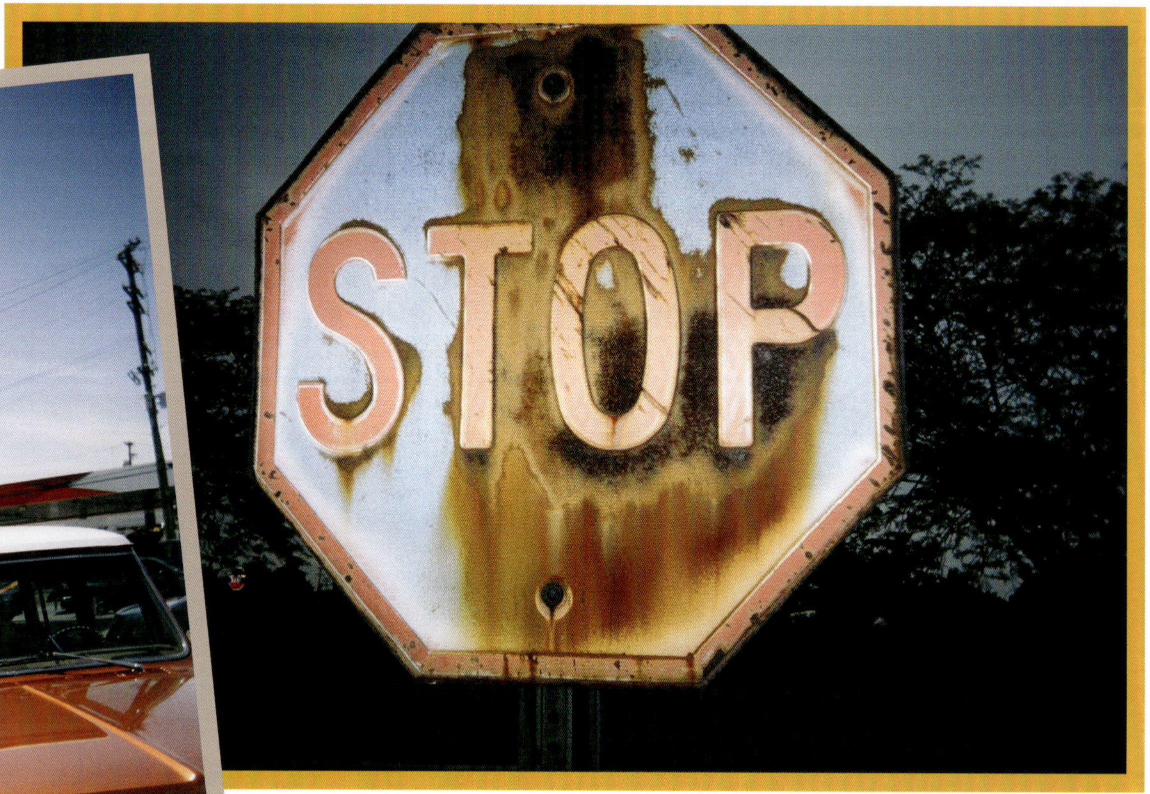

—Awesome News Taskforce

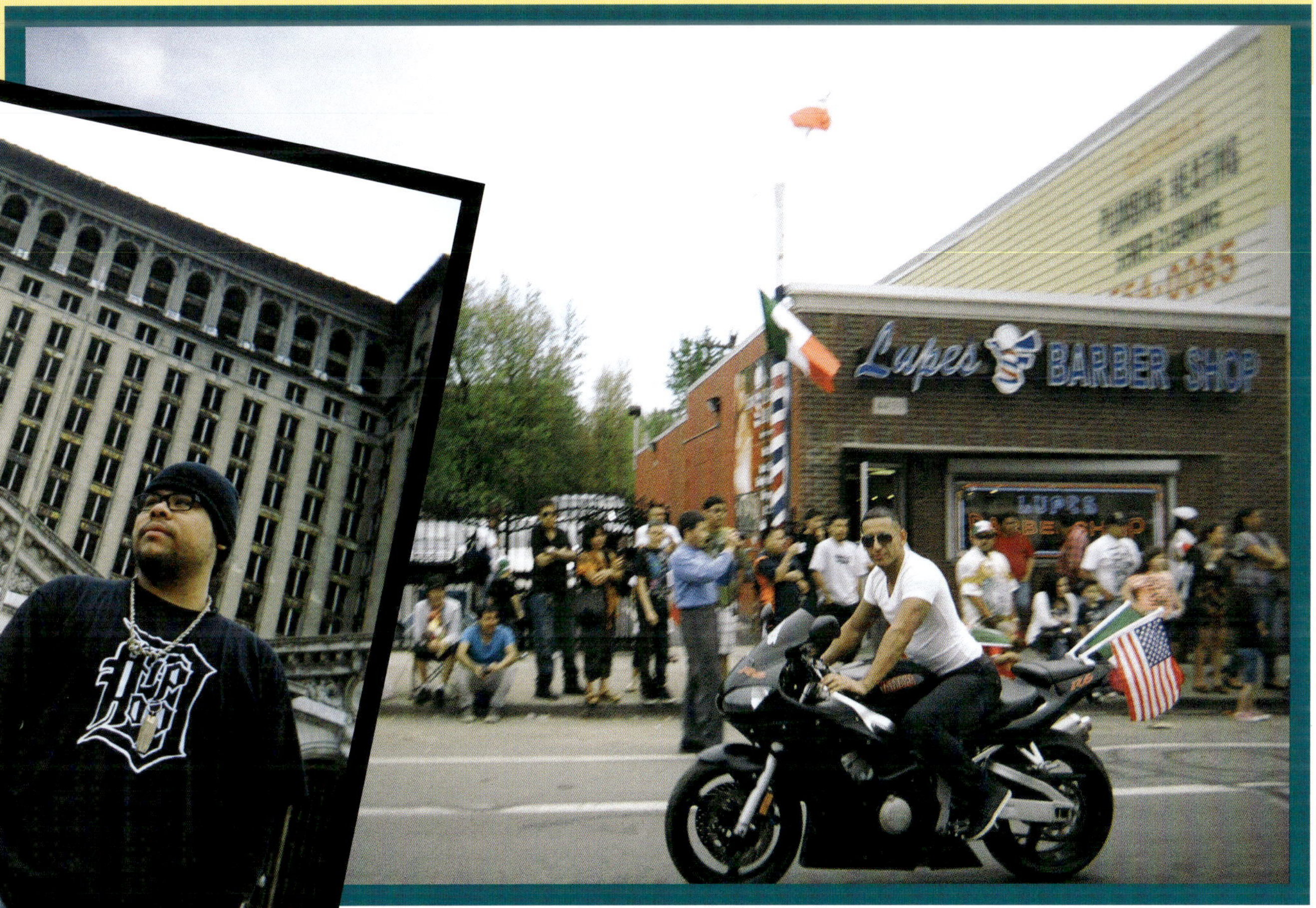

A festive time in Mexicantown. —Awesome News Taskforce

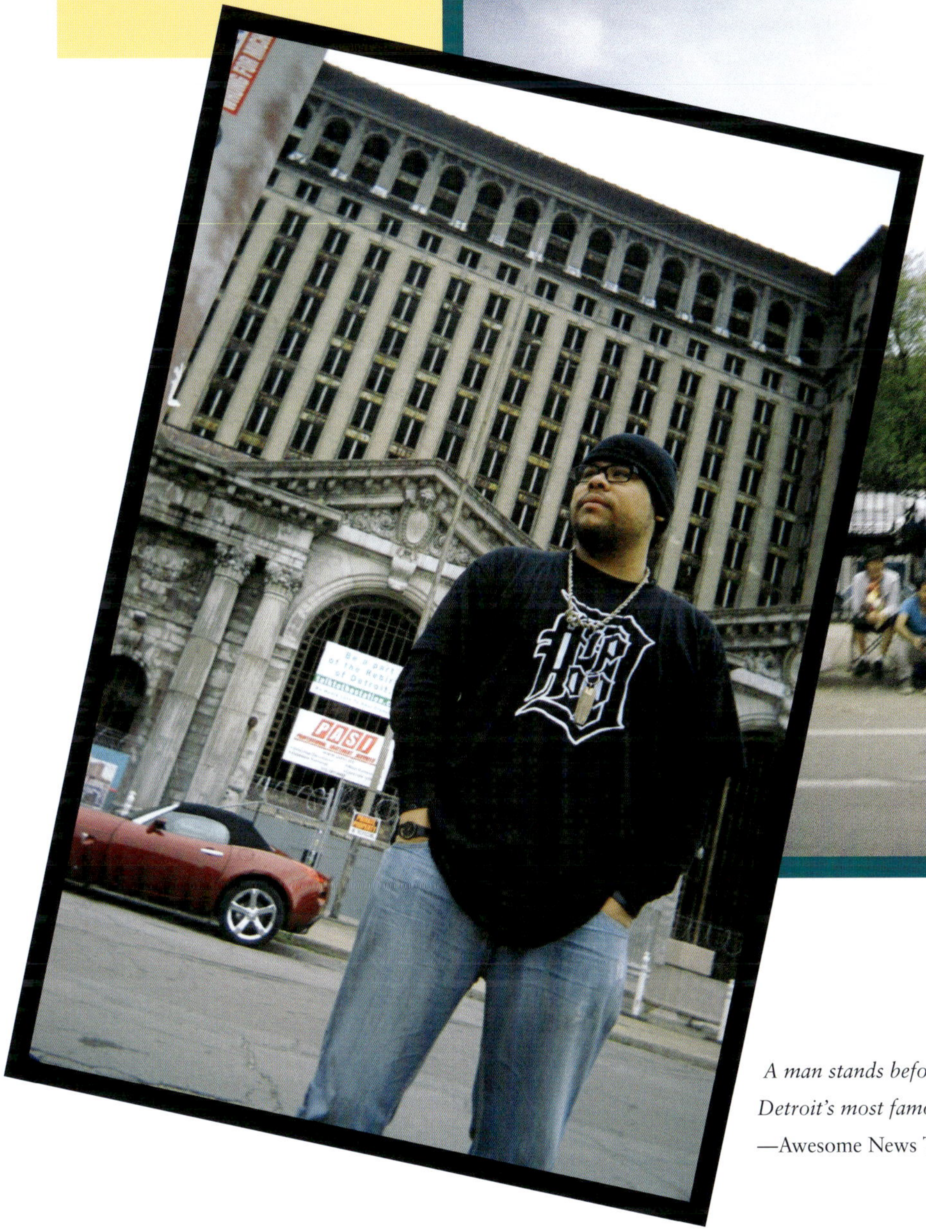

A man stands before Michigan Central Station, Detroit's most famous derelict building.
—Awesome News Taskforce

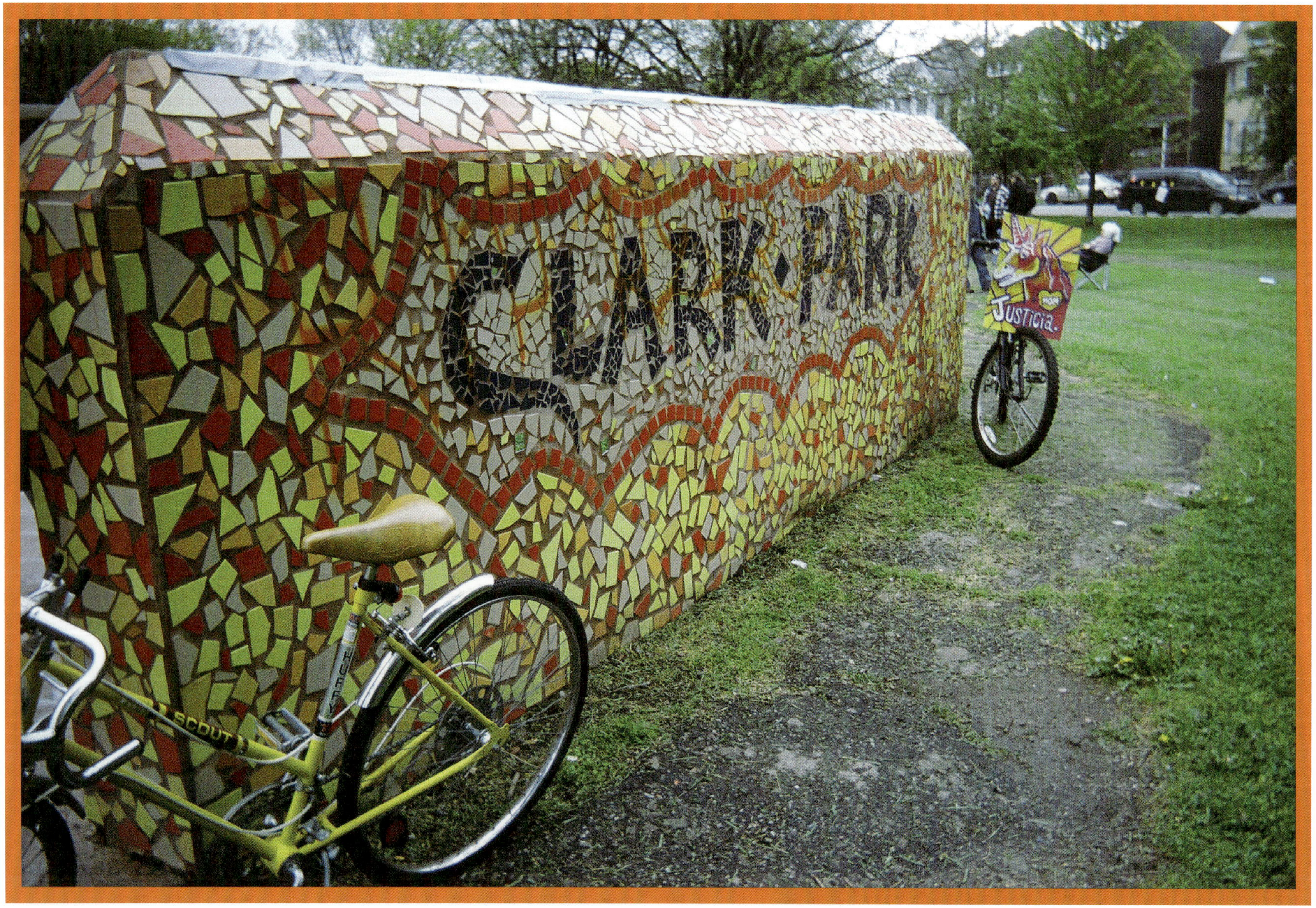

Clark Park is a favorite family destination in southwest Detroit. —Awesome News Taskforce

BE CULTURALLY EXPOSED

Leader: Bonnie E. Odom-Brown

Participants: 45

www.becultural.org

BE CULTURALLY EXPOSED provides positive alternatives for youth by offering cultural activities such as art exhibits, musical concerts, and theatrical performances. We help youth build character and instill confidence and a sense of purpose in their lives.

It was also a great experience for our youth to think critically about their environment. Reveal Your Detroit was a win-win for BE Culturally Exposed.

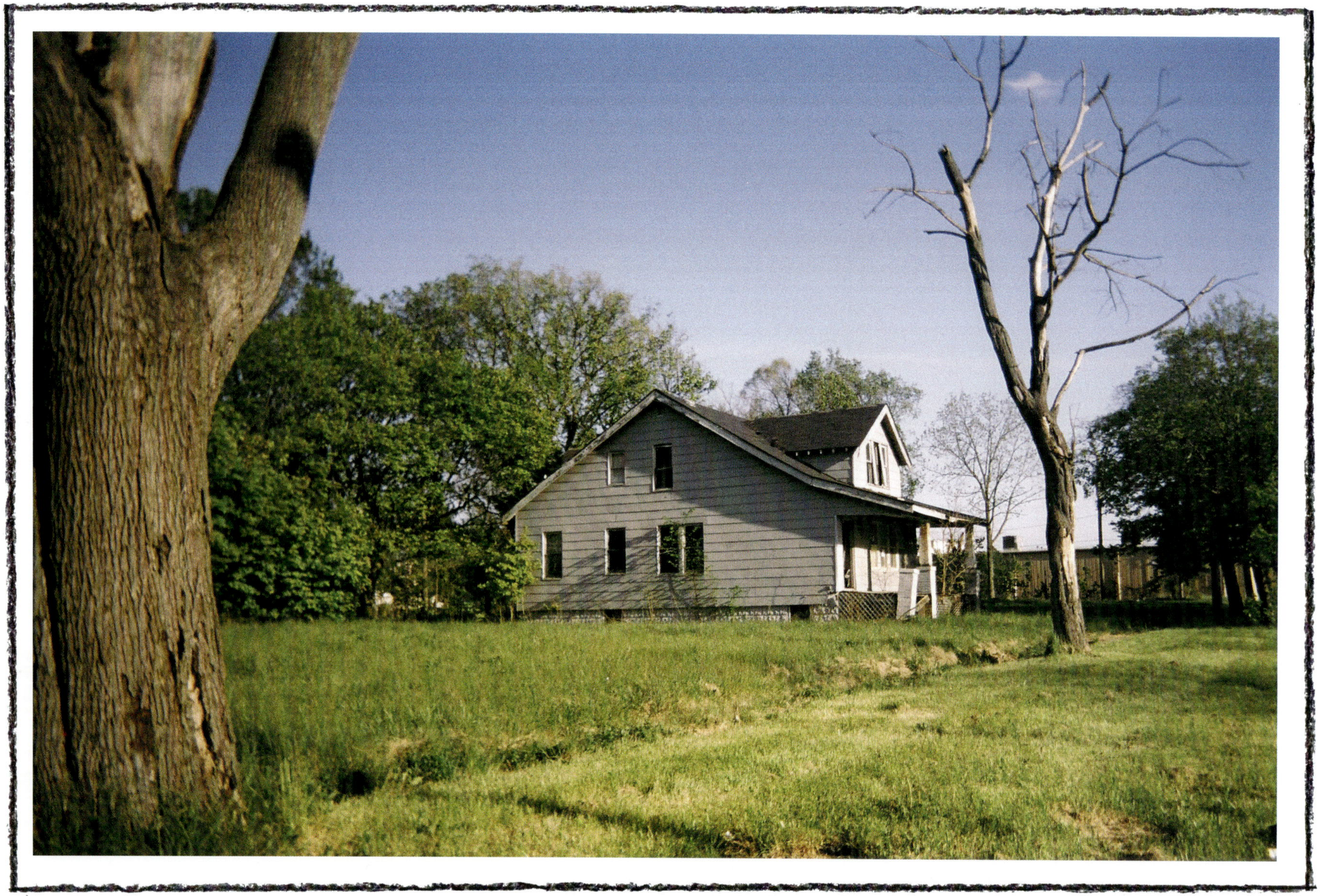

A lonely house. —BE Culturally Exposed

BE EXPOSED: DETROIT

Leader: Miguel Pope

Participants: 15

BE EXPOSED: DETROIT is a youth enrichment and development program that exposes youth to the world around them, allowing boys and girls the opportunity to see "STUFF" up close and personal.

Reveal Your Detroit provided BE EXPOSED: DETROIT an opportunity for youth from different parts of the city to come together to explore the community. It helped our youth see that neighborhoods are the same and different at the same time and that east and west Detroit are merely geographic divisions that can easily be crossed. The project encouraged youth from different communities, different schools, and different backgrounds to connect and to look beyond the surface when we visit other places.

It was so fun to hear the children exclaim: "They got a blue camera; they must be part of Reveal Your Detroit!"

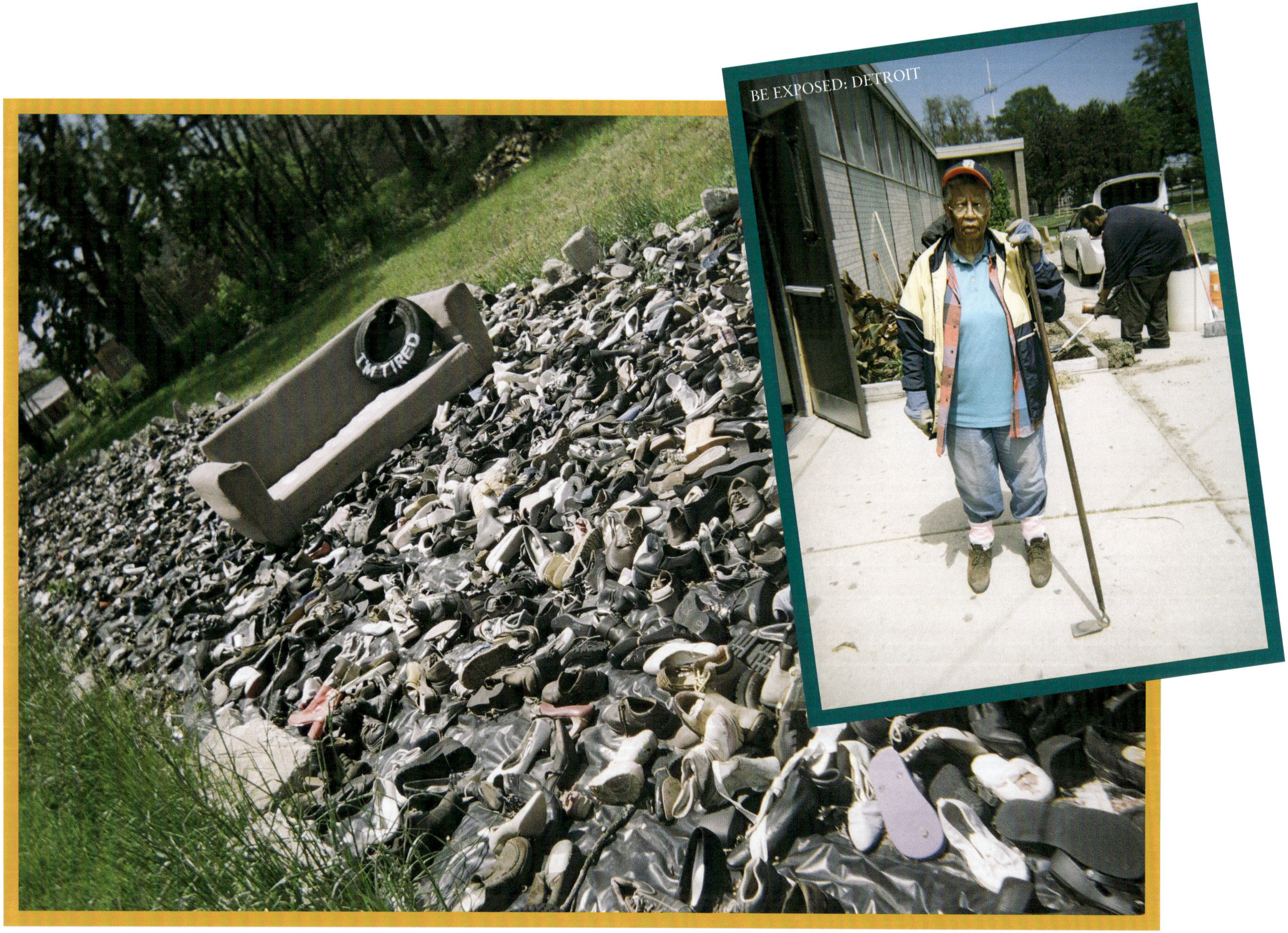

Art installation covering an abandoned street. —BE EXPOSED: DETROIT

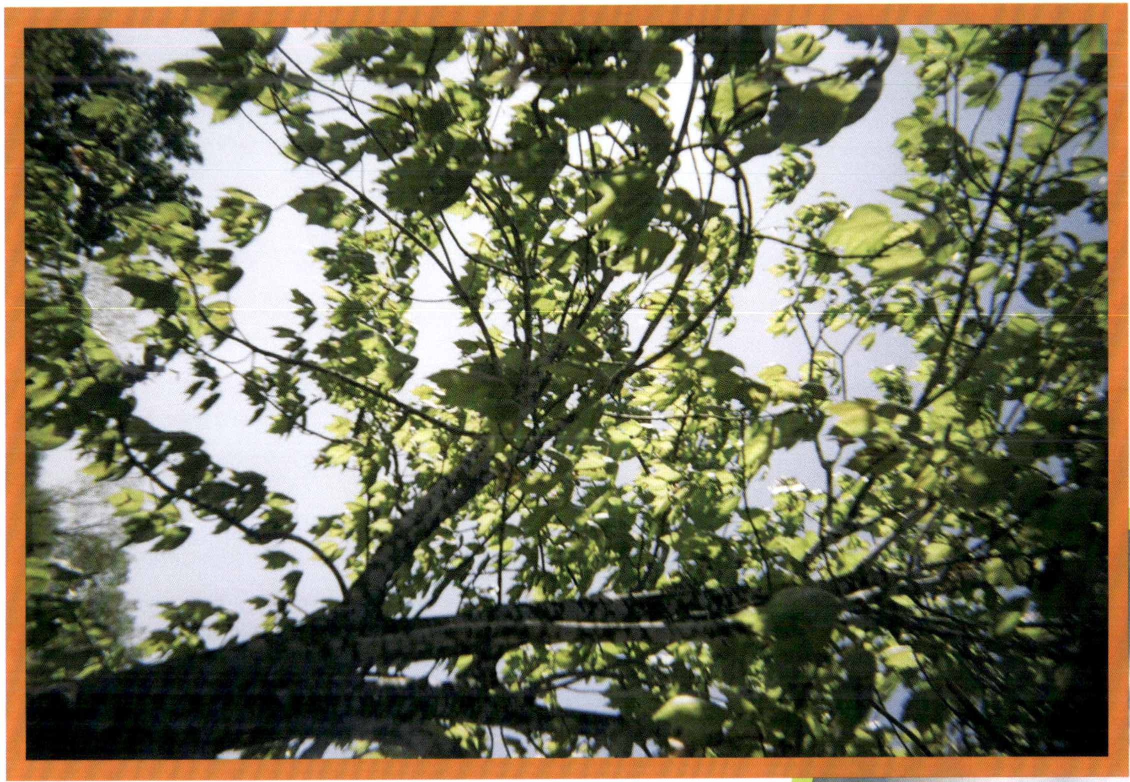

A burst of light through trees in Detroit. —BE EXPOSED: DETROIT

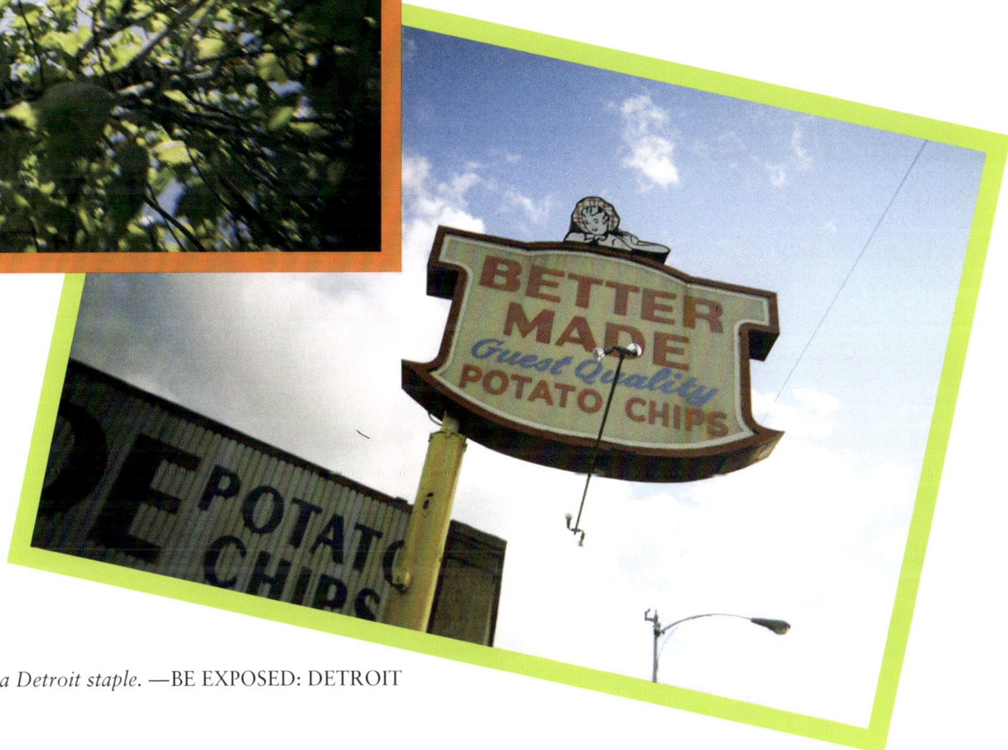

Better Made Chips, a Detroit staple. —BE EXPOSED: DETROIT

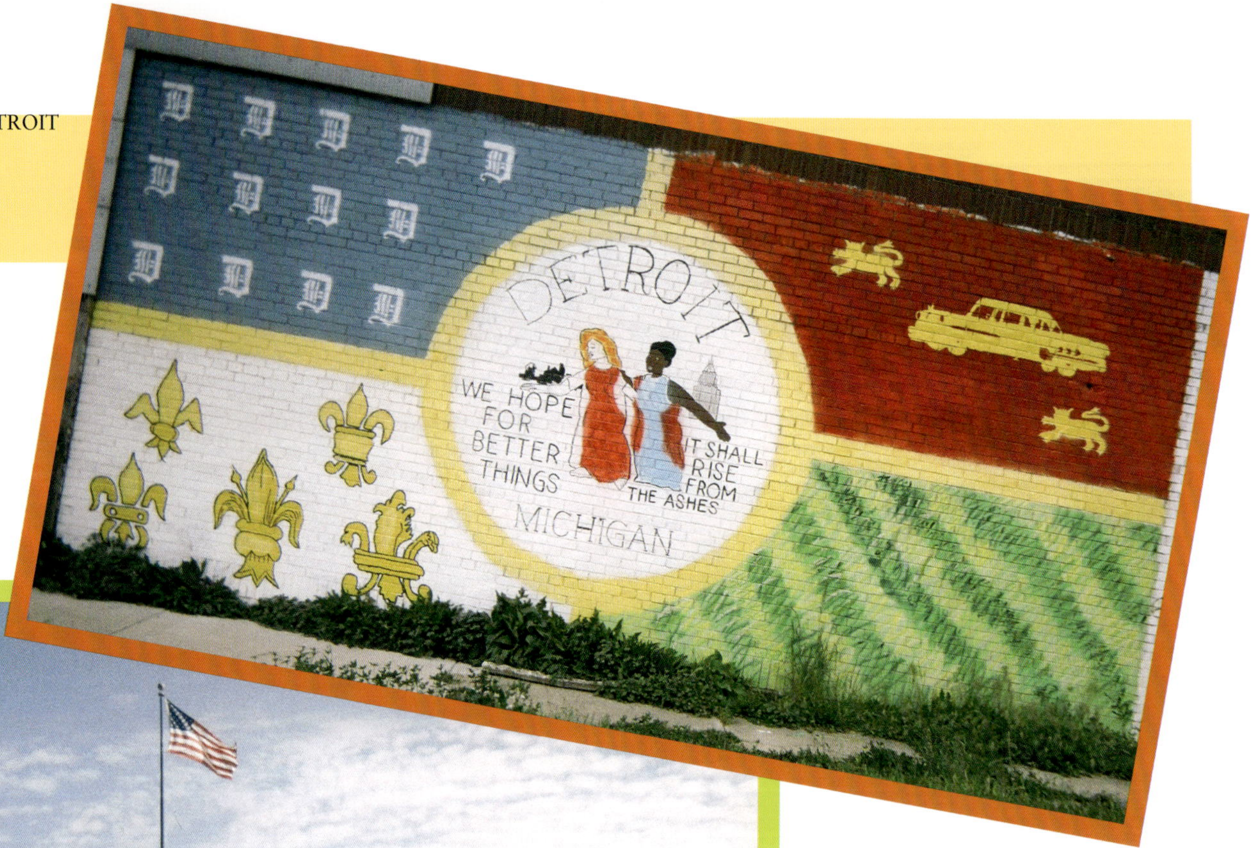

Mural of the Detroit city flag. —BE EXPOSED: DETROIT

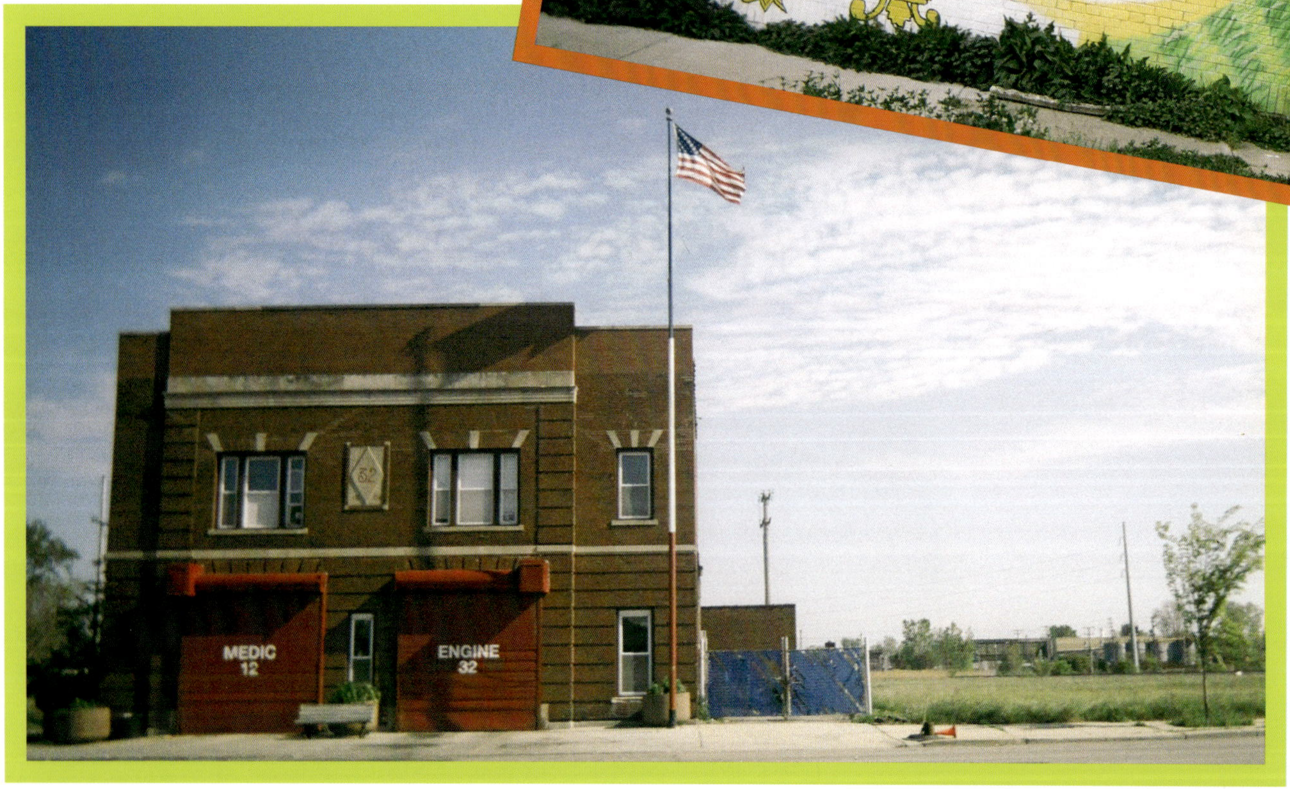

A Detroit firehouse.
—BE EXPOSED: DETROIT

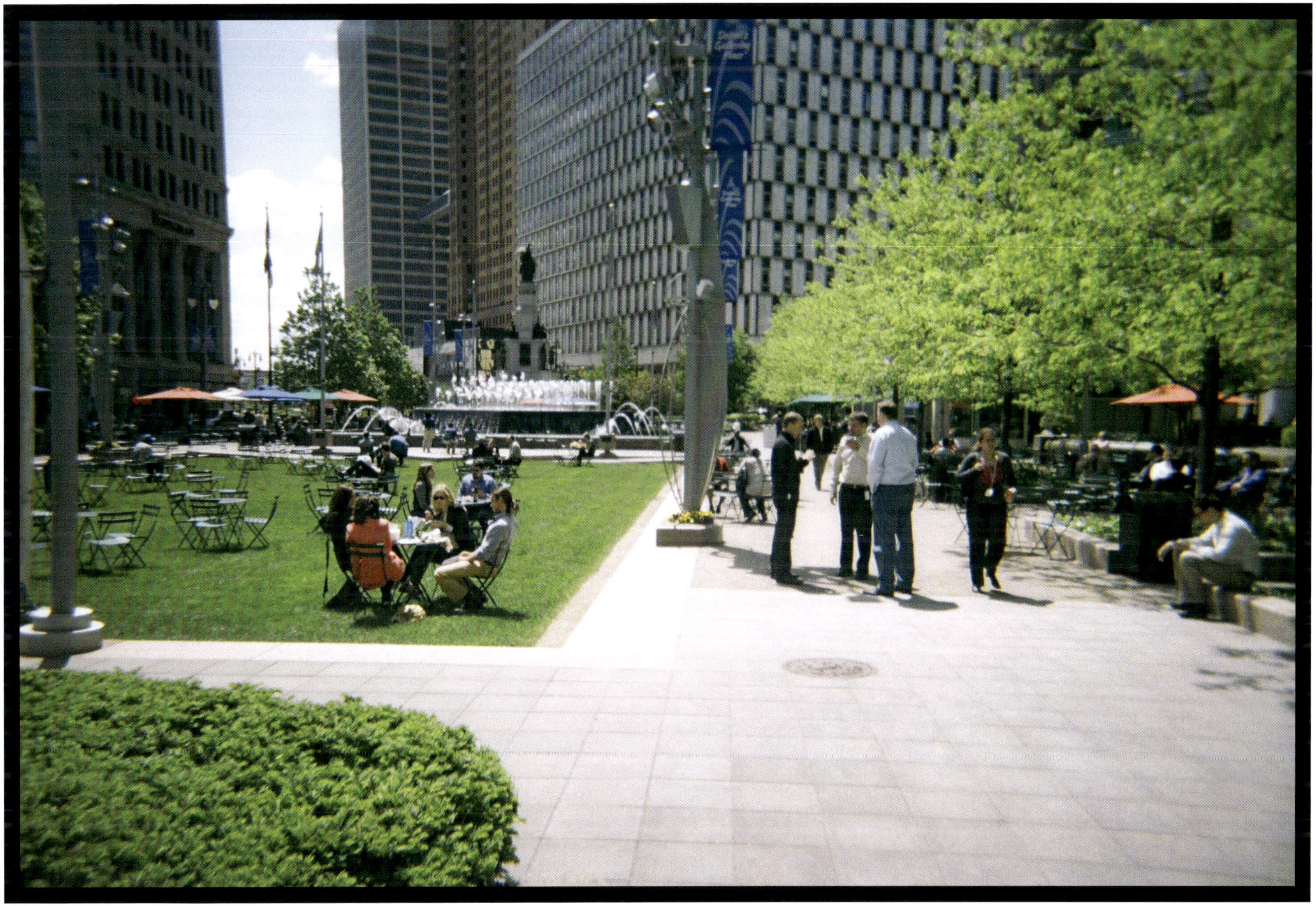

Campus Martius at lunchtime. —BE EXPOSED: DETROIT

BECKHAM WILLIAM ACADEMY ELEMENTARY SCHOOL

Leader: Kalleen Clark

Participants: 20

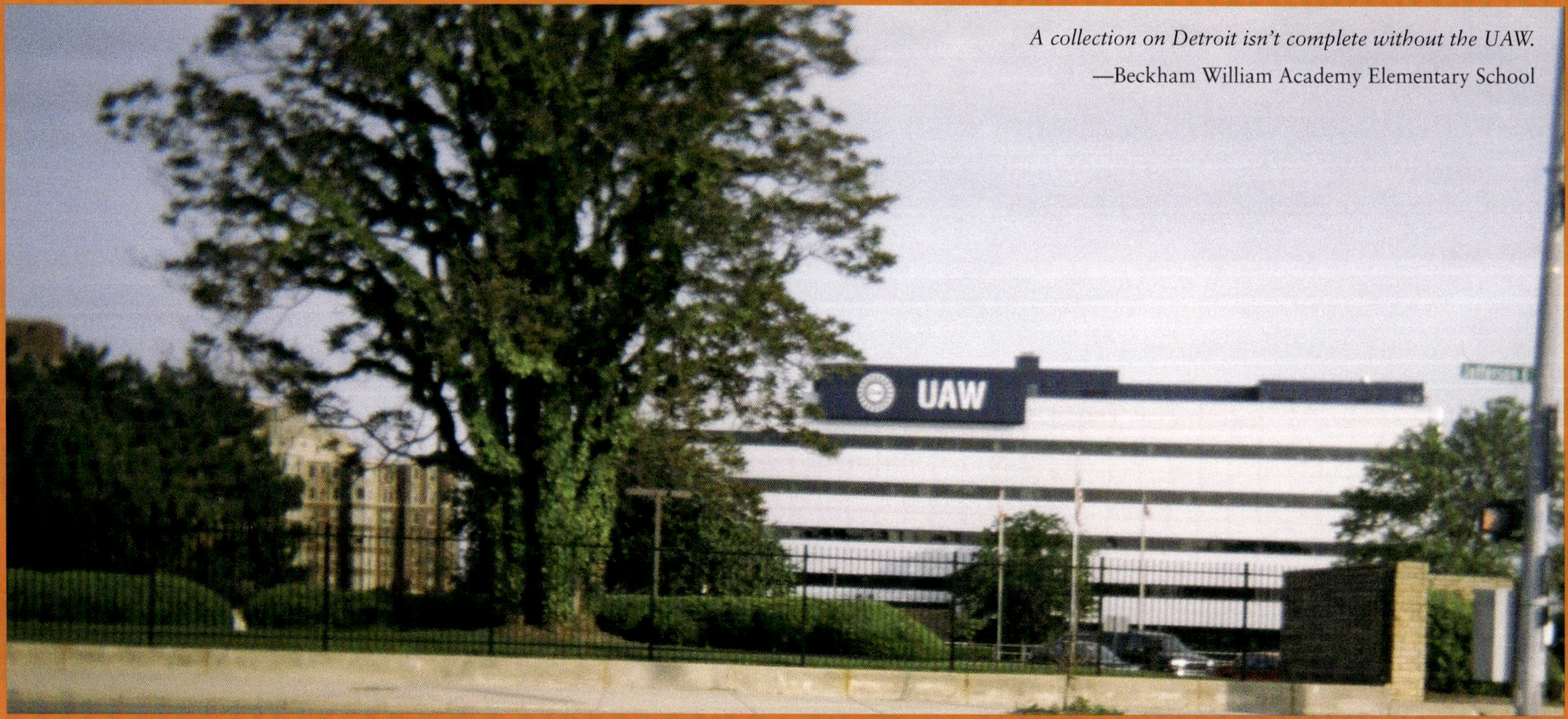

A collection on Detroit isn't complete without the UAW.

—Beckham William Academy Elementary School

CALVIN EAST PRESBYTERIAN CHURCH W.O.R.D. LITERACY PROGRAM

Leader: Andree J. Tarrant

Participants: 7

THE W.O.R.D. PROGRAM serves elementary and middle school children on the eastside of Detroit near Calvin East Presbyterian Church. Our trip to the DIA was the first field trip undertaken by the W.O.R.D. literacy program. Many of the children had never visited the DIA. After the field trip the children wrote and drew pictures about their experiences. They also took imaginative photographs to submit to the DIA's Reveal Your Detroit photography project.

The Reveal Your Detroit experience encouraged the children to explore various types of art at the DIA and then express their own artistic creativity through the capture of color, light, shape, and texture on film.

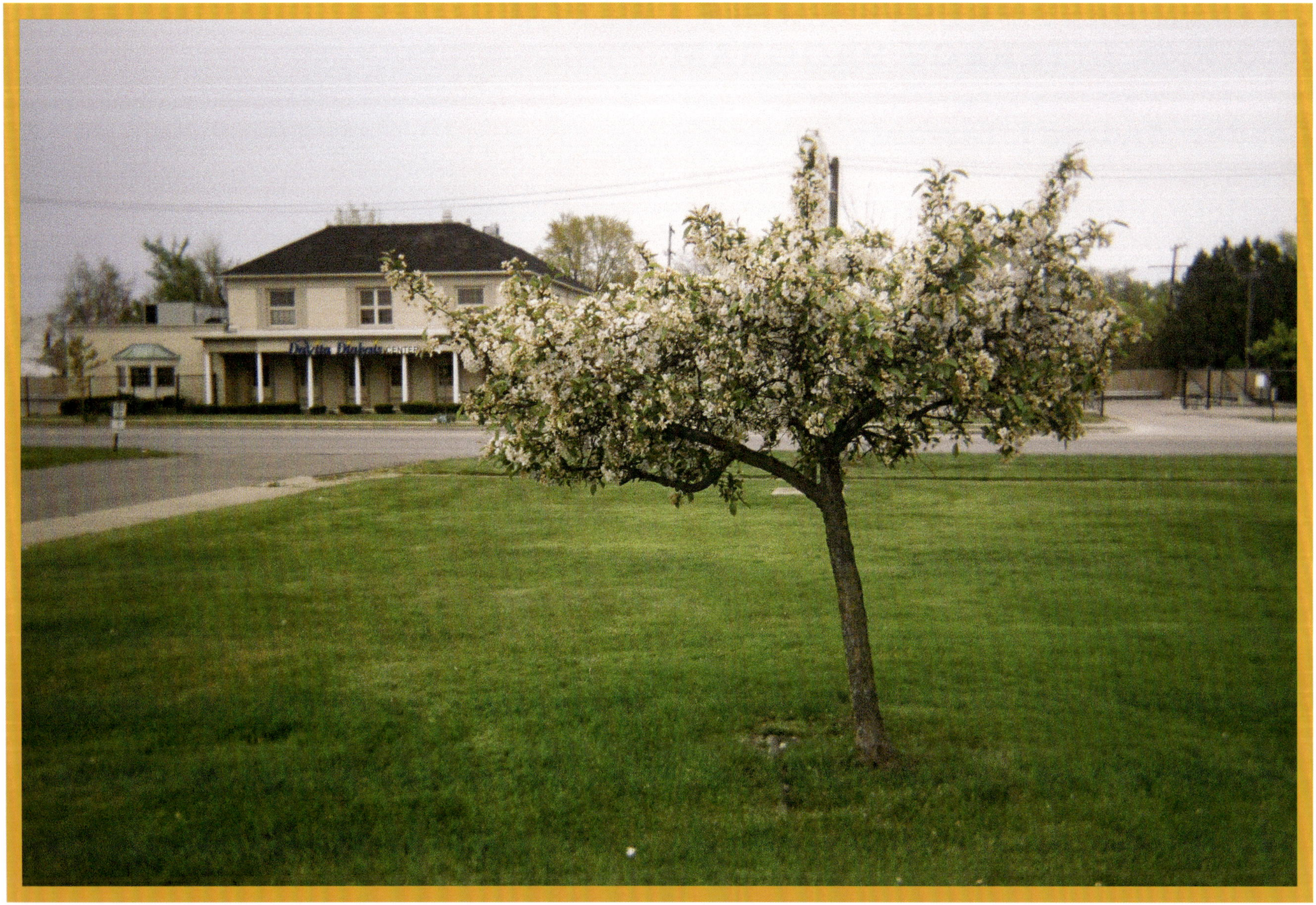

This tree is outside the church grounds on Detroit's eastside. —Calvin East Presbyterian Church W.O.R.D. Literacy Program

COMMUNITY DEVELOPMENT PROGRAM SCHOOL OF ARCHITECTURE, UNIVERSITY OF DETROIT MERCY

Leader: Libby Balter Blume

Participants: 10

www.architecture.udmercy.edu

UNIVERSITY OF DETROIT MERCY'S Masters of Community Development (MCD) program provides a holistic approach to the theory and practice of community development.

The educational and experiential aspects of the DIA exhibition, panel discussion, and community outreach project provided invaluable opportunities to discuss the important question of "What is community?" with diverse participants.

Reveal Your Detroit was exemplary in its level of community engagement, diversity of organizational participation, and use of digital media to reflect unique and compelling images of Detroit through the eyes of residents of all ages, ethnicities, and neighborhoods.

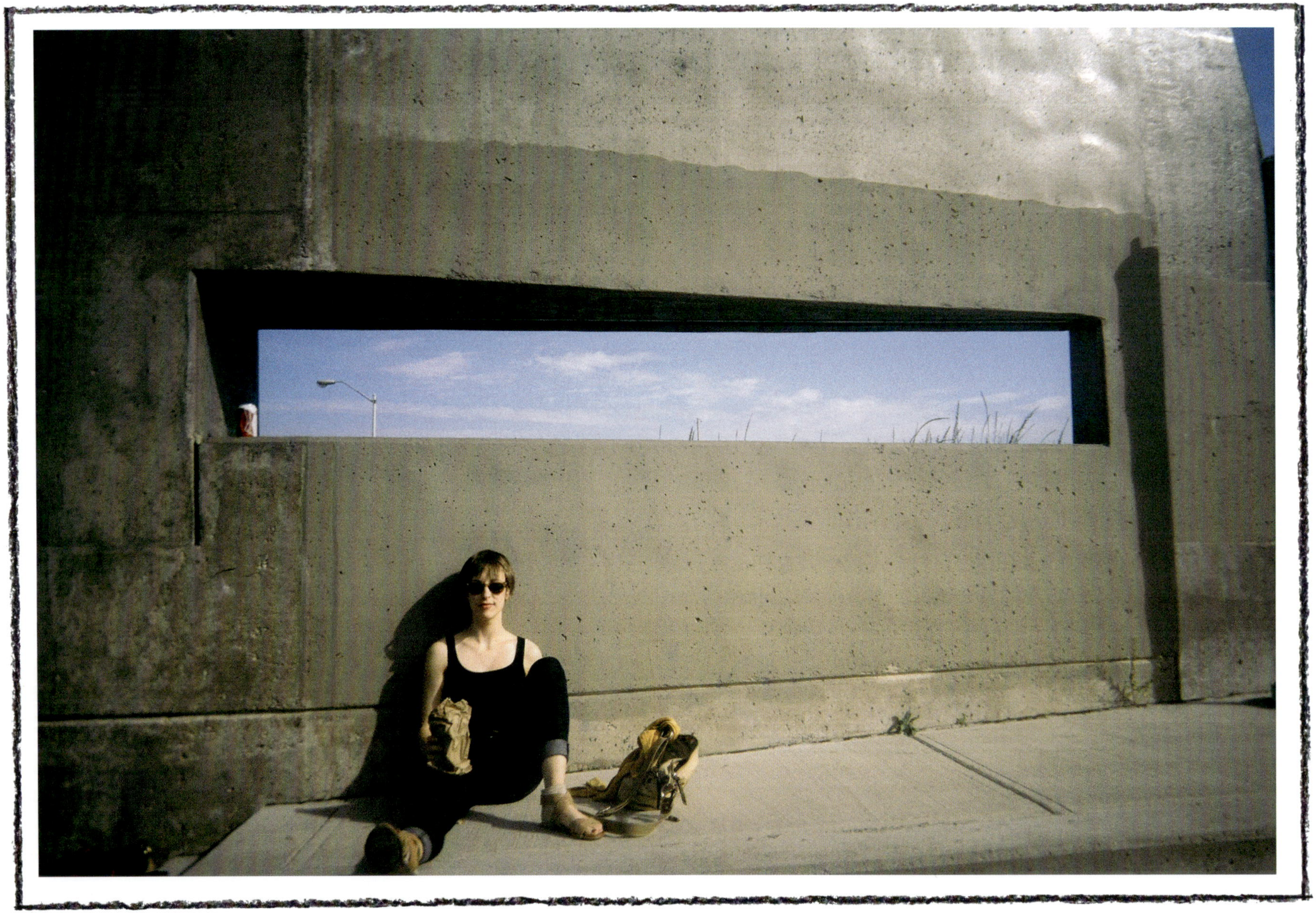

Community Development Program, University of Detroit Mercy

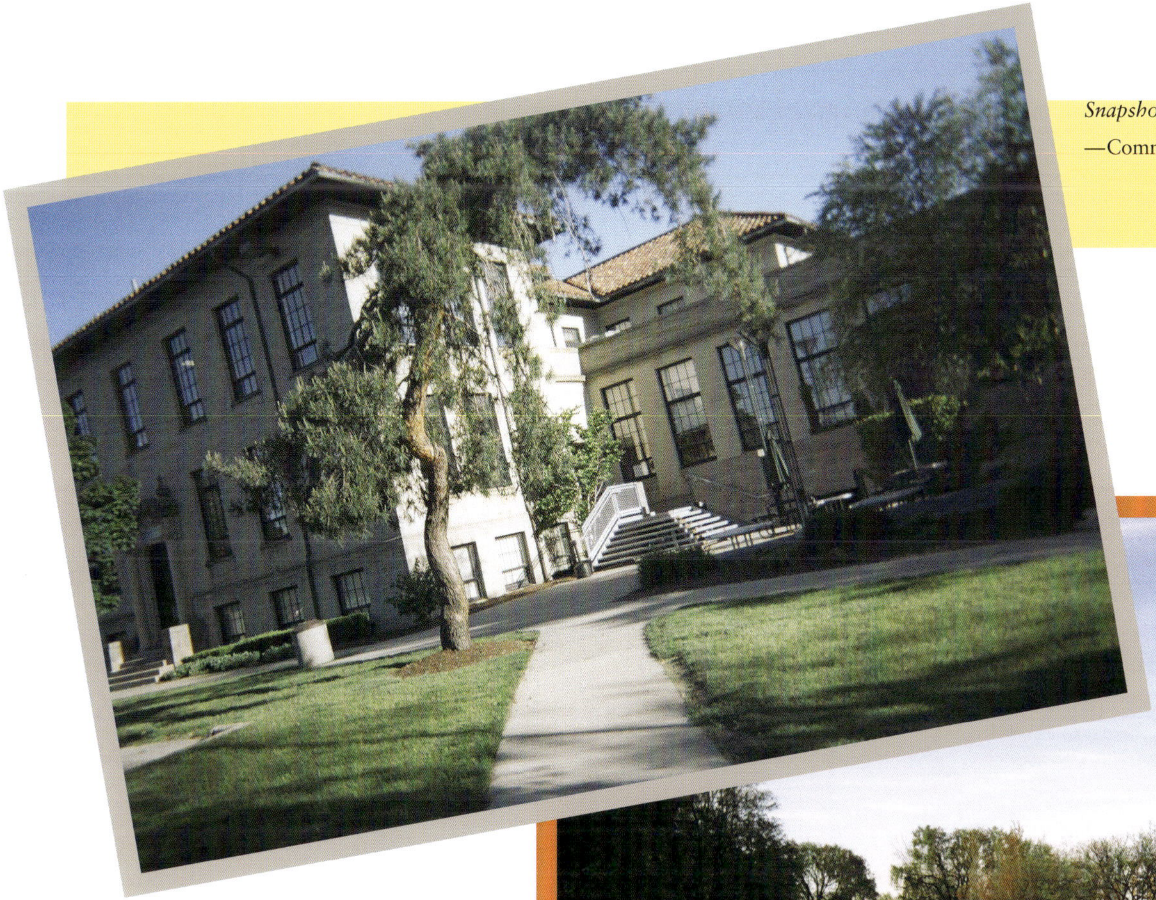

Snapshot of University of Detroit Mercy's campus.
—Community Development Program, University of Detroit Mercy

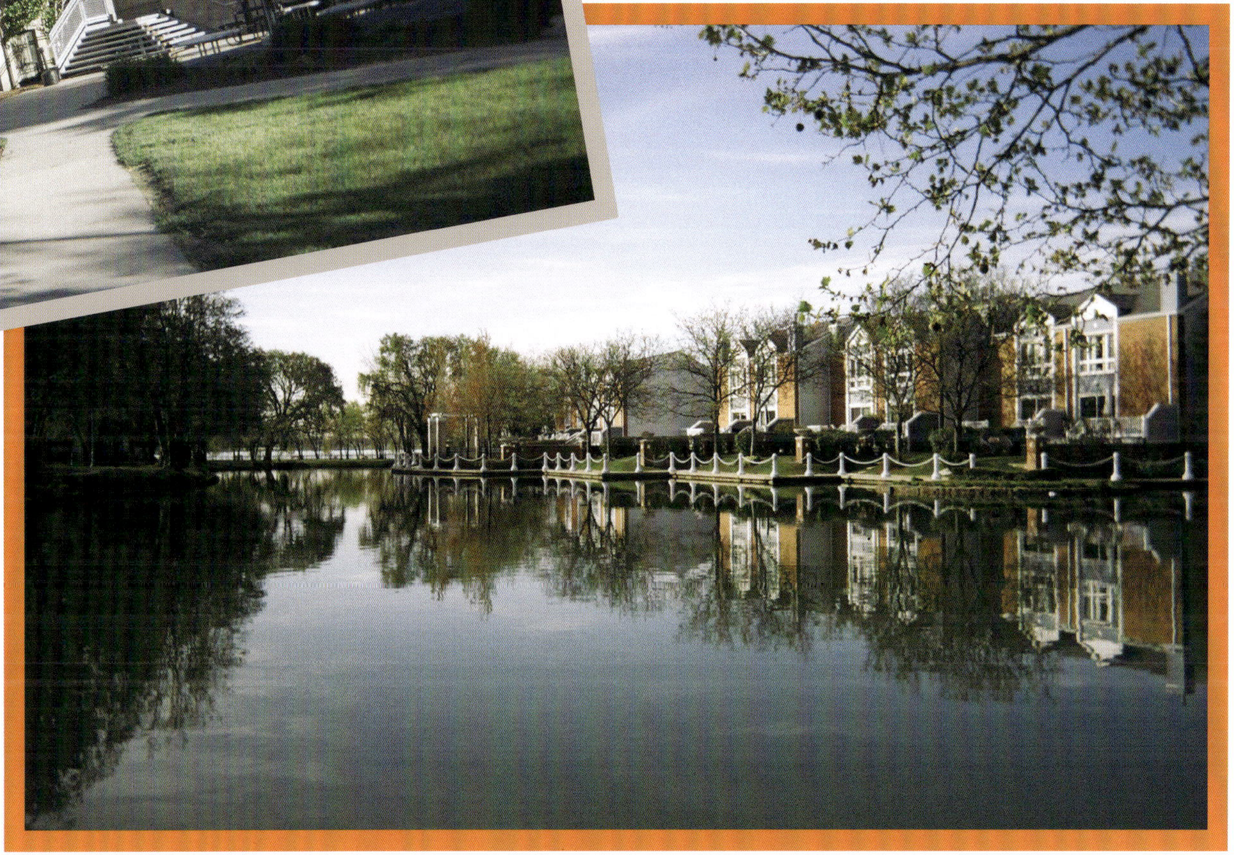

Harbor Town residence.
—Community Development Program,
University of Detroit Mercy

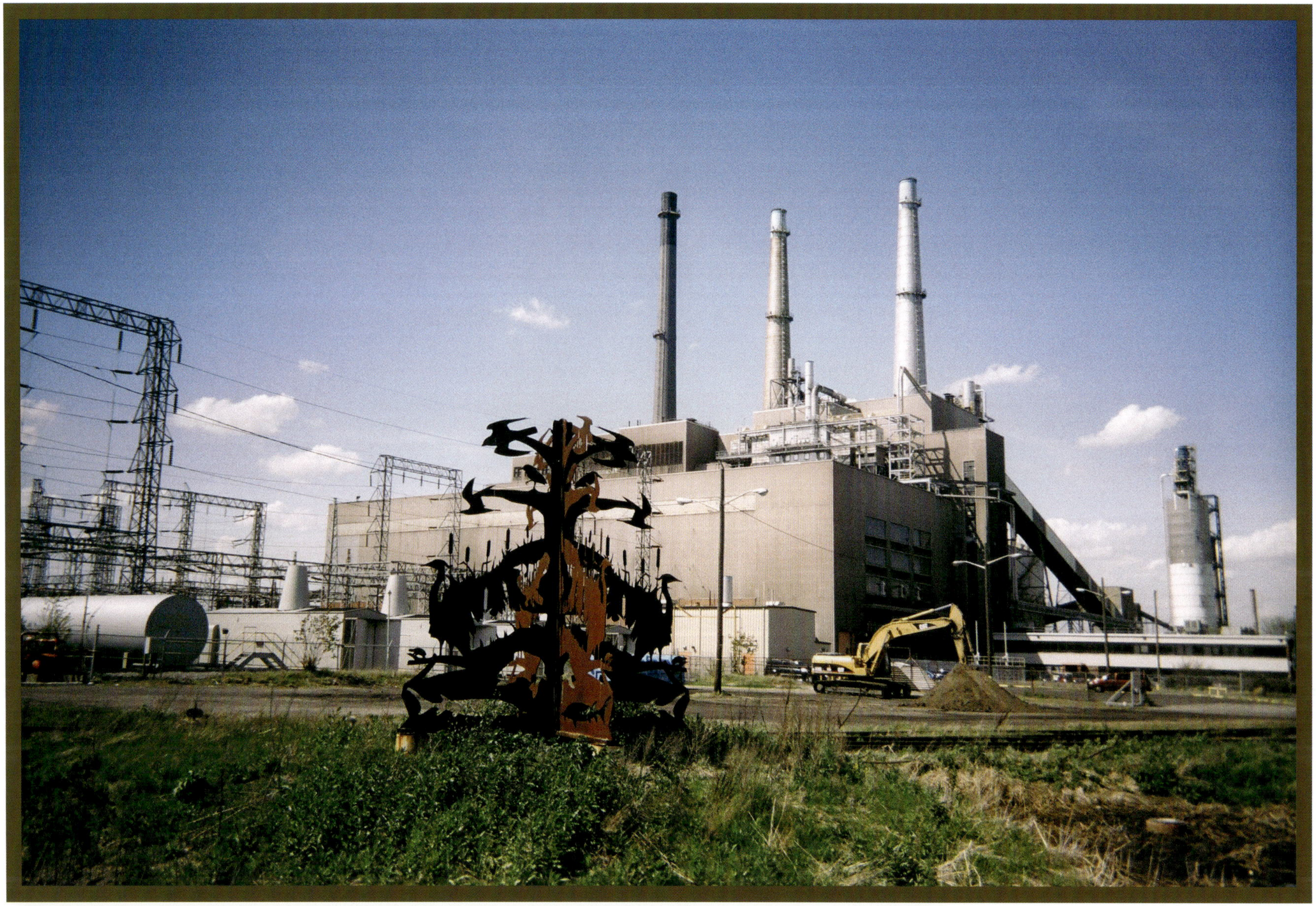

Industry and art sculptures meet. —Community Development Program, University of Detroit Mercy

CREATIVE SPIRITS

Leader: Shirley Lolles

Participants: 17

CREATIVE SPIRITS is a group of senior artists all over age sixty. The group's purpose is to promote Detroit artists who work in a variety of mediums.

While none of the Creative Spirits are professional photographers, all were excited about being involved in a project that exposed them to many ethnic groups in Detroit that they previously had little or no interaction with. Creative Spirits looks forward to being part of other projects that promote community advancement and togetherness.

While participating in this project we learned about areas of Detroit other than our own that are beautiful, interesting, and enlightening.

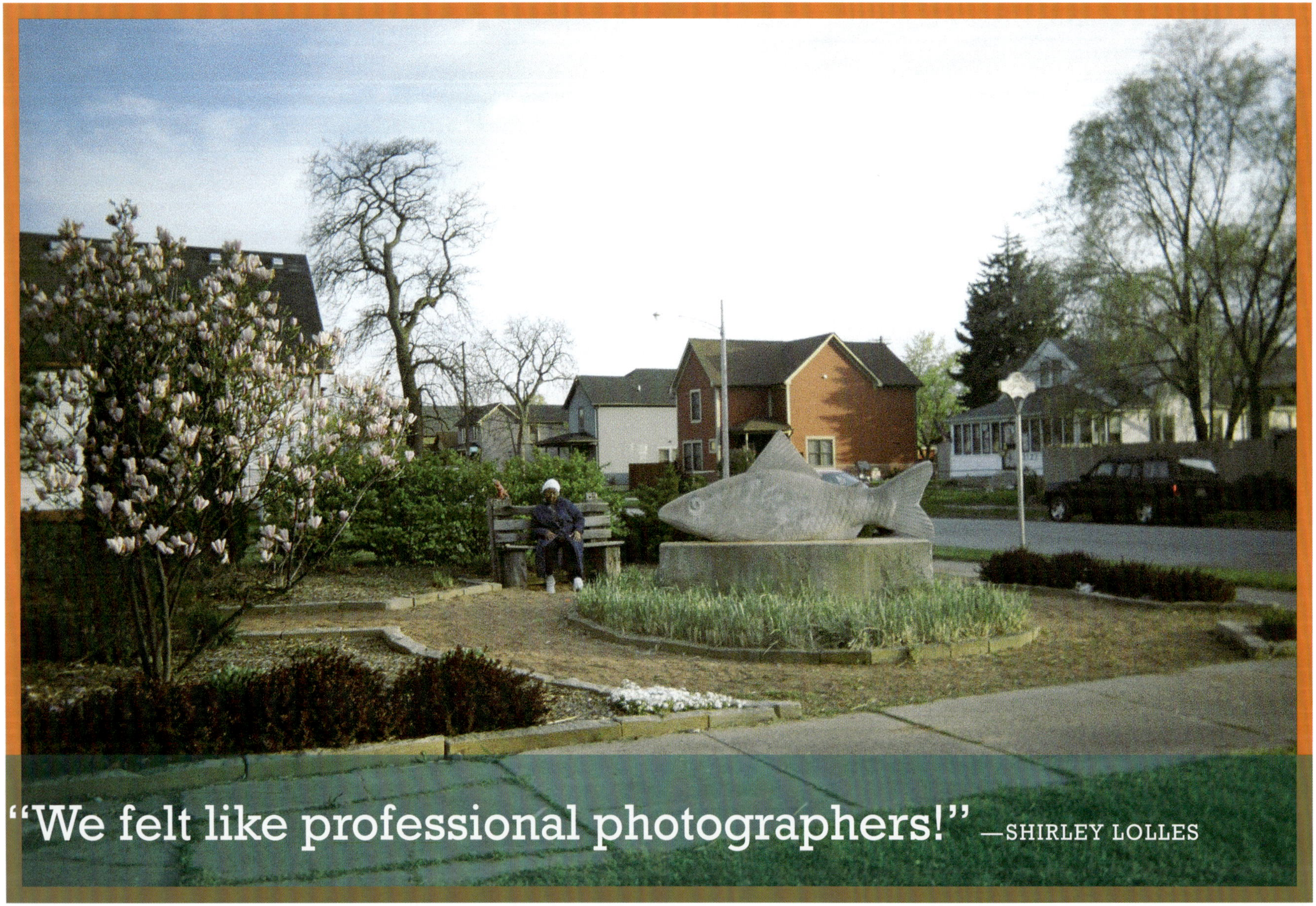

"We felt like professional photographers!" —SHIRLEY LOLLES

Shirley Lolles, group leader for Creative Spirits, recaptured an image from her youth of her sitting on this porch as a young girl. —Creative Spirits

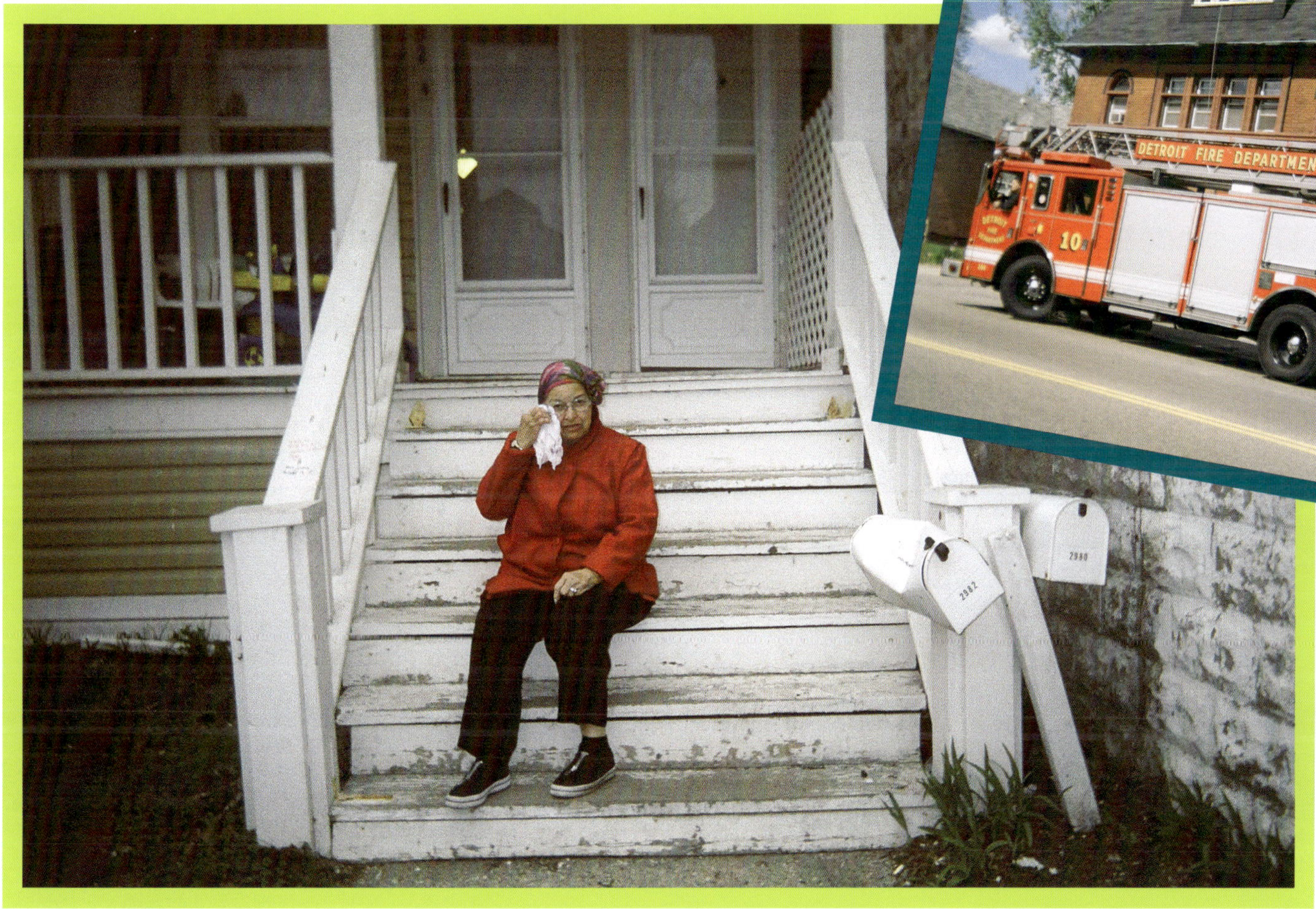

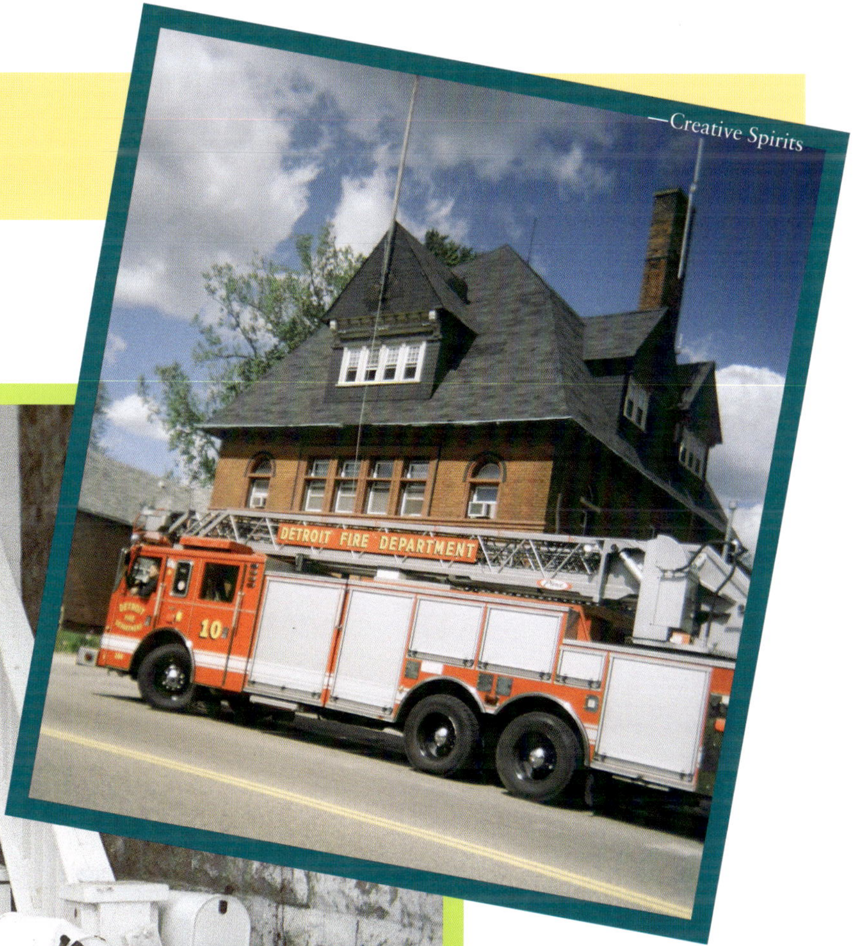

—Creative Spirits

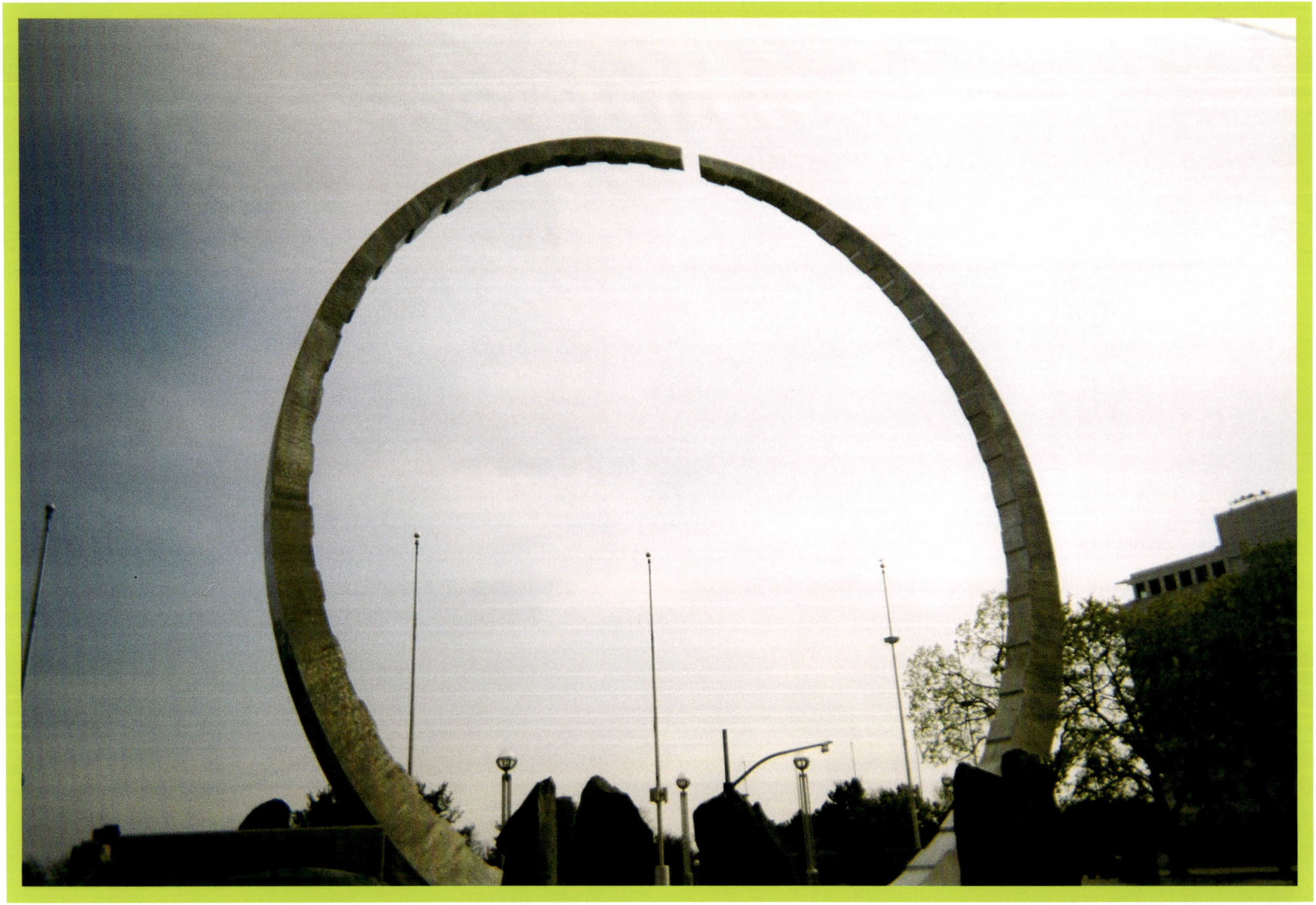

Hart Plaza sculpture Transcending *by David Barr and Sergio De Giusti.* —Creative Spirits

DETROIT LEISURE LEAGUE

Leader: Steve Shaw

Participants: 5

THE IDEA THAT all citizens have value appealed to our group. Whether you are working for an attorney at the top of the Penobscot building or living in an abandoned home without electricity or running water, or are a working artist, a student, or a small business owner who is a lifelong Detroiter, Reveal Your Detroit was from the eyes of residents. It was a great look into the city of Detroit.

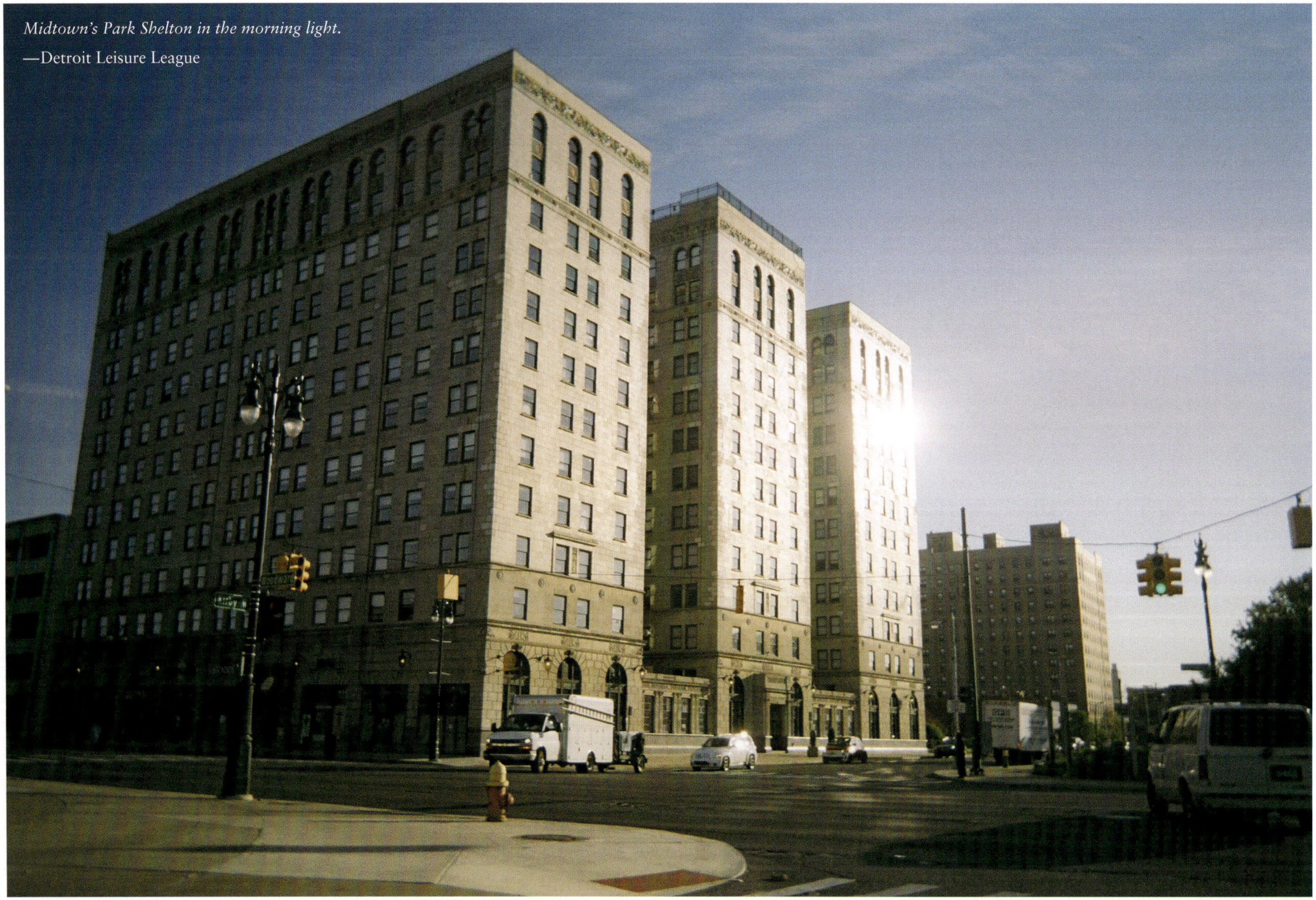

Midtown's Park Shelton in the morning light.
—Detroit Leisure League

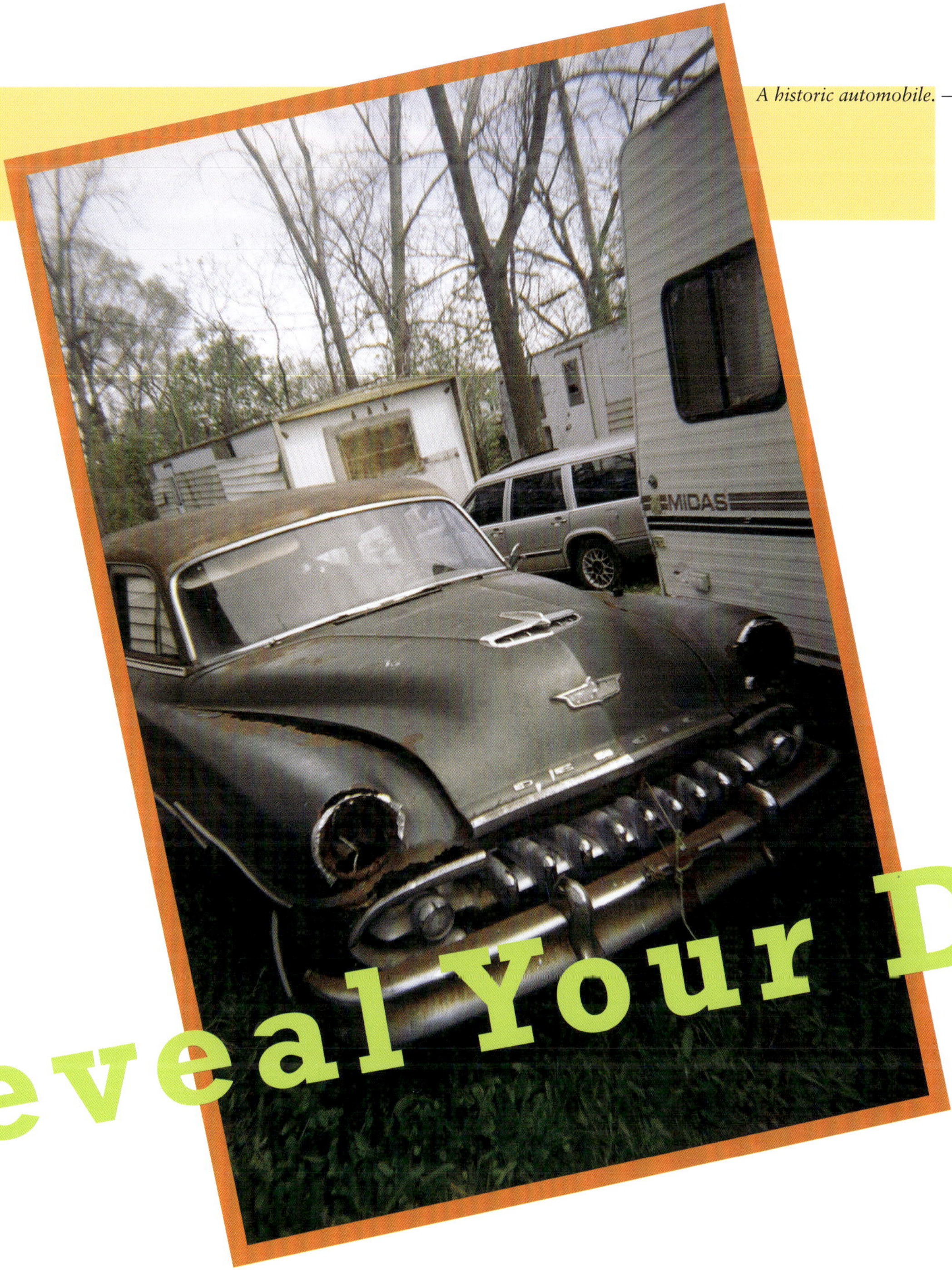

A historic automobile. —Detroit Leisure League

Reveal Your Detroit

DETROIT MERIT ACADEMY

Leader: Natasha Barsakova

Participants: 13

www.detroitmeritcharteracademy.com

Russell Industrial Center. —Detroit Merit Academy

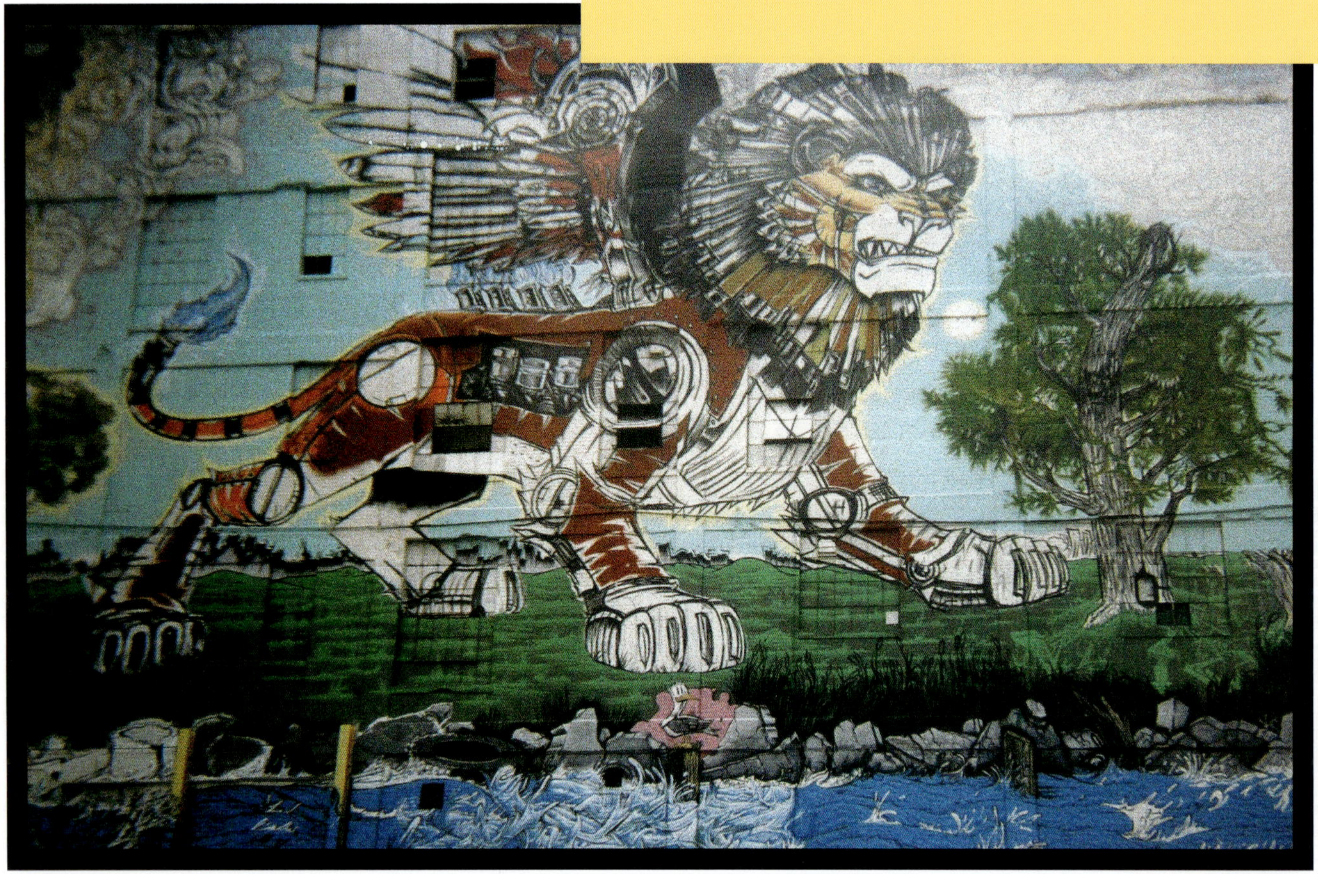

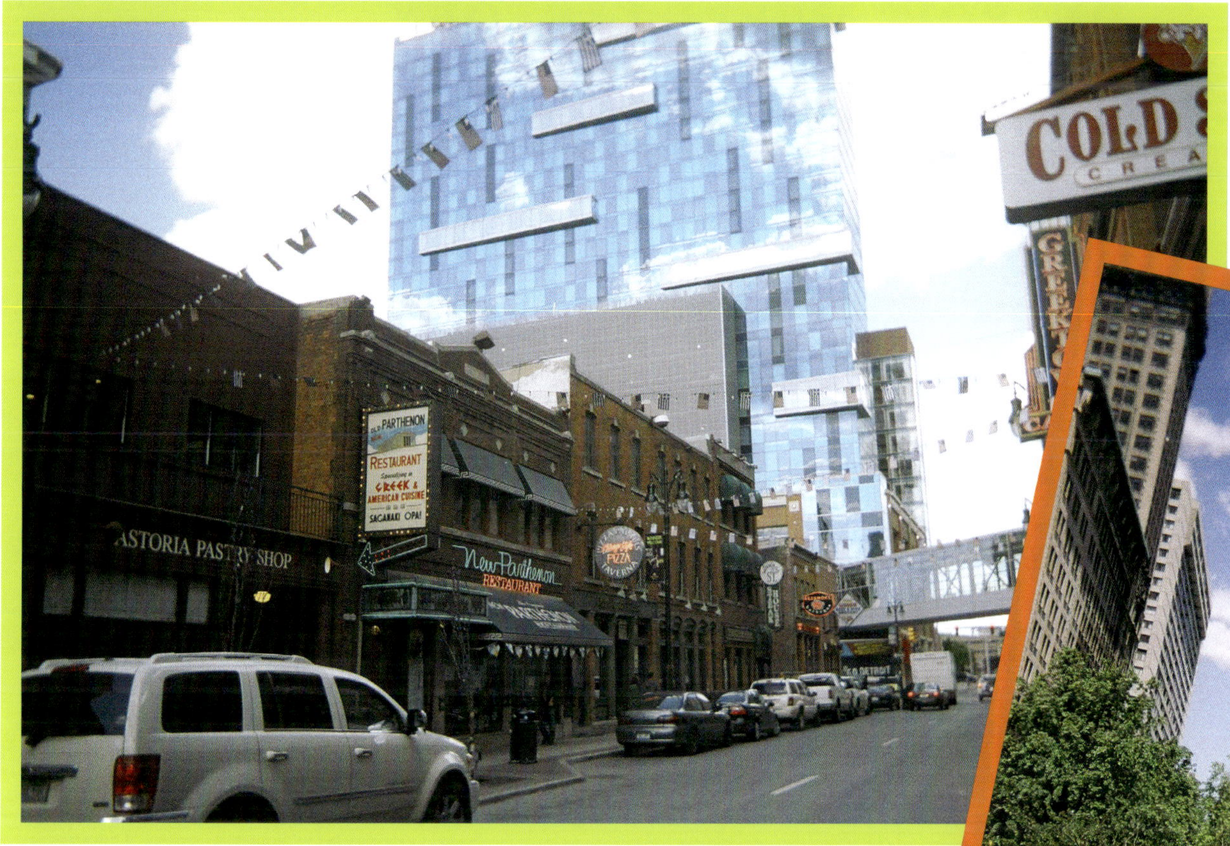

Greektown. —Detroit Merit Academy

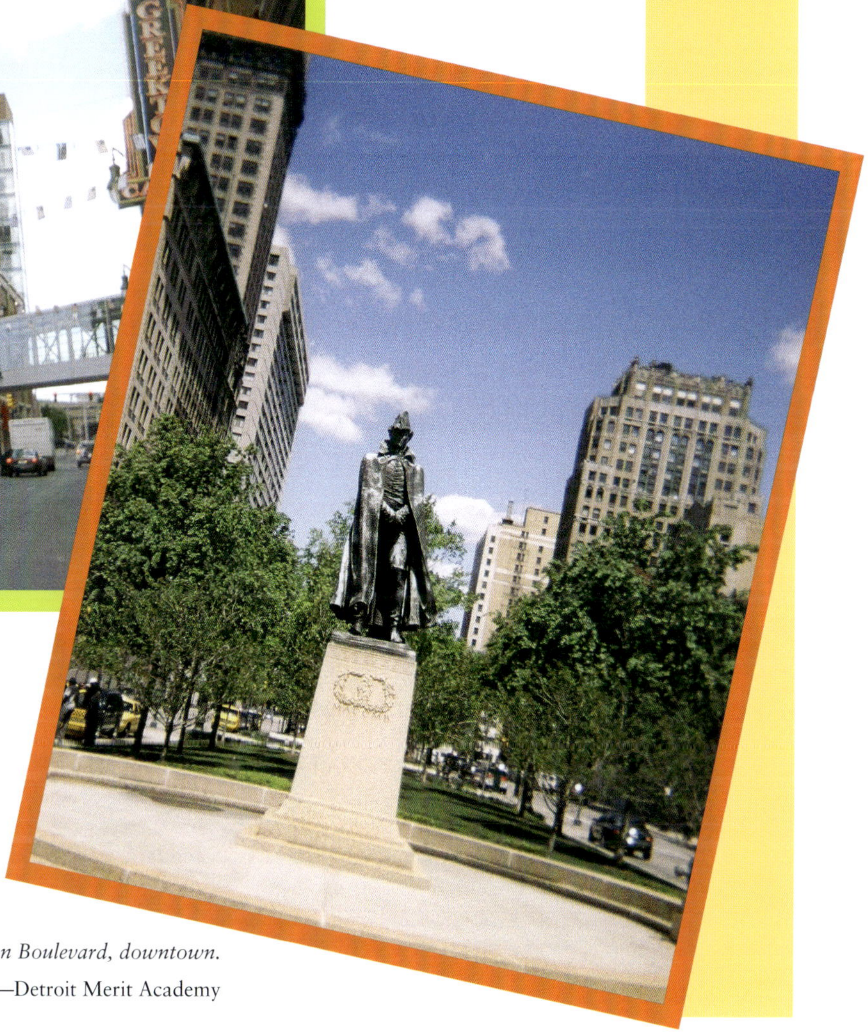

Statue of General Alexander Macomb on Washington Boulevard, downtown. —Detroit Merit Academy

DETROIT MURAL FACTORY

Leader: Halima Cassells

Participants: 26

www.detroitmuralfactory.com

Opposite: *Belle Isle Conservatory.*
—Detroit Mural Factory

DETROIT MURAL FACTORY creates beauty in Detroit and empowers youth through public participatory art experiences.

Detroit Mural Factory partnered with the HERU Organization to bring an intergenerational group to the DIA to view the Detroit Revealed exhibit. Meandering together through a photographic history of Detroit, talking, laughing—we all enjoyed the experience. Before we left, one of our adult allies gave a brief lesson on framing a shot and then many of us began capturing our perspectives on camera. When we met again at the show opening it was great to see how so much positive work intersects in our city.

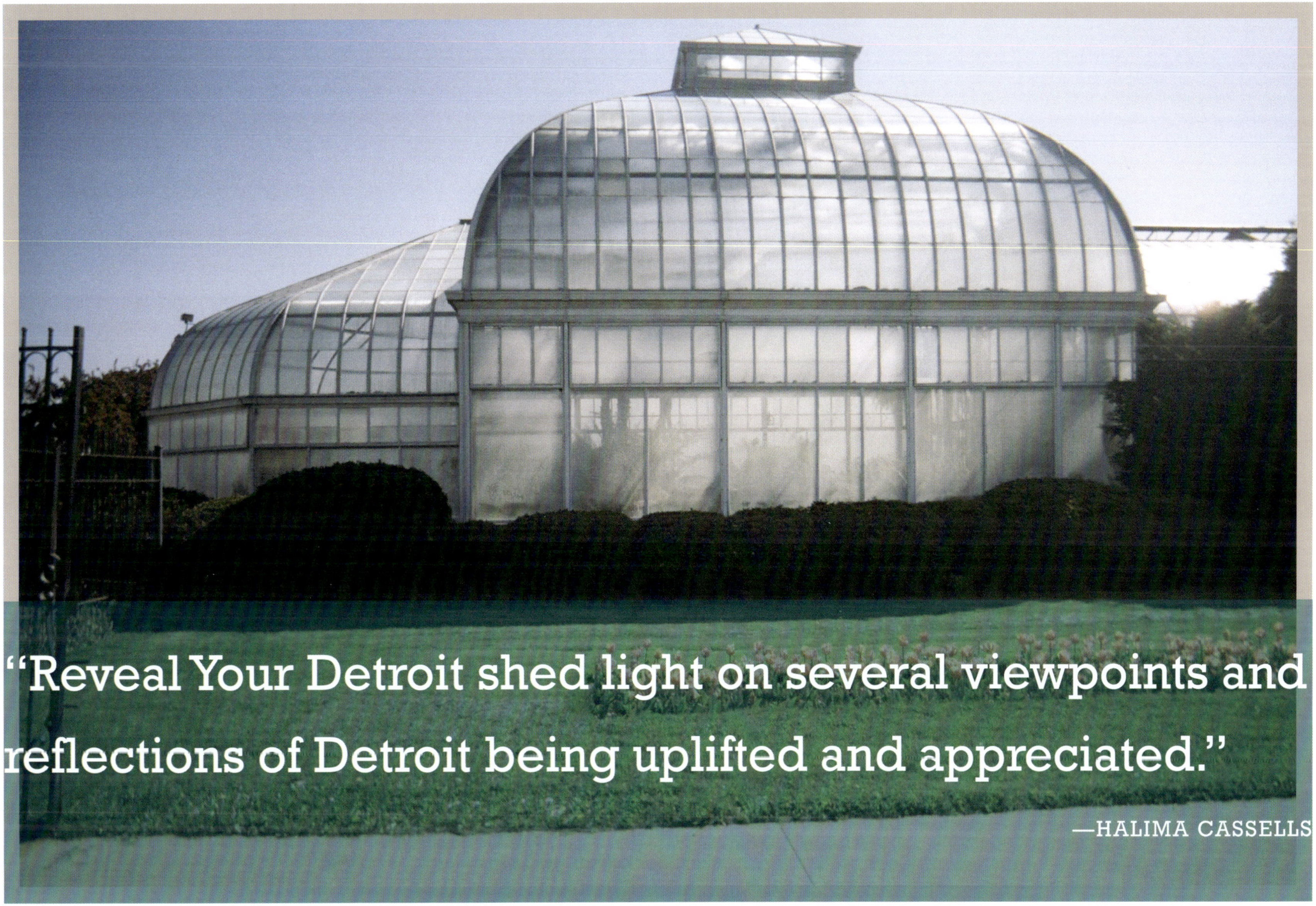

"Reveal Your Detroit shed light on several viewpoints and reflections of Detroit being uplifted and appreciated."

—HALIMA CASSELLS

DETROIT WORKERS FOR ENVIRONMENTAL JUSTICE GREEN JOBS ALUMNI CLUB

Leader: Charles Stokes

Participants: 9

www.dwej.org

DETROIT WORKERS FOR ENVIRONMENTAL JUSTICE (DWEJ) works with communities to create cleaner, safer, and healthier neighborhoods. The Green Jobs Alumni Club was established to improve and beautify the city of Detroit and provides DWEJ's job-training alumni with continued professional and personal development as well as opportunities for community engagement.

Reveal Your Detroit was an eye-opening experience because it allowed us to look at the city from an outsider's perspective. The discussion over the photos also encouraged our group members to engage with each other in a really different way than we normally do—more spiritual and artistic because our responses to each image were very personal. Working on this project brought Alumni Club members closer together and instilled a sense of ownership and pride in our community.

Reveal Your Detroit had true value in connecting the outsider's perspective with the insider's perspective and pushed each person to step outside of his or her own self by hearing or seeing someone else's perspective.

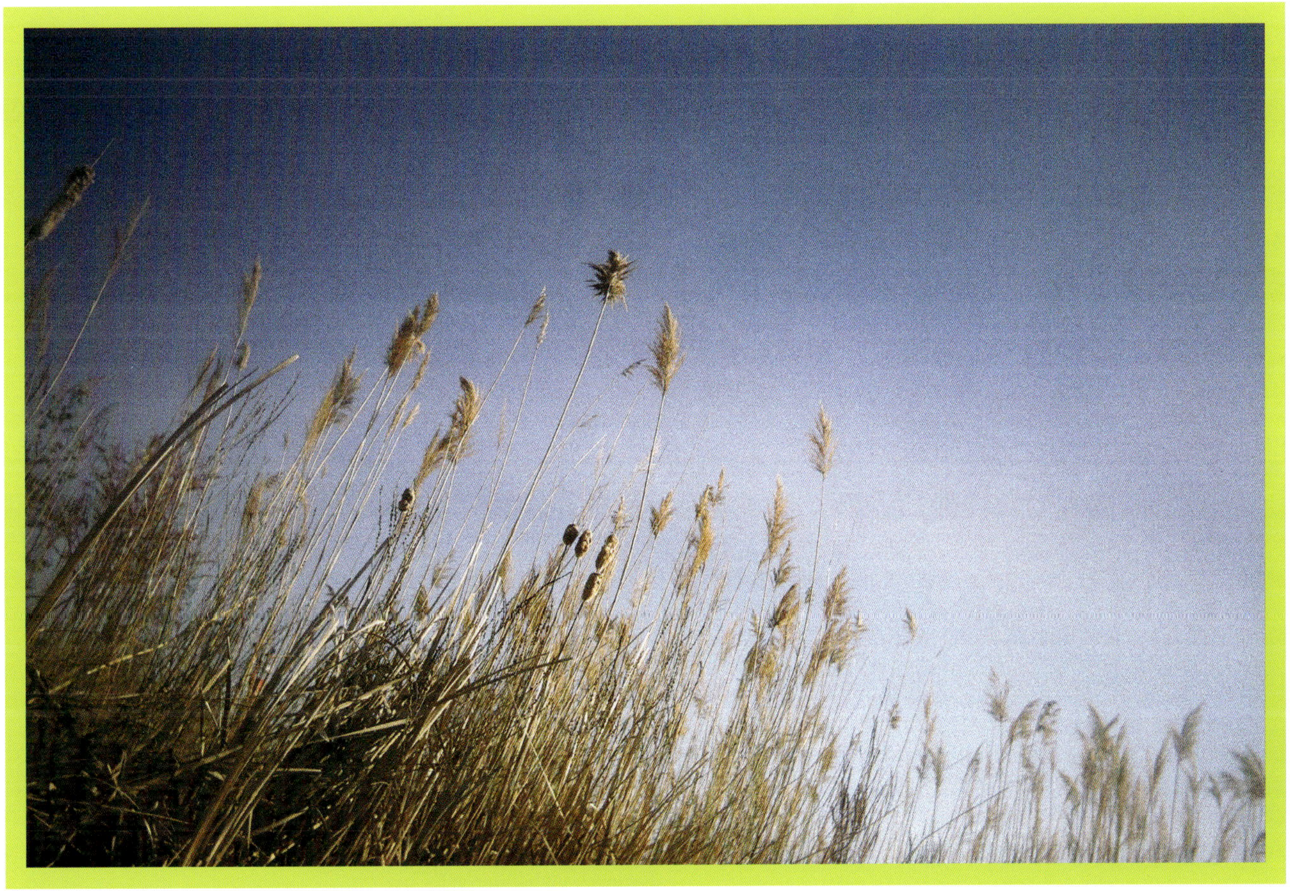

Prairie grass. —Detroit Workers for Environmental Justice

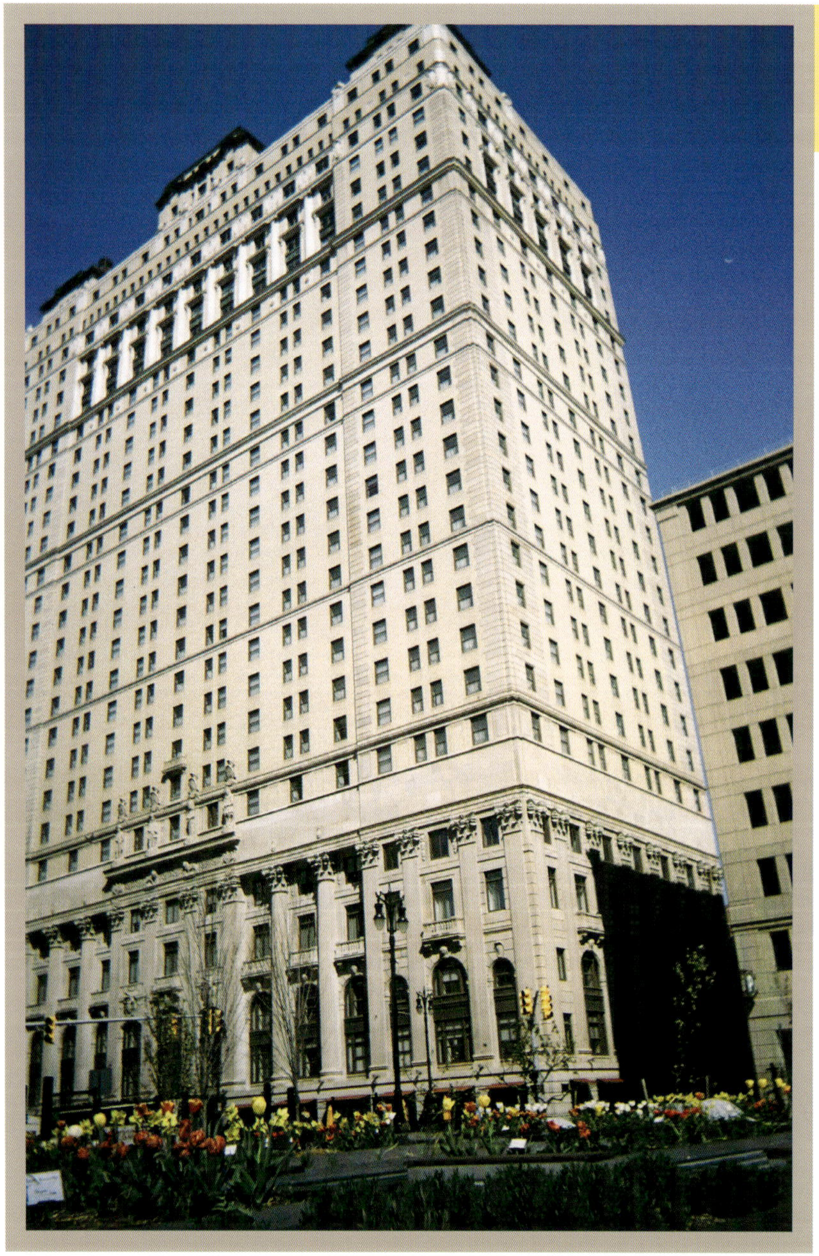

Book Cadillac Hotel from the Central Business District Community Garden.
—Detroit Workers for Environmental Justice

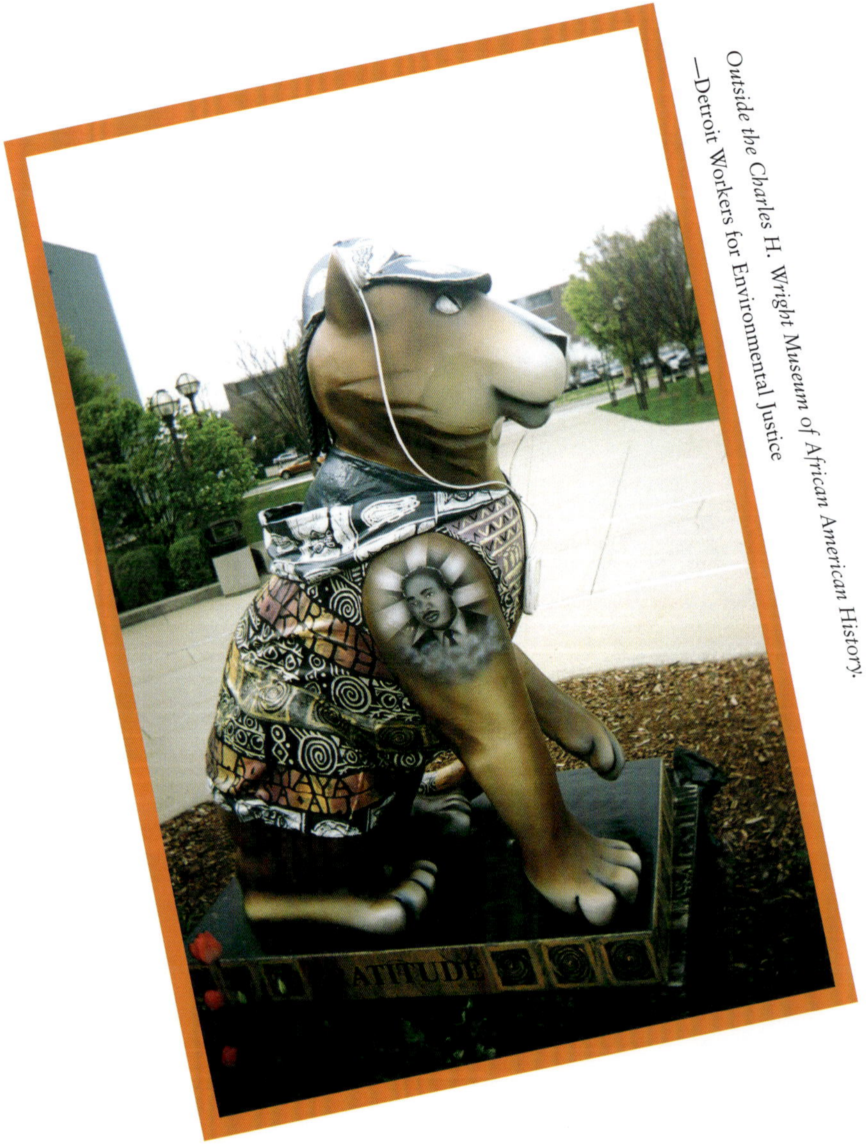

Outside the Charles H. Wright Museum of African American History.
—Detroit Workers for Environmental Justice

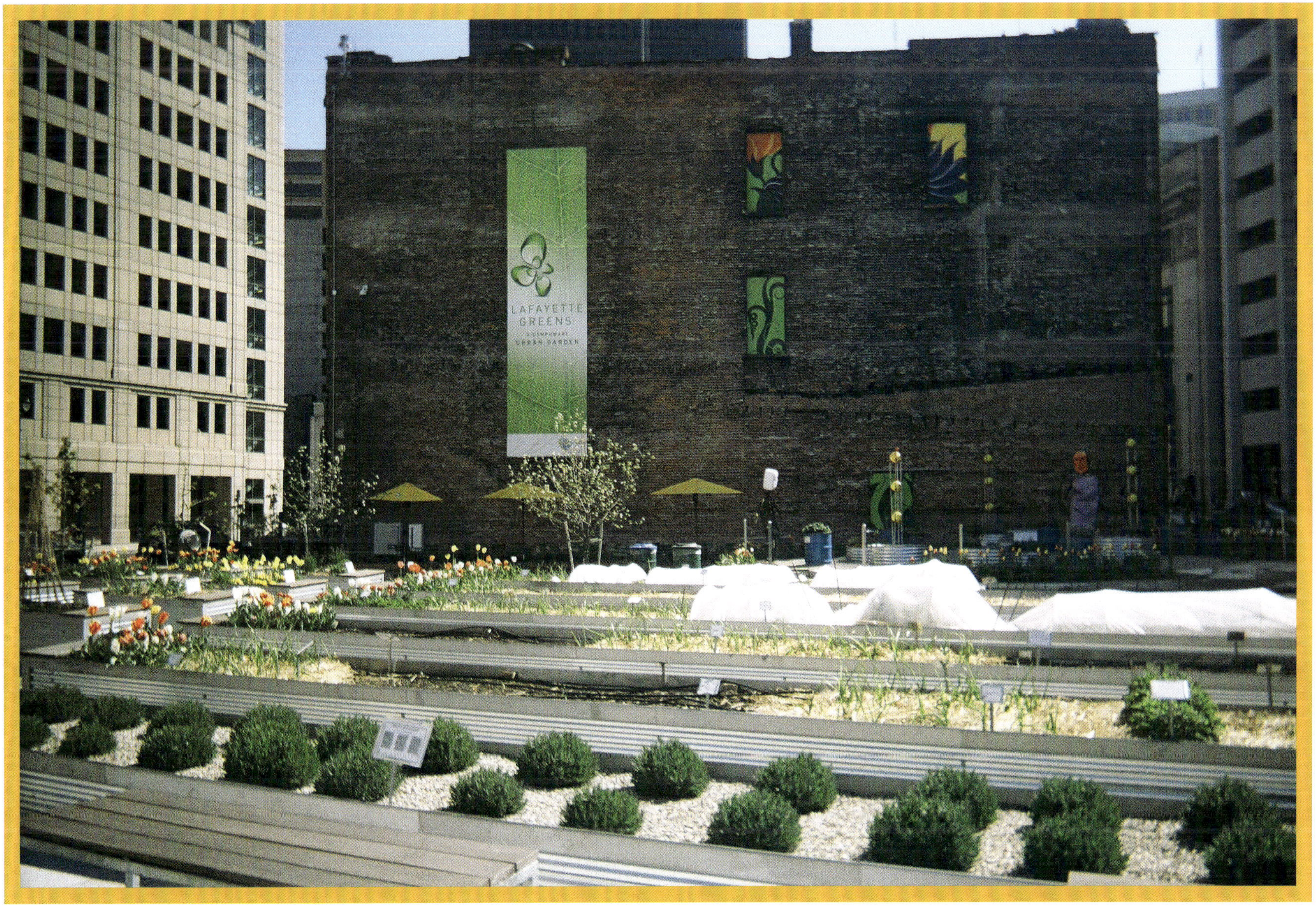

Central Business District Community Garden. —Detroit Workers for Environmental Justice

DENT HISTORICAL SOCIETY

Leader: Ms. L. Black

Participants: 9

Opposite top:
Heidelberg Project.
—Dent Historical Society

Opposite bottom:
The Fairmont Creamery Company on Milwaukee Street.
—Dent Historical Society

OUR MISSION was to submit pictures of Detroit from our eyes!

We hoped to highlight some of the architecture and geometric shapes that represented Detroit's style "back in the day." We searched for the old-style structures, century-old homes, and today's fine art.

We took pictures of things we take for granted: places of leisure activity, the local playground, Detroit's beautiful parks, and skyline venues.

The elders in our group enjoyed pointing out Detroit's past. It was exciting to take pictures that would be shared with others as we worked across multiple generations in families to complete this project.

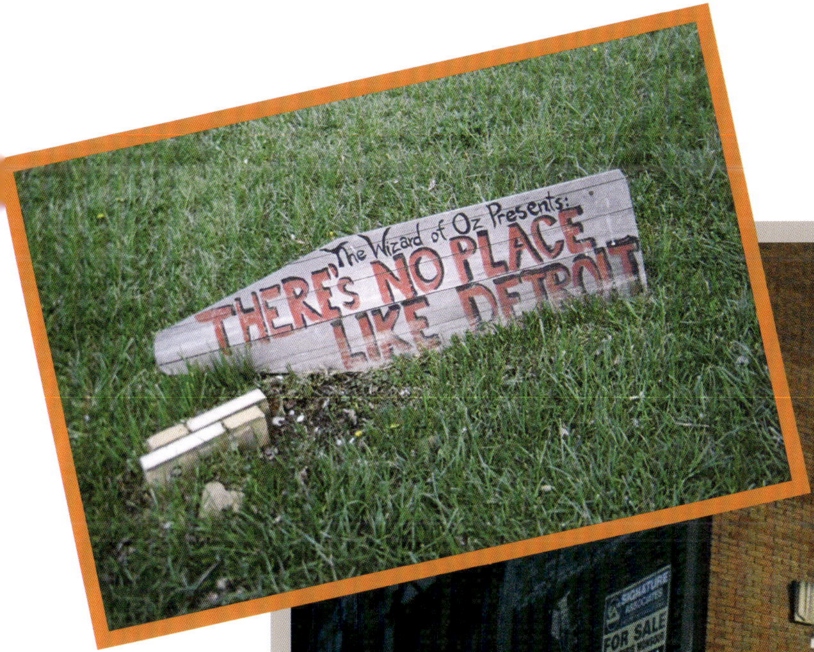
The Wizard of Oz Presents:
THERE'S NO PLACE
LIKE DETROIT

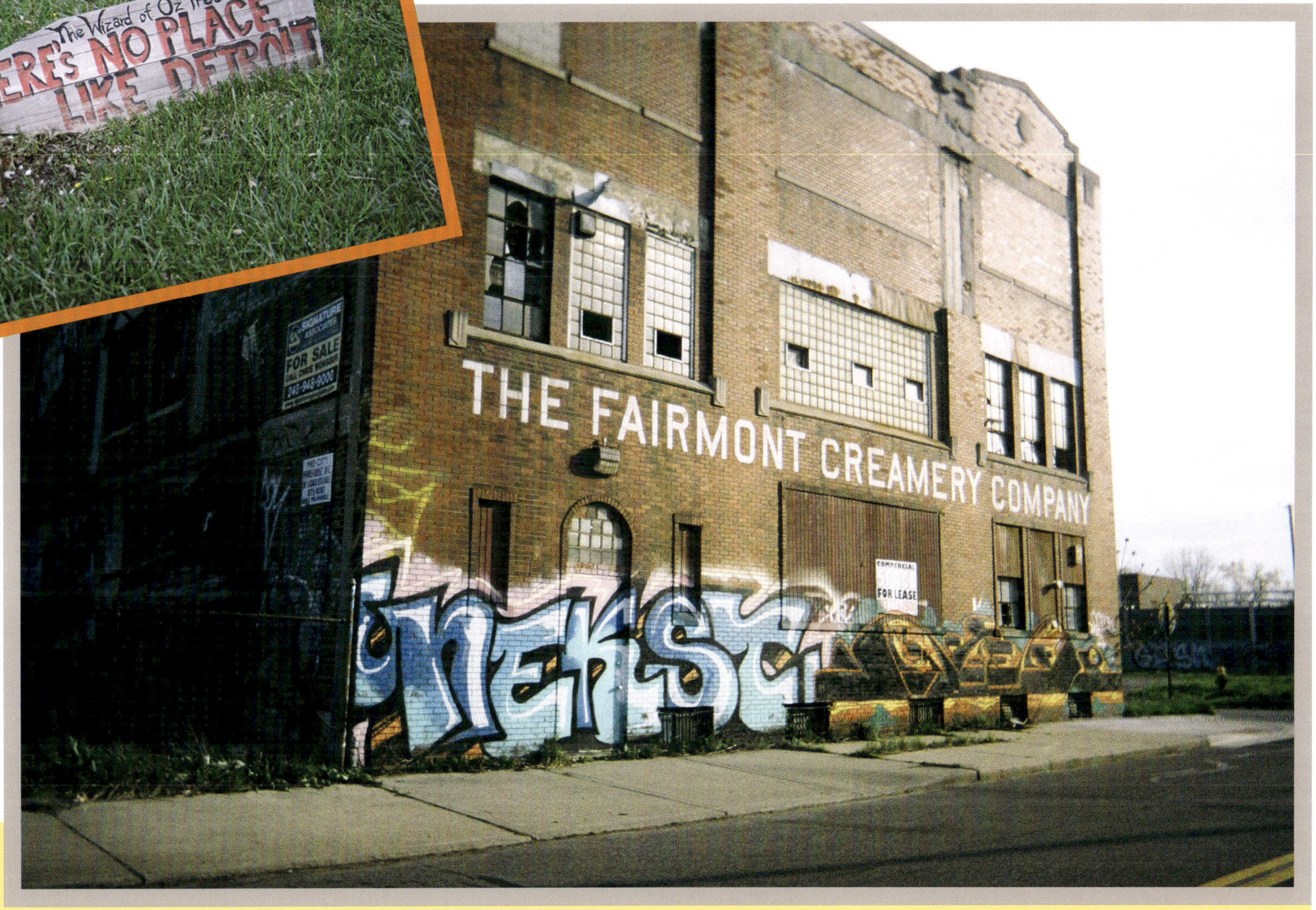
THE FAIRMONT CREAMERY COMPANY
FOR SALE
FOR LEASE

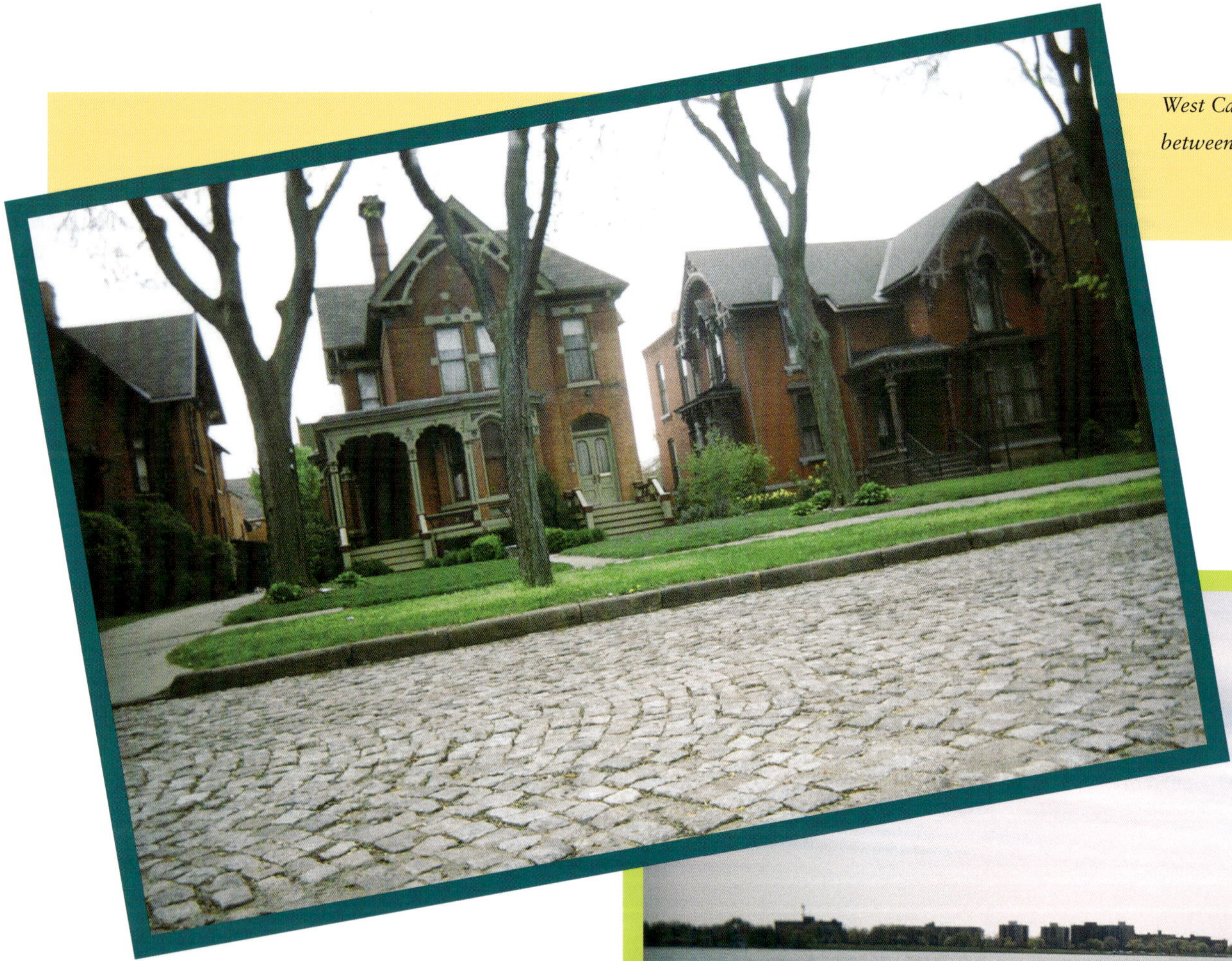

West Canfield is Detroit's Cobblestone Street in Midtown between Second and Third. —Dent Historical Society

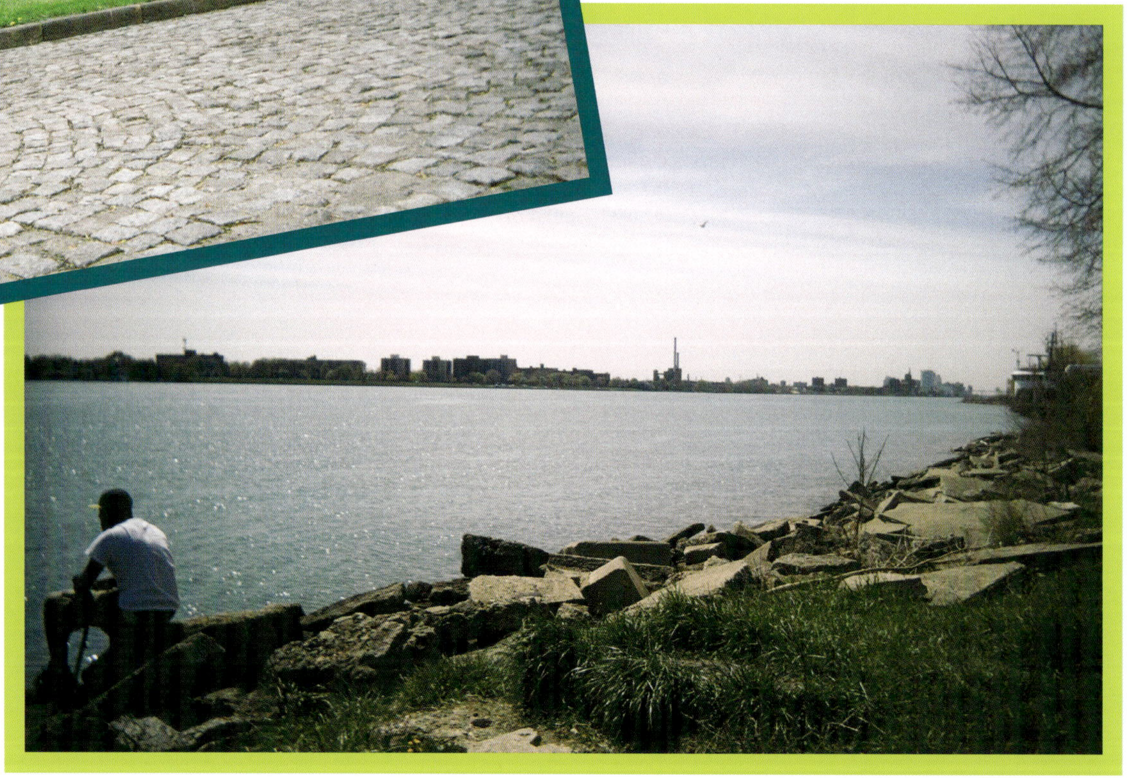

A man looks on at the Detroit River.
—Dent Historical Society

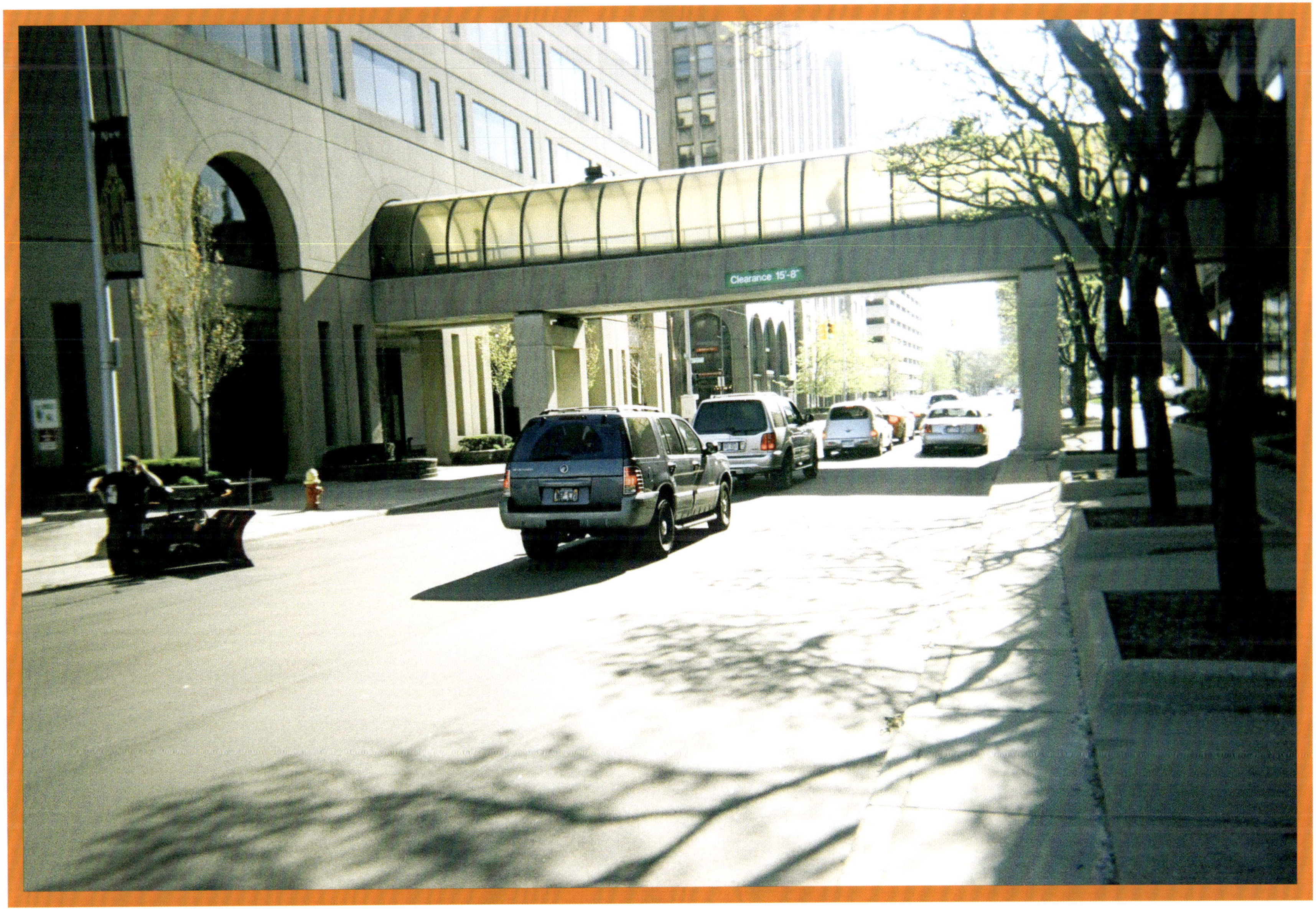

Pedestrian bridge in Detroit's New Center. —Dent Historical Society

FELLOWSHIP NONPROFIT HOUSING CORPORATION

Michelle Lee

Participants: 9

www.facebook.com/fellow.detroit

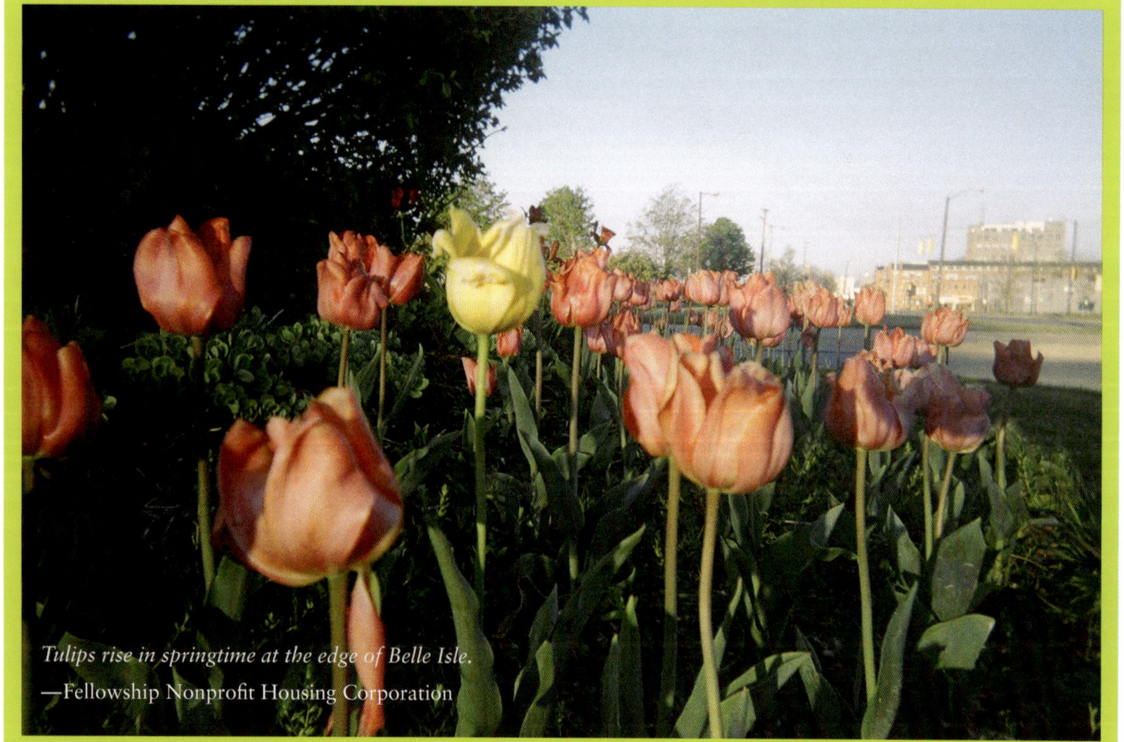

Tulips rise in springtime at the edge of Belle Isle.
—Fellowship Nonprofit Housing Corporation

FELLOWSHIP NONPROFIT HOUSING CORPORATION aims to revitalize eastside Detroit.

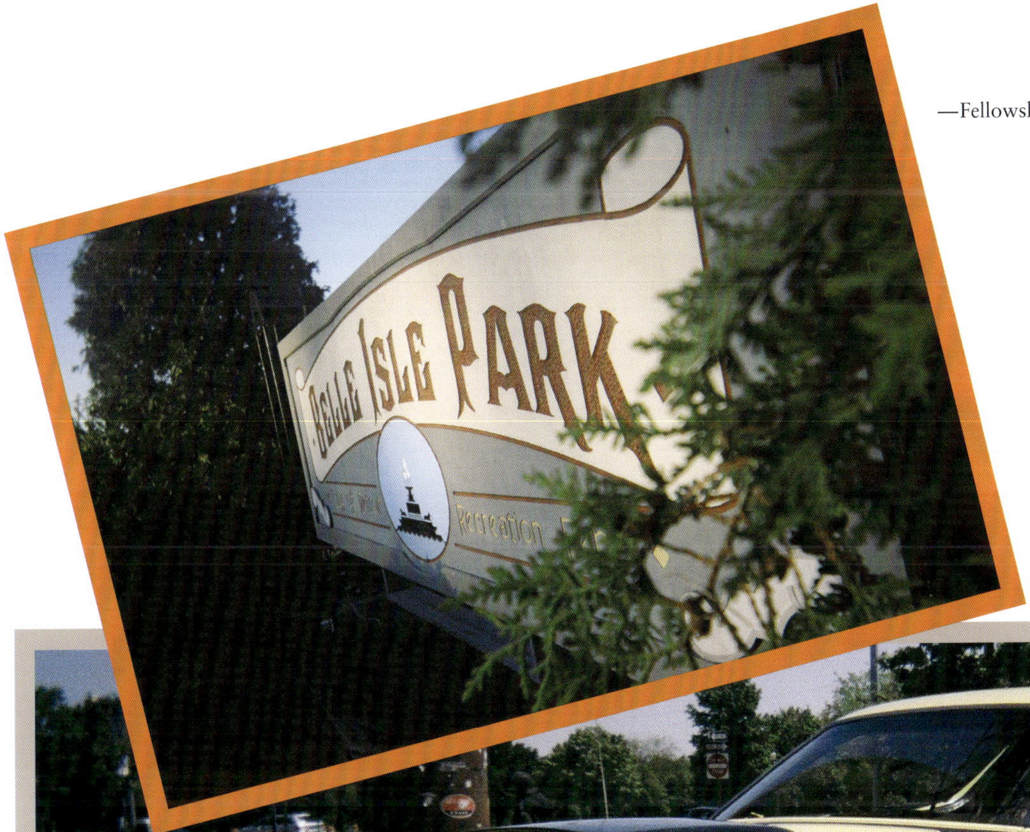

—Fellowship Nonprofit Housing Corporation

Hot rod. —Fellowship Nonprofit Housing Corporation

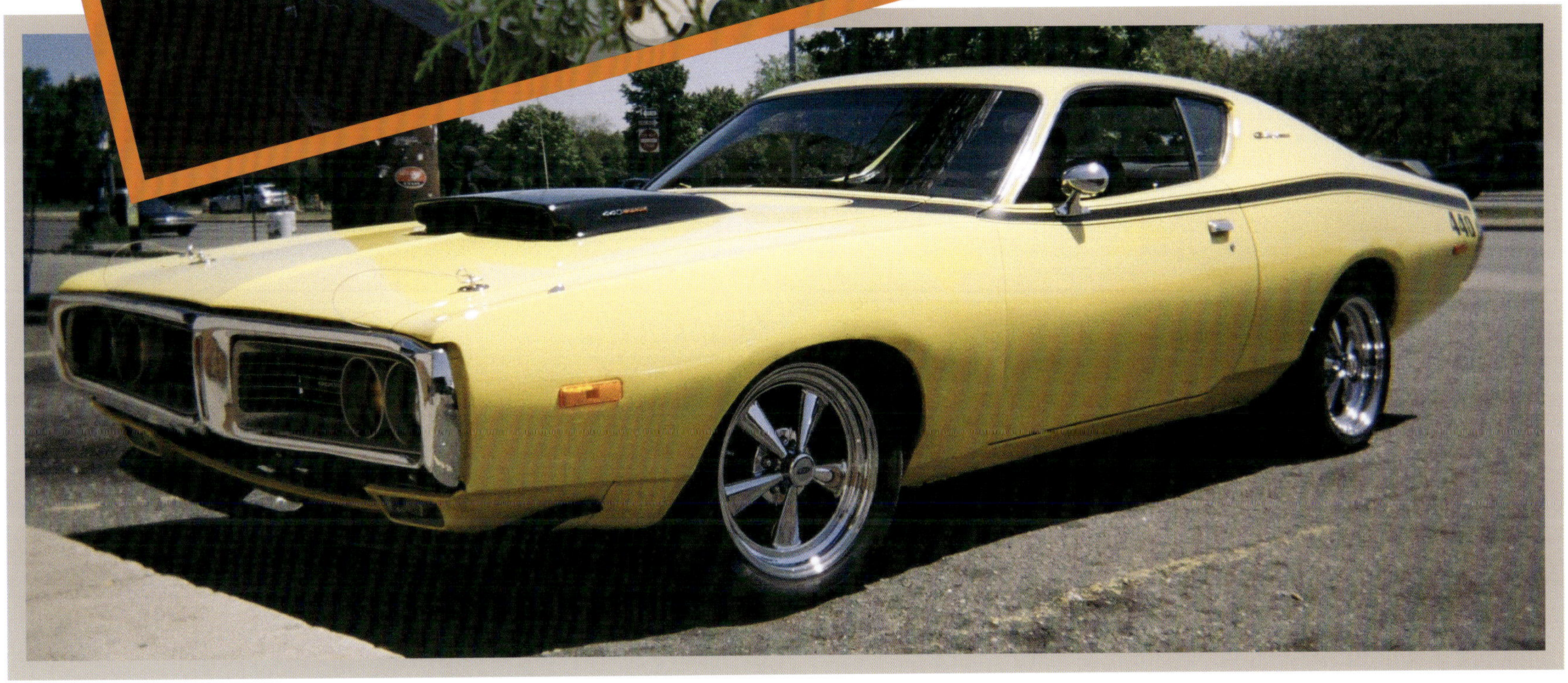

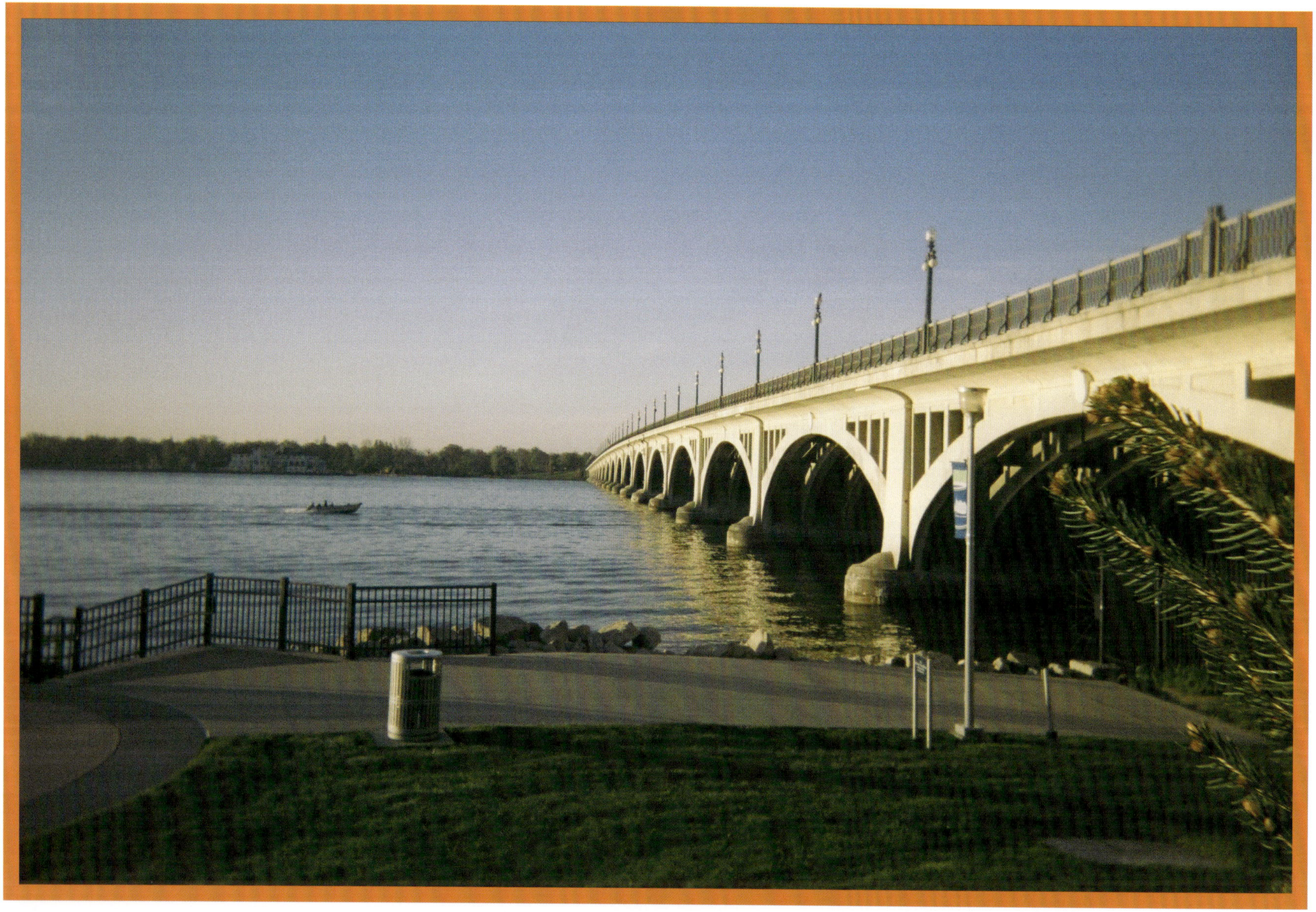

Sunrise on the Belle Isle Bridge. —Fellowship Nonprofit Housing Corporation

FENDER BENDER

Leader: Nora Mandray

Participants: 10

www.facebook.com/fender.bender

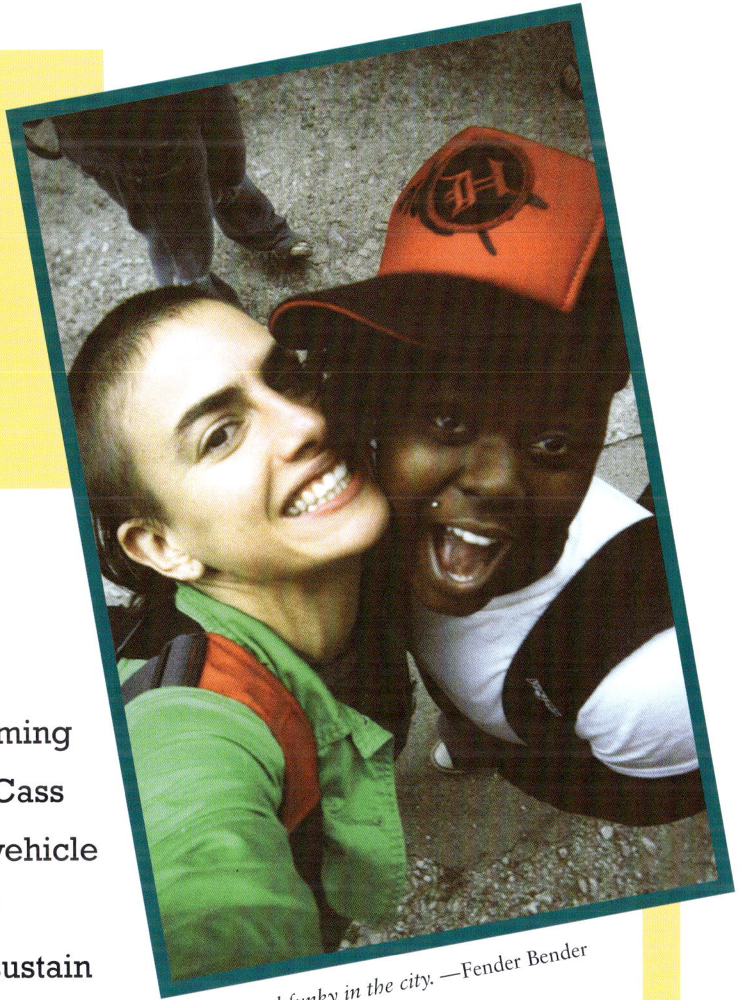

Fun and funky in the city. —Fender Bender

FENDER BENDER is a women's, queer, and gender-nonconforming collaborative bike shop and mechanic training experience in the Cass Corridor. We know the bicycle is accessible transportation and a vehicle of transformation. We work toward empowering ourselves and our community through skill building and engagement to create and sustain long-lasting relationships that contribute to and secure solid foundations in Detroit and its future.

FOCUS: HOPE EXCEL PHOTOGRAPHY PROGRAM

Leader: Annette Vanover

Participants: 25

www.focushope.edu

THE EXCEL PHOTOGRAPHY PROGRAM allows Detroit teens to develop their knowledge of film and digital photography. Excel participants are exposed to exemplary works of art and artists through field trips to museums, galleries, and professional studios. The program also promotes social and personal growth, creative self-expression, teamwork skills, high school academic achievement, and postsecondary education. The program creates positive peer support groups and effective youth-adult partnerships and advocates for community involvement.

The Reveal Your Detroit project was a chance for students to further their work using symbolism and to convey their relationship to Detroit through images.

Reveal Your Detroit was an awesome opportunity for Detroit youth to creatively explore their relationship to their city and to be involved in a major community project.

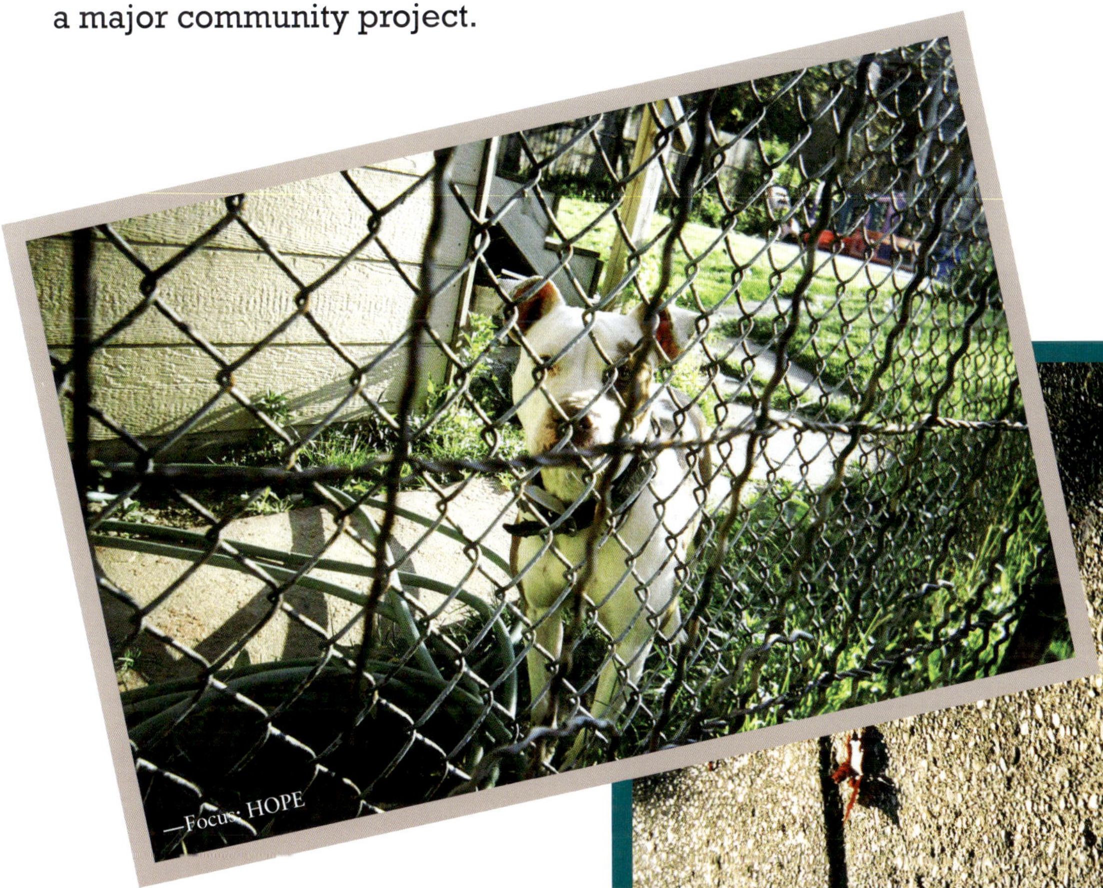

—Focus: HOPE

—Focus: HOPE

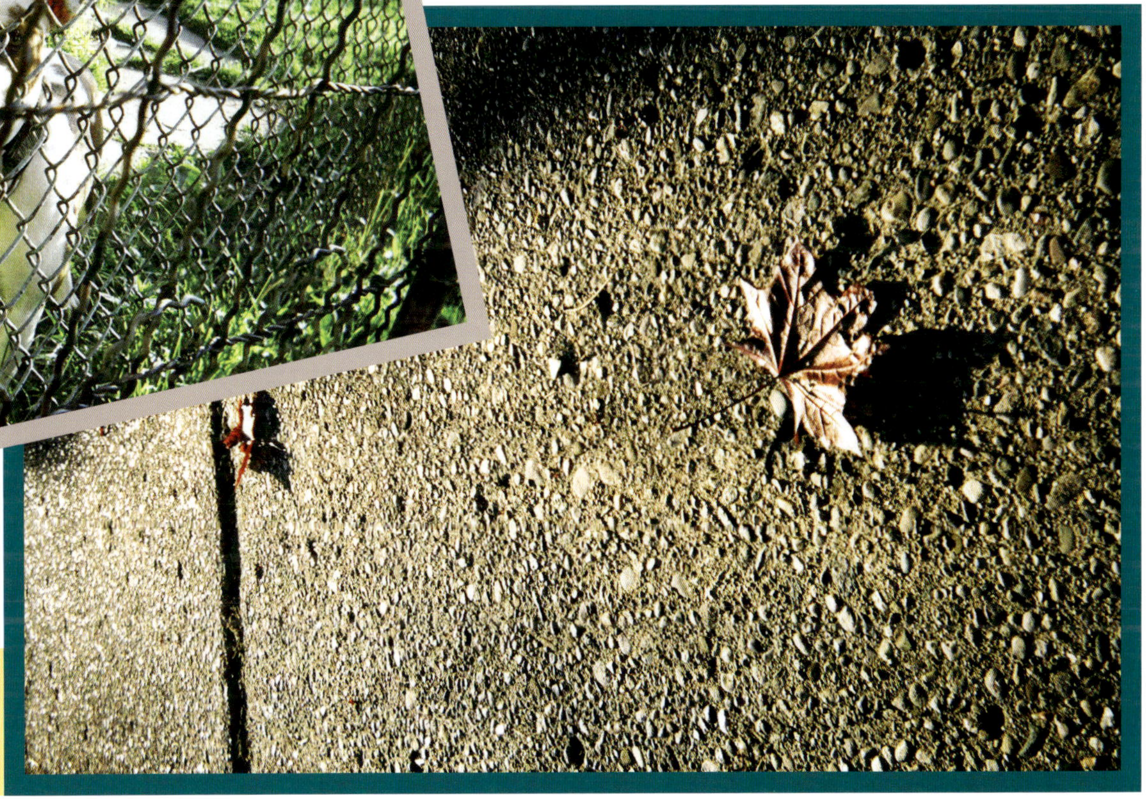

—Focus: HOPE

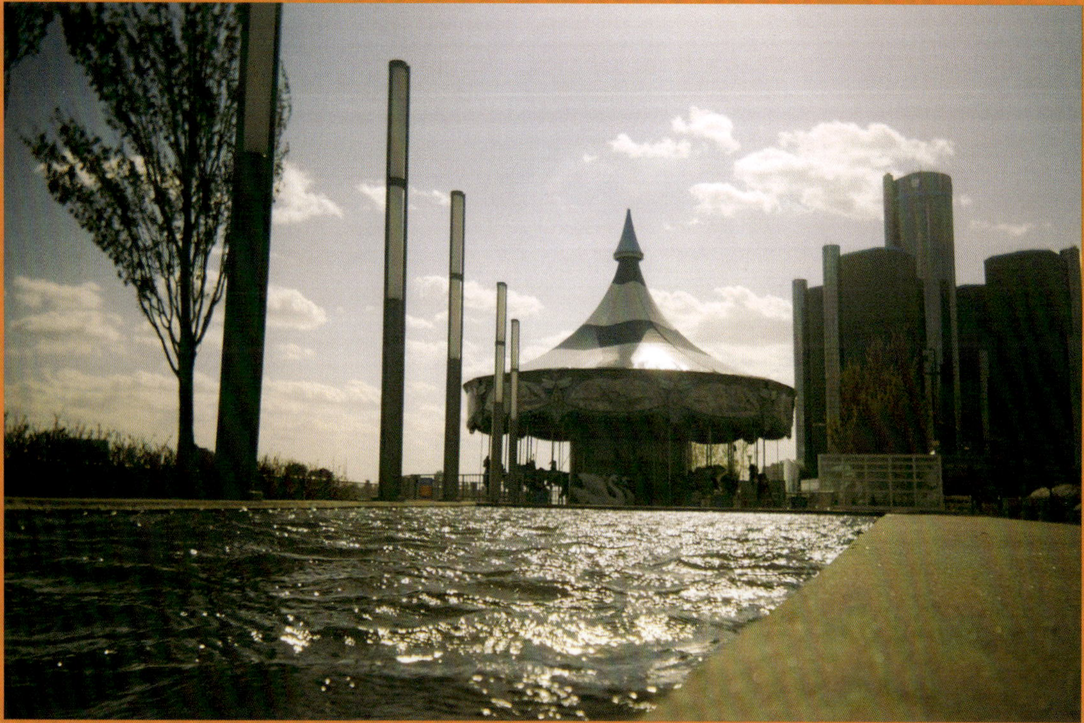

MARQUEZ BELL

I took this photograph because I believe that we as Detroit residents are on a carousel ride. We are slowly but steadily moving toward change and, as we move, we see parts of our community that we love and admire but parts that could use some work as well.

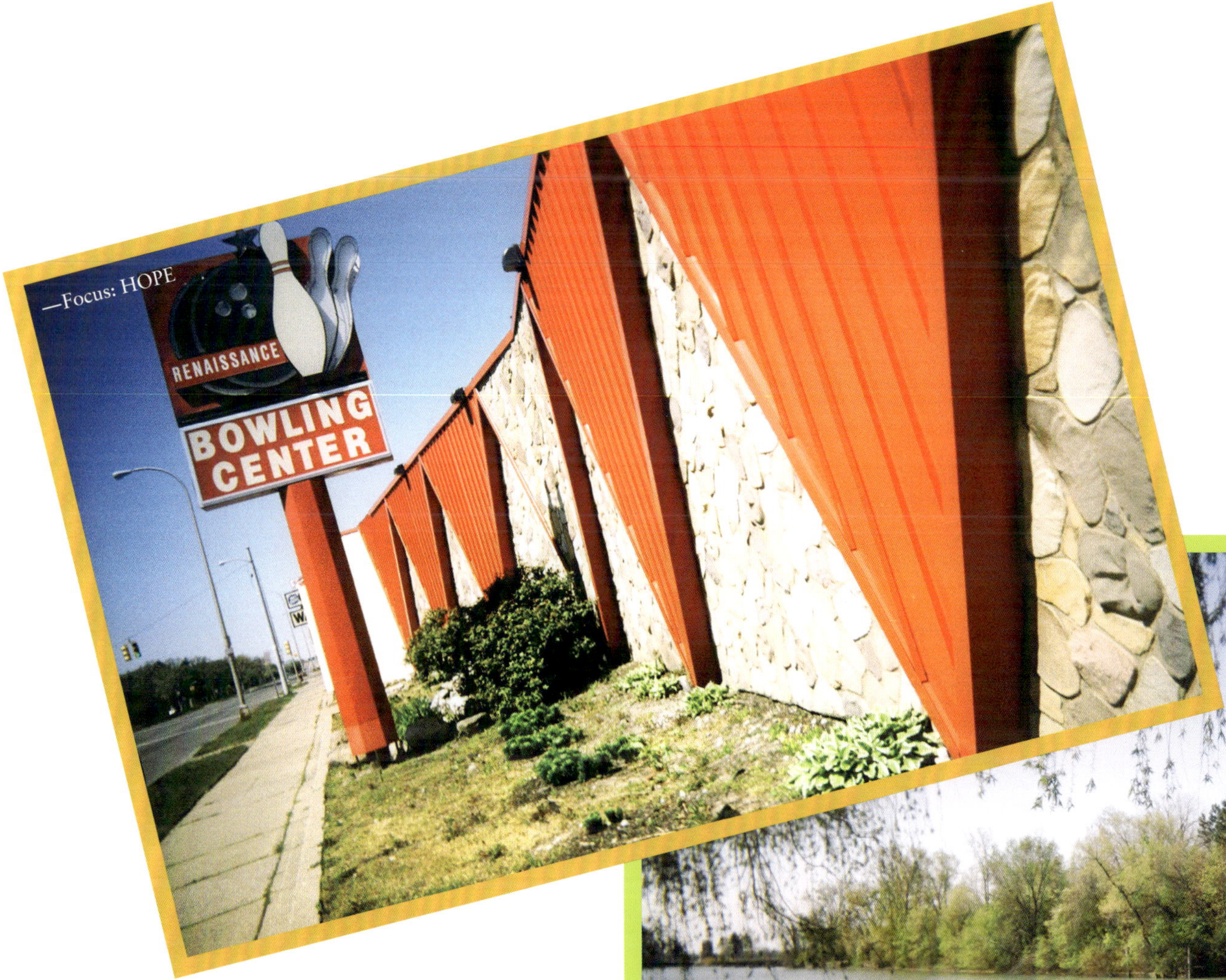

—Focus: HOPE

—Focus: HOPE

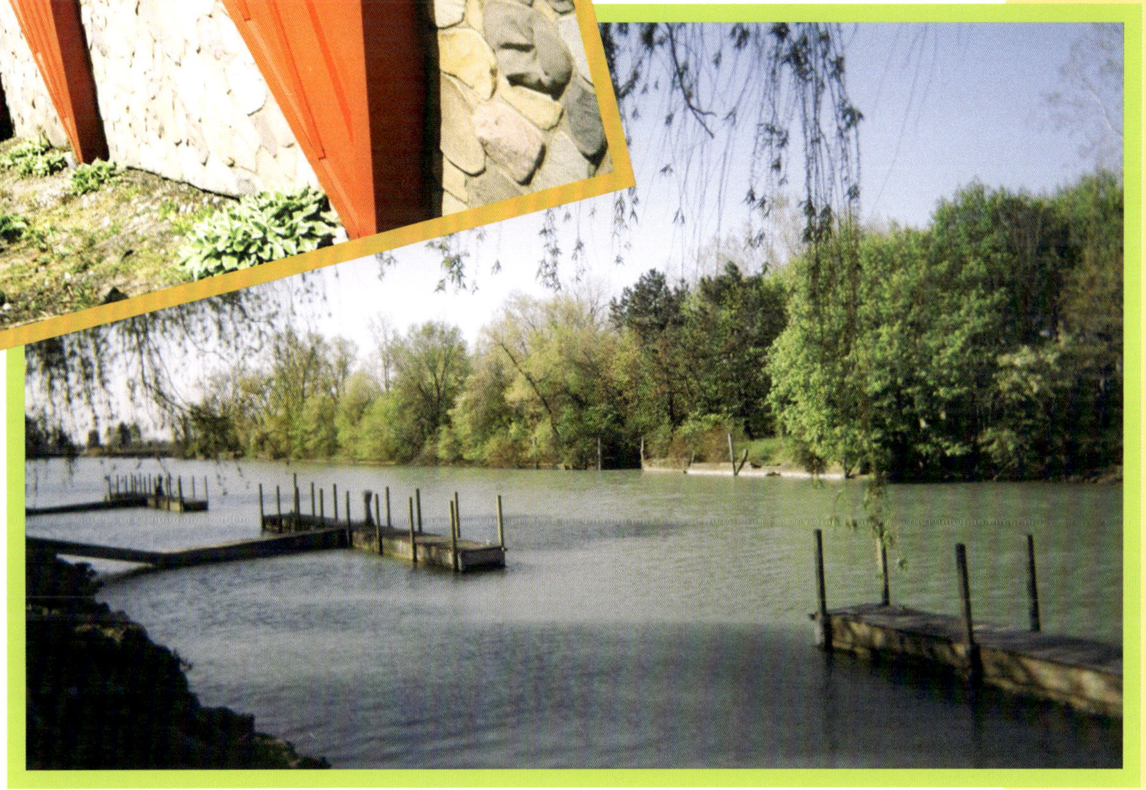

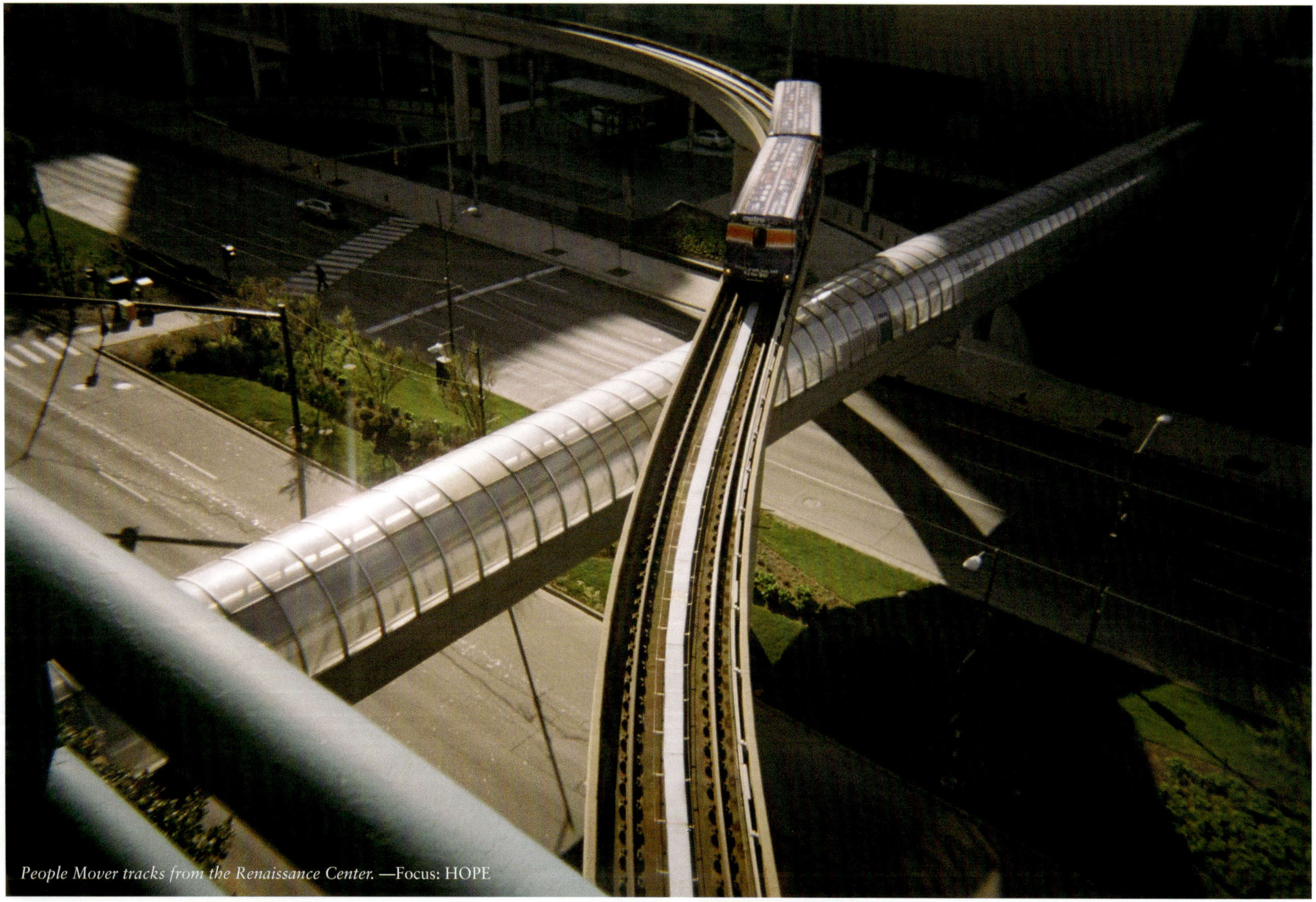

People Mover tracks from the Renaissance Center. —Focus: HOPE

While I am no longer a resident of Detroit, this photograph is symbolic of my daily journey into the city where I have the honor of working with many young people on arts-based youth development projects. Reveal Your Detroit Project was a wonderful opportunity for Detroiters to show off their city and all of its diversity.

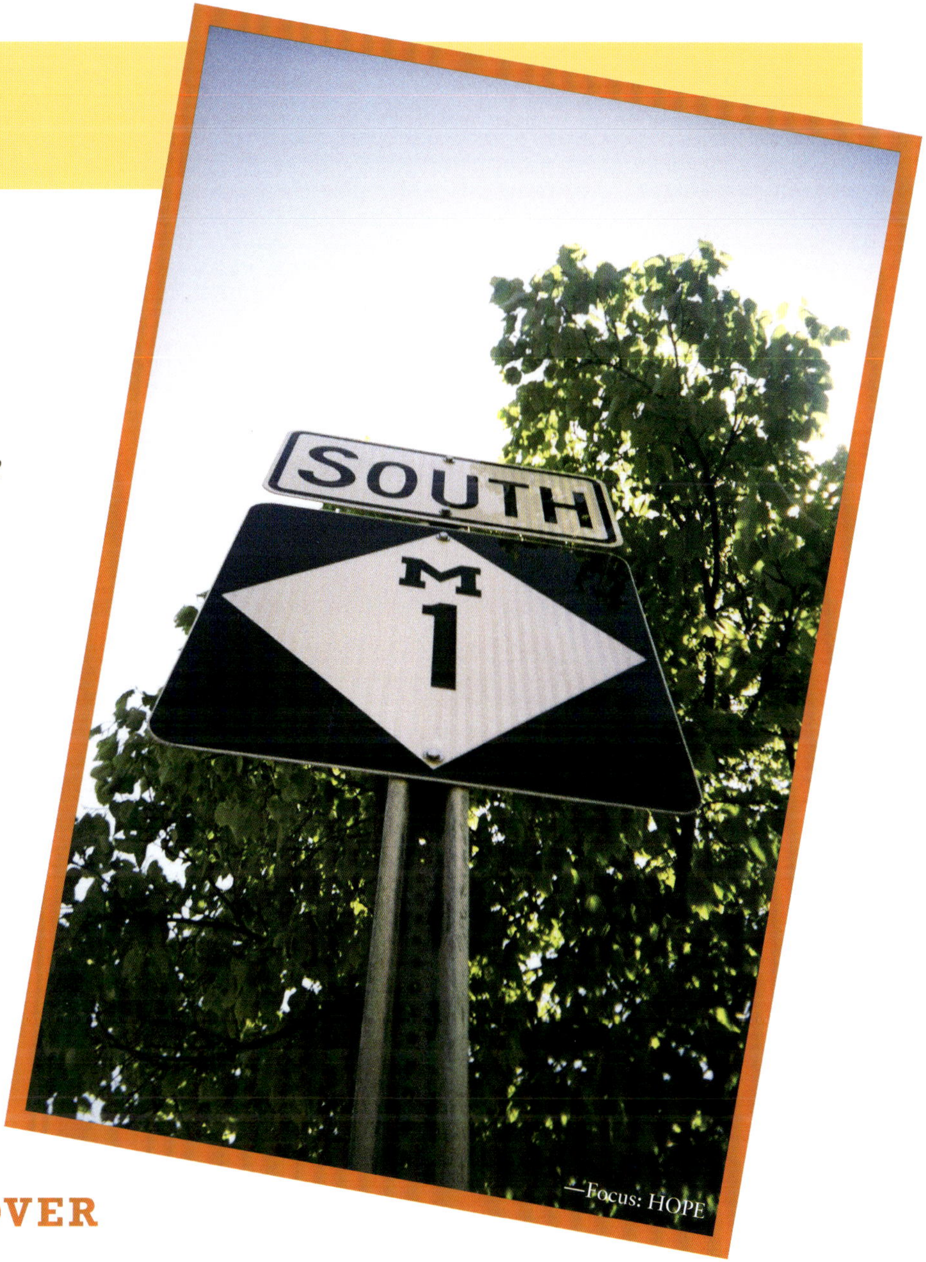

—Focus: HOPE

ANNETTE VANOVER

GENESIS HOPE

Leader: Renee Wallace

Participants: 15

www.genesishope.org

GENESIS HOPE scribed these words on April 21, 2012, when our group visited the DIA Detroit Revealed exhibit:

Why reveal our Detroit?

We the people of the community of Detroit's eastside are "building power." We have come together to create a safe, cleaner, healthier, sustainable community.

Through our photos we reveal the life of our community. The people from babe to elder. The places we gather. The small and great things we are doing. The assets present and possible.

Through our photos we reveal our hopes and dreams. Through our photos we reveal our power to transform our present reality into our desired glorious future.

Through our photos we reveal and declare our truth.

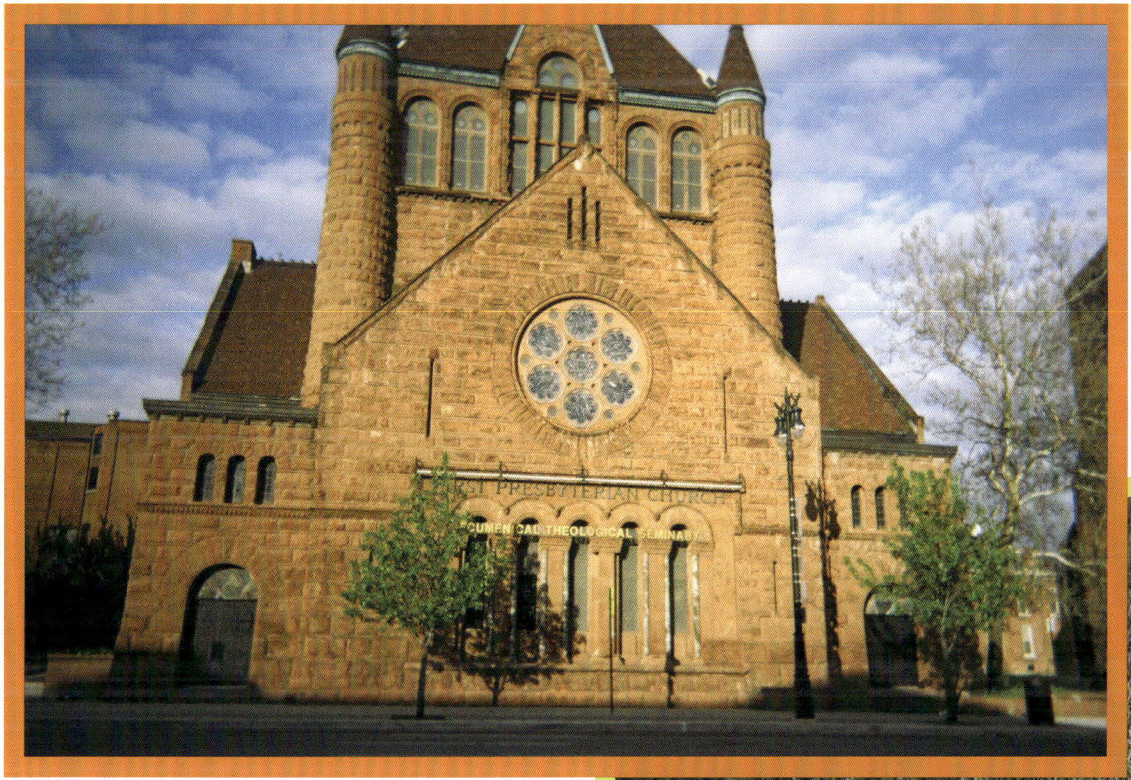

First Presbyterian Church aglow off Woodward near Brush Park. —Genesis Hope

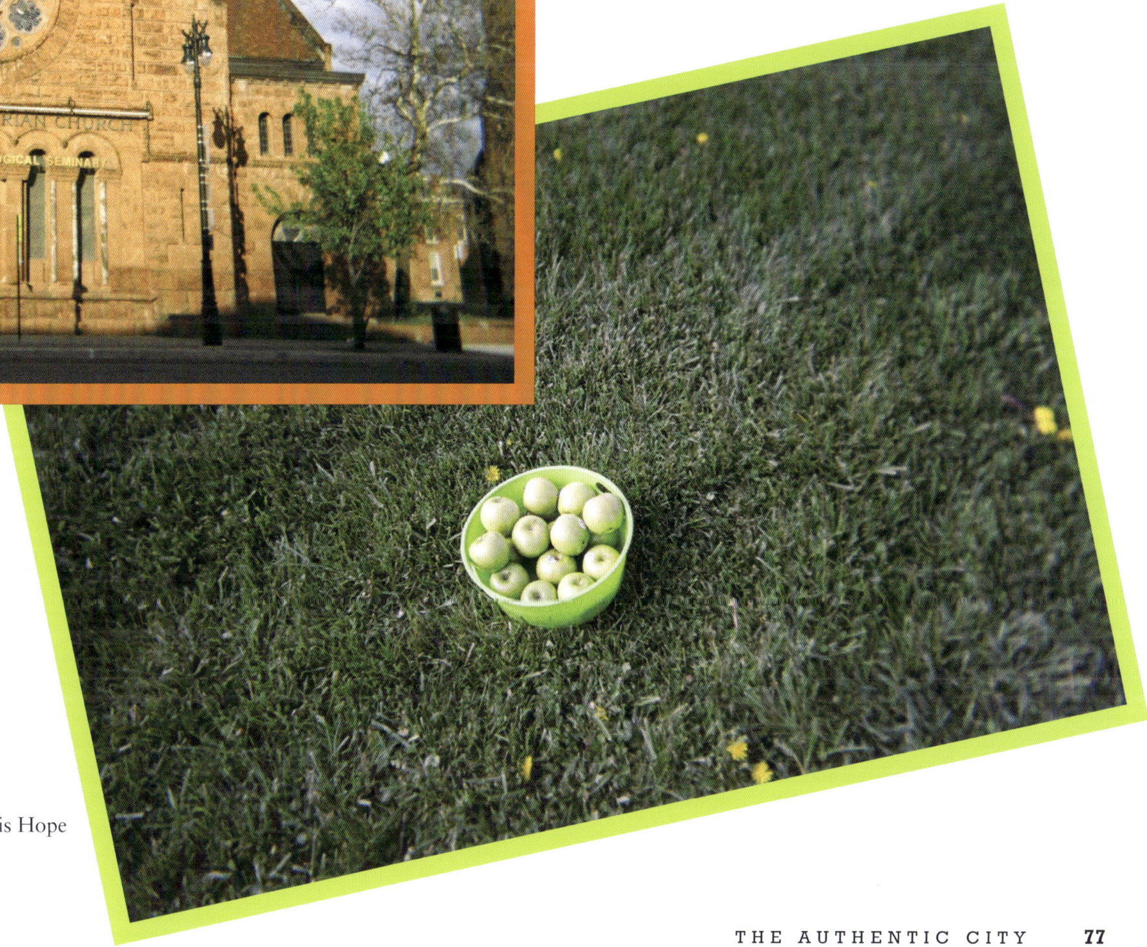

Apples from an orchard outing. —Genesis Hope

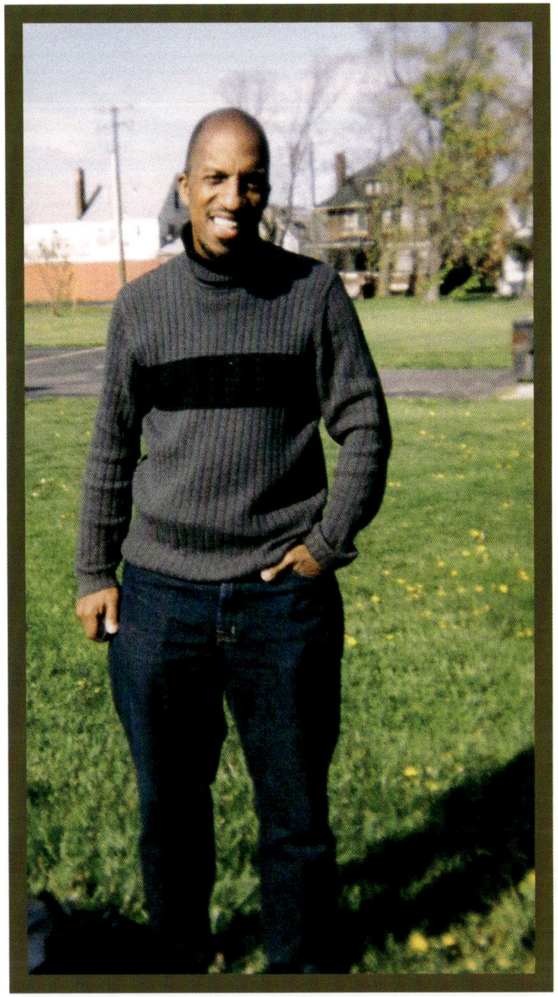

I saw the Reveal Your Detroit project as an opportunity to be part of a shared experience that would help promote all things Detroit, and I wanted to get as many people involved as possible. The project was a great tool to engage individuals in shared conversation about Detroit and a catalyst that prompted participants to take an honest look at the city. Being part of the Reveal Your Detroit project allowed individuals an opportunity to help shift paradigms about what's good in Detroit.

—Genesis Hope

MIGUEL POPE

Miguel Pope helped lead and support four community groups that partnered with Reveal Your Detroit

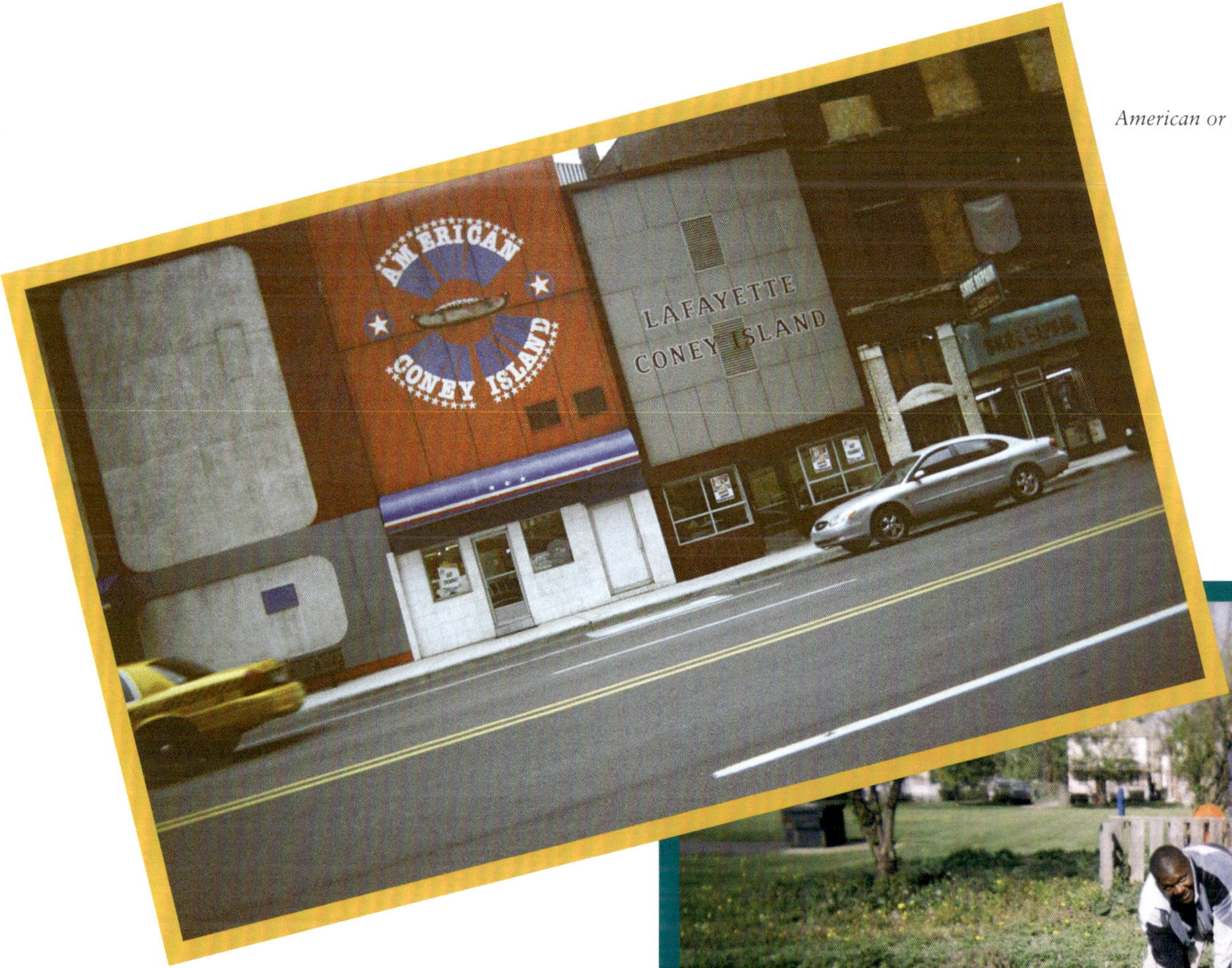

American or Lafayette? —Genesis Hope

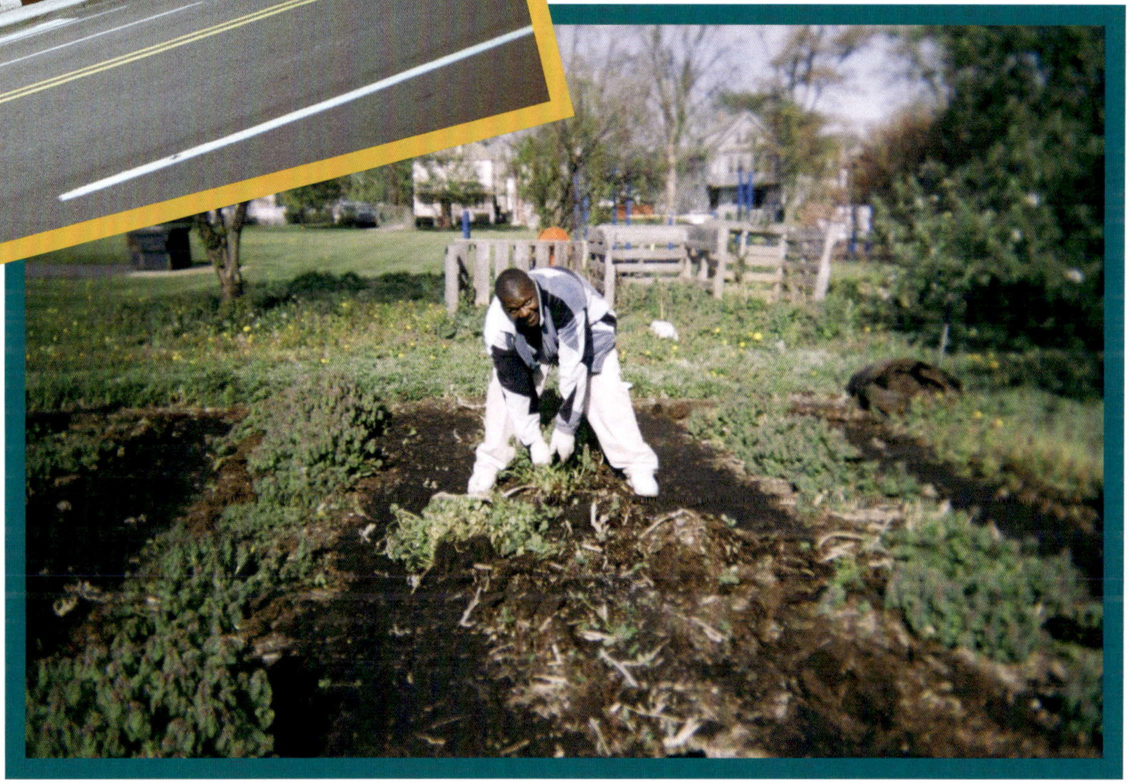

—Genesis Hope

GRANDMONT 1

Leader: Oliver Cole

Number of Participants: 10

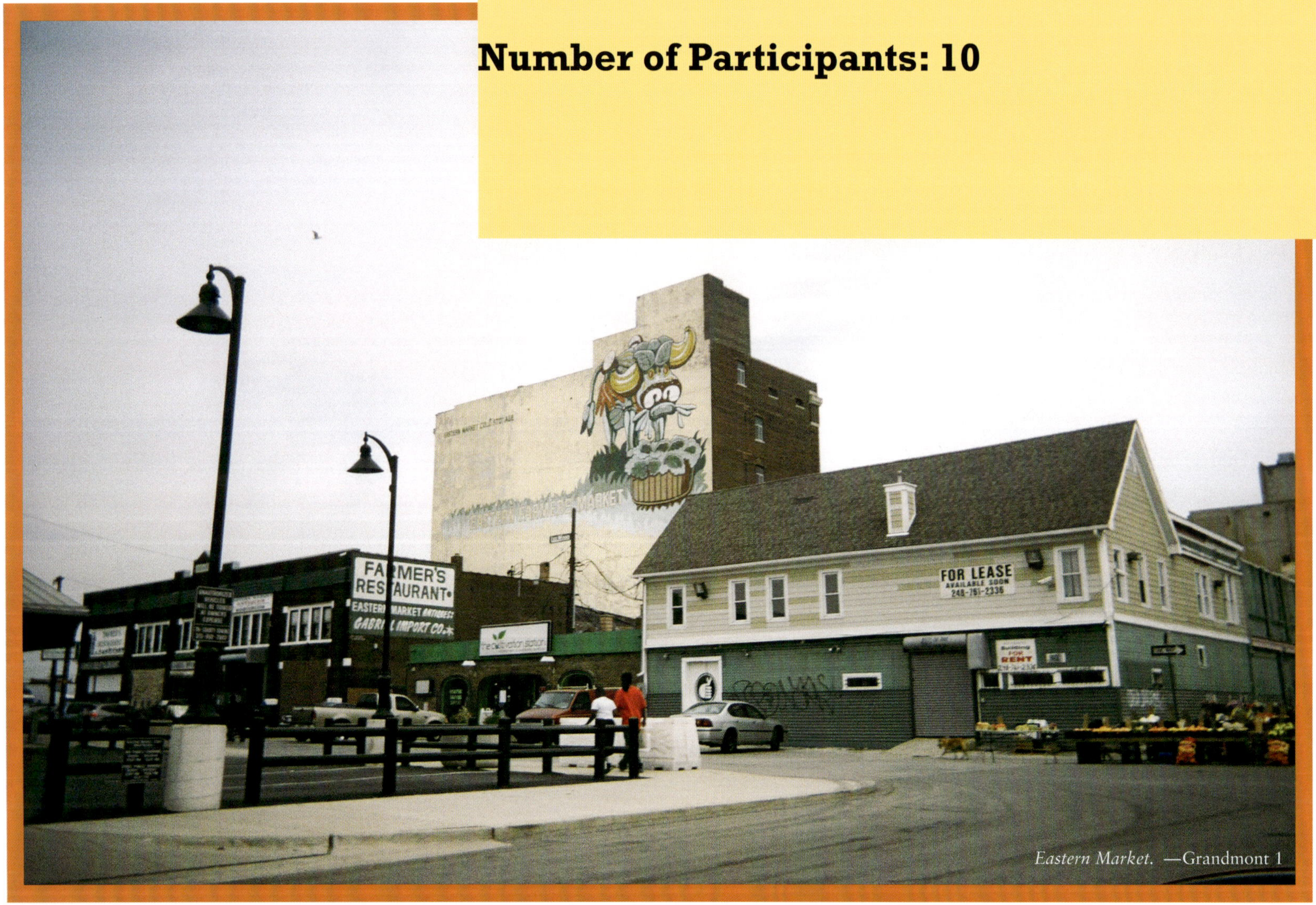

Eastern Market. —Grandmont 1

—Grandmont 1

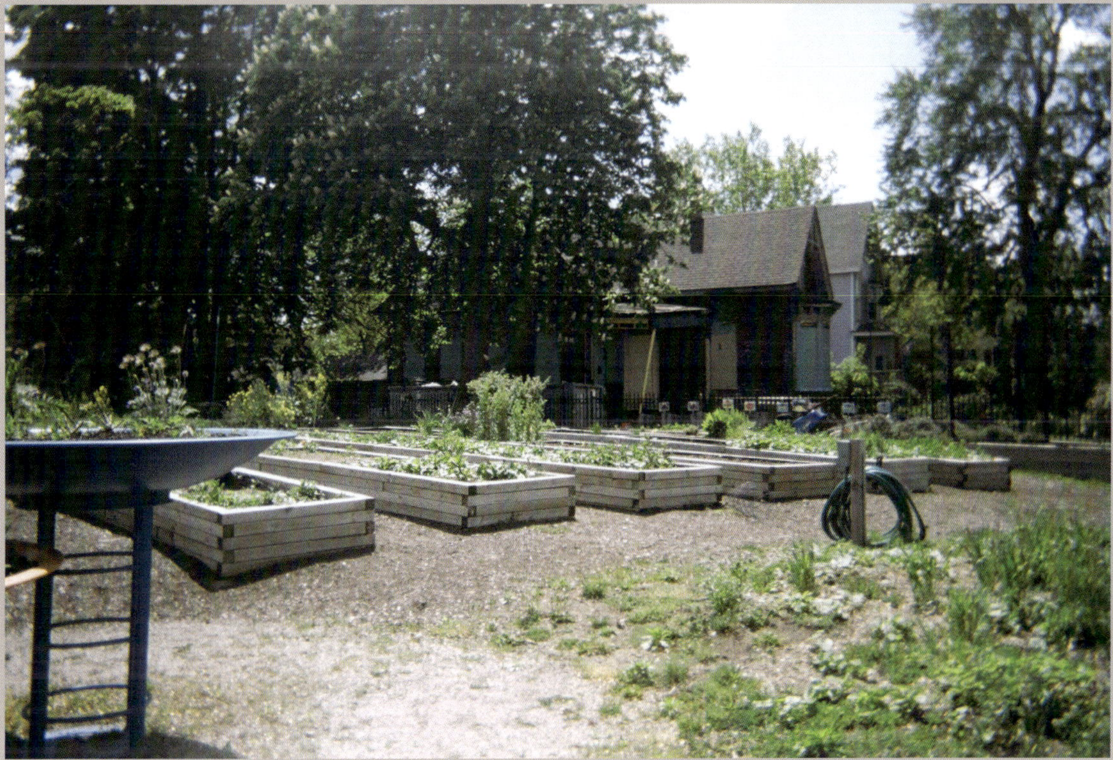

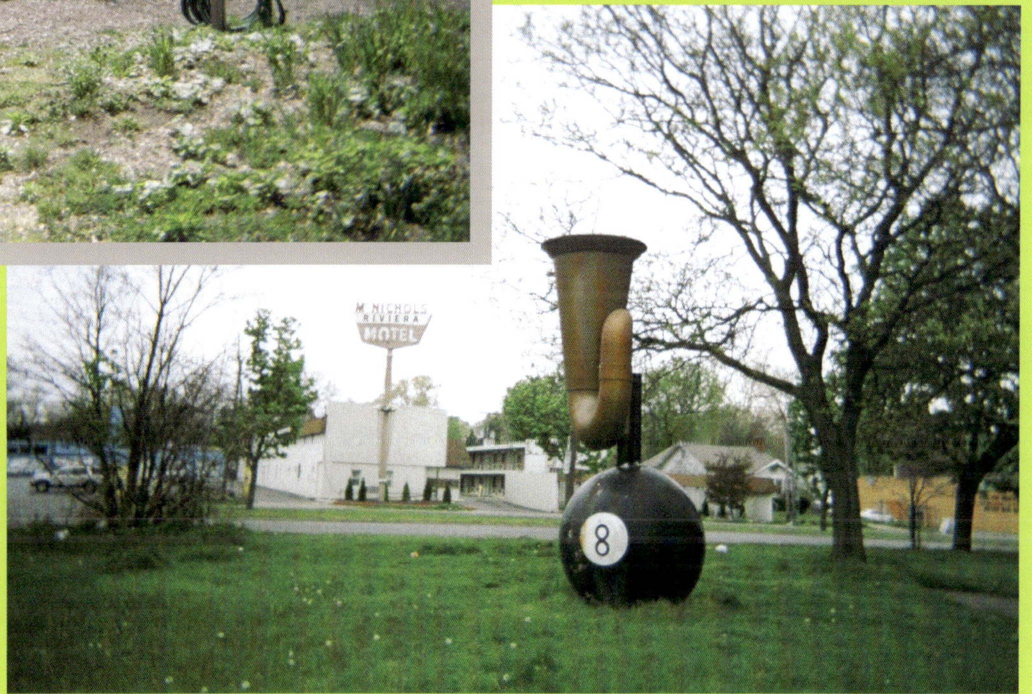

Detroit 8-Ball at McNichols and Grand River.
—Grandmont 1

GRANDMONT ROSEDALE DEVELOPMENT CORPORATION

Leader: Jessica Iwankoski

Participants: 10

www.grandmontrosedale.com

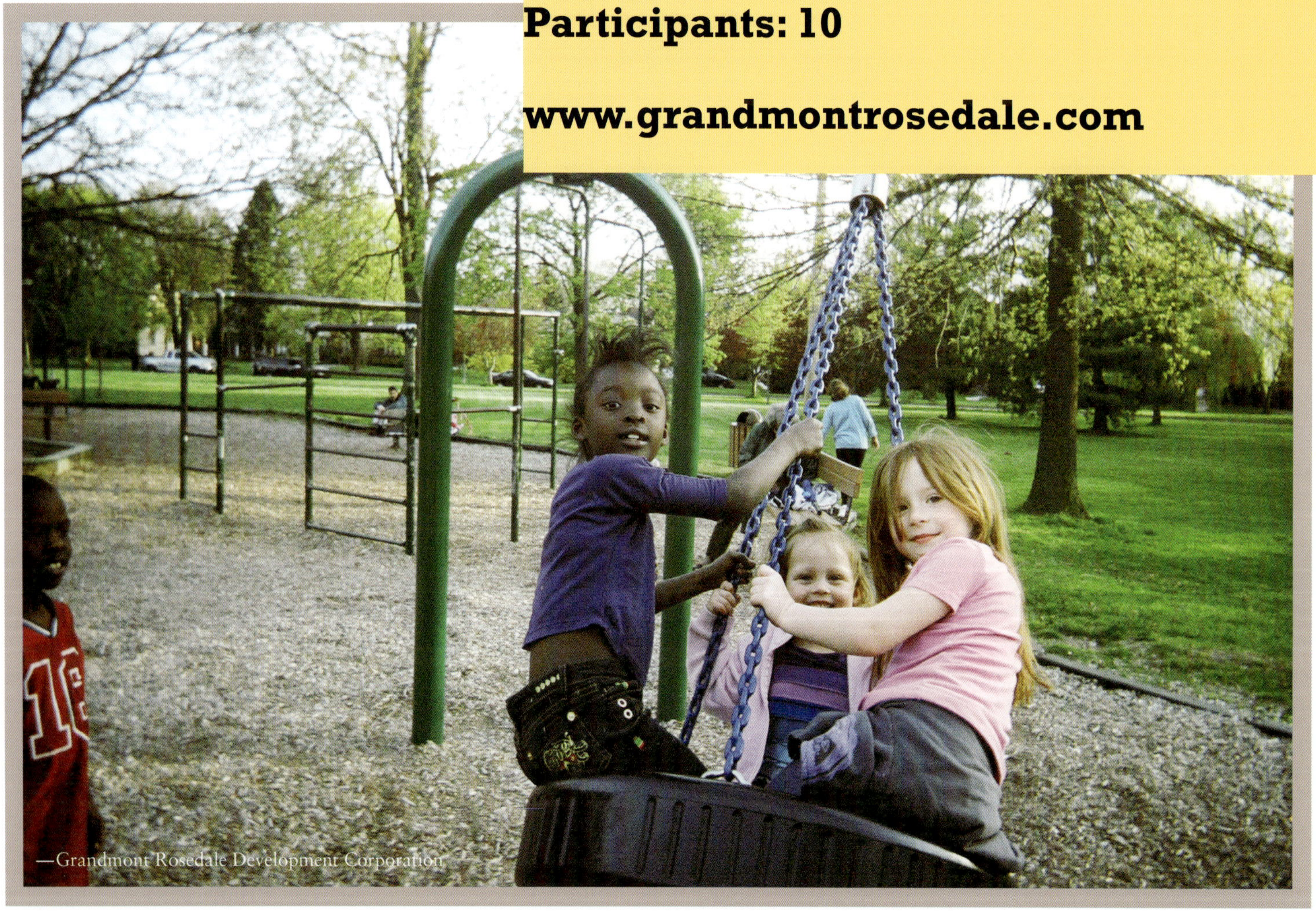

—Grandmont Rosedale Development Corporation

Reveal Your Detroit

This is a shot of two of my niece's daughters and another young girl they were playing with. It was just the perfect Detroit evening. The weather was really nice and children were playing as their families took in an evening at the park. It really describes to me what my neighborhood is all about. A place where all kids can come to spend time playing together. That's Detroit to me.

KATHY MARSHALL

HOSTEL DETROIT

Participants: 20

Leader: Michel Soucisse

www.hosteldetroit.com

Opposite: —Hostel Detroit

HOSTEL DETROIT was founded in November 2010 with the main purpose of providing safe, affordable accommodations in Detroit while educating patrons about the city. Hostel Detroit was made possible by countless donations and thousands of hours of volunteer work. Hostel Detroit is truly a community and collaborative effort, taking ideas from community members and Hostel Detroit committee members.

Hostel Detroit is one block west of Rosa Parks and three blocks north of Michigan Avenue, in North Corktown.

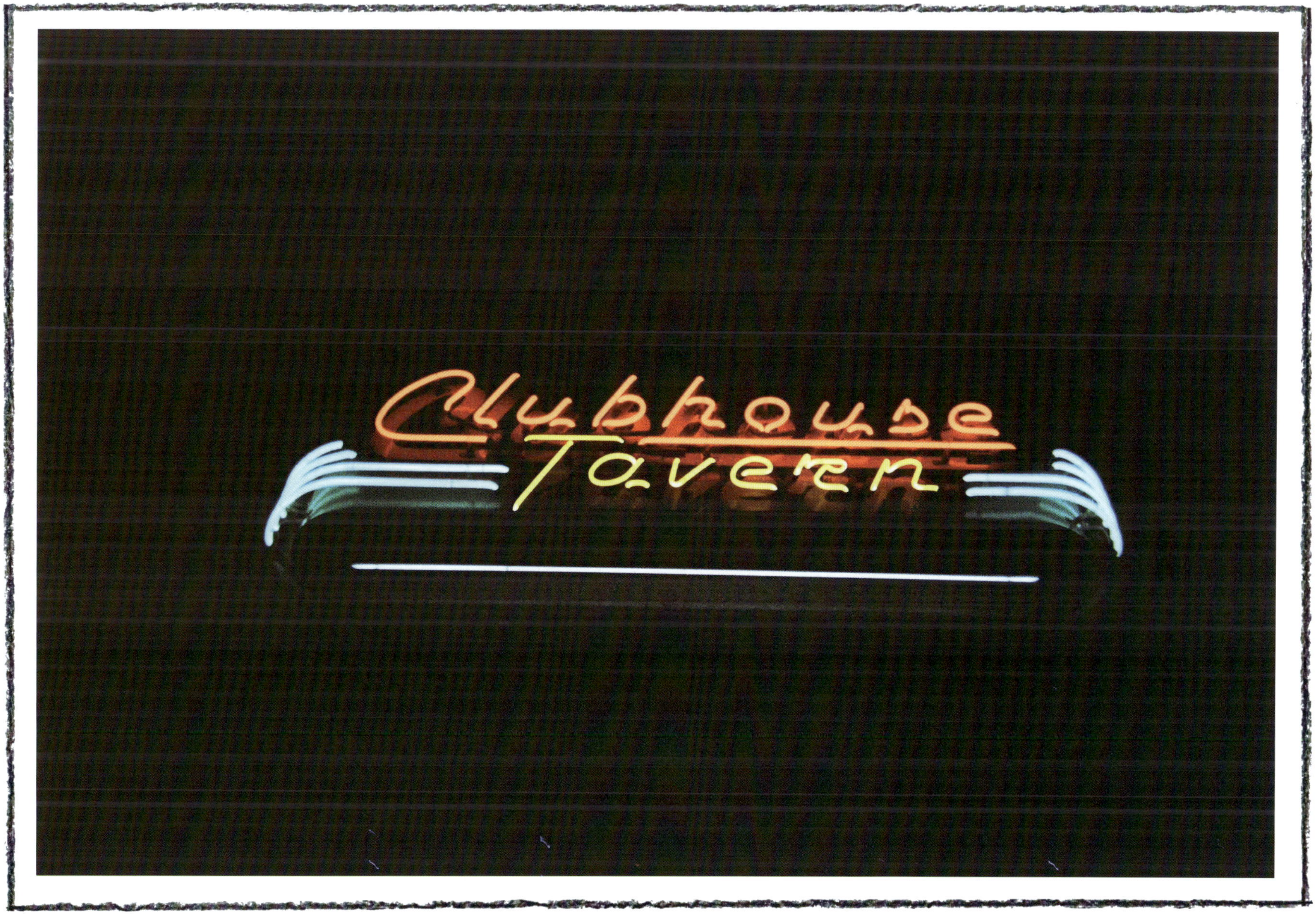
Clubhouse
Tavern

ISLANDVIEW COMMUNITY–FIELD OF OUR DREAMS BLOCK CLUB

Leader: Maria Martin-Thomas

Participants: 6

WE ARE NOT a dying community but a vibrant, diverse, motivated, progressive, caring, interesting, intelligent, and faith-filled people. We seek to strengthen our neighborhood and city, sustain our environment, and work toward a more just society filled with opportunity for all.

Most of the members of our group live on one block of the lower eastside on Detroit's Gold Coast. Together we represent young and old, white and black, healthy and health-challenged. By bringing this diverse group of people together we strengthened our neighborhood and have continued to grow relationships on our block and beyond. This project was a catalyst for greater things.

Reveal Your Detroit was an incredible, fantastic, beautiful, wonderful, awesome, powerful, lovely, and enlightening experience!

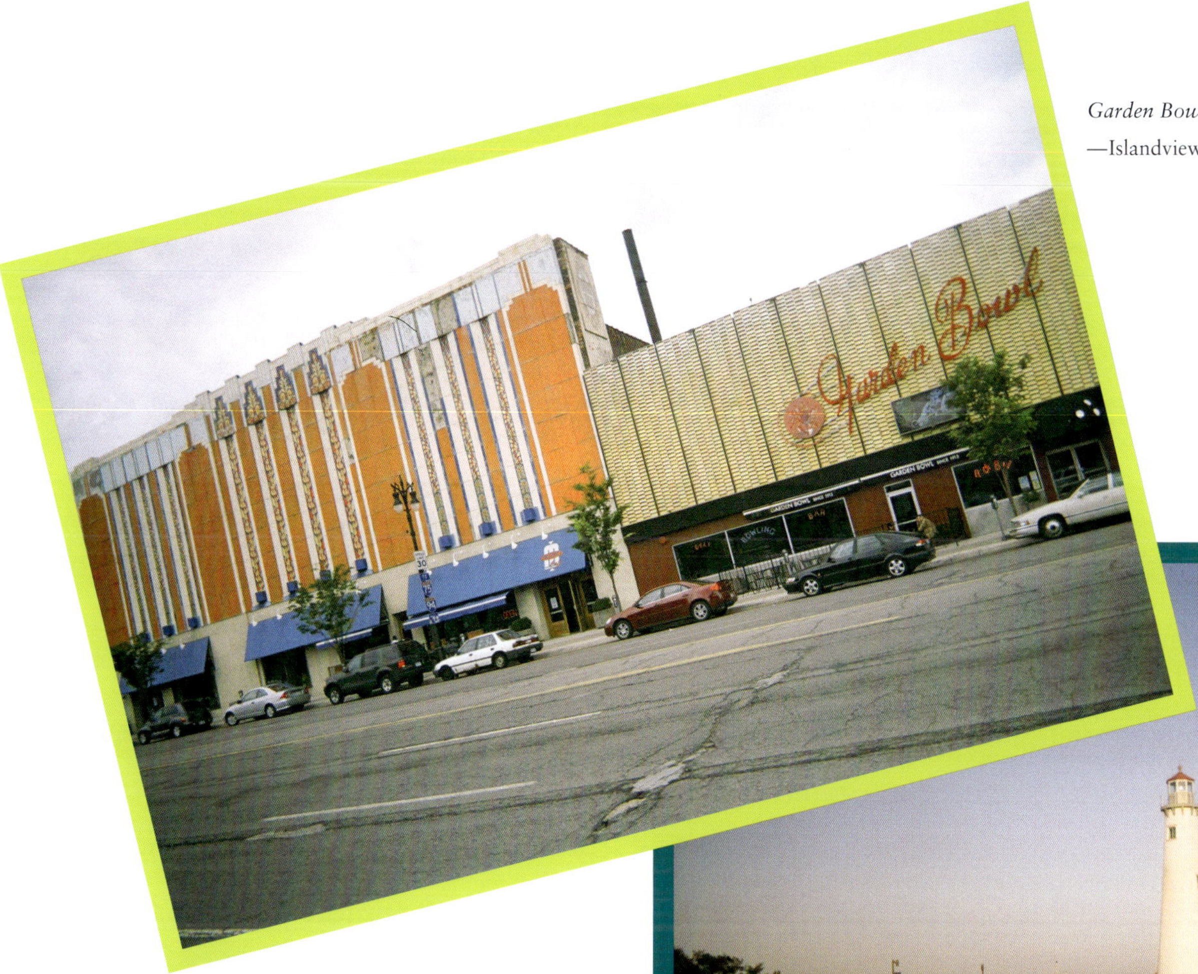

Garden Bowl and the Majestic in Midtown.
—Islandview Community

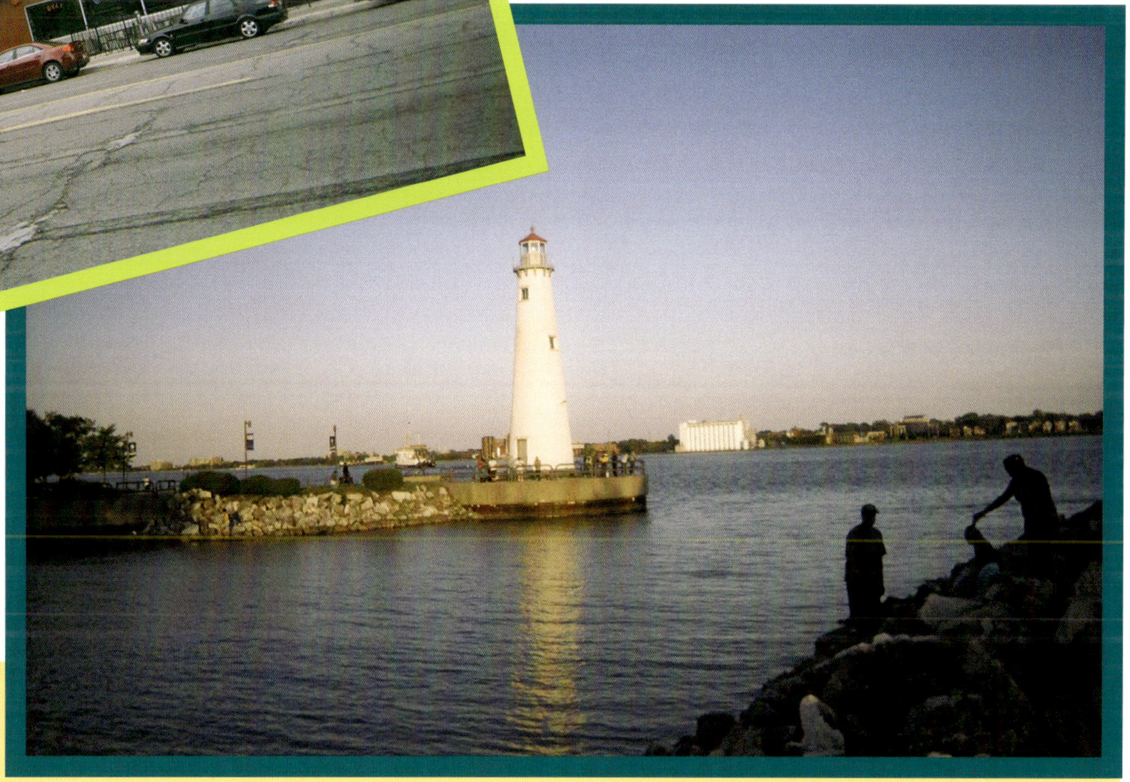

Harbor lighthouse, Milliken State Park and Harbor.
—Islandview Community

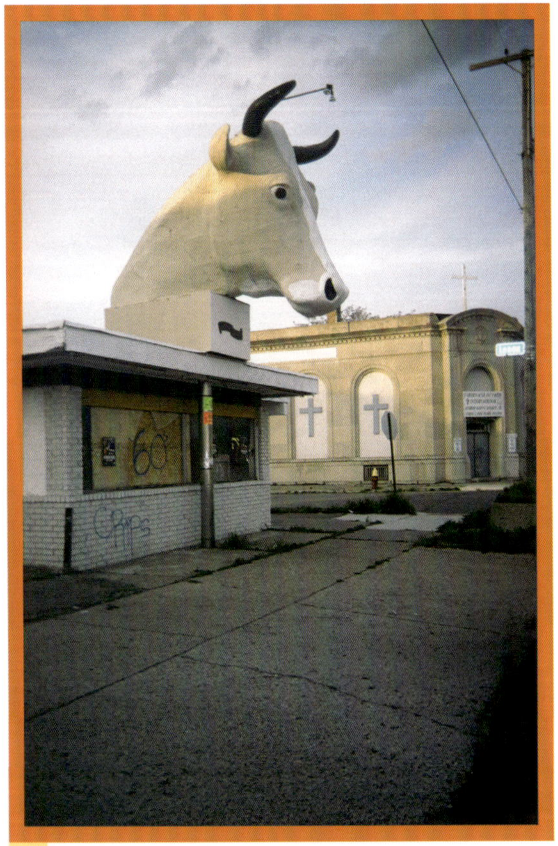

This bull can be found on Detroit's eastside near Warren and Conner. —LEAP

LOWER EASTSIDE ACTION PLAN (LEAP)

Leader: Khalil Ligon

Participants: 33

www.facebook.com/leapdetroit

THE LOWER EASTSIDE ACTION PLAN (LEAP) is a community-driven project to transform vacant land and property into uses that improve the quality of life in our neighborhoods and surrounding areas. Focusing on the area bound by I-94, the Detroit River, Alter, and Mt. Elliott, LEAP convened residents and community stakeholders, neighborhood and technical agencies, universities and government officials to generate a plan that addresses the vacant land crisis on the lower eastside of Detroit.

Participants in LEAP's community planning project were invited to take part in the DIA's Reveal Your Detroit. Stakeholders were asked to photograph their place from their perspective. Even though the physical landscape is dotted by blight, the people who have remained are a testament to the resiliency of the community to transform itself into a better place to live and thrive. Our photographs represent Detroit's beauty as we see it.

Reveal Your Detroit gave LEAP participants an opportunity to capture and share the many hidden gems of beauty throughout Detroit's lower eastside.

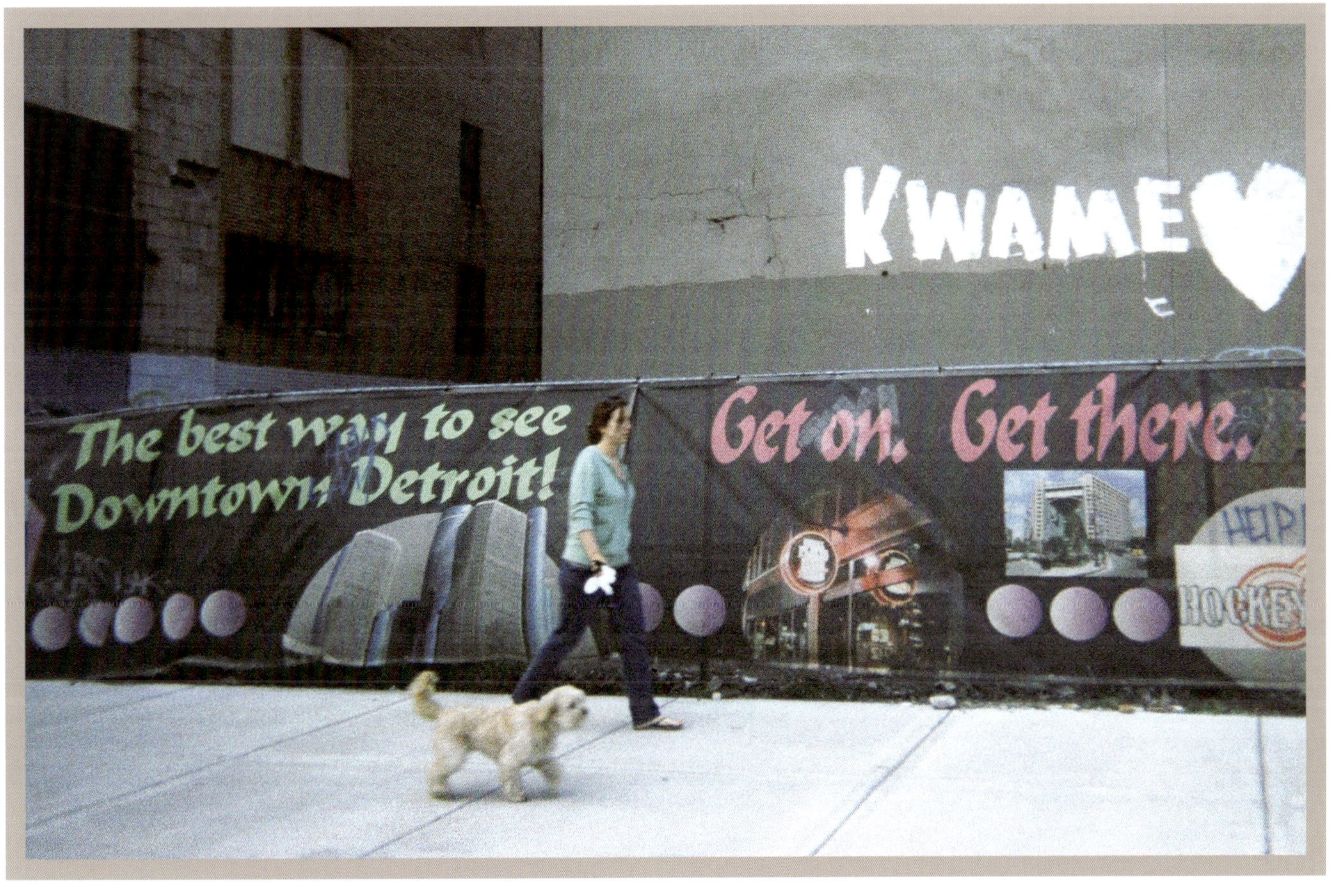

Walking downtown. —LEAP

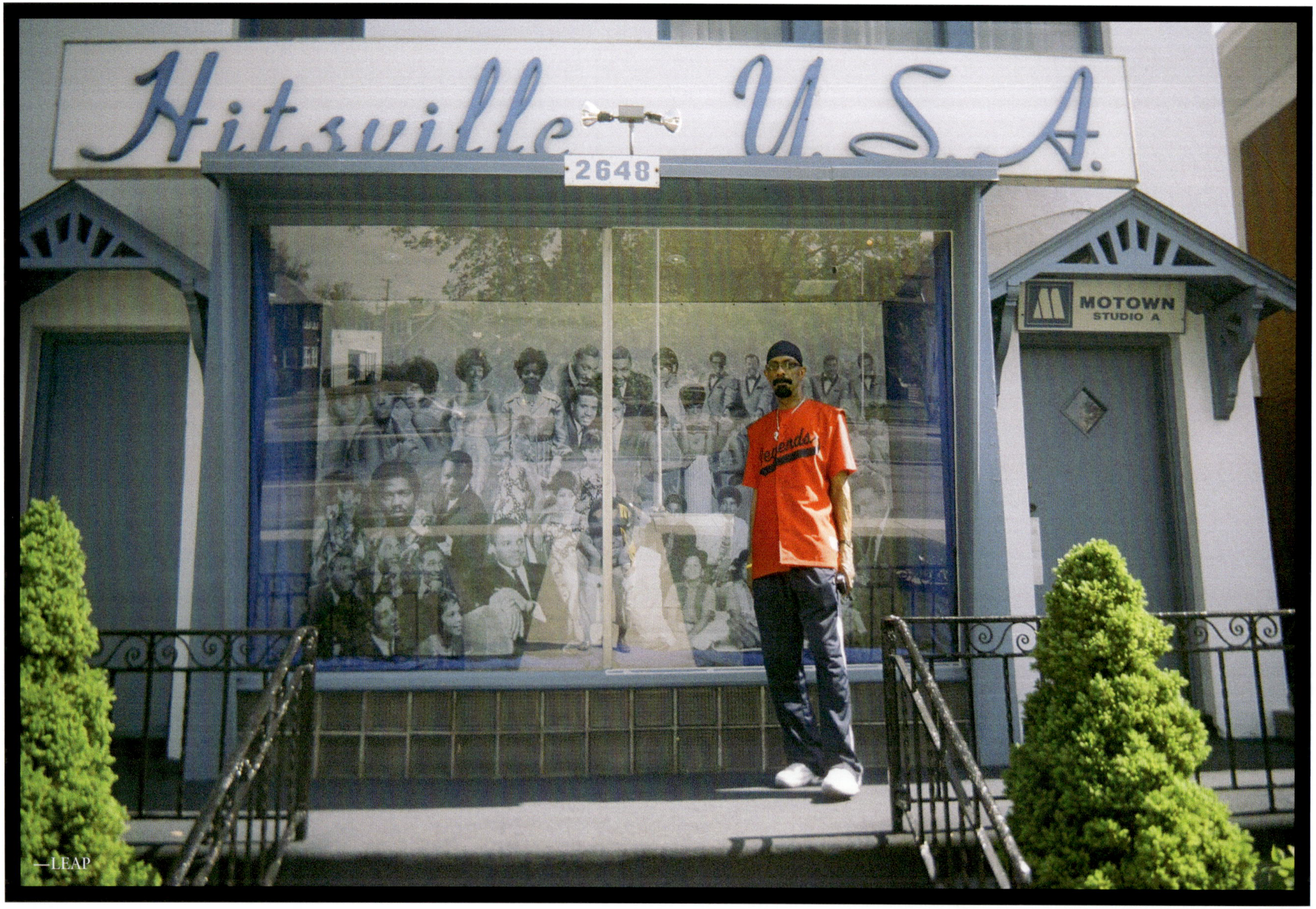
Hitsville U.S.A.
2648
MOTOWN
STUDIO A
Legends
—LEAP

Reveal Your Detroit

Motown is nostalgic. I grew up listening to the greatest hits in America. Marvin Gaye, Smokey Robinson, The Temptations, Stevie Wonder, and many, many more! I was insistent on being photographed at Motown Museum because that was a place for family outings as a child. The Motown Museum is one of the great things about this city.

GREG WELCH

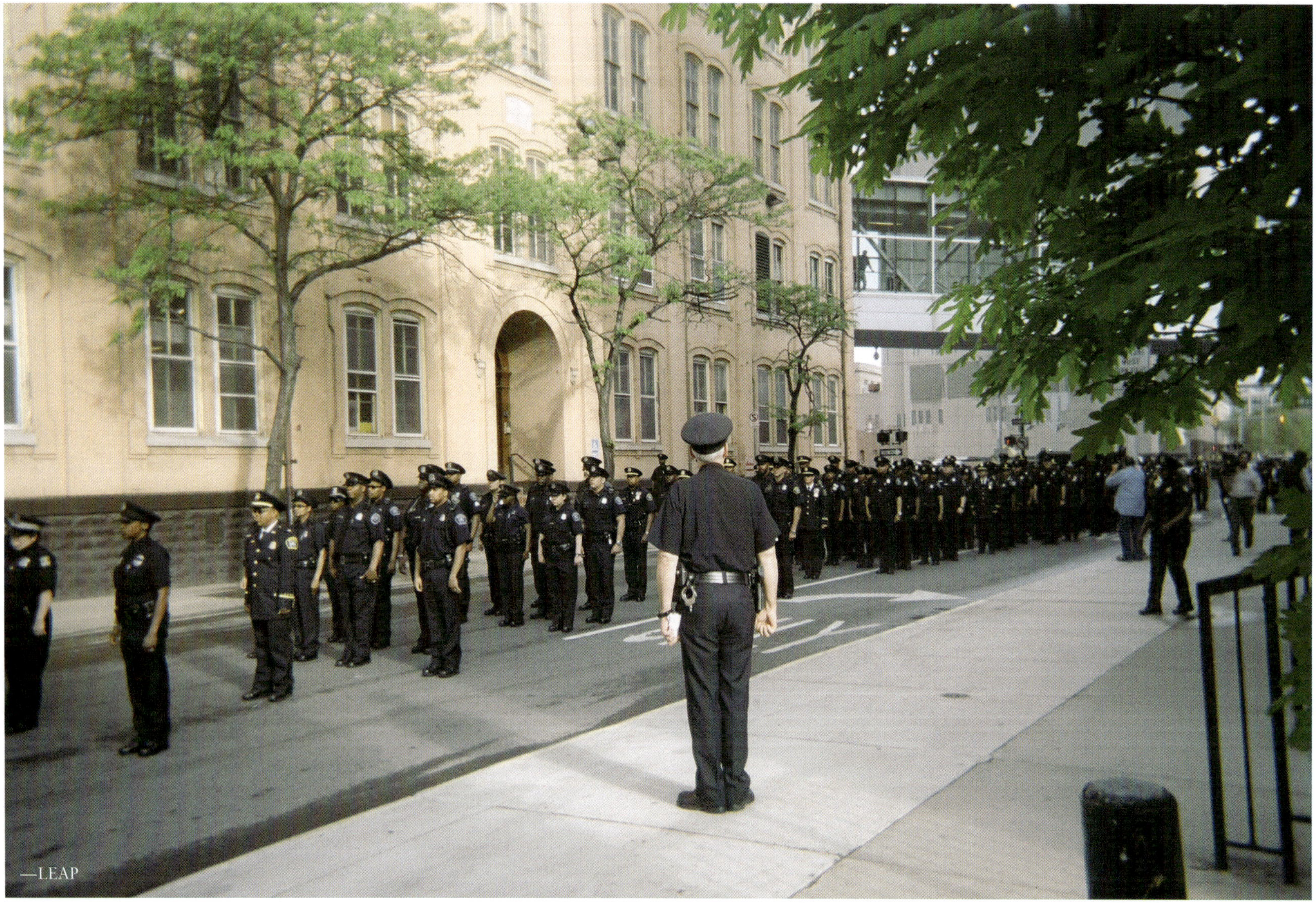

—LEAP

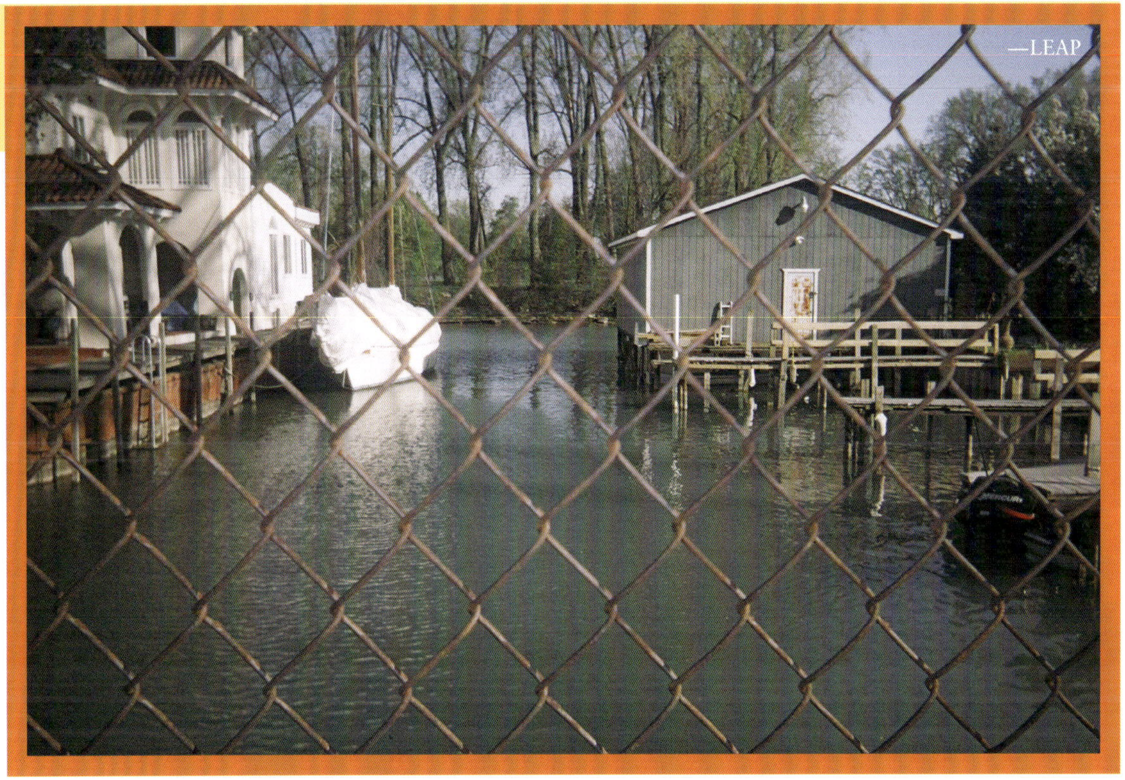
—LEAP

I took this picture because I grew up a few blocks from the canal but was never allowed to go near the water as a child. It is one of my childhood landmarks that always reminds me why I love Detroit.

LYTANGA YARBOR

MARYGROVE COLLEGE PHOTOGRAPHY CLASS

Robert Stewart

Participants: 15

www.marygrove.edu

Opposite: *The FOX Theater marquee.*
—Marygrove College Photography Class

MARYGROVE COLLEGE'S Division of Visual & Performing Arts believes that artists impact their community through visionary, innovative practice within or across creative disciplines. Often this work effects change. The artist, writer, director, composer, or choreographer has historically challenged and reinvented how contemporary society views and understands itself. This drama plays itself out in the urban arena. This is leadership through practice and is the core of the very nature of the creative impulse. Often this practice, whether by an individual artist or a group of artists working together, is really the moving force for community change and improvement.

Reveal Your Detroit engaged students and the surrounding community in ongoing discussions on Detroit's past, present, and future through film.

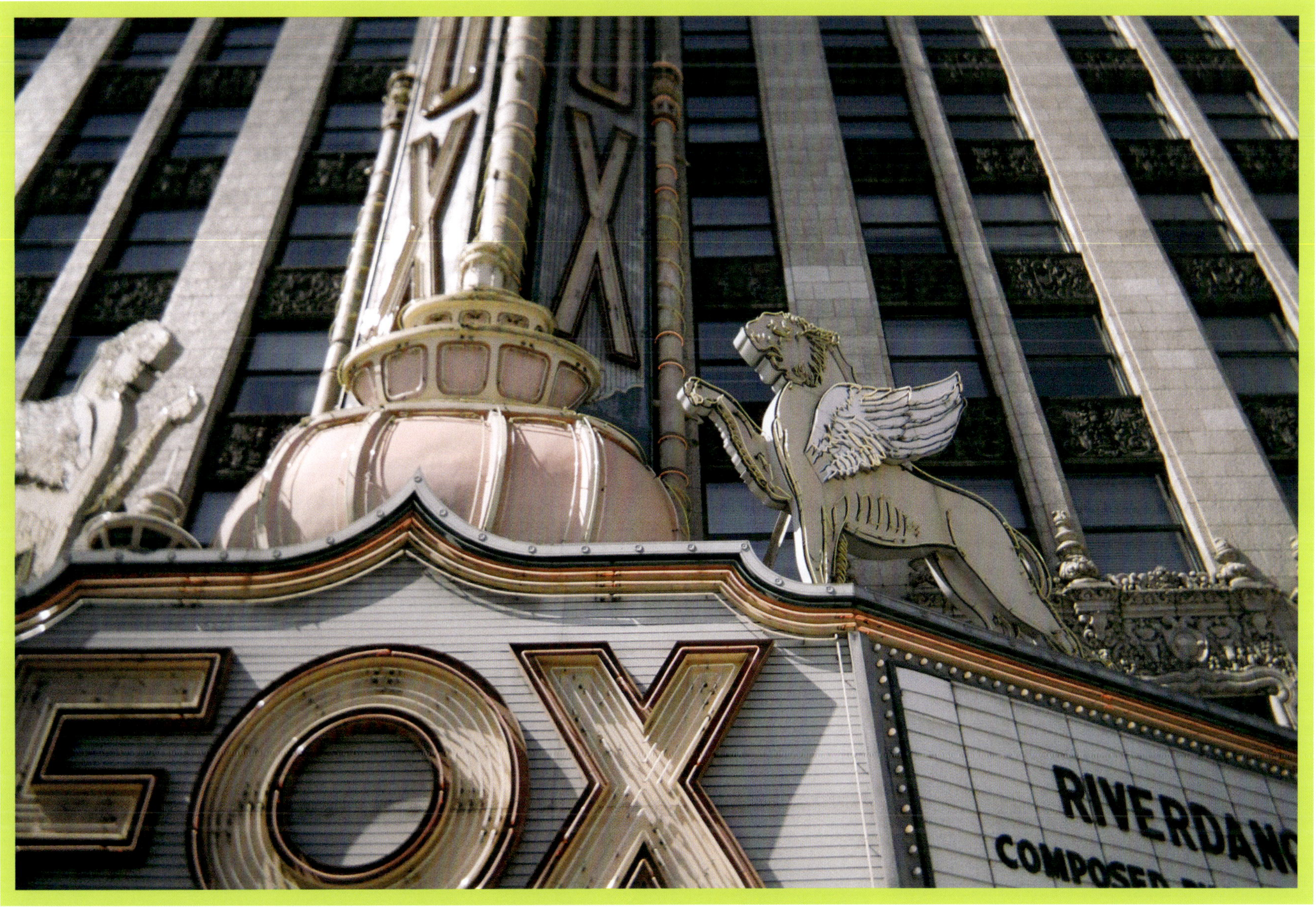

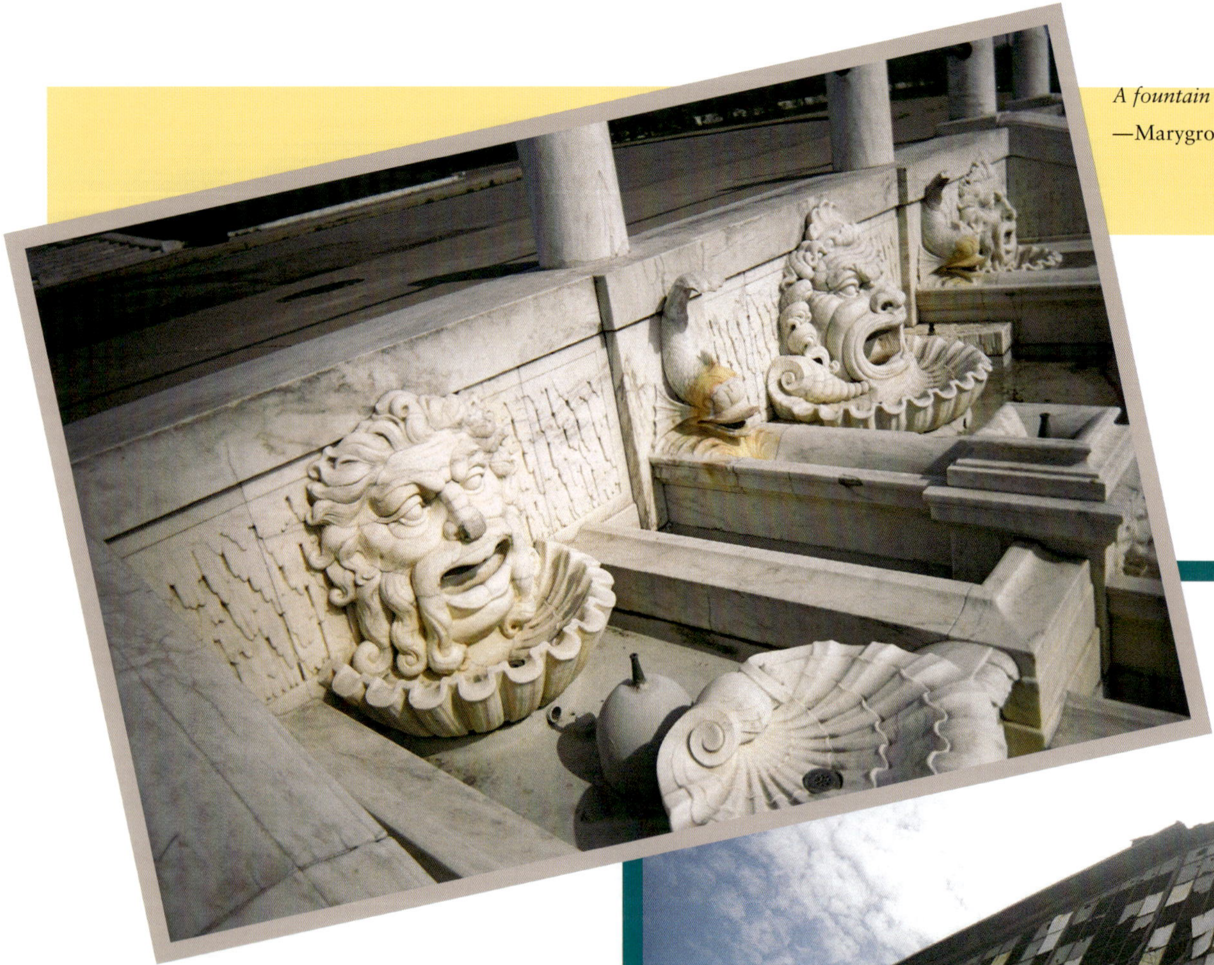

A fountain on Belle Isle.
—Marygrove College Photography Class

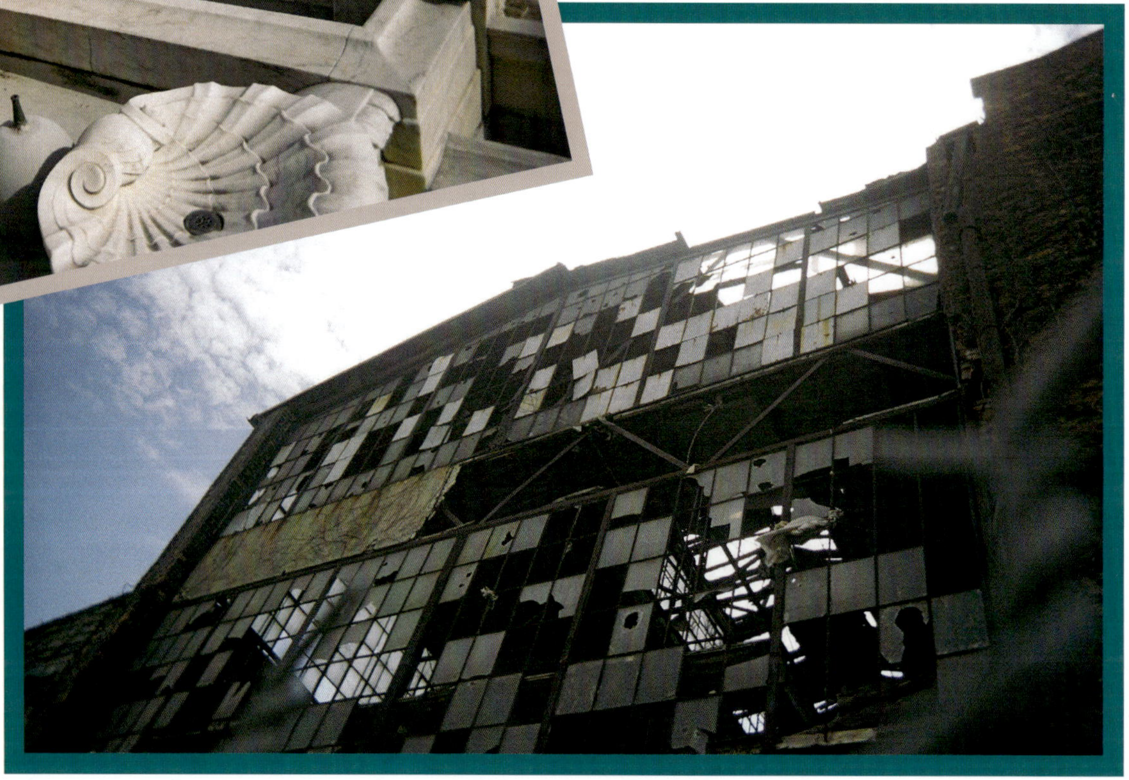

The Globe Trading Building from the Dequindre Cut.
—Marygrove College Photography Class

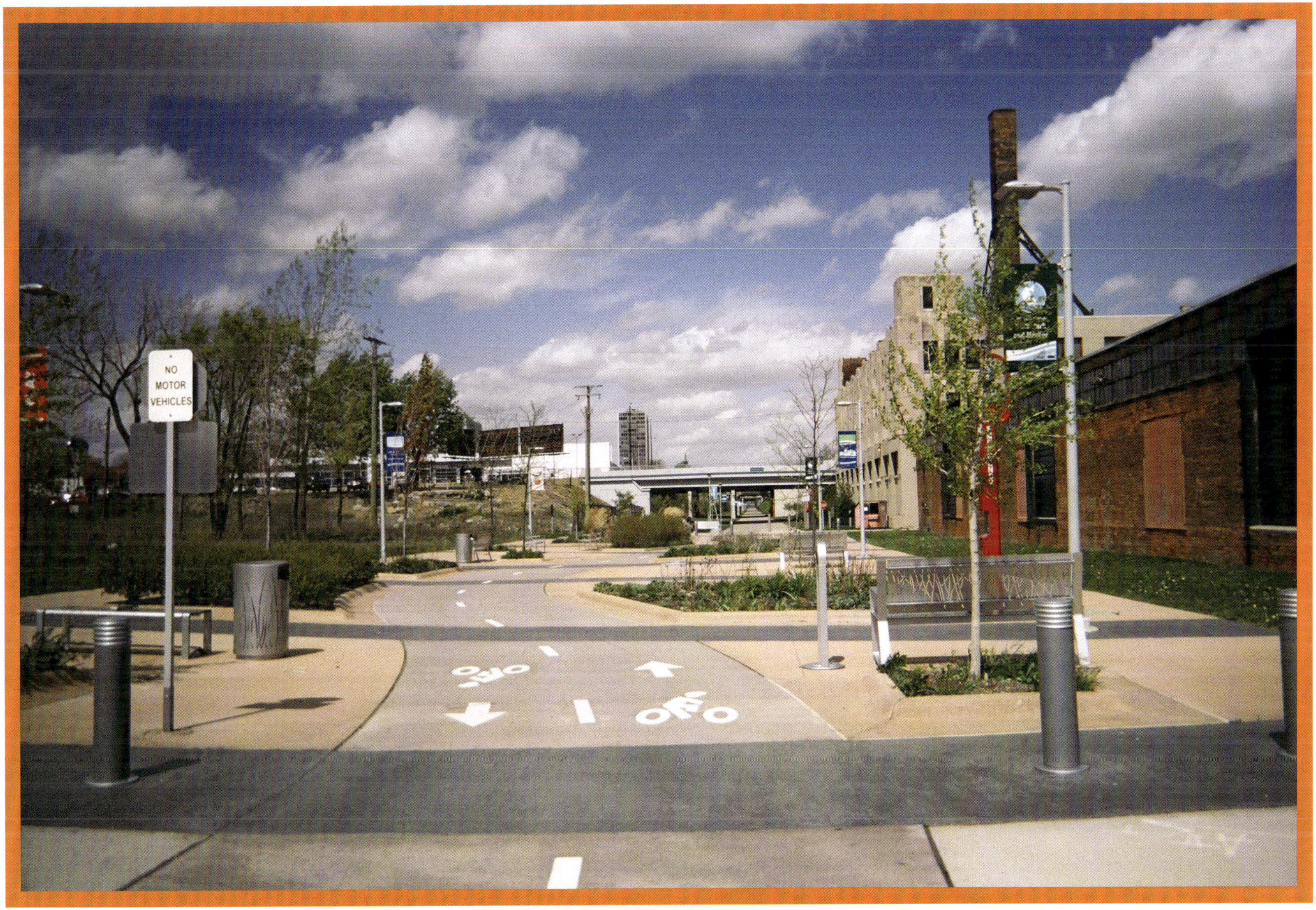

The bottom of the Dequindre Cut, a new greenway that leads from the Detroit Riverwalk to Eastern Market. —Marygrove College Photography Class

MCDOUGAL HUNT CITIZENS DISTRICT COUNCIL

Leader: Anthony Dicus

Participants: 4

www.mdhcdc.com

Opposite: *Faygo pop.*
—McDougal Hunt Citizens District Council

MCDOUGAL HUNT CITIZENS DISTRICT COUNCIL encouraged its membership to walk the neighborhood it represents and find the beauty and document it via photography. Reveal Your Detroit gave our members a tool for discovery, a tool to use to get more personally involved with the community in which we serve. If more institutions would form such partnerships, I truly believe this city would move forward with more of a sense of understanding.

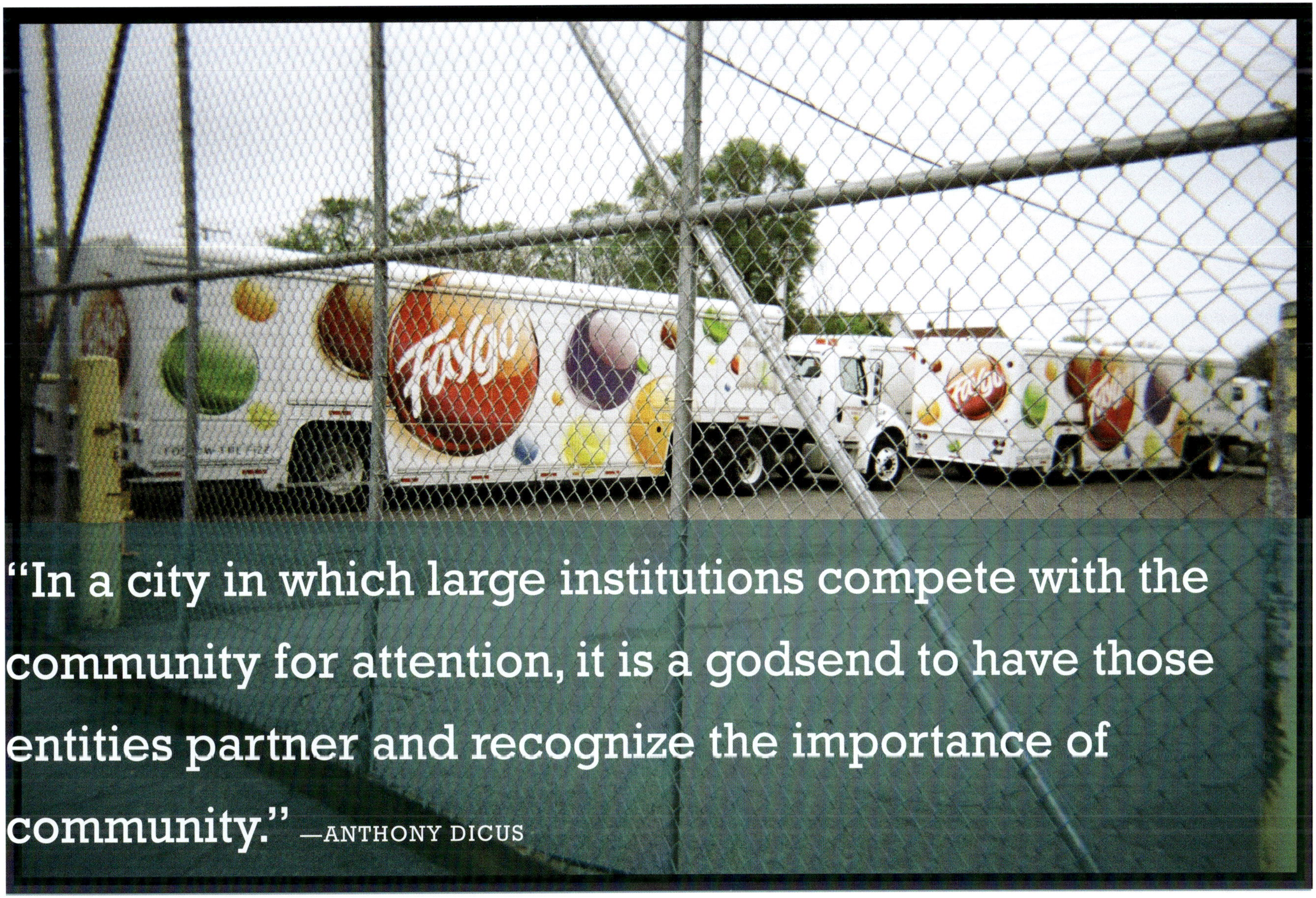

"In a city in which large institutions compete with the community for attention, it is a godsend to have those entities partner and recognize the importance of community." —ANTHONY DICUS

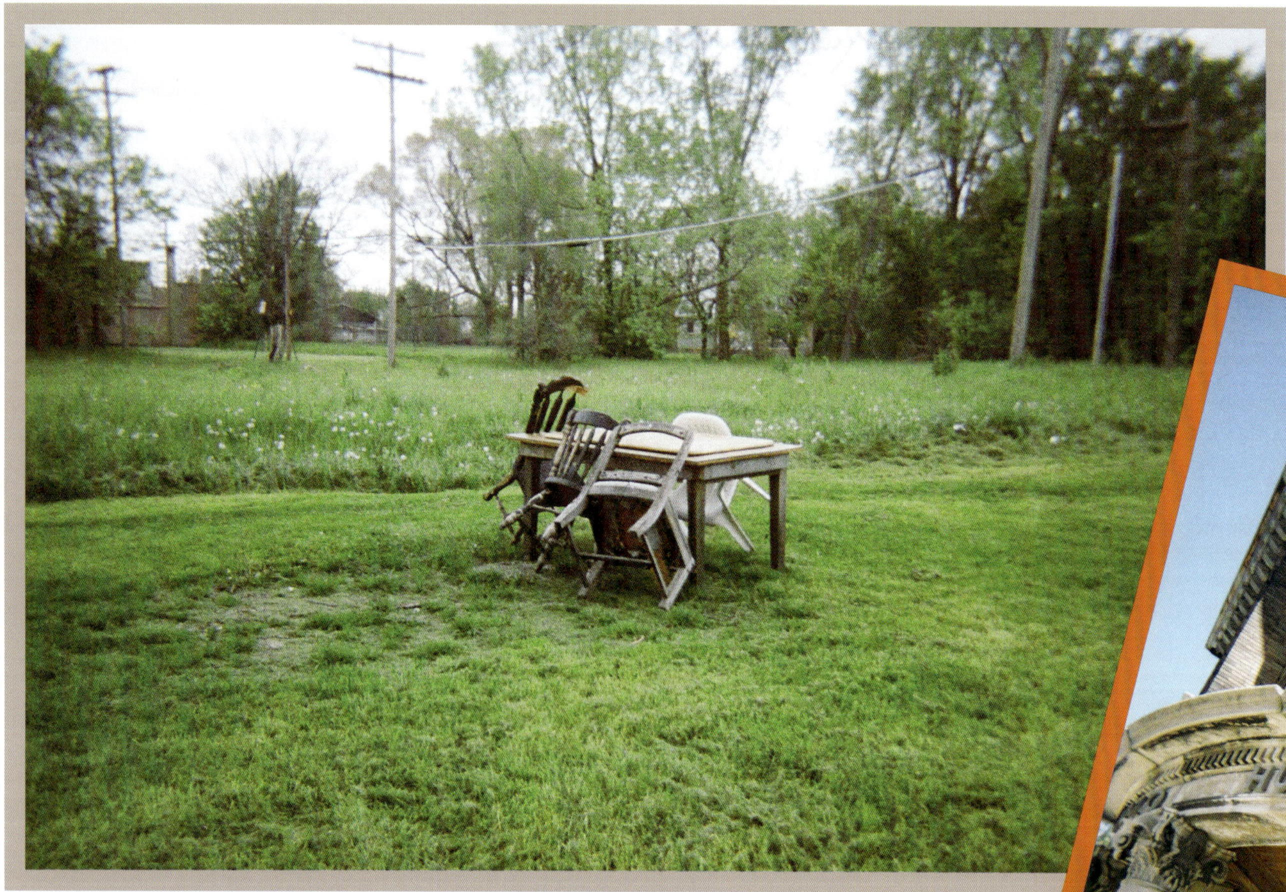

Picnic chairs.

—McDougal Hunt Citizens District Council

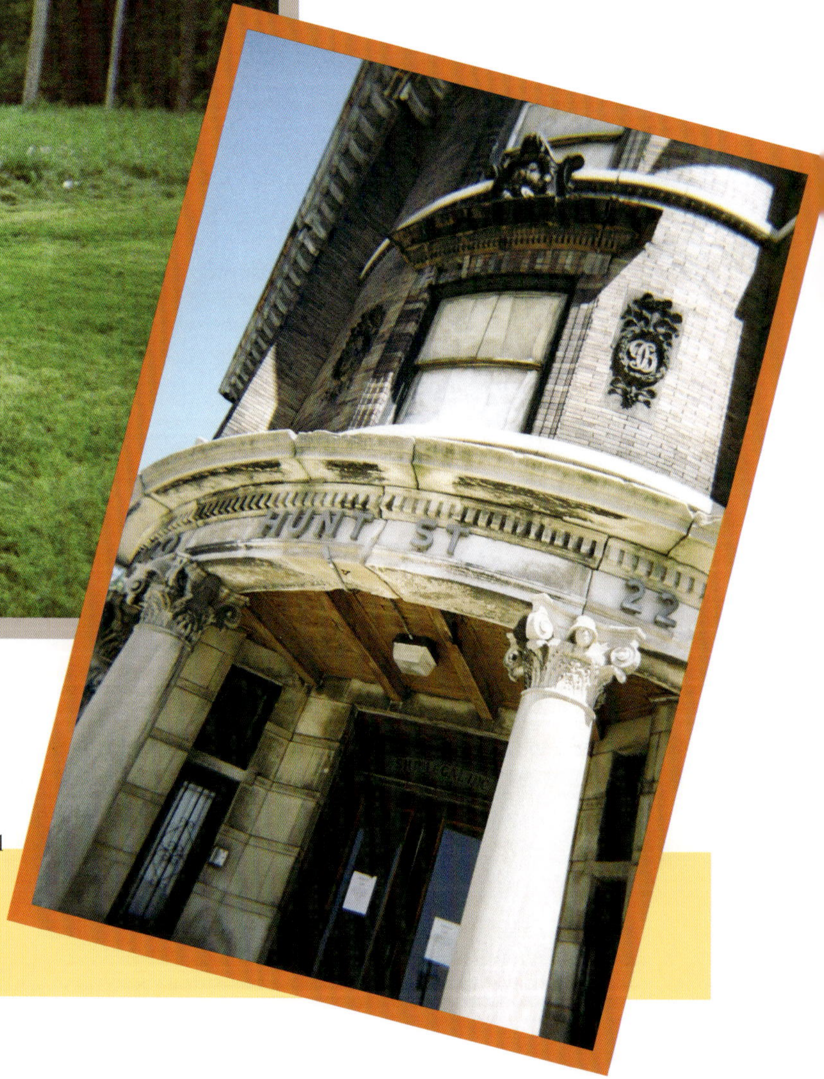

—McDougal Hunt Citizens District Council

MT. ELLIOTT BUSINESS & COMMUNITY ASSOCIATION (MEBCA)

Leader: Miguel Pope

Participants: 15

MEBCA is a community organization that dedicates its efforts to all aspects of neighborhoods within the boundaries of Mt. Elliott, Jefferson, Vernor, and Bellevue. Our focus is on quality of life issues and the physical environment that impacts all who live, work, and worship within the MEBCA community.

This project provided an opportunity for both residents and business owners to explore the community together. Stakeholders found a renewed sense of community as each discovered shared commonalities in photos that indicate similar vision, hopes, and desires for our community.

The Reveal Your Detroit project was powerful in linking communities and organizations across the city; the blue cameras spotted in someone's hand sparked conversations.

At least two kinds of saviors in Detroit.

—Mt. Elliott Business & Community Association

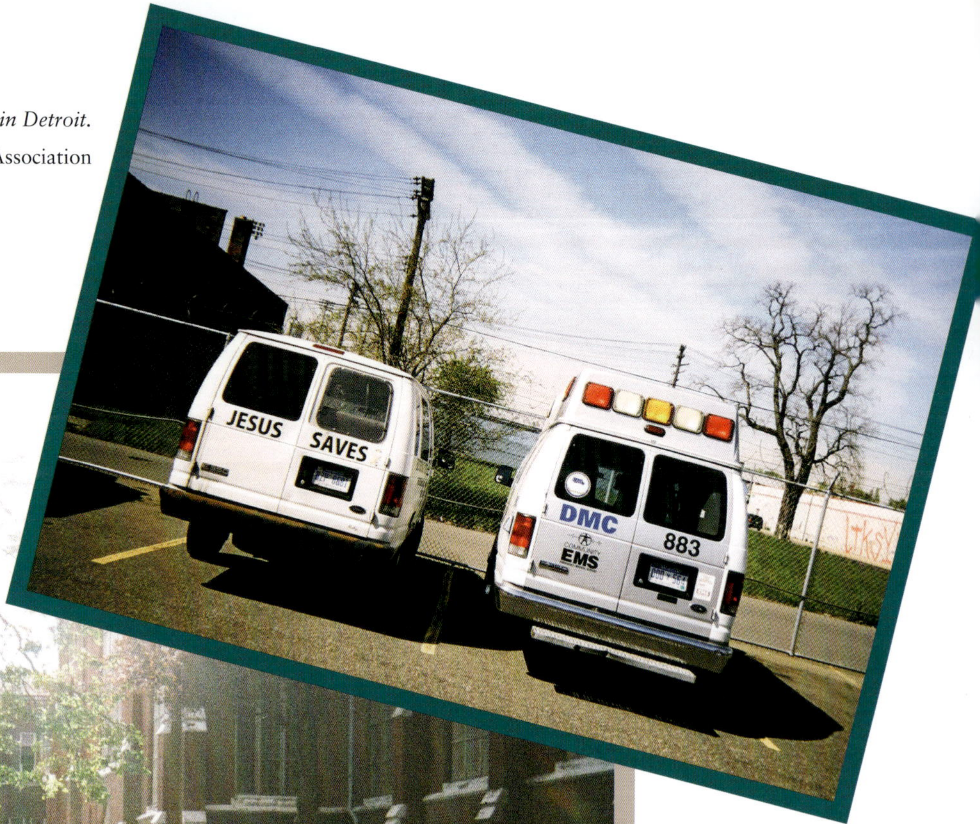

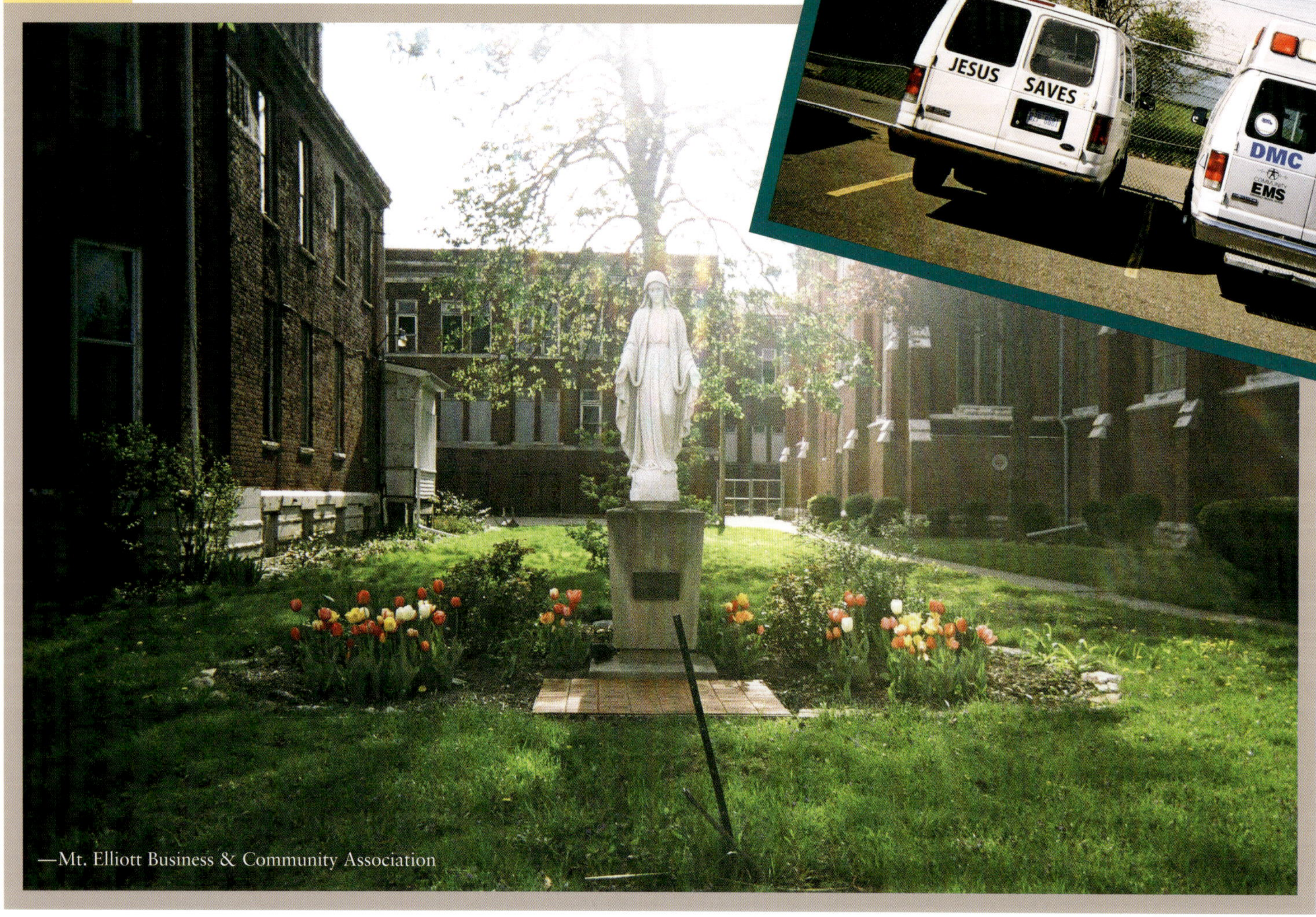

—Mt. Elliott Business & Community Association

NORTH ROSEDALE PARK CIVIC ASSOCIATION

Leader: Gloria Y. Adebayo

Participants: 10

www.northrosedalepark.org

ESTABLISHED IN 1924, the North Rosedale Park Civic Association is a community organization that promotes the interests and welfare of North Rosedale Park residents.

The Reveal Your Detroit Project allowed neighbors in North Rosedale Park an opportunity to share their vision of Detroit. Each participant "revealed" neighborhood-inspired pictures of community activities, landmarks specific to our neighborhood, children playing, and so forth.

Despite how people portray our city, it really is for the most part a quiet and peaceful place where we watch our leaves fall, come back, and fall again while we maintain and live our lives.

Reveal Your Detroit gave the citizens an opportunity to share with people outside our neighborhood and show them what Detroit life is like on a day-to-day basis.

The DIA and Reveal Your Detroit brought Detroiters together to give a unique perspective of our city and its talent. Plus, it was fun to do!

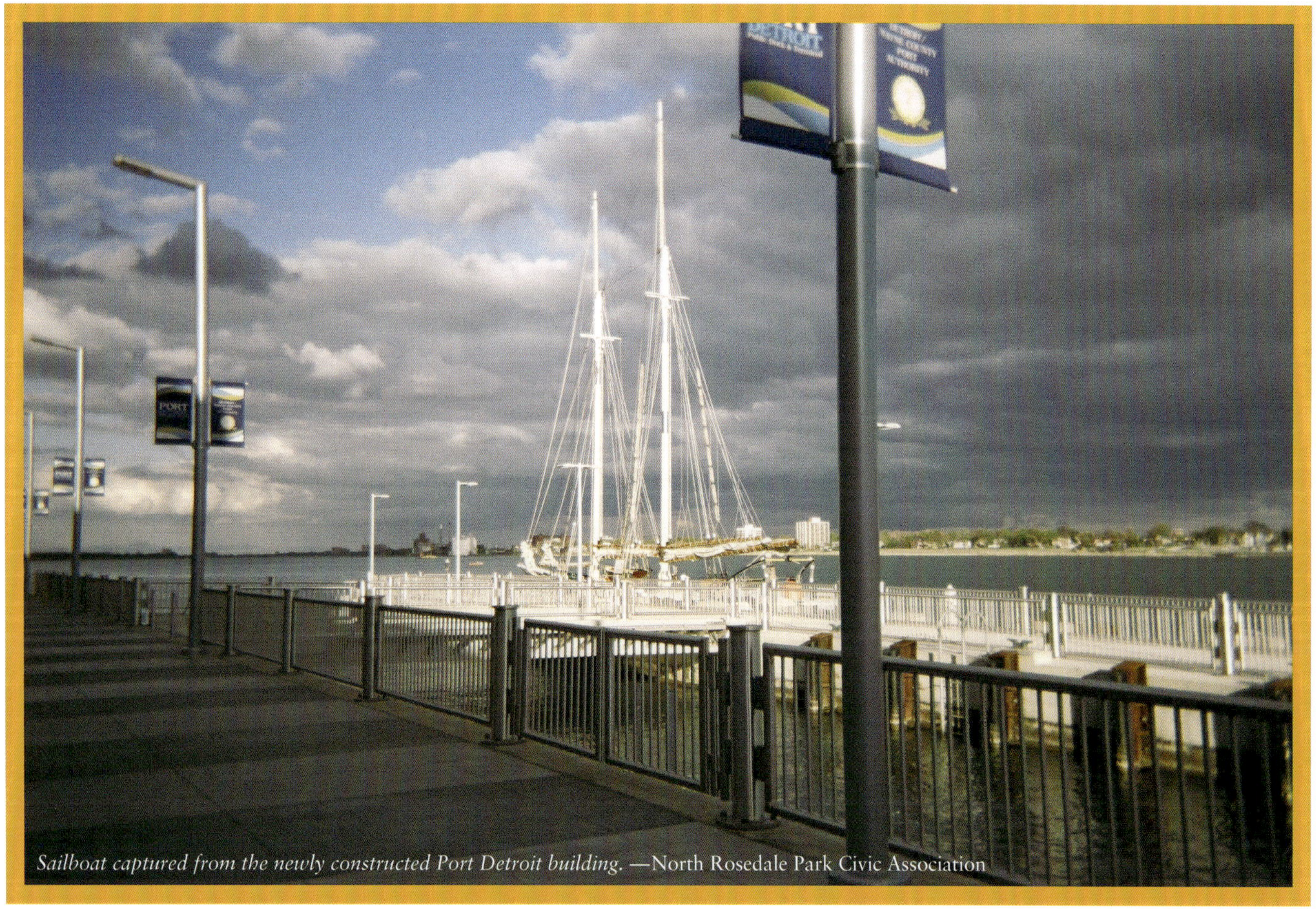

Sailboat captured from the newly constructed Port Detroit building. —North Rosedale Park Civic Association

OFFICERS OF THE DIA

Leader: Hasan Hasan

Participants: 10

www.dia.org

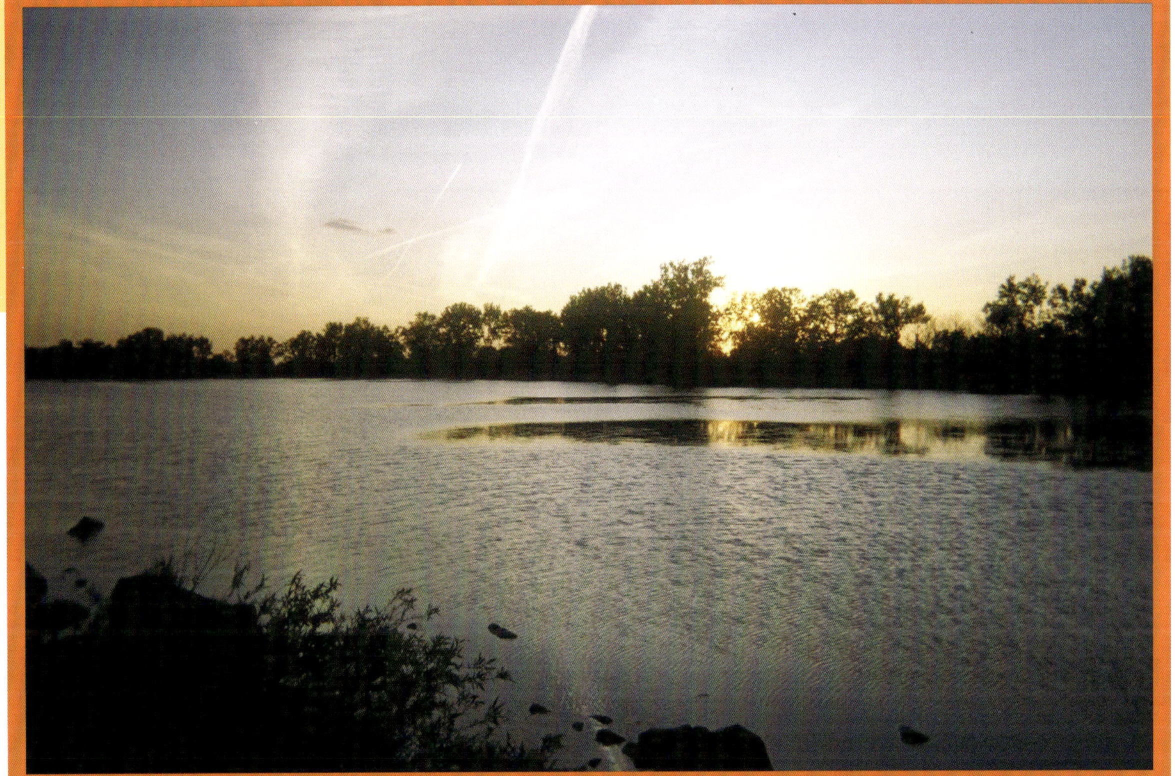

—Officers of the DIA

THE OFFICERS OF THE DIA oversee day-to-day security at the museum and were invited to participate in the Reveal Your Detroit project as representatives of the museum and our broader community.

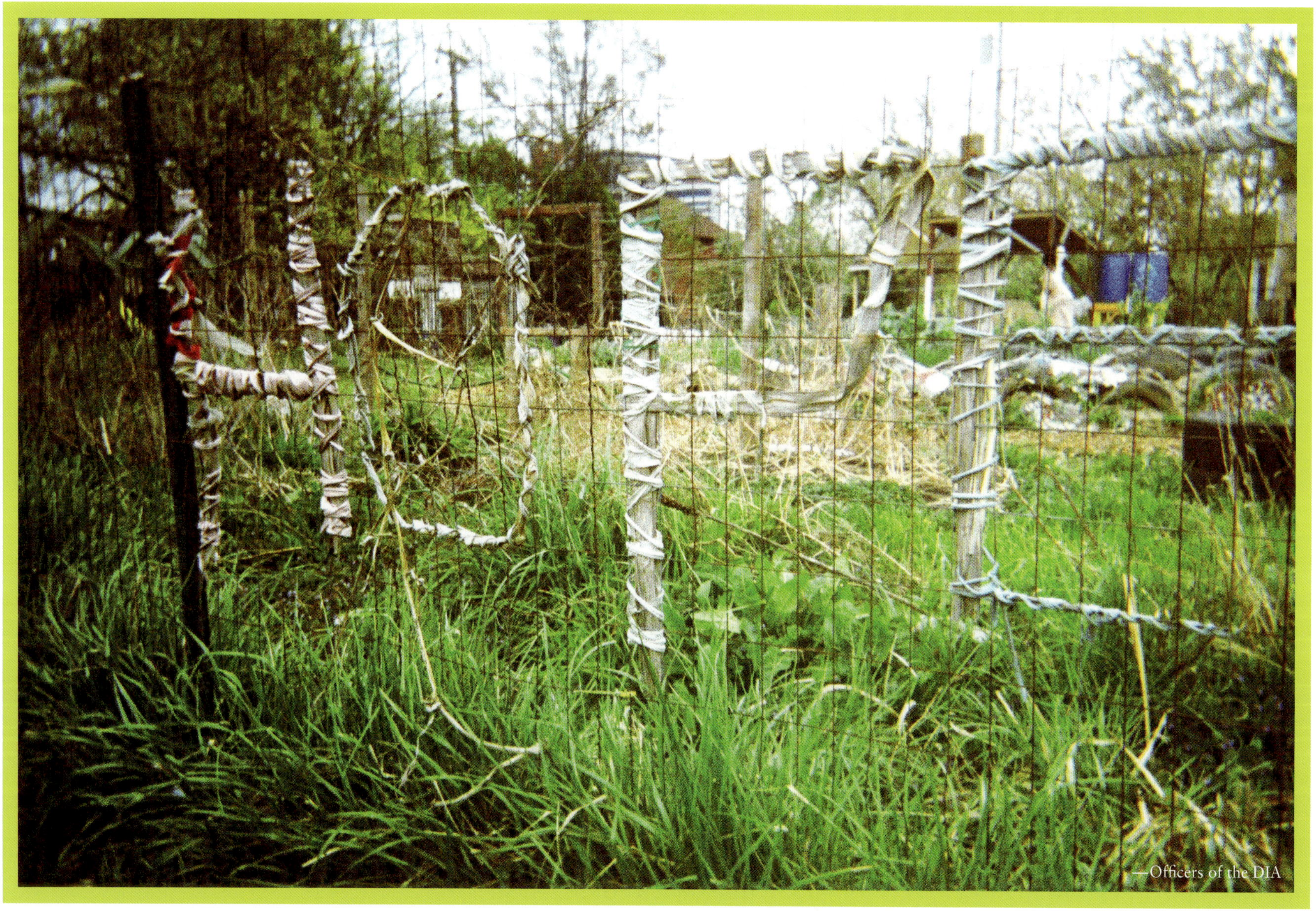

—Officers of the DIA

OUR LIFE IN THE D

Group Leader: China Cochran

Number of Participants: 10

www.ourlifeinthed.com

OUR LIFE IN THE D is a multimedia training and leadership project intended to provide young people living in Detroit with a voice as we explore issues we face in our communities. Our Life in the D has a special focus on the Skillman Foundation's six Good Neighborhood communities that include Chadsey-Condon, southwest Detroit, Cody-Rouge, Osborn, Northend-Central, and Brightmoor.

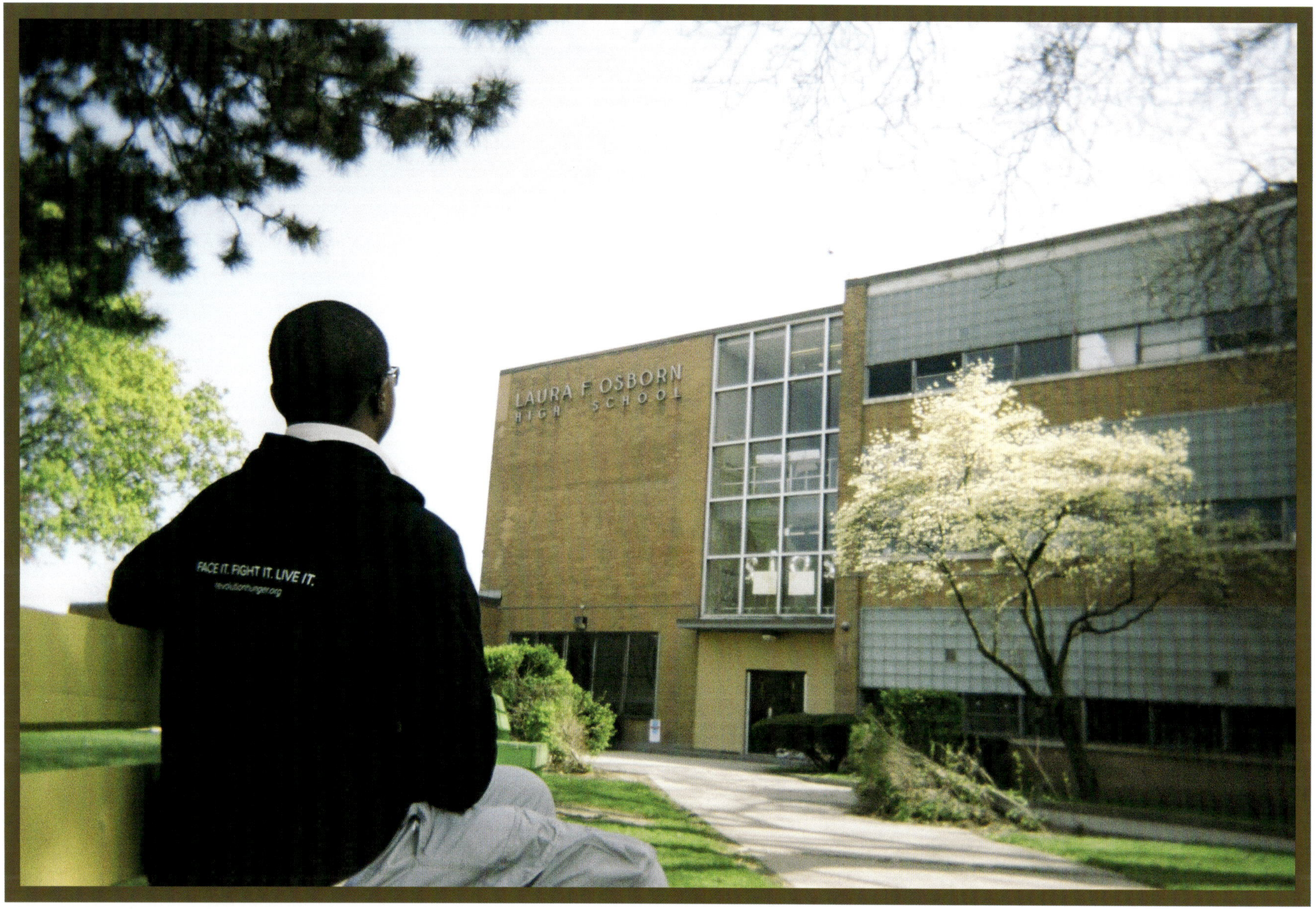

A teen looks on at Osborn High School. —Our Life in the D

PAY IT FORWARD INITIATIVE

Leader: Charlie Cavel

Participants: 7

www.facebook.com/pages/Pay-it-Forward-Initiative

THE PAY IT FORWARD INITIATIVE is a nonprofit organization that provides transformational services through employment, education, and empowerment. Our vision is to help the next generation of Detroit citizens develop their own viable framework for success.

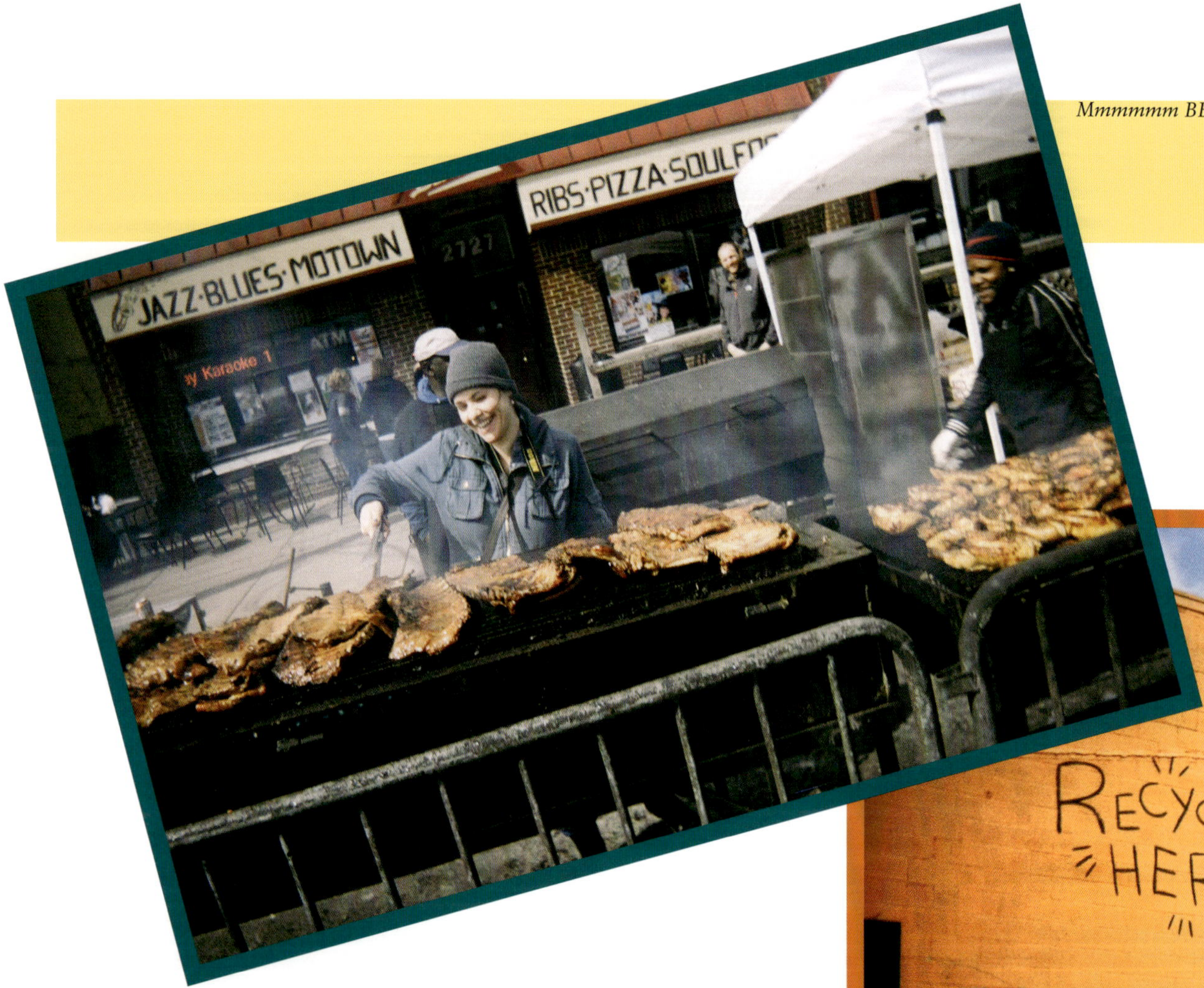

Mmmmmm BBQ at Bert's. —Pay It Forward Initiative

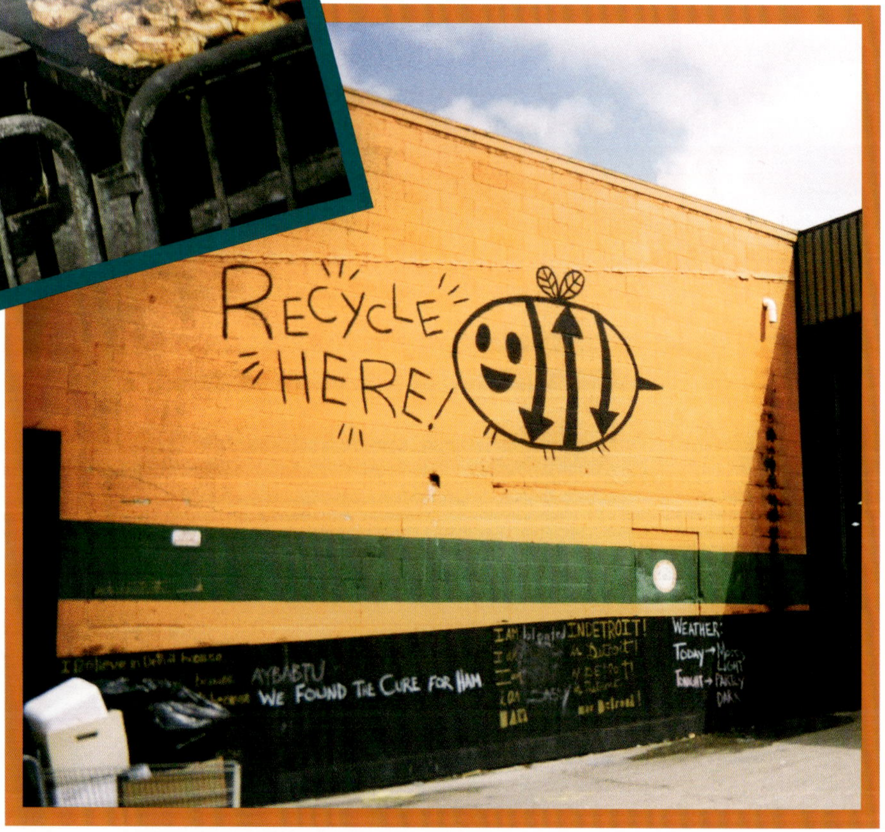

Recycle Here: BEE Green! —Pay It Forward Initiative

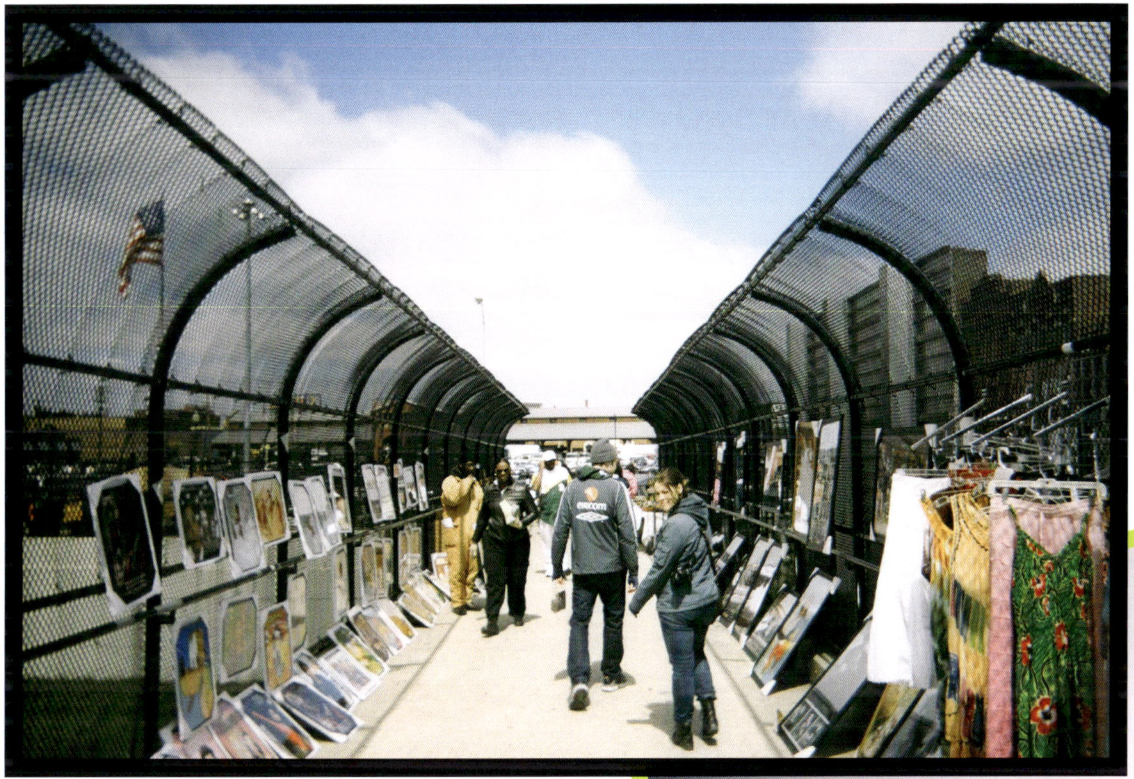

Eastern Market bridge shopping on Saturday.
—Pay It Forward Initiative

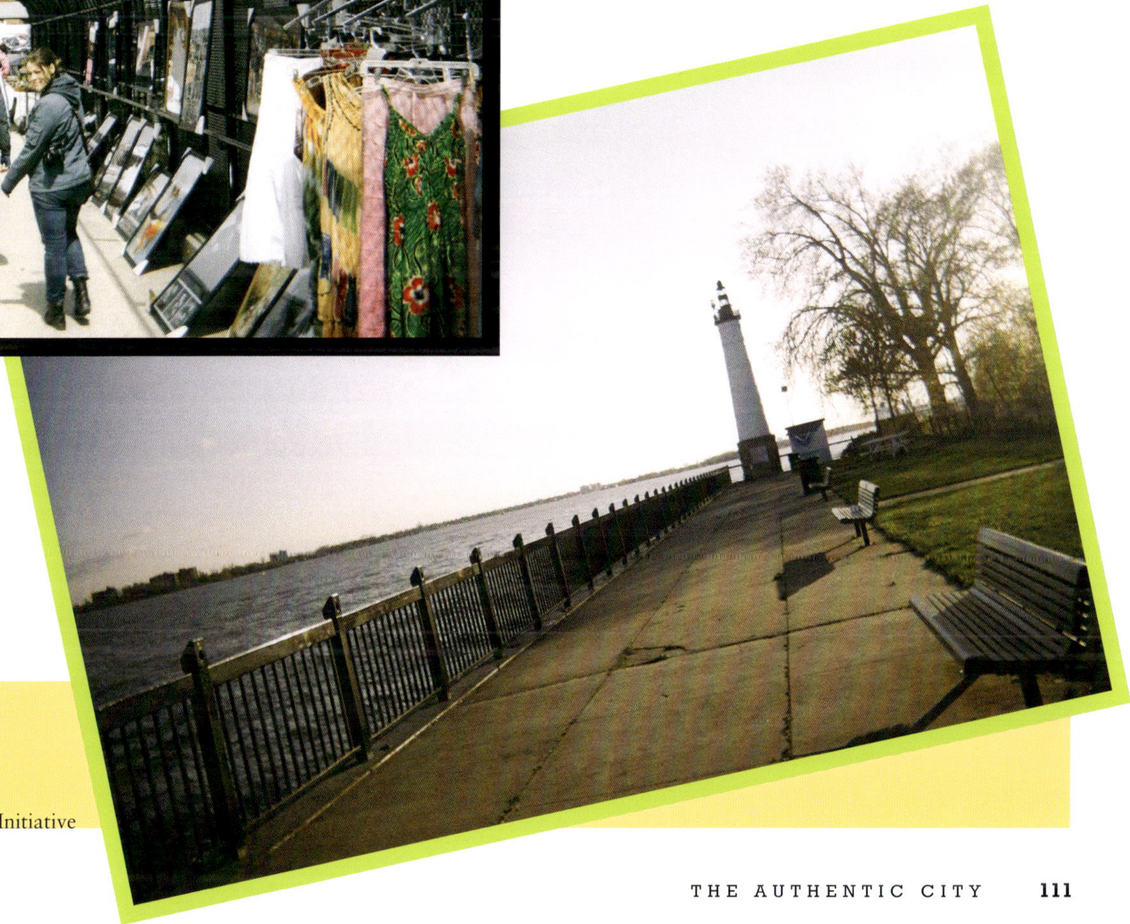

Park benches along the river. —Pay It Forward Initiative

PONYRIDE DETROIT

Leader: Phillip Cooley

Participants: 4

www.ponyride.org

PONYRIDE is a study to see how the foreclosure crisis can have a positive impact on our communities. Using an "all boats rise with the tide" rent subsidy, we are able to provide cheap space for socially conscious artists and entrepreneurs to work and share knowledge, resources, and networks.

Ponyride nurtures collaboration using shared resources, knowledge, and ideas to cultivate opportunities created by the strengths and crises of Detroit. Participants serve Detroit communities by sharing their craft and expertise.

Reveal Your Detroit allowed us to engage diverse groups of socially conscious entrepreneurs and give them opportunities for community outreach and education.

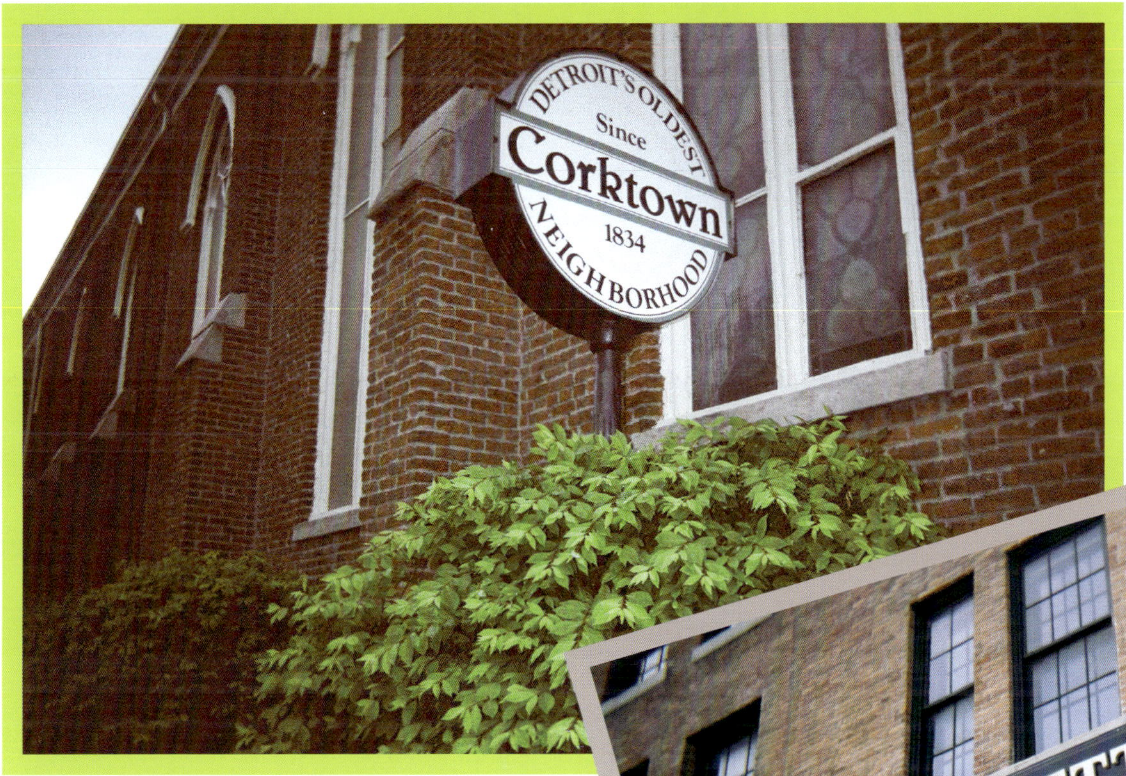

Corktown, home to Ponyride. —Ponyride Detroit

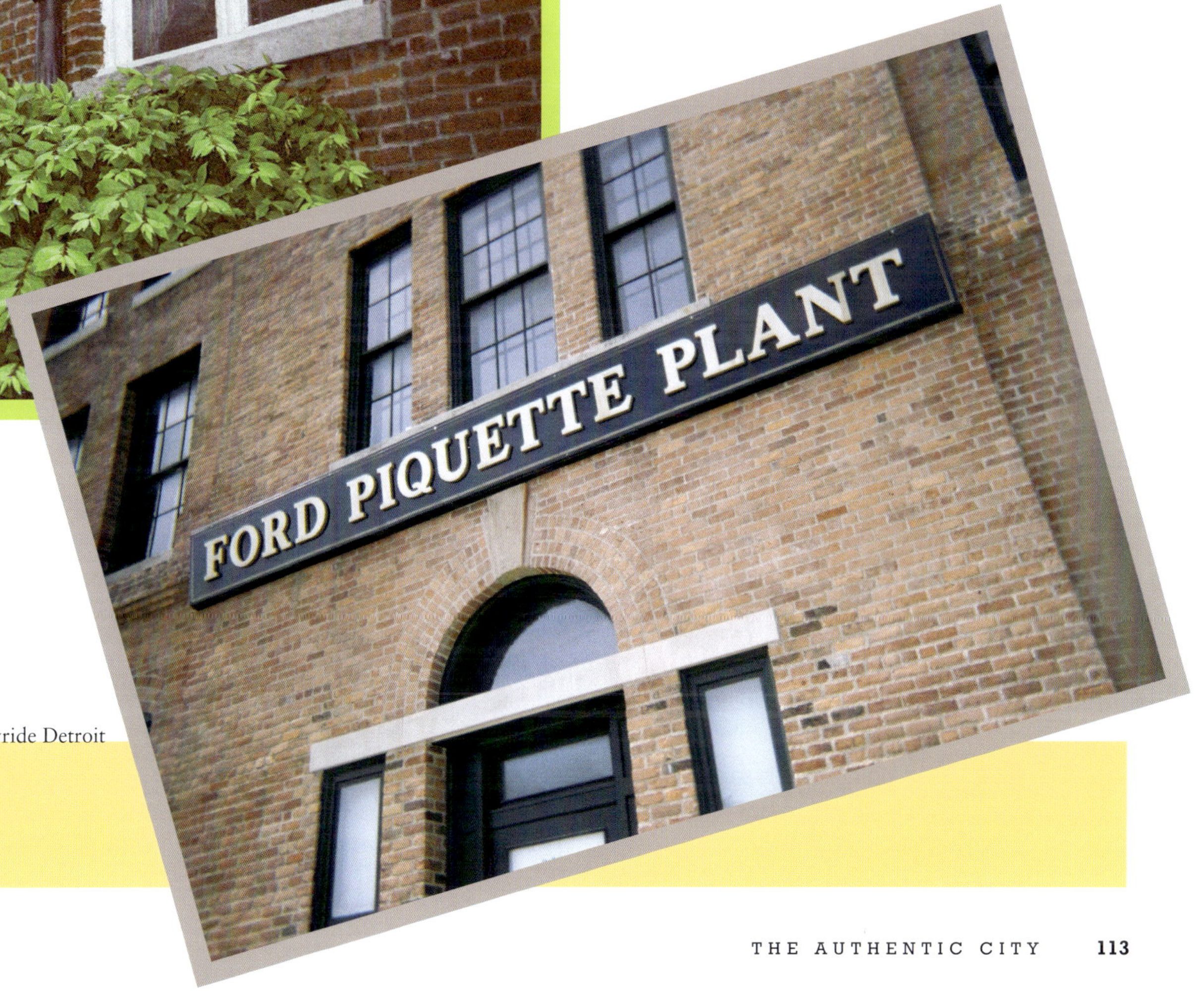

Ford Piquette Plant, Northend Detroit. —Ponyride Detroit

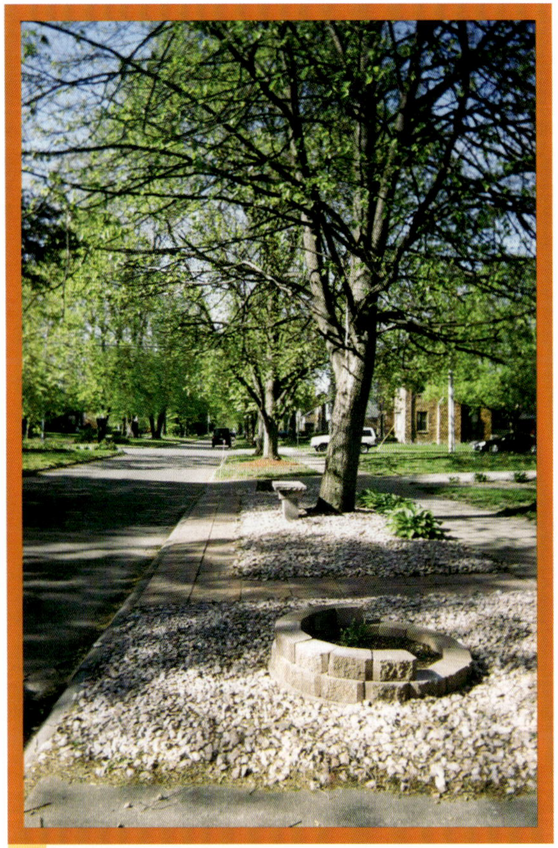

Big trees and green boulevards are a staple in the Rosedale Park neighborhood. —Rosedale Park Improvement Association

ROSEDALE PARK IMPROVEMENT ASSOCIATION

Leader: Mary McLeod

Participants: 12

www.rosedalepark.org

THE ROSEDALE PARK IMPROVEMENT ASSOCIATION is a neighborhood association representing almost 1,600 homes in northwest Detroit. We promote pride in home ownership, neighborhood beautification, civic engagement, commitment to community, and social activism.

Rosedale Park residents took this opportunity to capture on film images that meant something to them about living in our neighborhood and the city of Detroit in general. Young and old alike were engaged in seeing their usual surroundings in a different way. This also provided another link to the DIA, bringing an artistic edge to our community.

This cross-generational, cross-cultural experience contributed to a sense of pride in a city that is often struggling to identify what is worthy of praise.

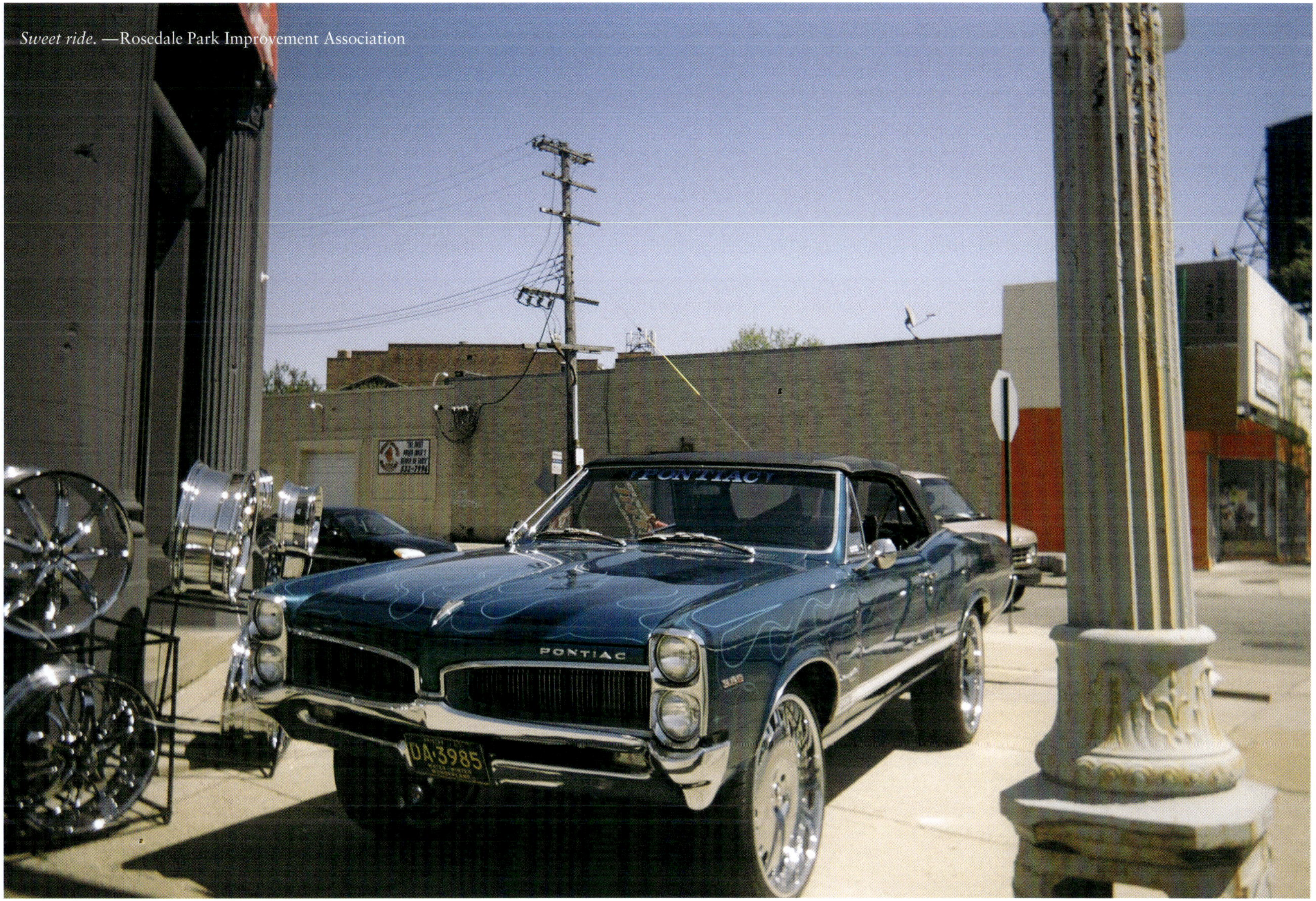

Sweet ride. —Rosedale Park Improvement Association

ST. PAUL AFRICAN METHODIST EPISCOPAL CHURCH

Leader: Miguel Pope

Participants: 15

THIS WAS A multigenerational project that involved individuals from the same church who live in the various communities of metropolitan Detroit. The photos captured were seen through the eyes of those who have observed the city at its best and the youthful eyes that only know what they see in front of them. The project provided opportunities for conversation about the past, present, and future of Detroit.

This project provided an opportunity for members of the same faith community to come together and discuss and explore the city we all live in. It also sparked interest in returning to the DIA.

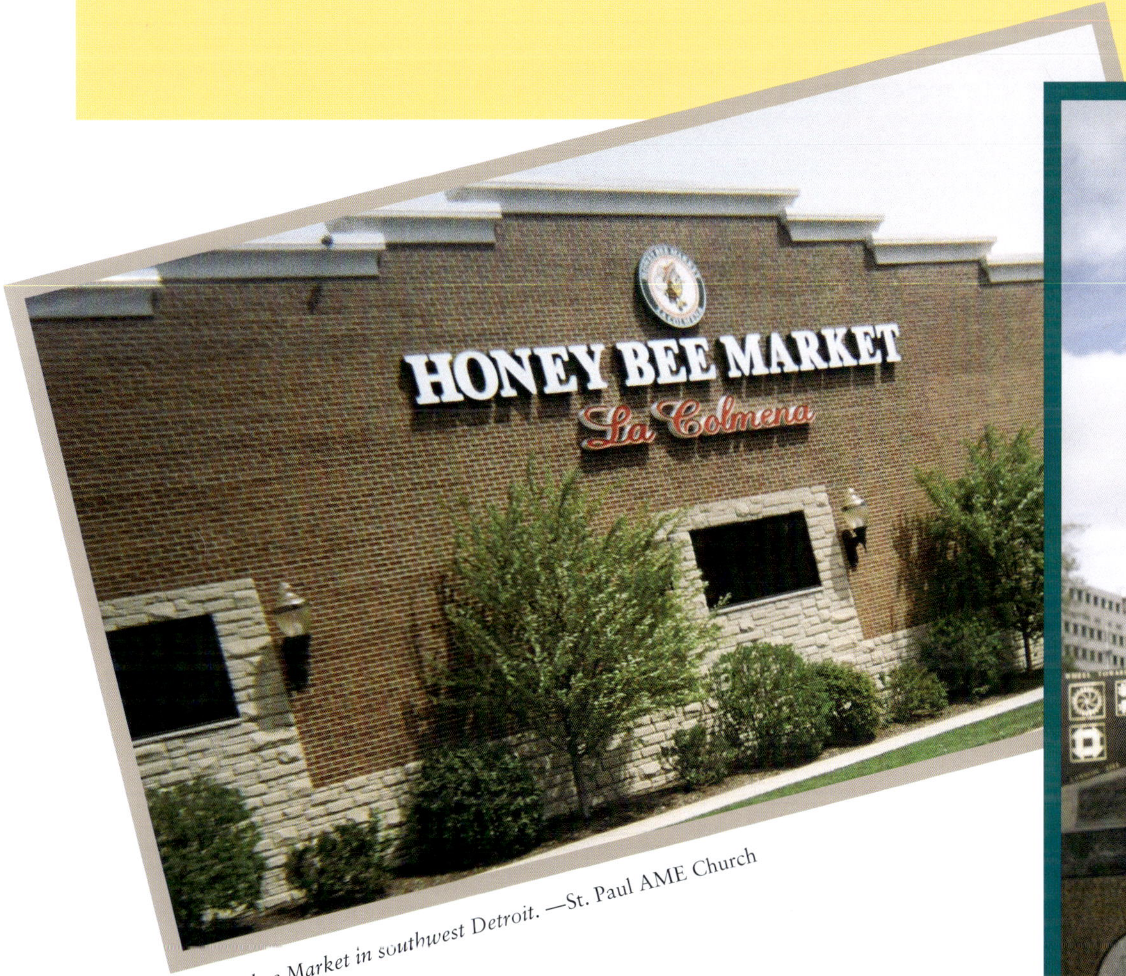

Honeybee Market in southwest Detroit. —St. Paul AME Church

Underground Railroad memorial. —St. Paul AME Church

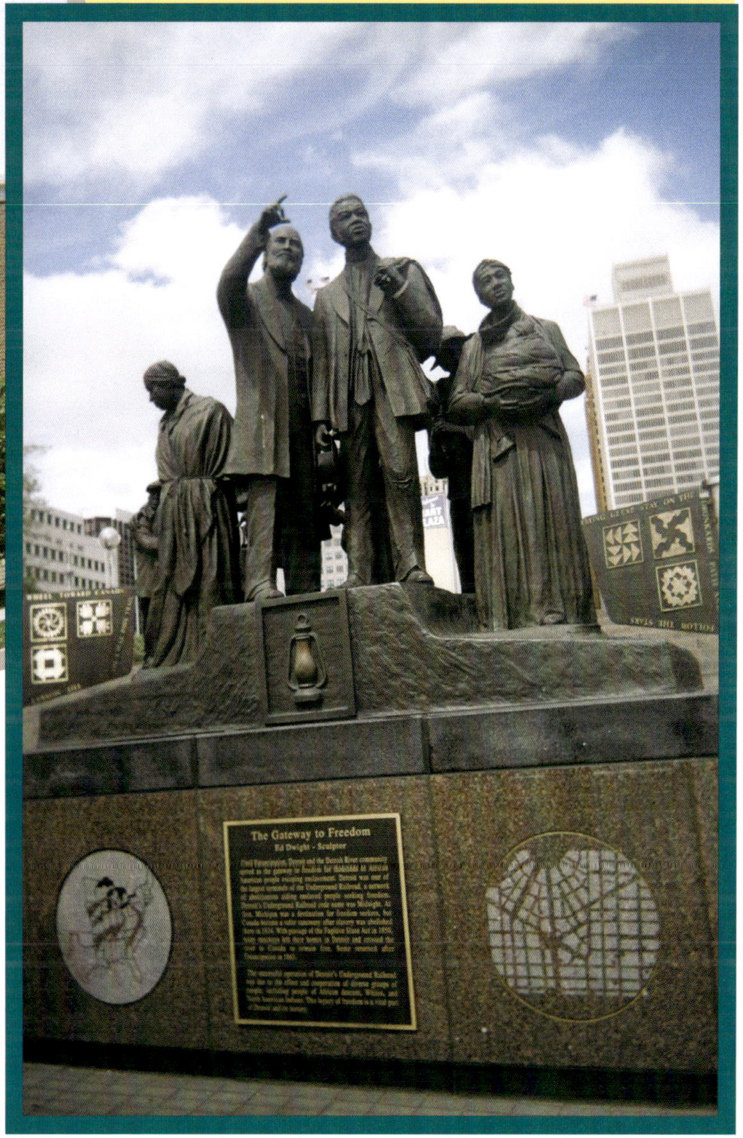

HERU ORGANIZATION

Leader: Bryce Anderson-Small

Participants: 5

www.theheru.org

Opposite: *Home in Brush Park near Comerica Park.*
—HERU Organization

THE HERU ORGANIZATION'S mission is to serve youth using media literacy for youth leadership and entrepreneurship. We develop youth's skills in digital media arts to serve our greater Detroit community through thought-provoking and socially transforming multimedia messages.

For this project, the HERU Organization engaged five young people between the ages of five and nineteen from our media literacy program to photo-document "their Detroit." This project created an opportunity for thousands of people in the metro Detroit community to be exposed to our youth's media project, which is part of our mission: sending positive and productive youth messages throughout the city and world.

Reveal Your Detroit provided the youth in our organization an opportunity to photo-document their unique story, through their own dynamic lens.

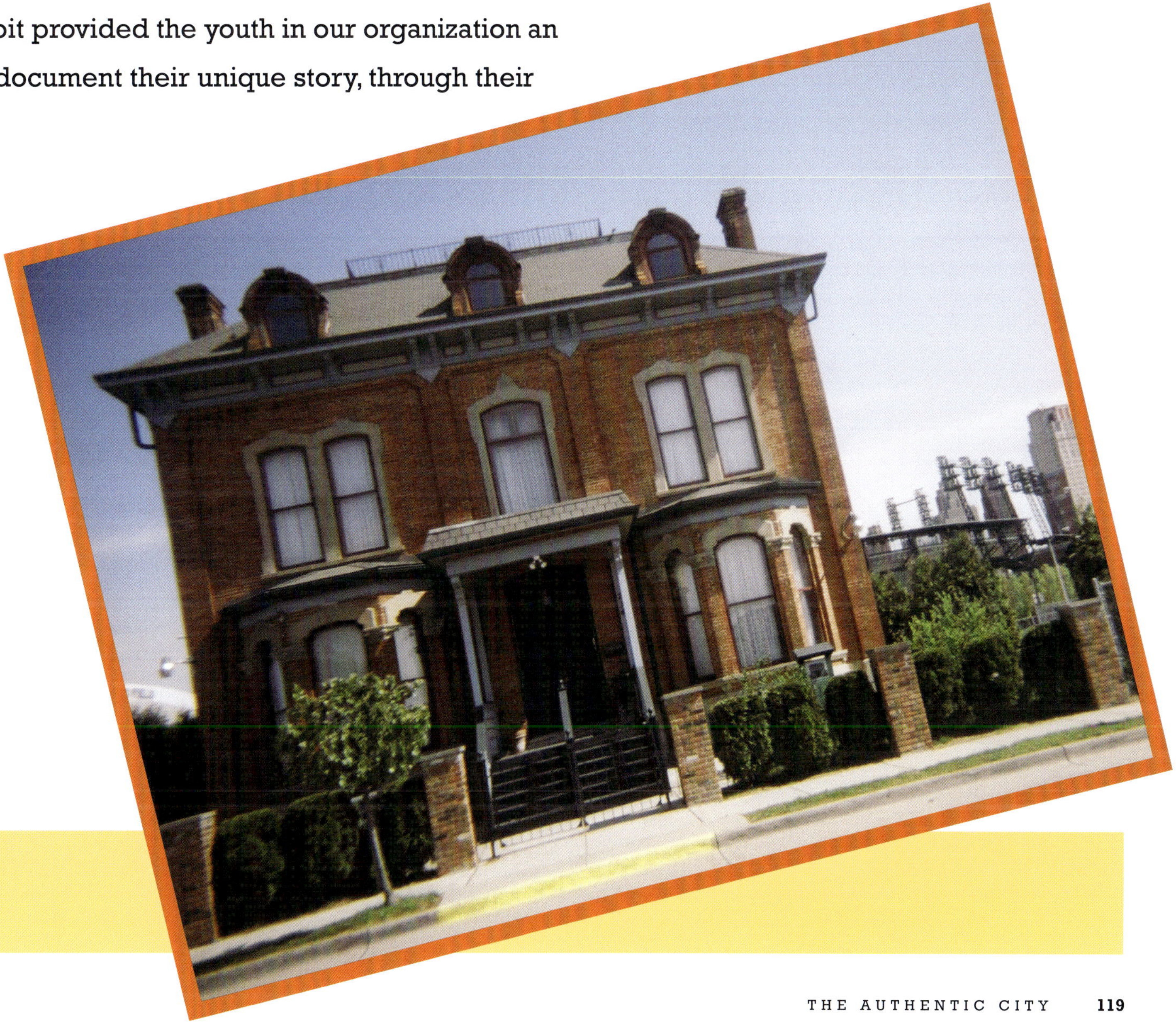

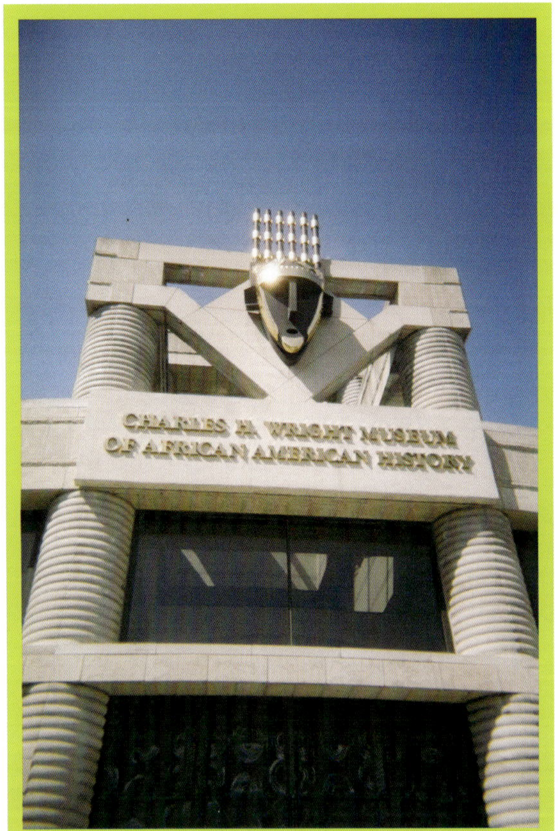

Charles H. Wright Museum of African American History.
—University Commons

UNIVERSITY COMMONS ORGANIZATION

Leader: Kim Tandy

Participants: 14

www.universitycommonsdetroit.org

THE MISSION OF UNIVERSITY COMMONS is to improve the physical and economic character of the Livernois and McNichols corridors and promote the quality of life within the area.

The DIA's Reveal Your Detroit let the community show Detroit as they see it. This in itself is unique. Reveal Your Detroit was a great opportunity for our community to show how we feel about Detroit, as well as see how others see their city.

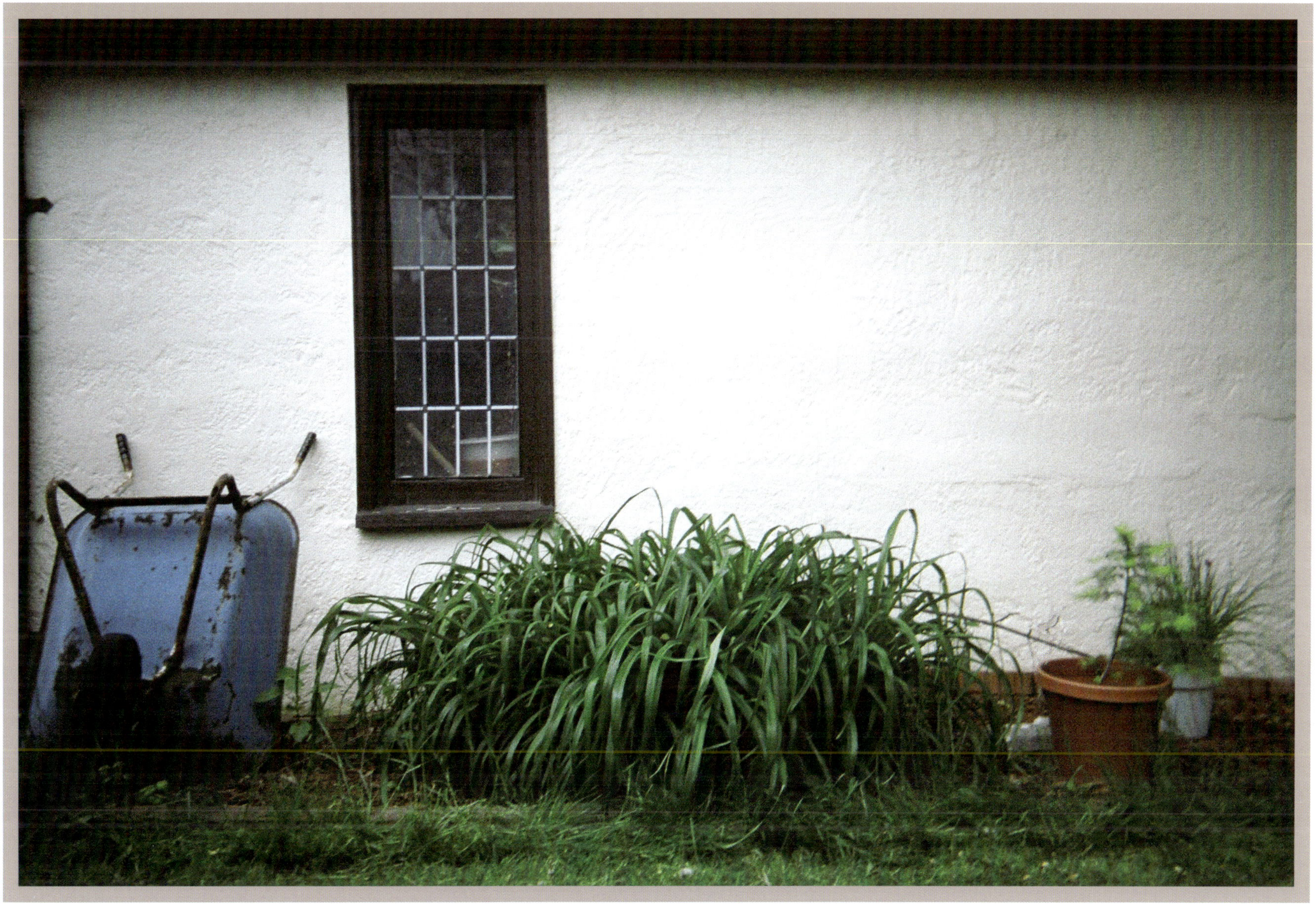

Backyard gardening. —University Commons

VANGUARD COMMUNITY DEVELOPMENT CORPORATION (CDC)

Leader: Dontai Mitchell

Participants: 11

www.vanguardcdc.org

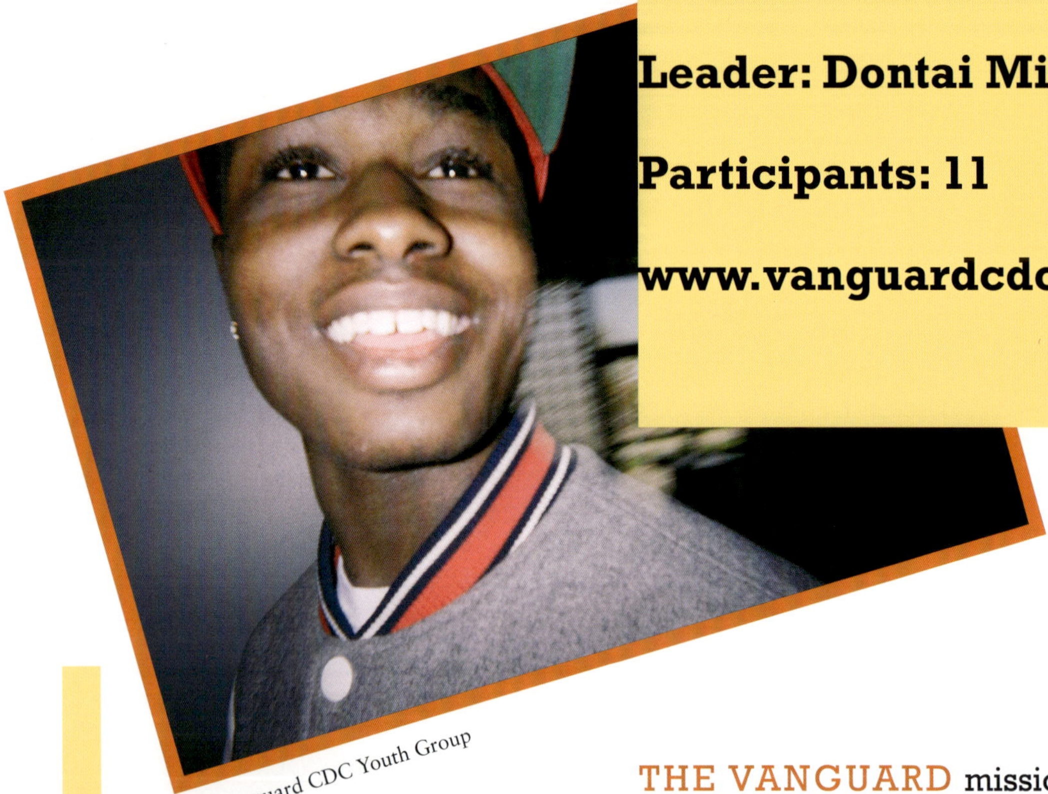

—Vanguard CDC Youth Group

THE VANGUARD mission is to facilitate the physical, social, and economic fabric of Detroit's Northend neighborhood.

Reveal Your Detroit

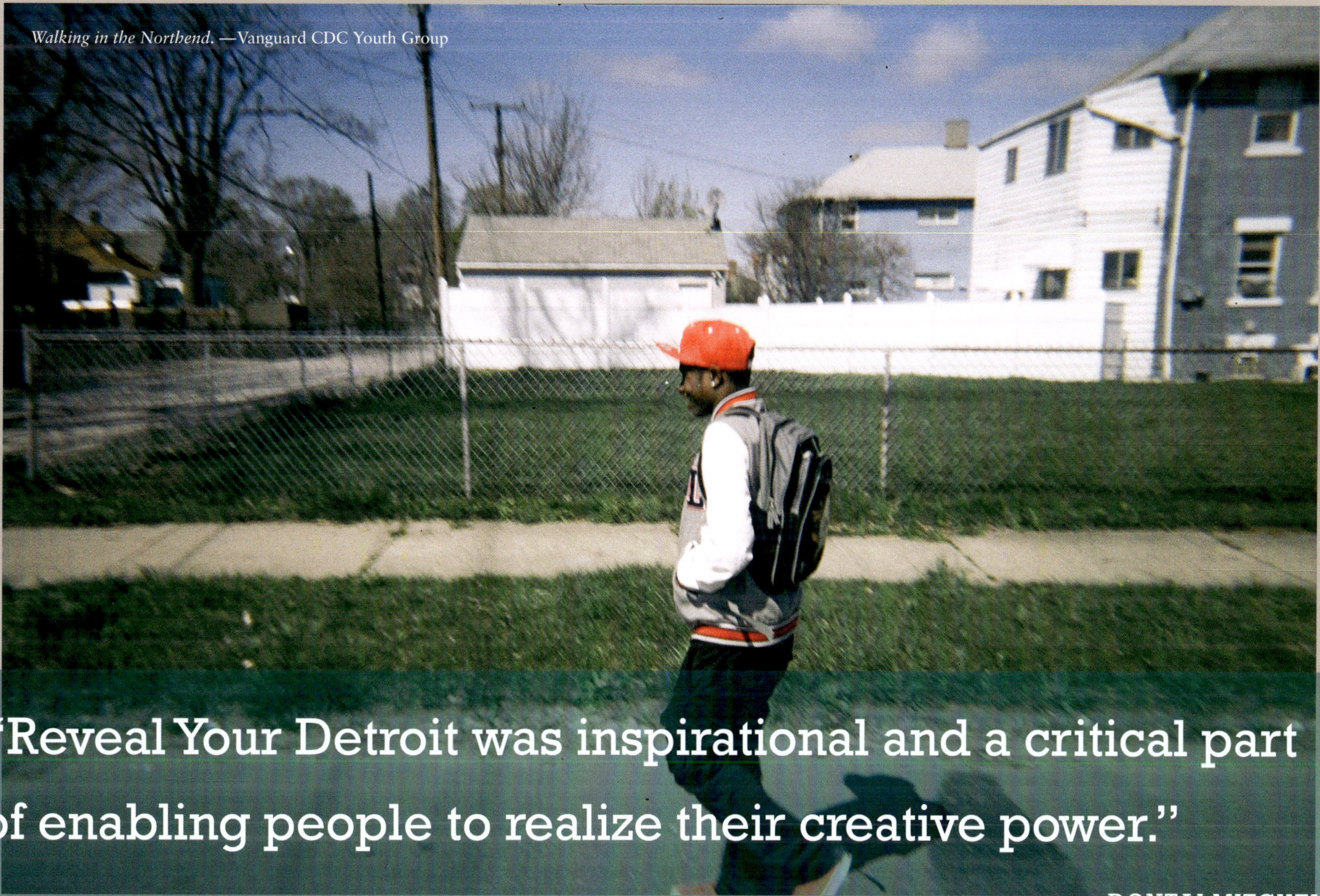

Walking in the Northend. —Vanguard CDC Youth Group

"Reveal Your Detroit was inspirational and a critical part of enabling people to realize their creative power."

—DONTAI MITCHELL

WARM TRAINING CENTER

Leader: Alicia Miller

Participants: 11

www.warmtraining.org

Opposite: *Food stand.*
—WARM Training Center

WARM TRAINING CENTER is a nonprofit organization that promotes the development of resource-efficient, affordable, healthy homes and communities through education, training, and technical assistance.

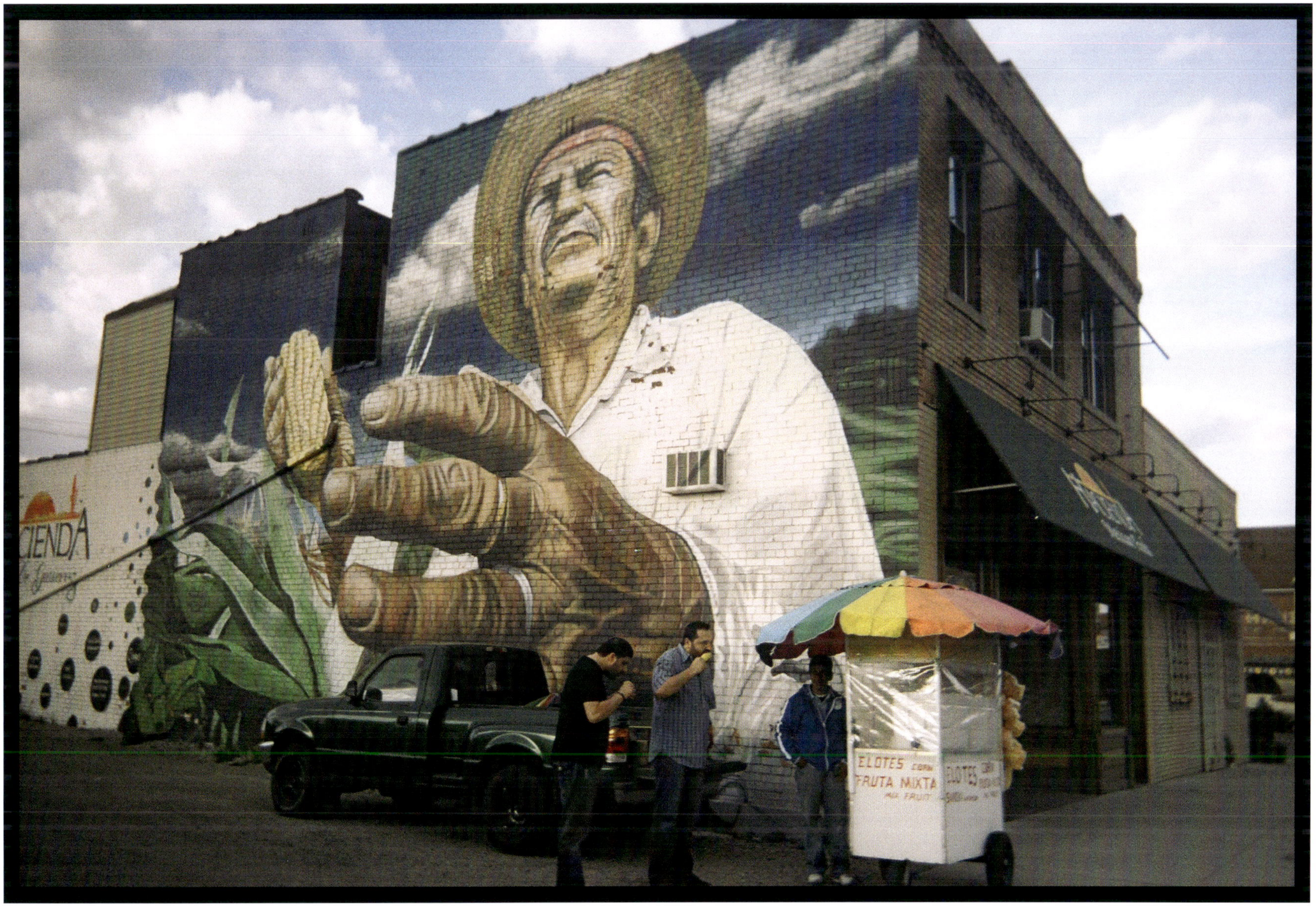
ELOTES
FRUTA MIXTA

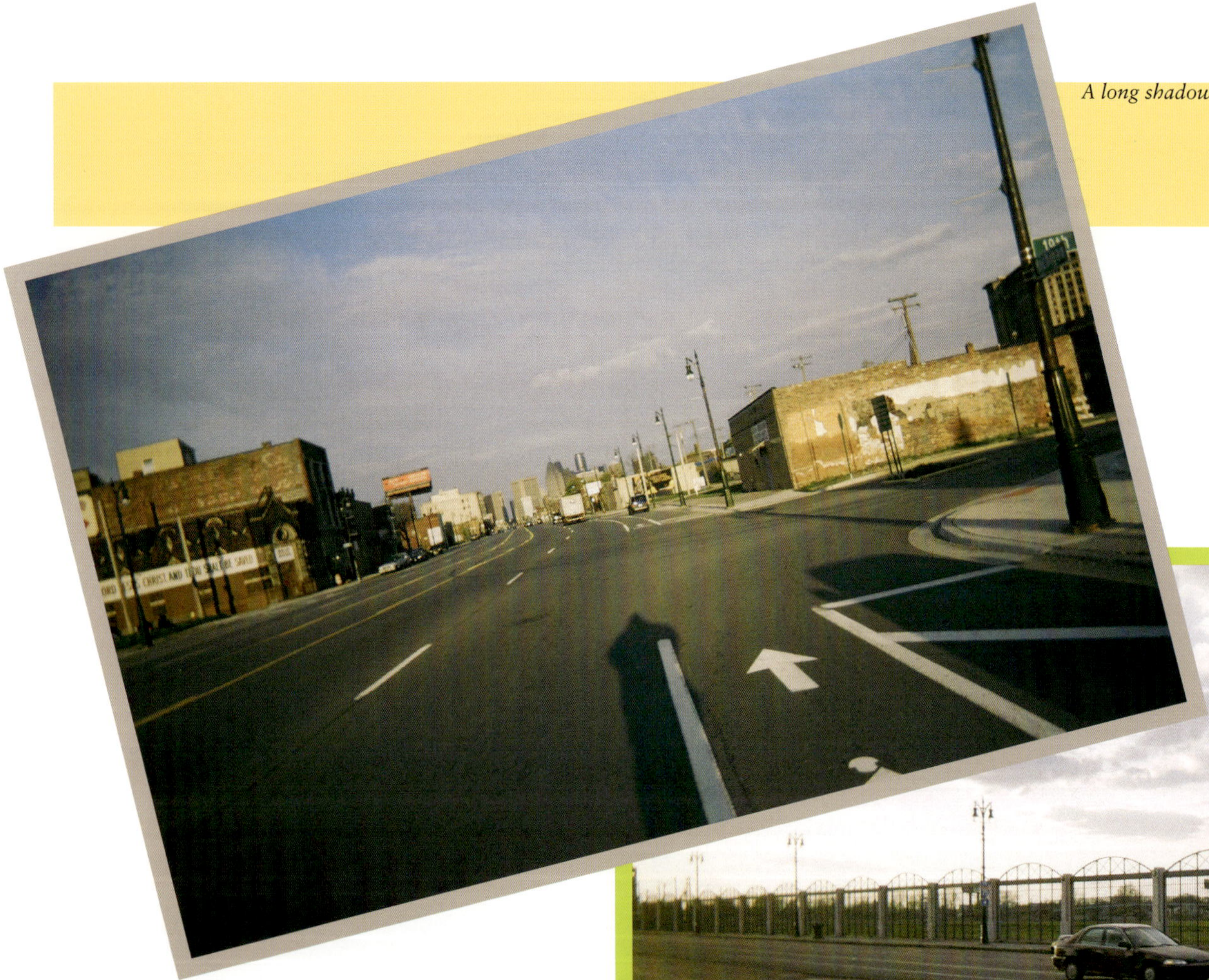

A long shadow downtown. —WARM Training Center

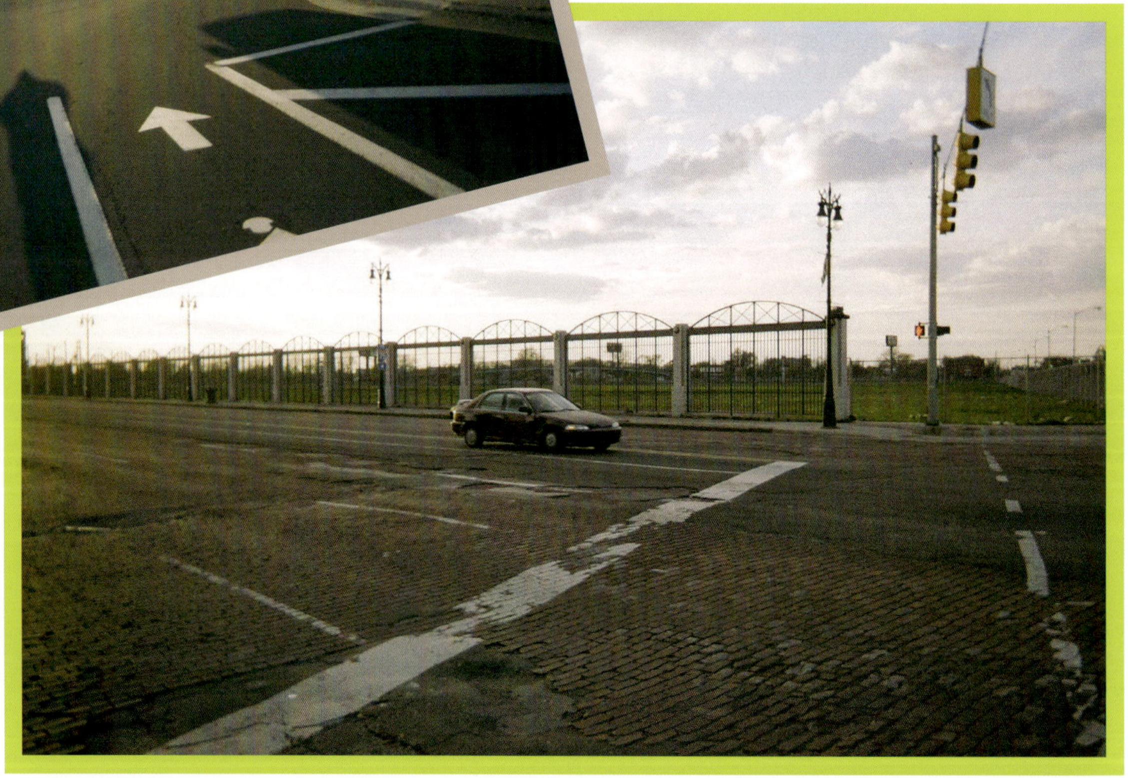

Old Tiger Stadium ball field in Corktown.
—WARM Training Center

WESTMINSTER KENILWORTH ASSOCIATION

Group Leader: Dana Hart

Participants: 10

Avalon Bakery, a Midtown staple.
—Westminster Kenilworth Association

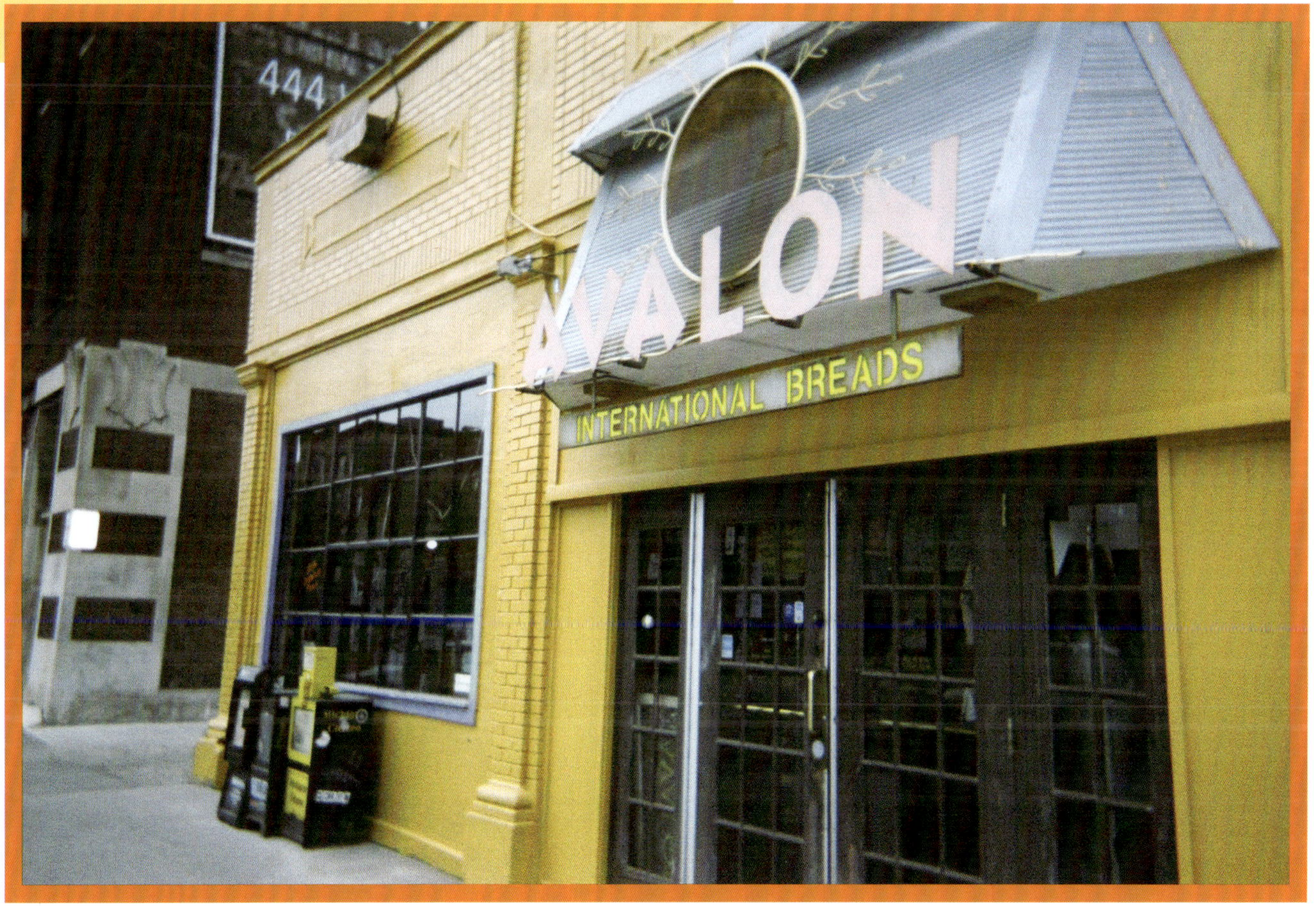

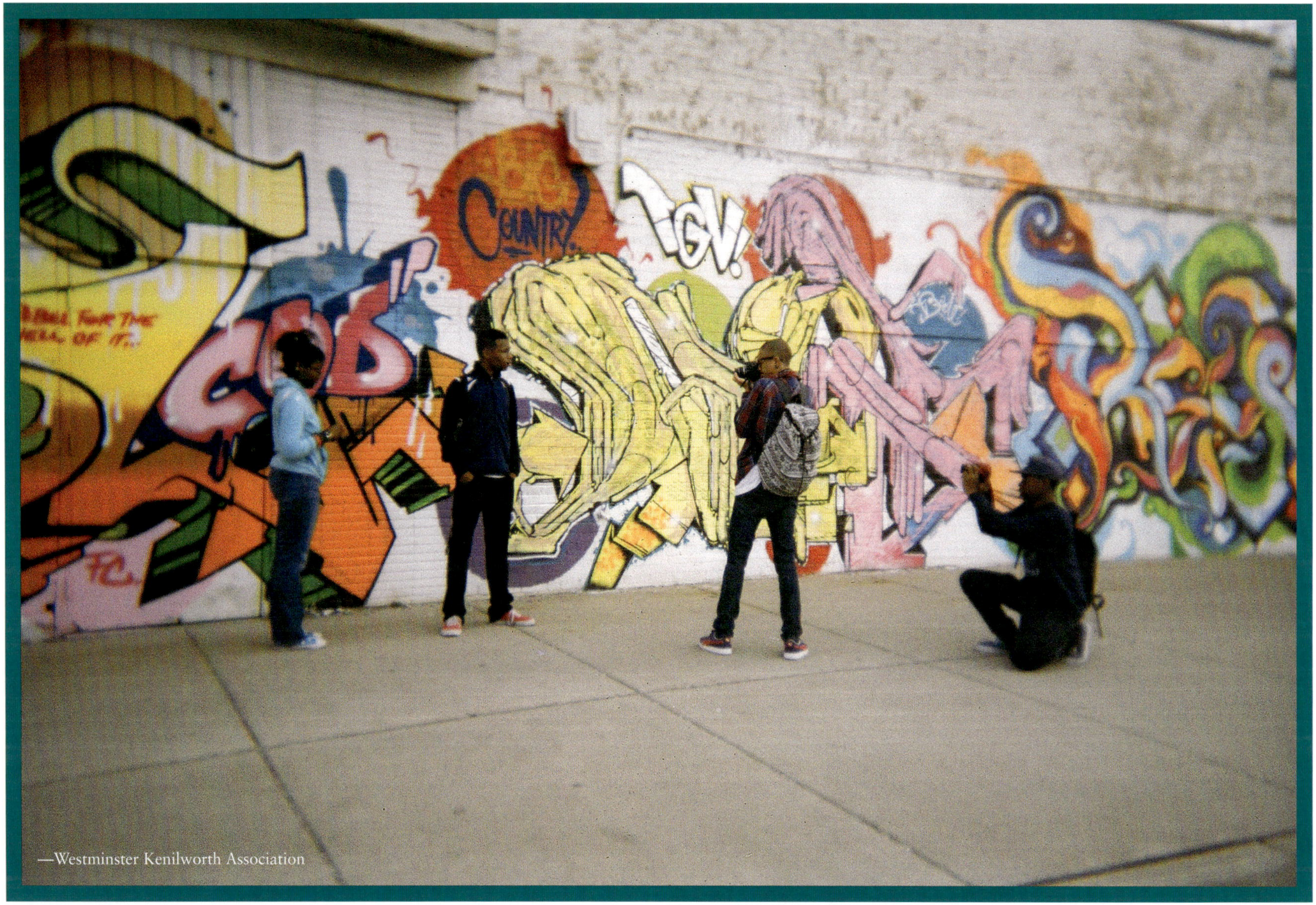

—Westminster Kenilworth Association

WOODWARD CORRIDOR INITIATIVE

Leader: Nicole Brown

Participants: 8

www.woodwardcorridorinitiative.org

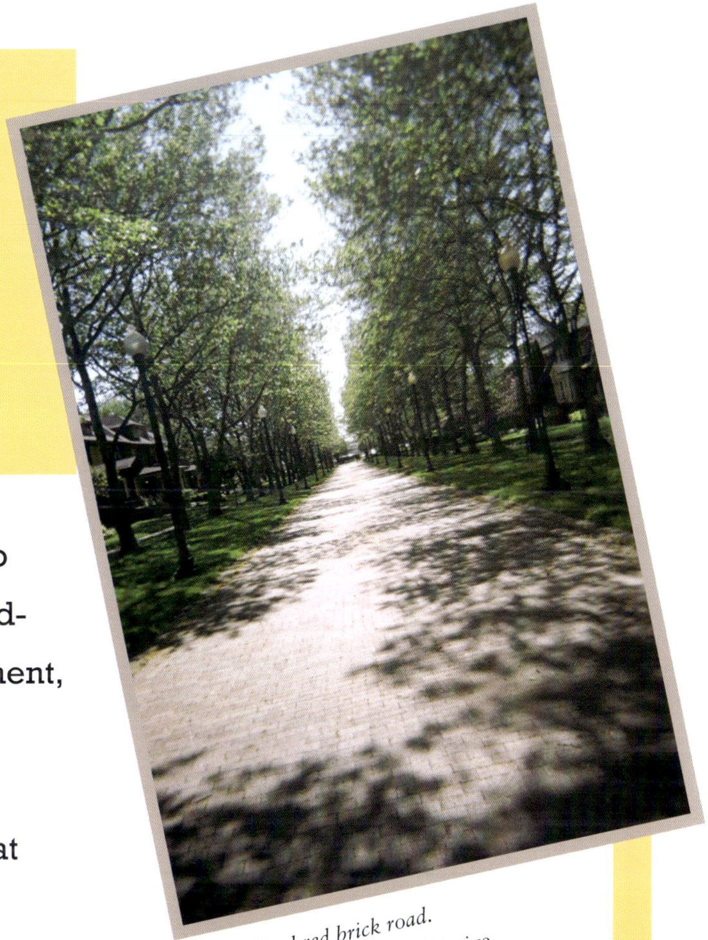

A tree-lined red brick road.
—Woodward Corridor Initiative

THE WOODWARD CORRIDOR INITIATIVE is committed to harnessing the power of public-private partnerships to revitalize Midtown, New Center, and Northend neighborhoods to increase investment, attract new residents, and provide access to quality education and work opportunities.

Proud. Inspired. Hopeful. These are just a few of the emotions that were shared by community members who participated in the DIA's Reveal Your Detroit. The project gave our participants the gift of being able to share their story of what makes them proud of the rich history of their neighborhood and the possibilities of its future and to share their stories through the visual arts.

This project crossed neighborhoods and bridged the gap between Detroiters and suburbanites.

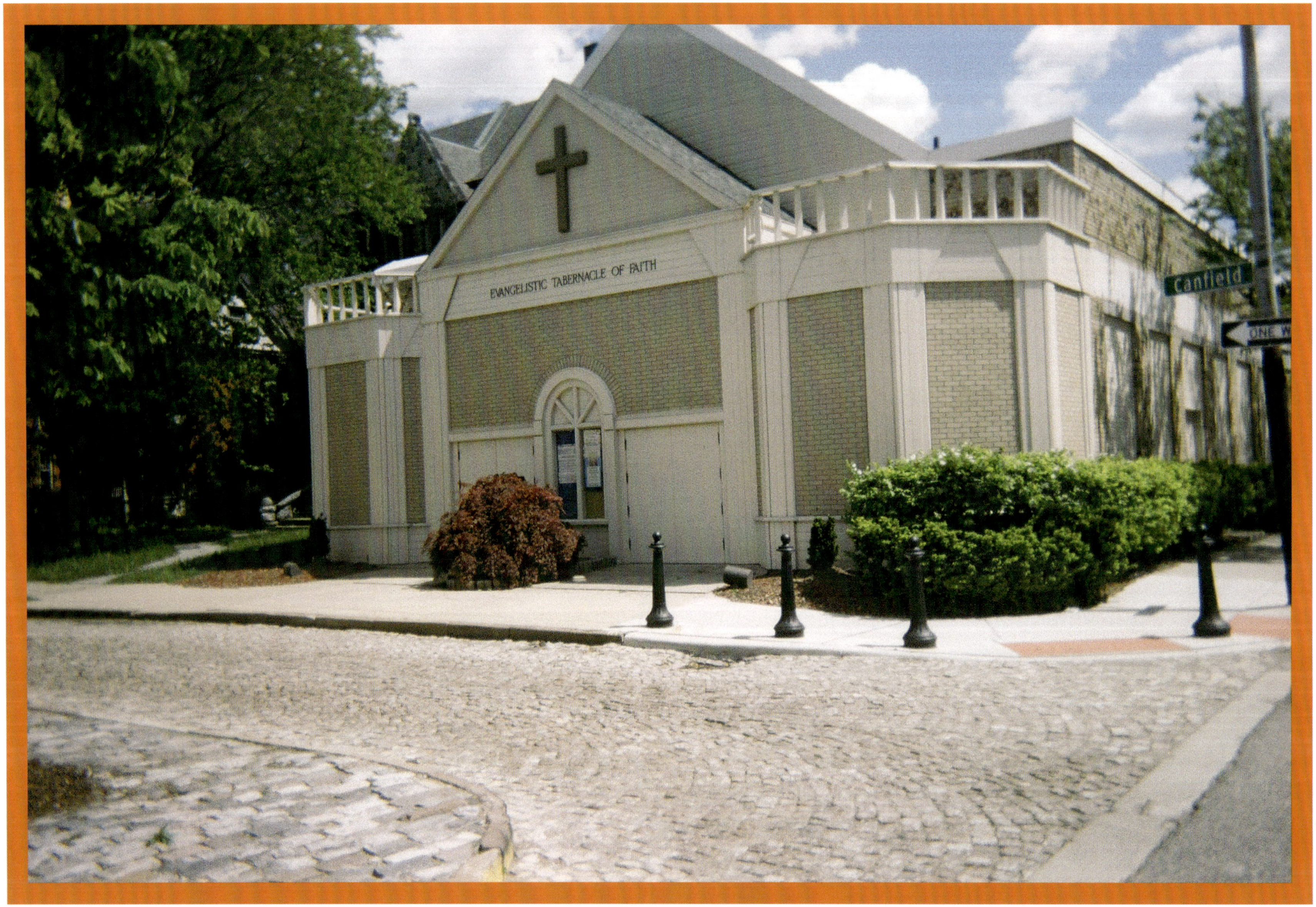

Many Detroiters pray for cobblestone dreams along West Canfield in Midtown. —Woodward Corridor Initiative

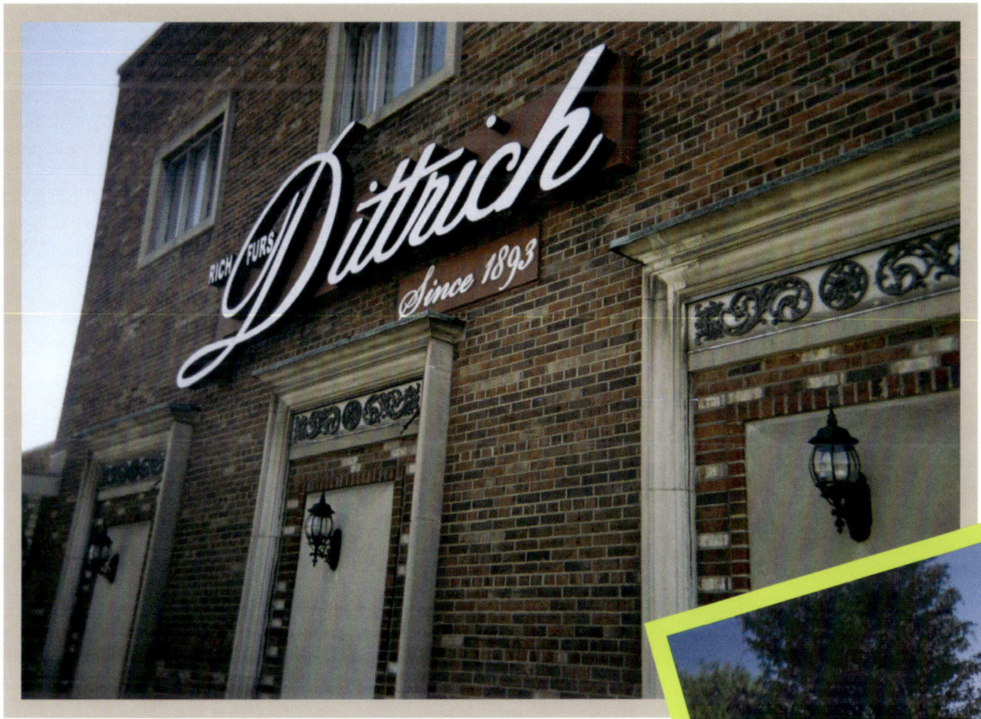

Famed Dittrich Furs. —Woodward Corridor Initiative

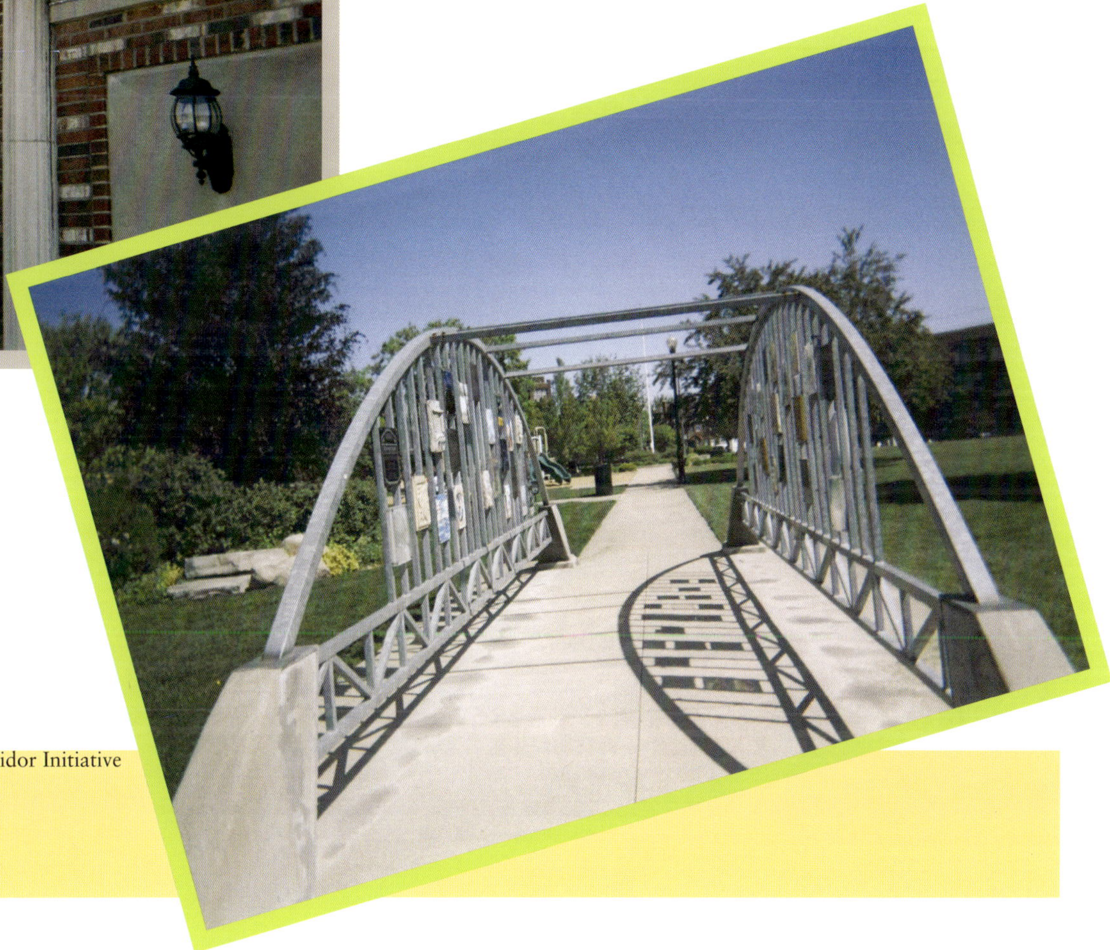

A walking bridge on Belle Isle. —Woodward Corridor Initiative

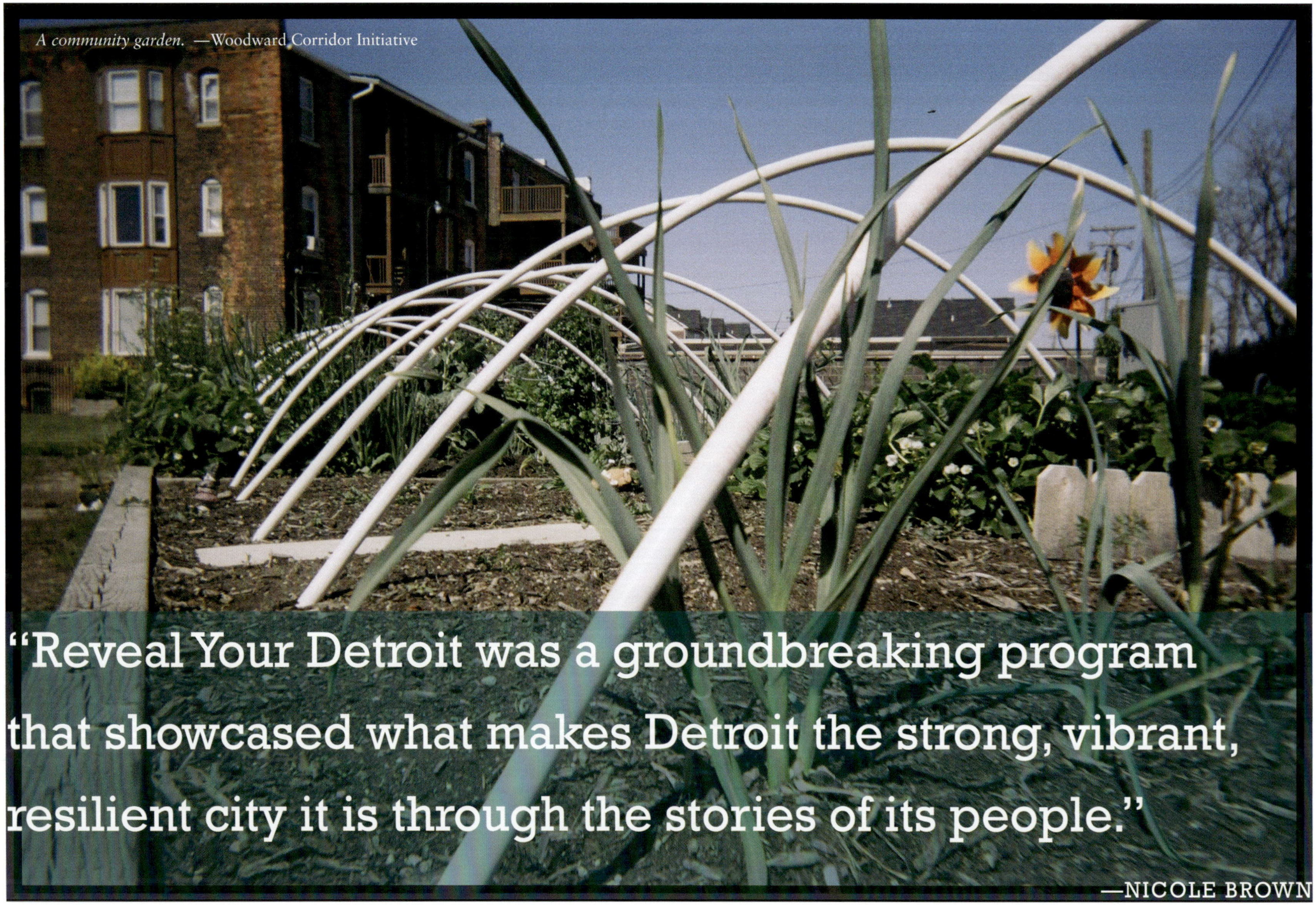

A community garden. —Woodward Corridor Initiative

"Reveal Your Detroit was a groundbreaking program that showcased what makes Detroit the strong, vibrant, resilient city it is through the stories of its people."

—NICOLE BROWN

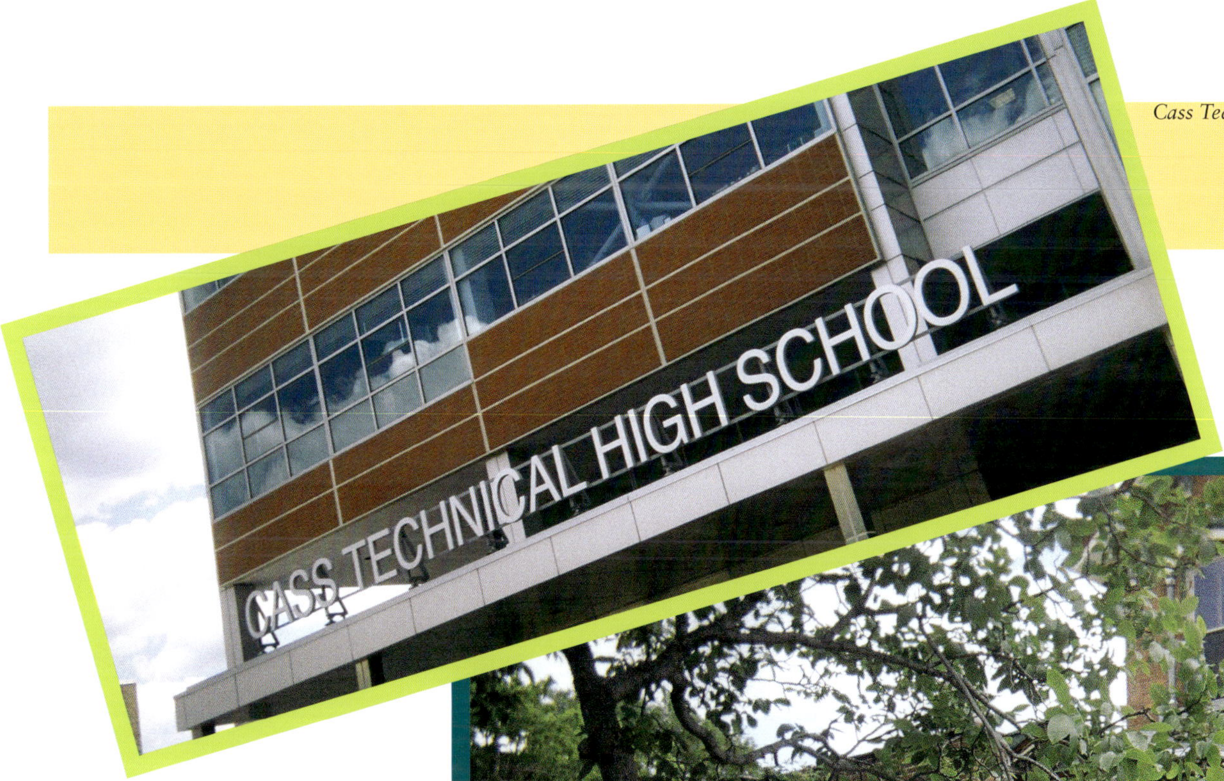

Cass Tech. —Woodward Corridor Initiative

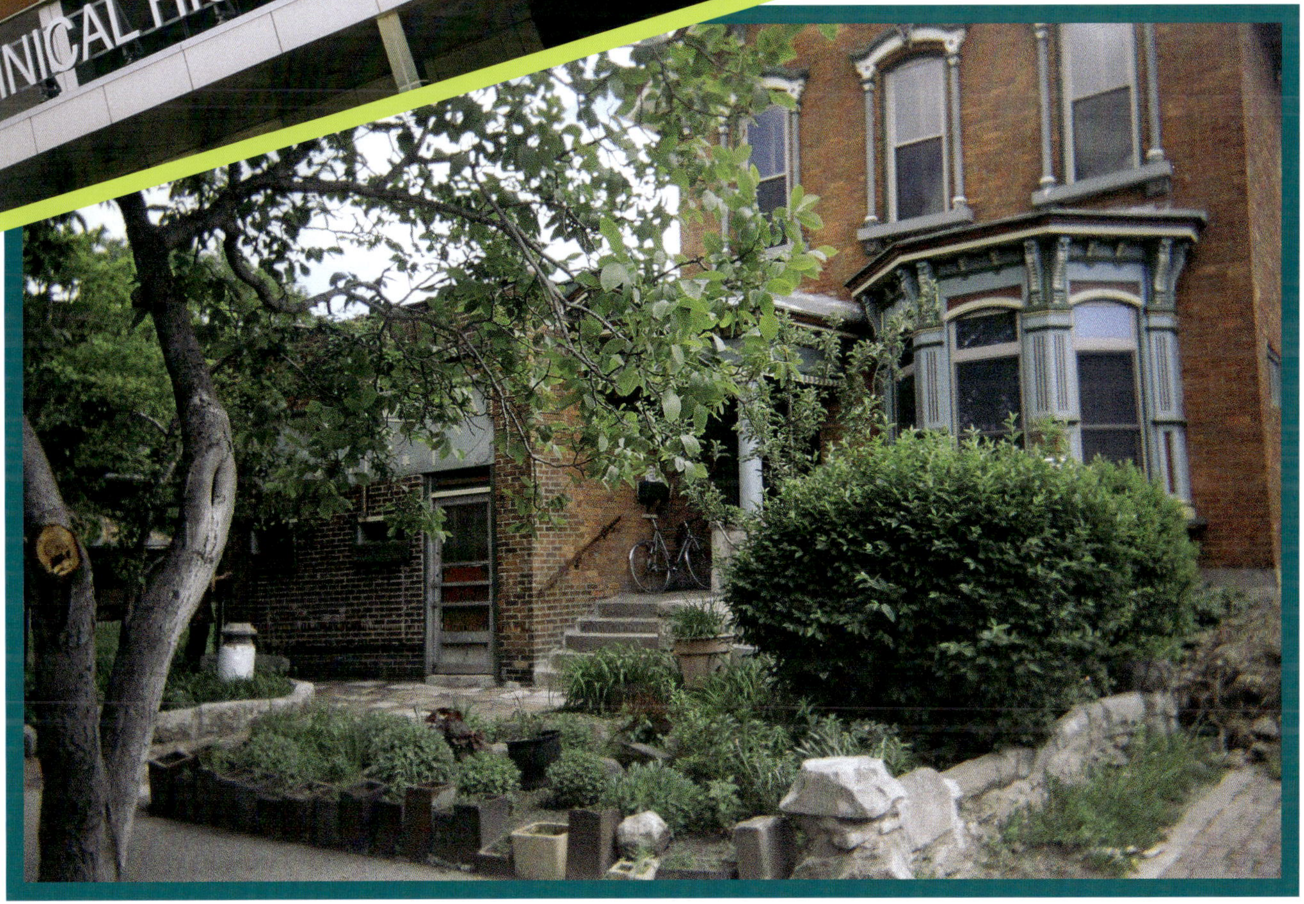

A Detroit home.
—Woodward Corridor Initiative

"A Future for Detroit."

—BE EXPOSED: DETROIT

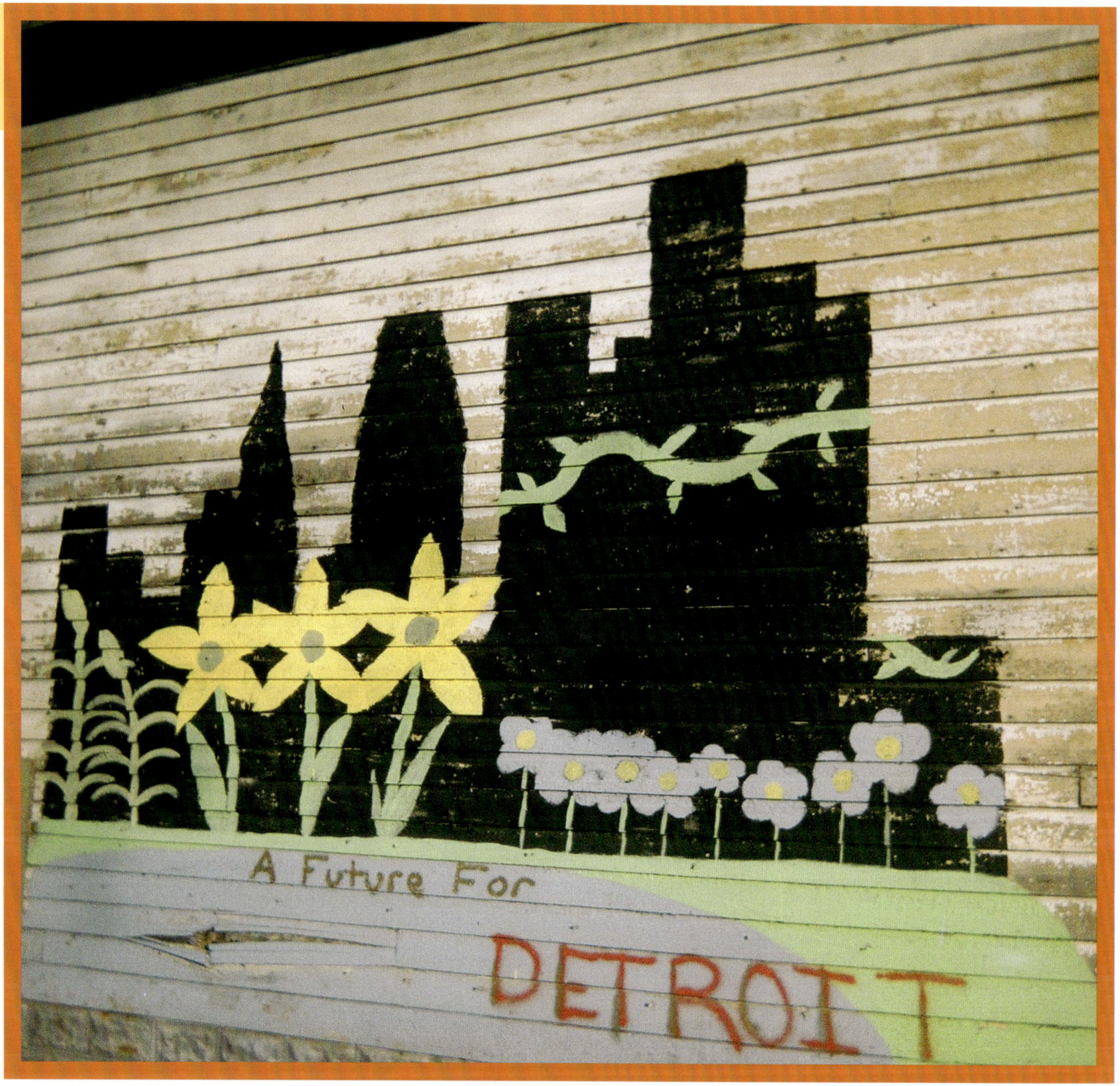

Detroit's Vital Transformation

TRANSFORMATION is hard work.

At its core, transformation is a process of seeking radical change while retaining the central DNA of the object being transformed. This is true whether witnessing the transformation of a butterfly, a mission-driven organization, or even a city.

This is the crux of Detroit's dilemma: we love the best of what Detroit is, and although we know it's a city that must transform, we fear losing its essence in the process.

Call it the big-town amenities and small-town feel. Or perhaps it's the midwestern ethos combined with urban grit, but Detroit leaves an indelible mark that its people hold dear in their hearts. The Detroit badge reflects something fundamental about who we are, what we value, and what we dare to do with our lives. Losing that ineffable quality the city holds would make transforming it worth little in the end.

We know Detroit must change. We aspire to it. We design programs, projects, civic groups, and massive citywide planning efforts around transforming Detroit. Although we're all a little wounded from the gluttony of pretty plans and past promises, we believe Detroit's transformation is not only possible but essential. Although plans for blight removal, new jobs, reduced crime, improved education, and so forth have yielded underwhelming results, Detroit's promise holds our attention rapt.

However unlikely it may seem, for most of the Reveal Your Detroit participants, Detroit is also a city with momentum rising. We recognize the severe challenges that must be met. We're aware of the unevenness of development, and we genuinely strive to ensure that all of Detroit's residents will be included in the transformation process and emerge better for it. Those aims bind us as we harness our collective energy to fill in the gaps wherever they are needed across this city. It is in this way that you begin to see art as community building in the form of public gardens, outdoor murals, and even graffiti installations. It also helps explain how professional cohorts like the Detroit Revitalization Fellows, advocacy groups like Declare Detroit, and efforts like the Detroit Works Project Long Term Planning are, like most of the Reveal Your Detroit partners, mobilizing to solve the complex array of Detroit's challenges.

This section takes a closer look at some of those groups and presents images from the Reveal Your Detroit project that evoke Detroit's transformation imperative.

Detroit breeds strong sentiments. For those who love it here, it's a city we love to love as much as it's a city we sometimes struggle to love. We hope to preserve the best of what makes up Detroit. And yet

Collectively, we know that Detroit must embrace widespread change across the city. It must be a safe, clean, and welcoming city.

we fear losing Detroit's soul in the revitalization process. Preserving Detroit's greatest strength—the passion of its people—will be the key to that transformational paradox of changing and yet staying the same.

In this section, you will read passages from a few partner leaders who were asked to delve deeper into this issue. Dan Pitera of Detroit Works Project Long Term Planning, Rob St. Mary of WDET, and Doxie Kaltz of Burners Without Borders, among the other partner voices shared in these pages, describe how Reveal Your Detroit helped accelerate their own transformative work in Detroit. These short essays and the group profiles that follow give credence to the ways in which Reveal Your Detroit empowered many across Detroit's community development landscape to further their revitalization objectives.

Collectively, we know that Detroit must embrace widespread change across the city. It must be a safe, clean, and welcoming city. Opportunity must be fostered. Detroit needs to invest in strong schools and vibrant neighborhoods. We also believe that Detroit's rich heritage will always remain worthy of celebration. But as we honor the footprints of our elders and those who came before us, let's continue to push for a boundless future together.

Our tenacity will be tested, but as these groups and the images that follow depict, there is little doubt: this is Detroit's Vital Transformation.

DETROIT WORKS PROJECT LONG TERM PLANNING

Leaders: Kaleen Clark and Dan Pitera

Participants: 20

www.detroitworksproject.com

DETROIT WORKS PROJECT LONG TERM PLANNING was a groundbreaking journey to create a guide for decision making—a strategic framework plan—with innovative strategies to improve the quality of life and business in Detroit.

We Need Respect.

—Detroit Works Project Long Term Planning

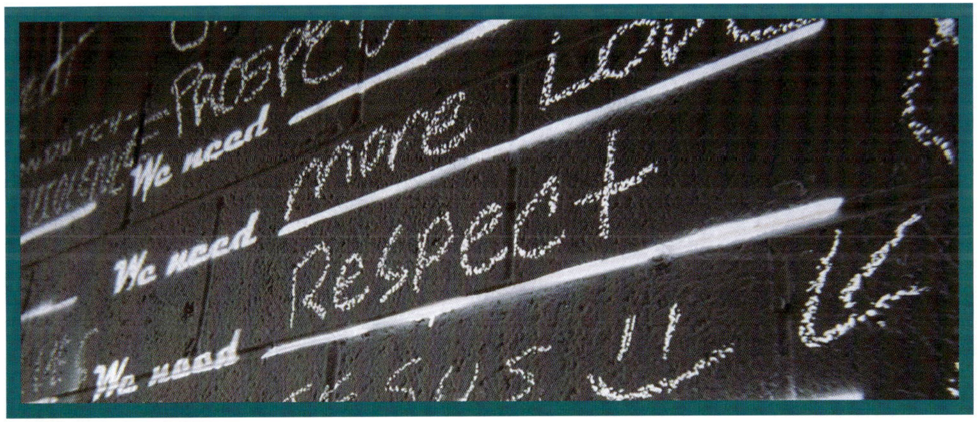

DAN PITERA

Co-Chair

Civic Engagement Team for Detroit Works Project Long Term Planning

REVEAL YOUR DETROIT reminds me of two things my mother would tell me when I was young. First was the South African slogan "Nothing about us, without us, is for us." Second were the general words of wisdom: "If you want to go fast, go alone. If you want to go far, go together." From our perspective at the Detroit Works Project Long Term Planning with our many partners, Reveal Your Detroit embodied these ethos.

When I see an old friend, one of the first things I do is show him or her a photo of my daughter and my spouse. This is natural. We all want to share the things that are special to us. Detroit is special to us. Yes, there are issues, large and small. But Detroiters will be the first to say: this is still a special place. Reveal Your Detroit asked us to share this personal view with each other. At the exhibit, I saw people waiting for the images they photographed to share with the people around them. The enthusiasm of everyone was electric. Laughter, sadness, and, most of all, memories connected everyone. All of these shared photos of people, places, and actions made for a shared vision of Detroit. I know that this is not a complete vision. But that is the beauty of it—this vision is a snapshot in time waiting for more photos and looking forward to the future.

The things we love about a place are often hidden, forgotten, or perhaps taken for granted. It takes someone to reveal them to us or remind us of their power. Discovering things together binds us together.

We live, work, play, and worship in a large city and region filled with assets. Reveal Your Detroit, through this visual collection, elevates many of these assets and reminds us of the rich and wonderful place we have around us. It is upon this foundation our city's future rests.

As we move into the future, we move together as a community. This community is rich with variety, much like a mosaic piece of art is made from many unique individual pieces working together to form a larger colorful picture. When we work together, play together, live together, and worship together, we build lasting relationships together. We at the Detroit Works Project Long Term Planning were inspired by Reveal Your Detroit's ability to bring people together to share their vision with one another.

This is key to our mission as well. Together we make our future. We may not get there fast, but we will go far. "Nothing about us, without us, is for us."

One last thought, which also comes from my mother: "A picture may be worth a thousand words, but as we share them with each other, words are never enough."

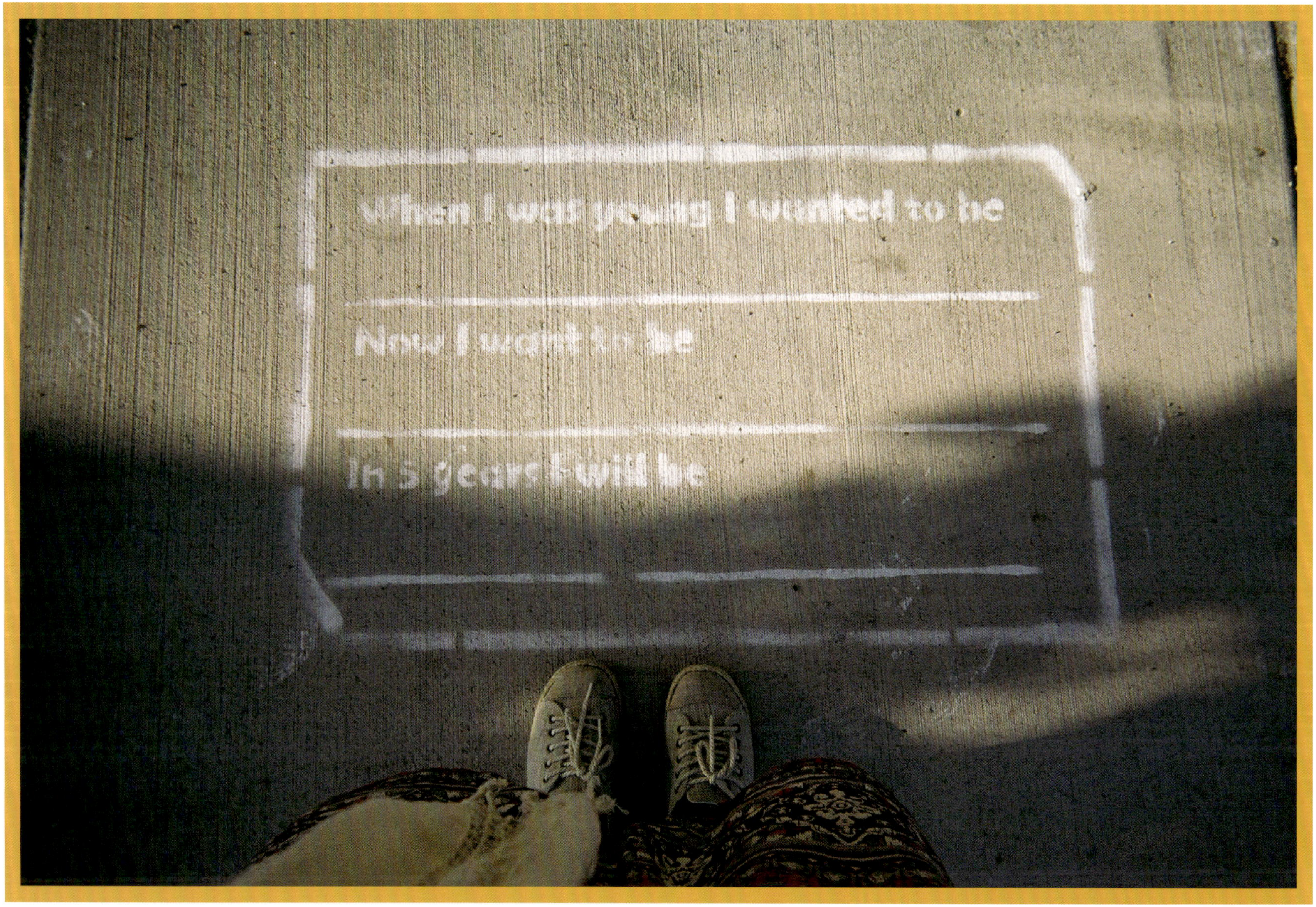

Life planning via sidewalk chalk. —Detroit Works Project Long Term Planning

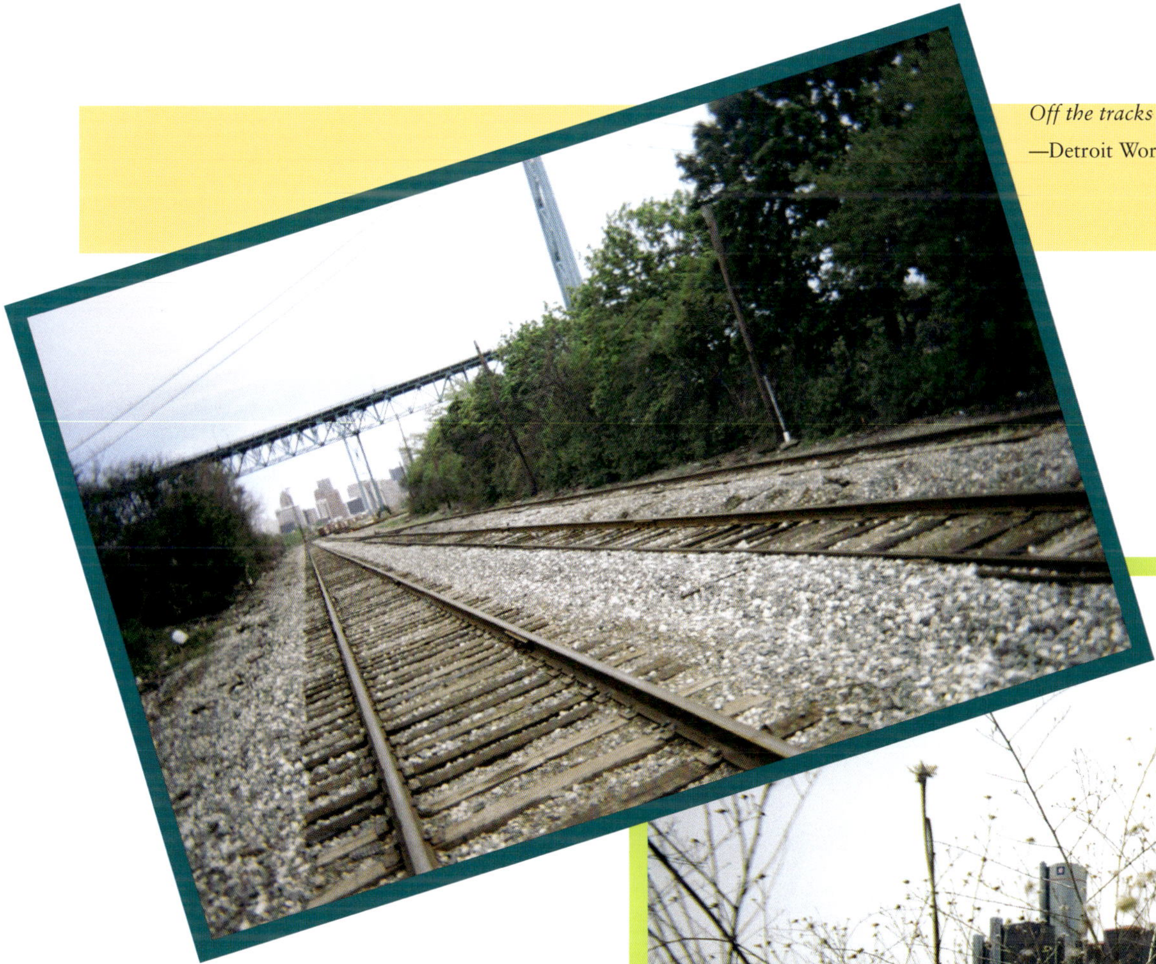

Off the tracks looking at the Ambassador Bridge in southwest Detroit.
—Detroit Works Project Long Term Planning

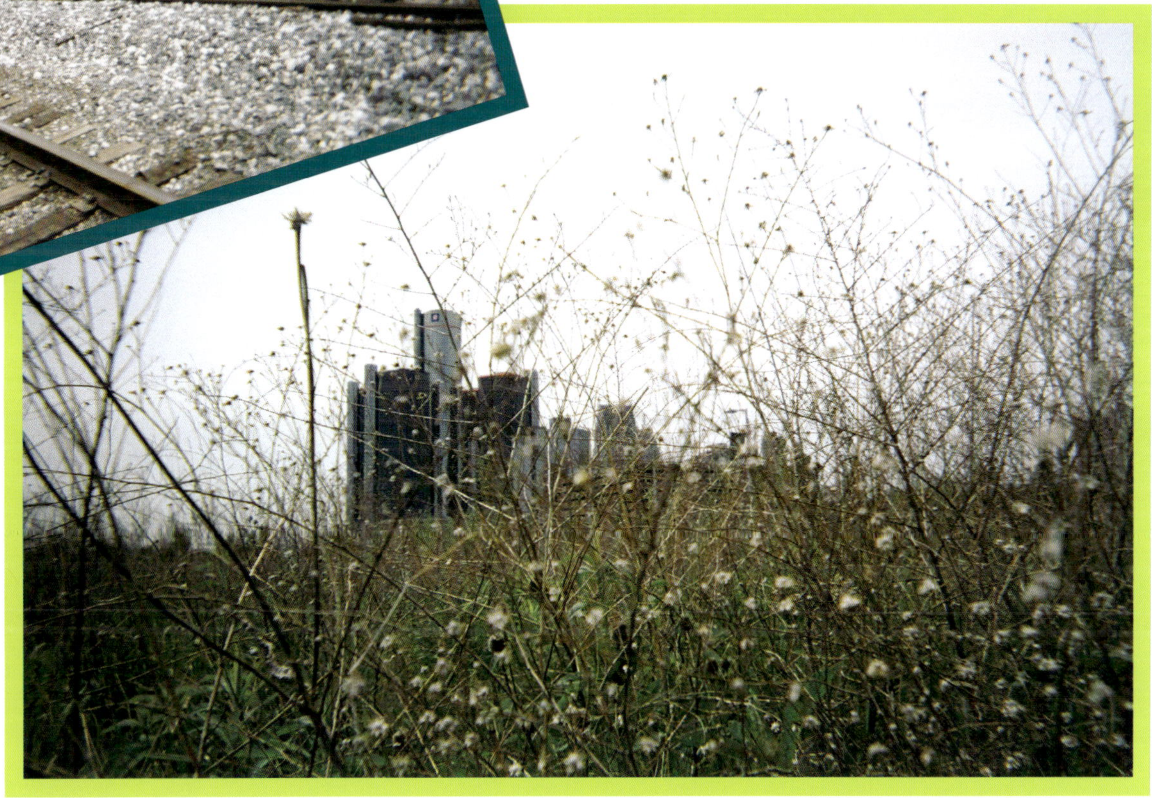

Renaissance Center from "The Mound."
—Detroit Works Project Long Term Planning

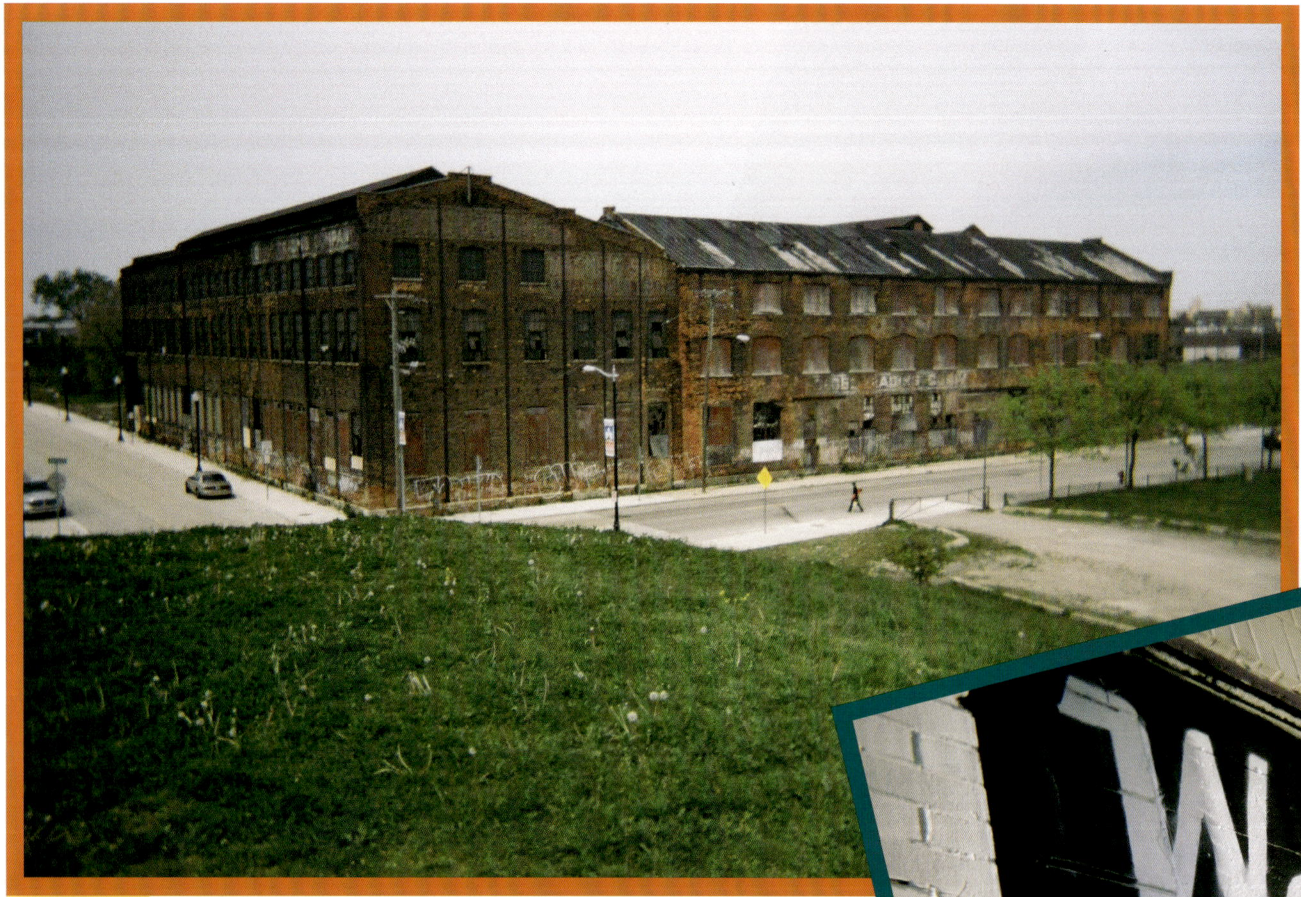

Globe Trading Building. —Detroit Works Project Long Term Planning

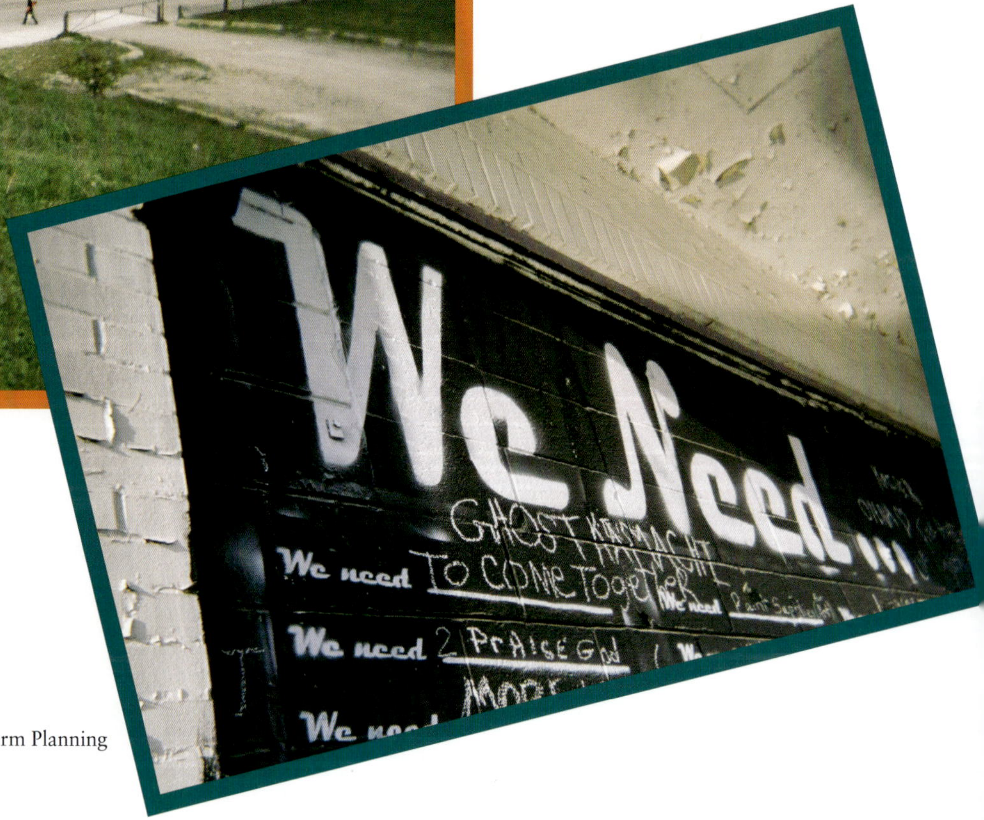

We Need. —Detroit Works Project Long Term Planning

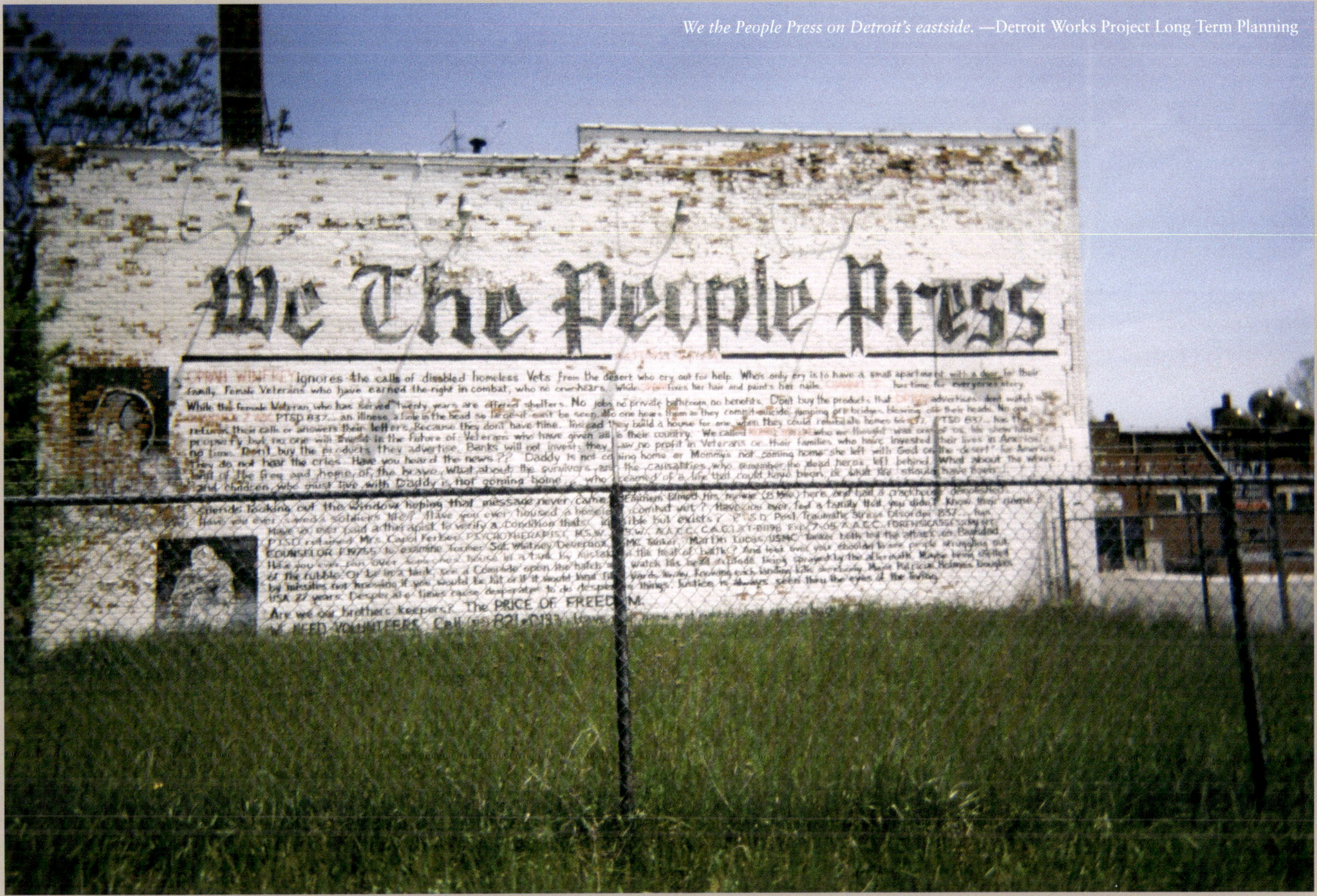

We the People Press on Detroit's eastside. —Detroit Works Project Long Term Planning

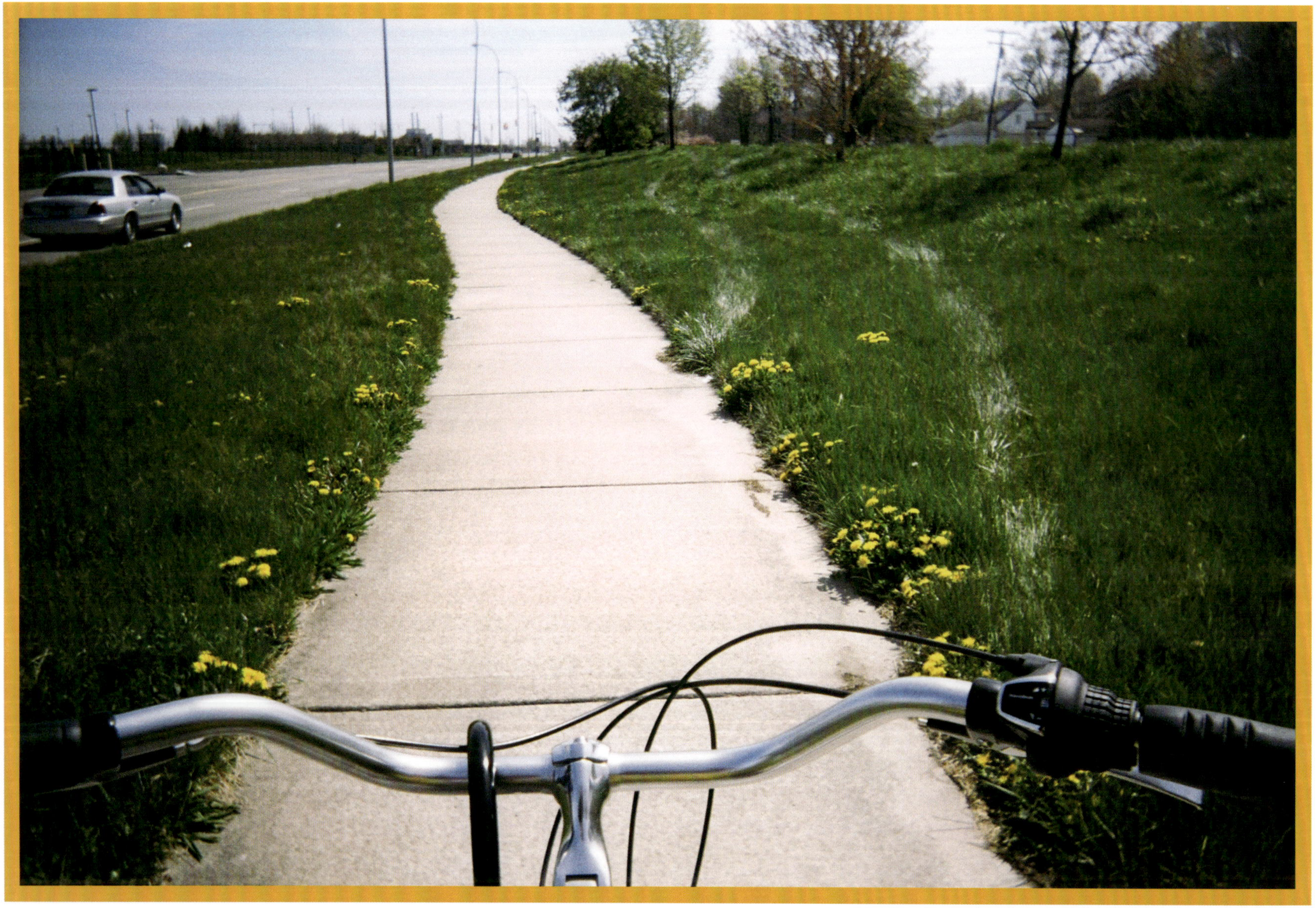

—Detroit Workers for Environmental Justice

Reveal Your Detroit

I was riding my bike from Midtown to the eastern district. I was on St. Jean. To the left was the Chrysler plant, but on St. Jean there was this big green space. I want to show how pretty it can be and how friendly green space can be. And, since I was biking, it was a really hard picture to take because you have to really scoot back to get the handlebars in—it was just a really nice scene.

SANDRA YU

DETROIT YOUNG PROFESSIONALS

Leader: Eddie Lee

Participants: 10

www.detroityoungprofessionals.org

Opposite: *Motor City Brew Works.*
—Detroit Young Professionals

DETROIT YOUNG PROFESSIONALS (DYP) is a nonprofit organization that provides professional development, social networking, and civic engagement opportunities. We are dedicated to making metro Detroit a better place and developing our region's next generation of leaders.

Launched in January 2008, DYP began as a grassroots collective of diverse, forward-thinking individuals with a passion for cultivating creativity, entrepreneurship, and a spirit of community in metropolitan Detroit. Since then, we've evolved into one of the largest networks of young leaders, innovators, and change makers in Southeast Michigan.

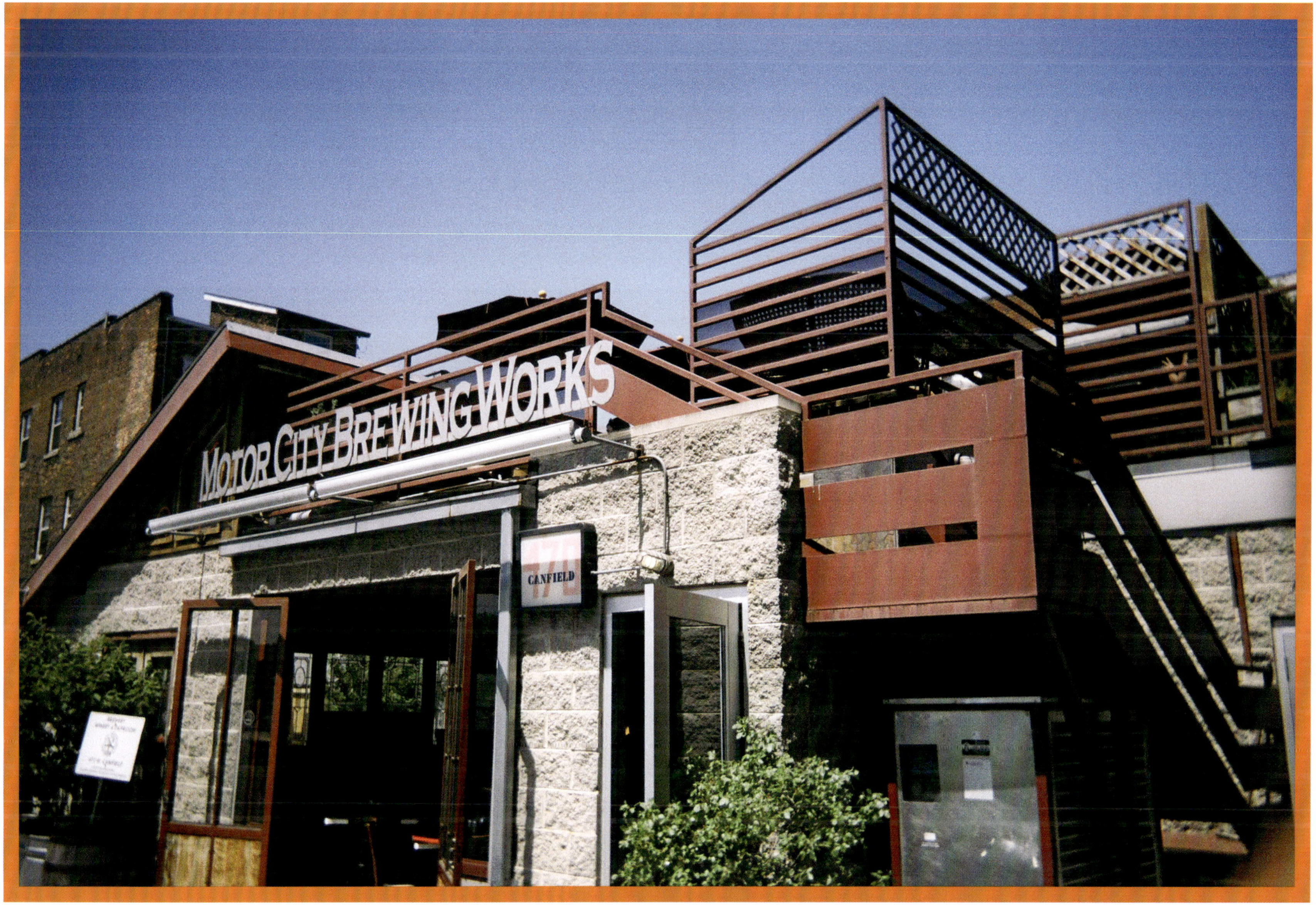
MOTOR CITY BREWING WORKS
CANFIELD

A look down the Green Garage's Green Alley. —Detroit Young Professionals

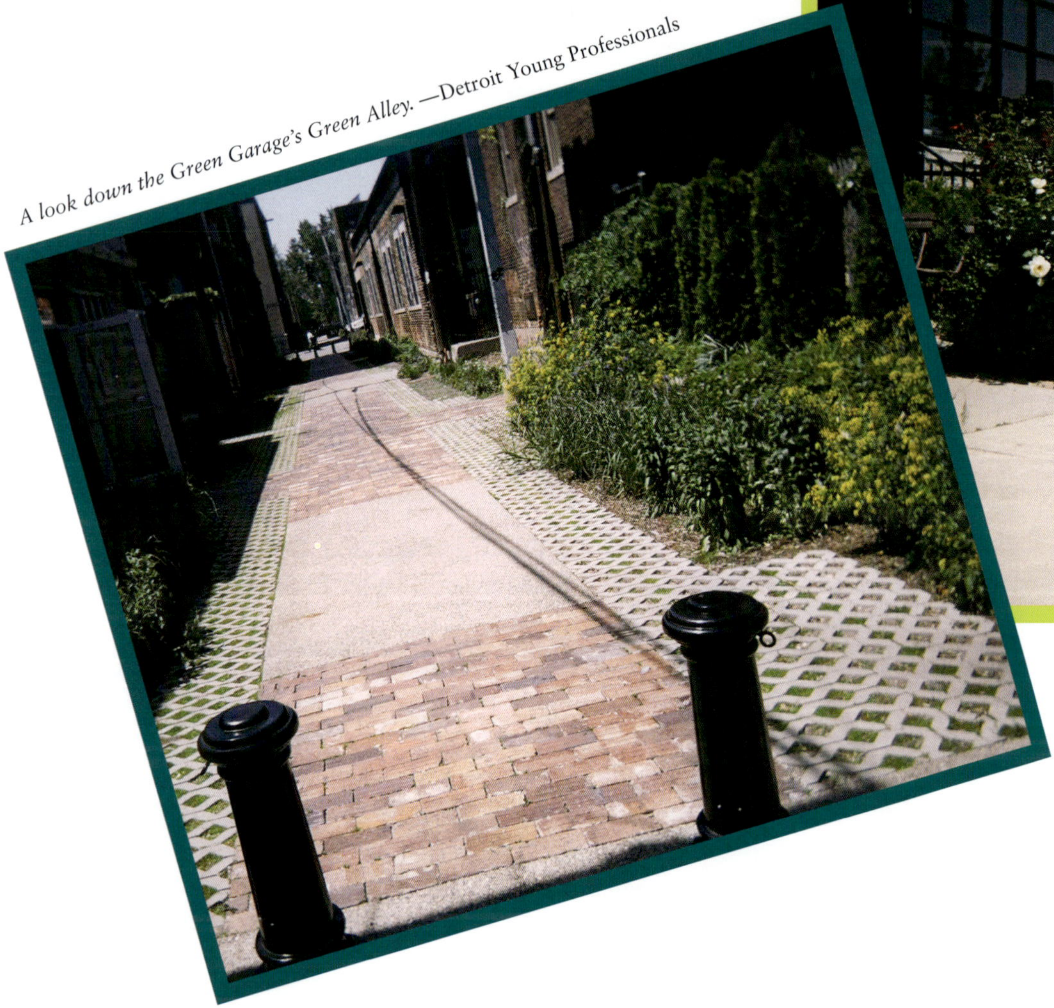

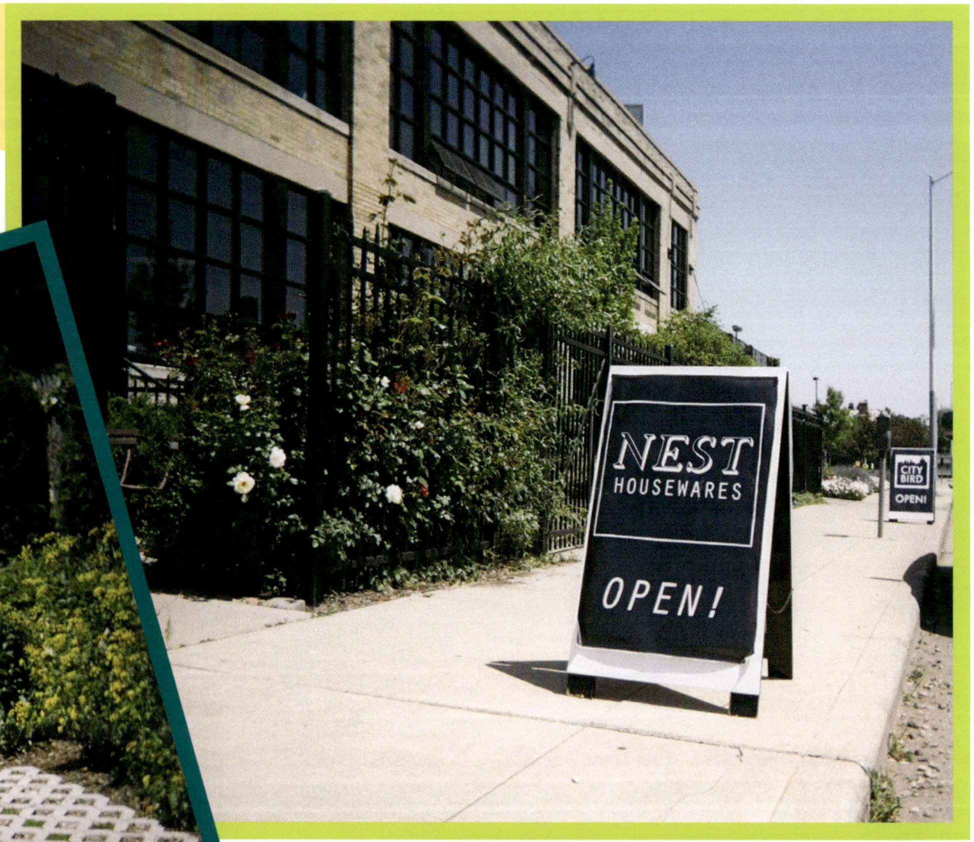

City Bird and Nest retail shops off Canfield Avenue in Midtown.
—Detroit Young Professionals

DECLARE DETROIT

Leader: Roland Leggett

Participants: 20

www.declaredetroit.wordpress.com

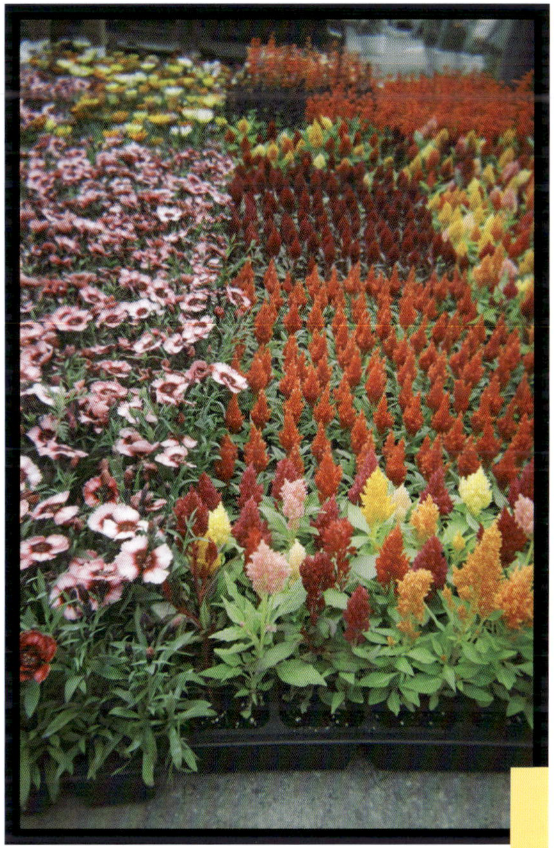

Flower Day at Eastern Market. —Declare Detroit

DECLARE DETROIT is a movement to empower engaged citizens to support bold new leadership in Detroit. Forged through twelve principles, the group's declaration emphasizes Detroit's assets to create opportunity and a prosperous city on a transformative scale. The principles seek leaders citywide who will embrace our diversity, preserve Detroit's authenticity, cultivate creativity, enhance quality of place, and demand government accountability.

Declare Detroit asked its fifteen thousand followers to help shine a bright light on the declaration principles through film.

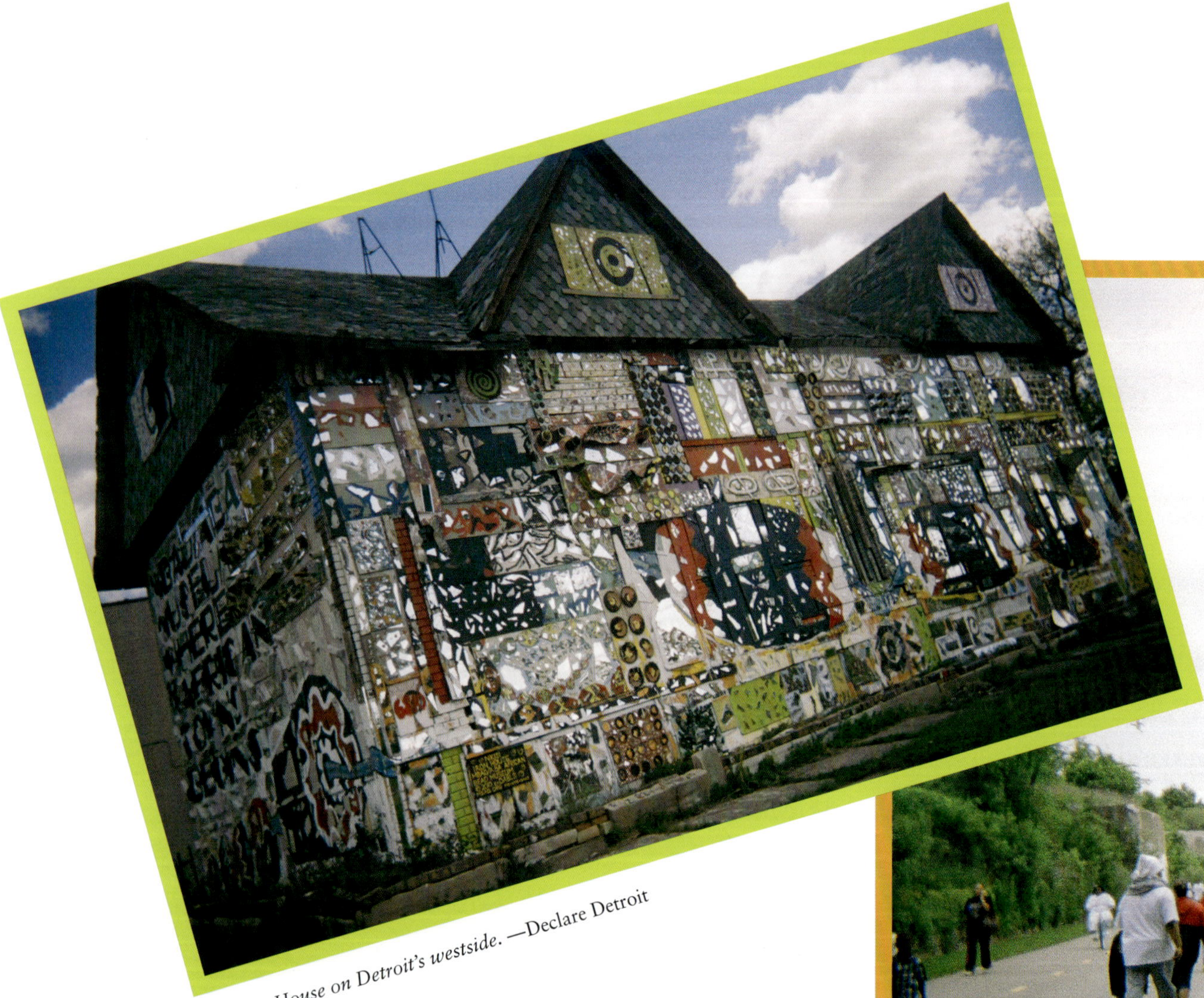

Mirror House on Detroit's westside. —Declare Detroit

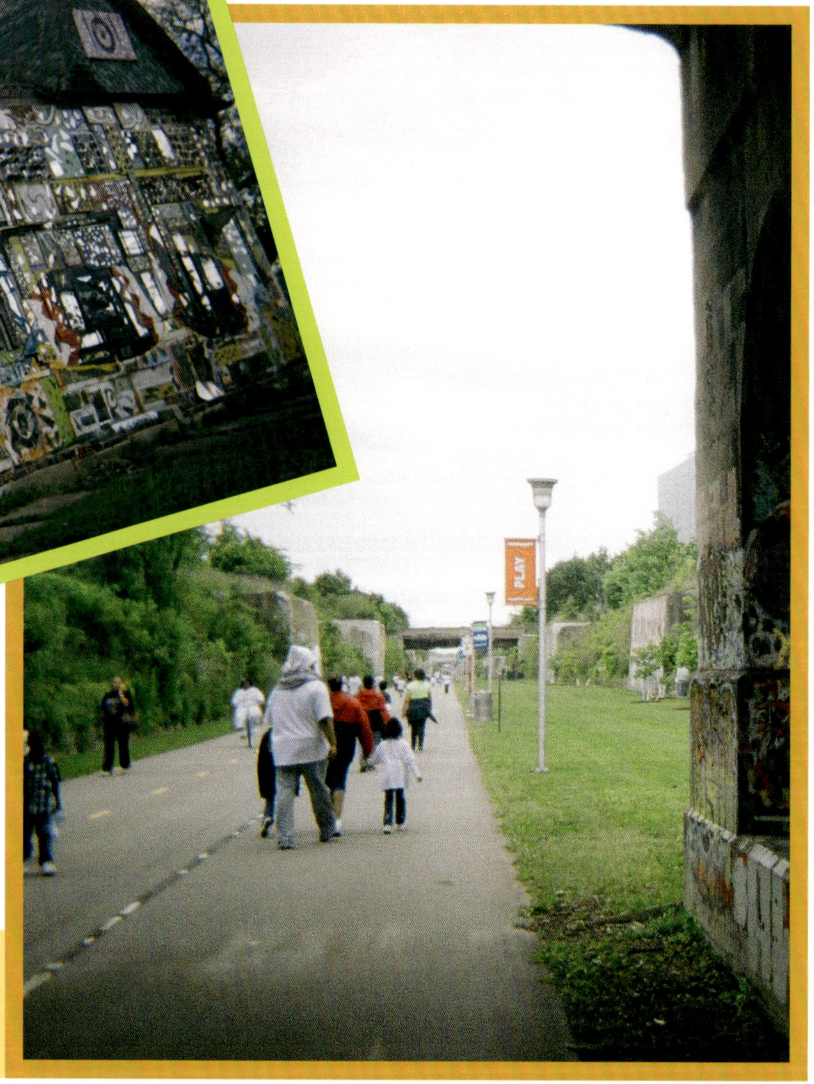

Families strolling the Dequindre Cut. —Declare Detroit

—Declare Detroit

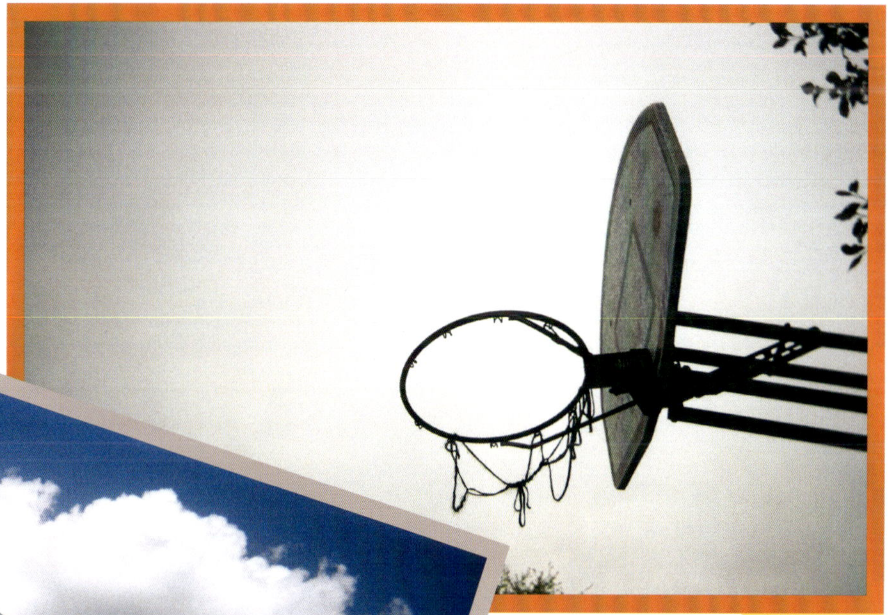

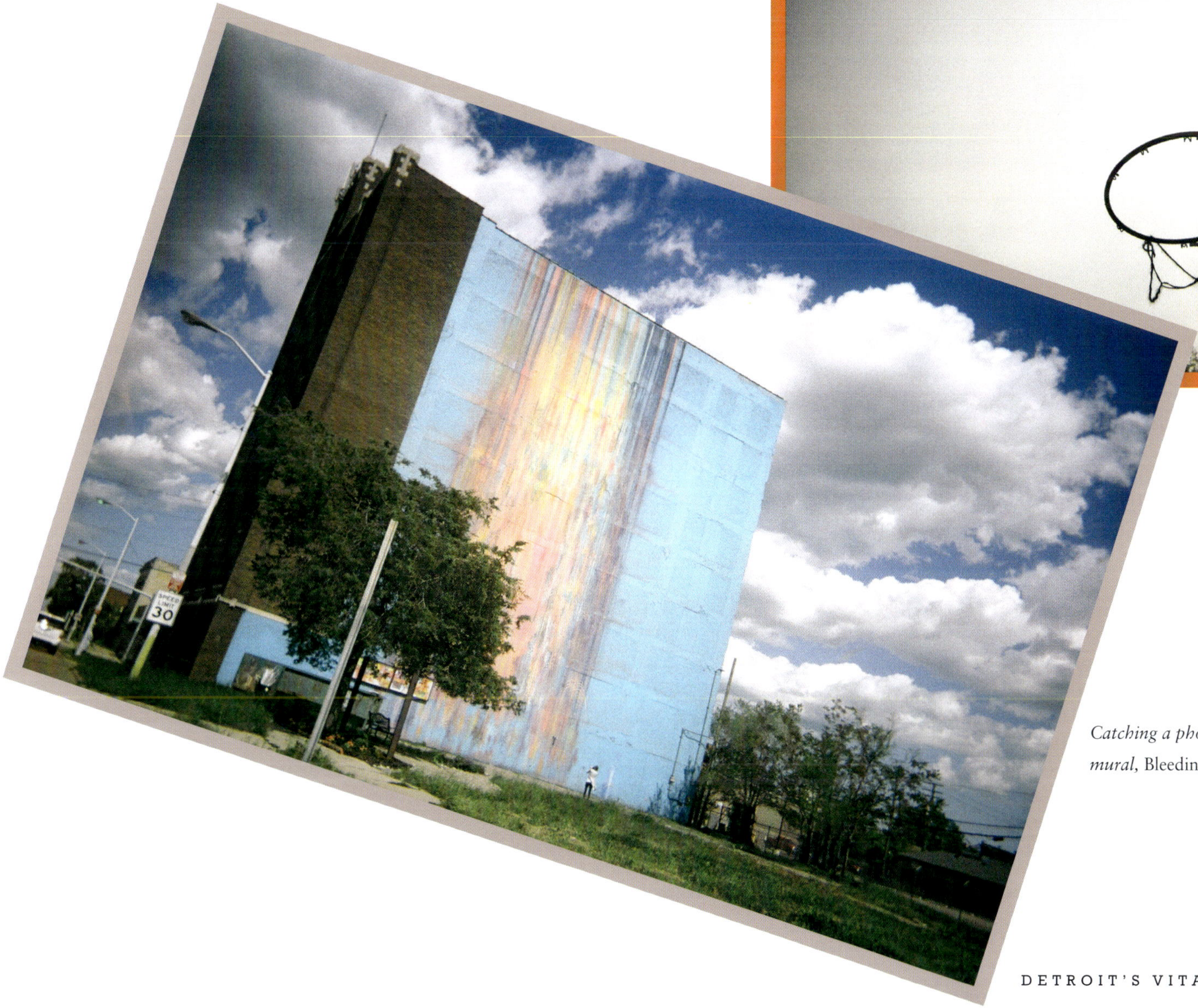

Catching a photographer at Katie Craig's Northend mural, Bleeding Rainbow. —Declare Detroit

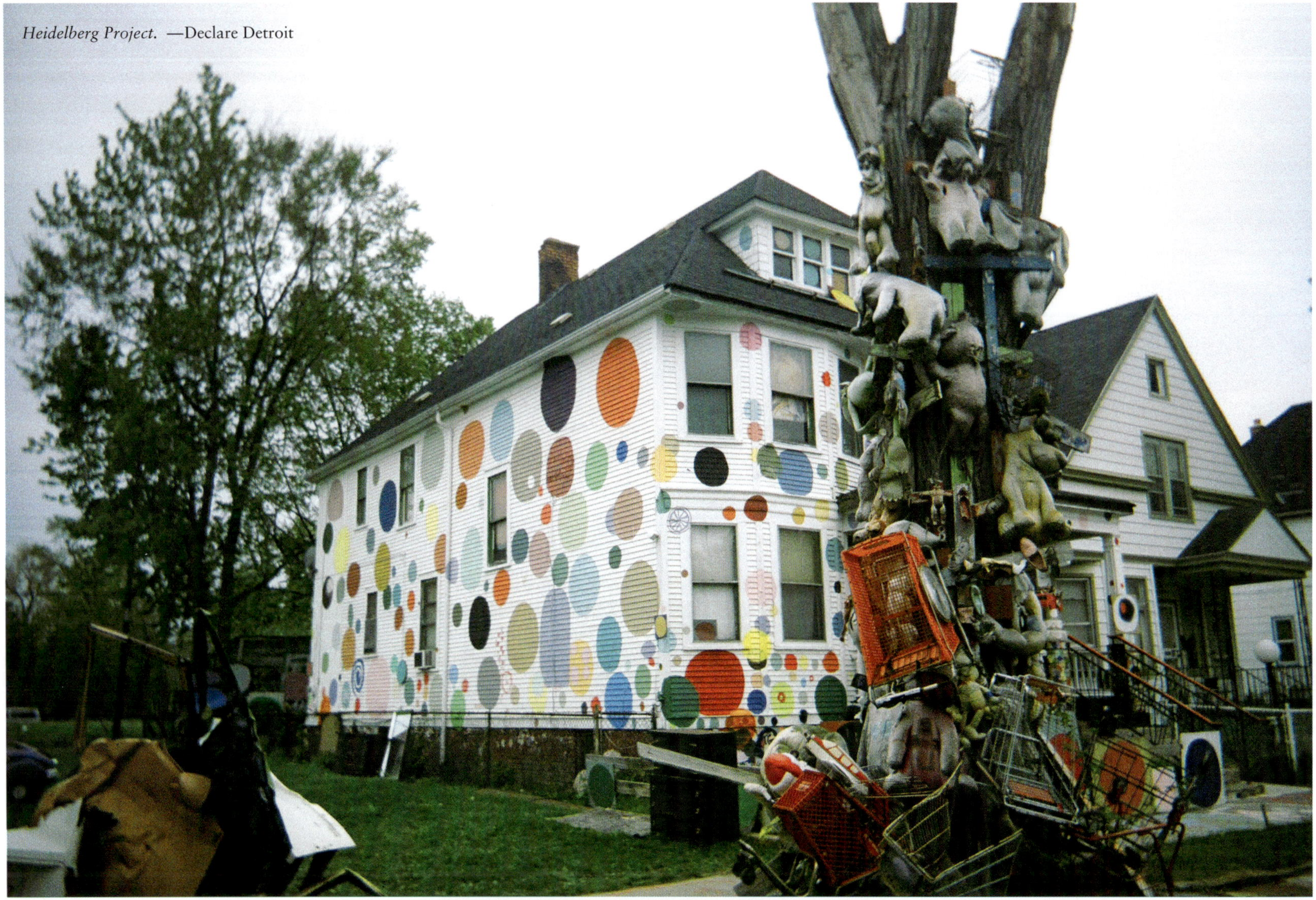

Heidelberg Project. —Declare Detroit

DETROIT REVITALIZATION FELLOWS

Leader: Kennis Wooten

Participants: 29

www.DetroitFellows.com

THE DETROIT REVITALIZATION FELLOWS are a network of professionals who work to build capacity, cultivate relationships, foster collaboration, and accelerate progress across organizations engaged in revitalizing Detroit. The first fellowship cohort ran from August 2011 to July 2013 and included twenty-nine fellows working at twenty-five organizations throughout Detroit.

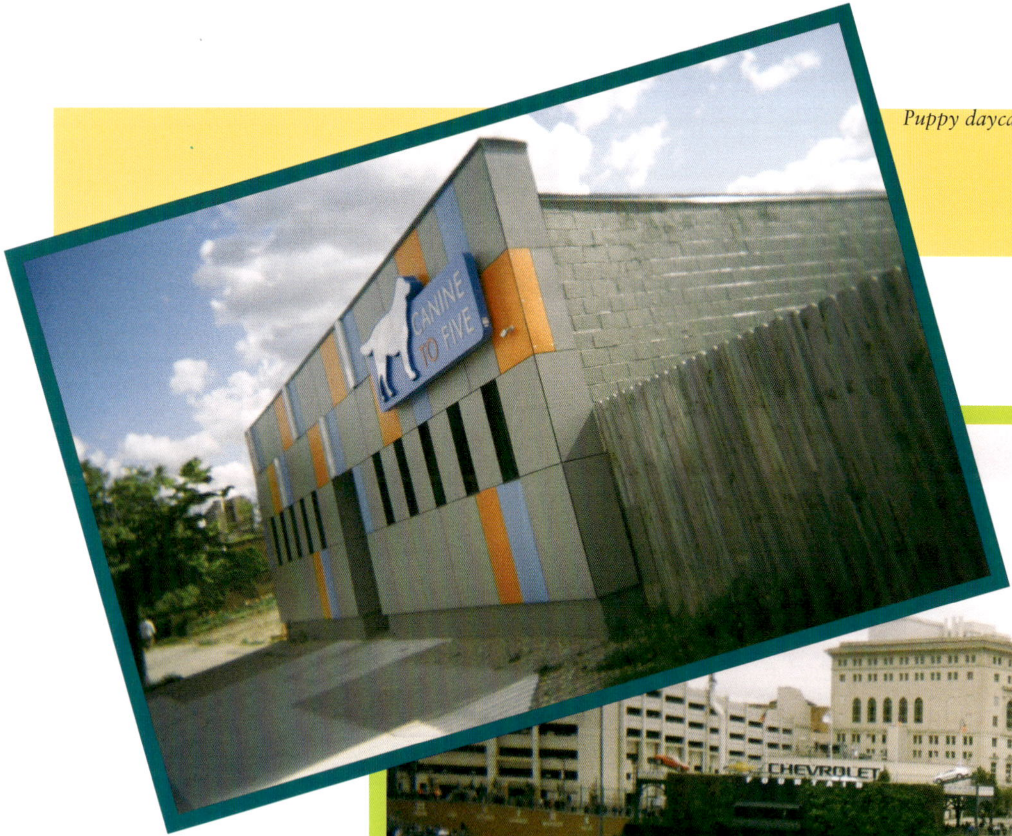

Puppy daycare at Canine to Five. —Detroit Revitalization Fellows

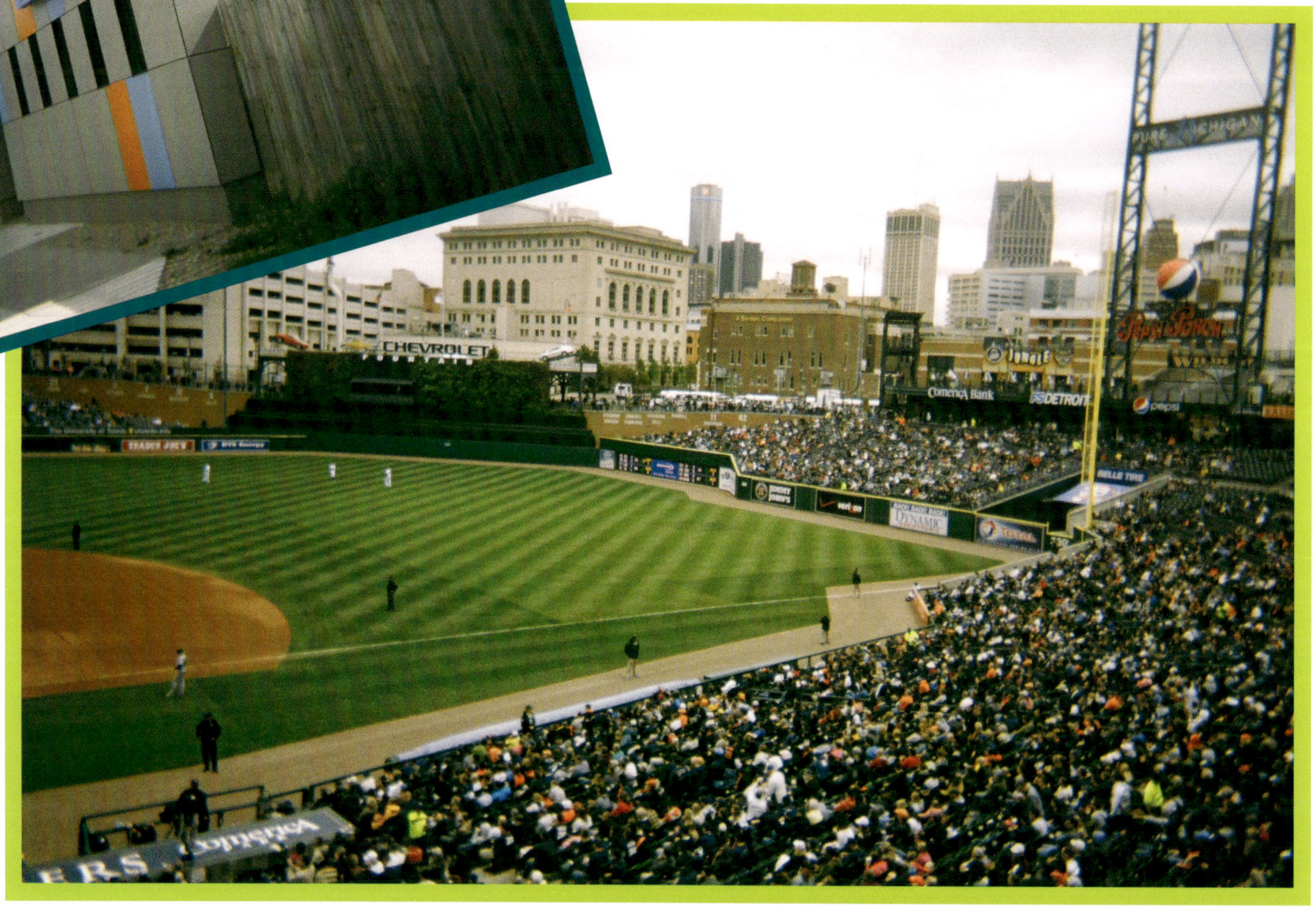

Tigers game day and downtown view. —Detroit Revitalization Fellows

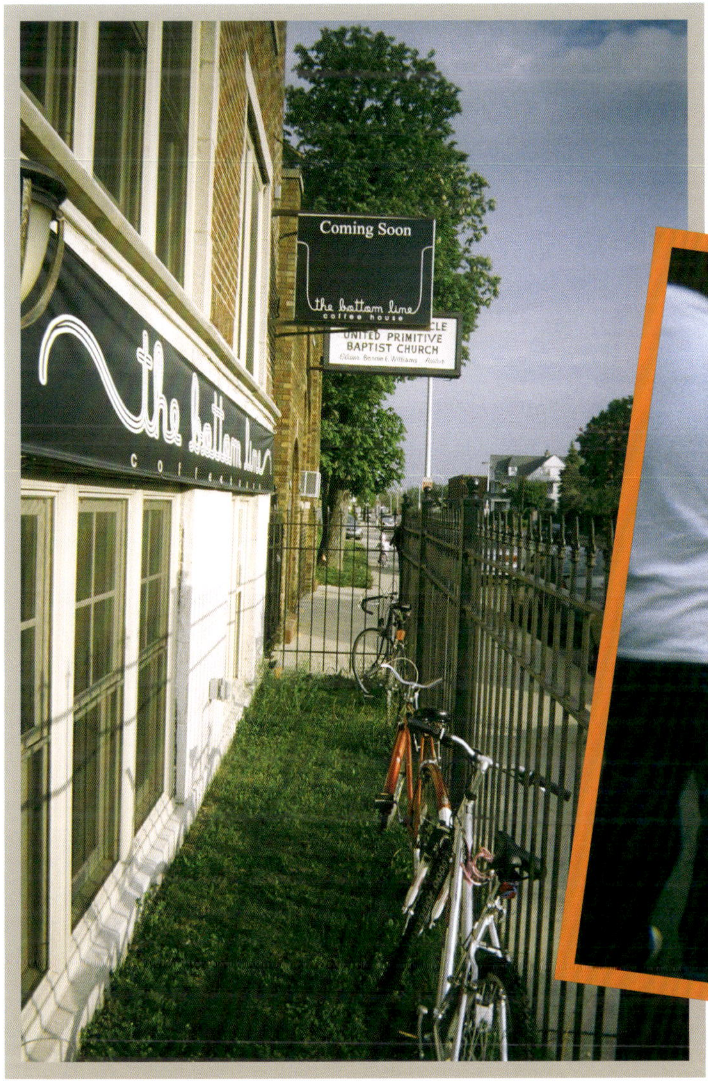

Happy bikes. —Detroit Revitalization Fellows

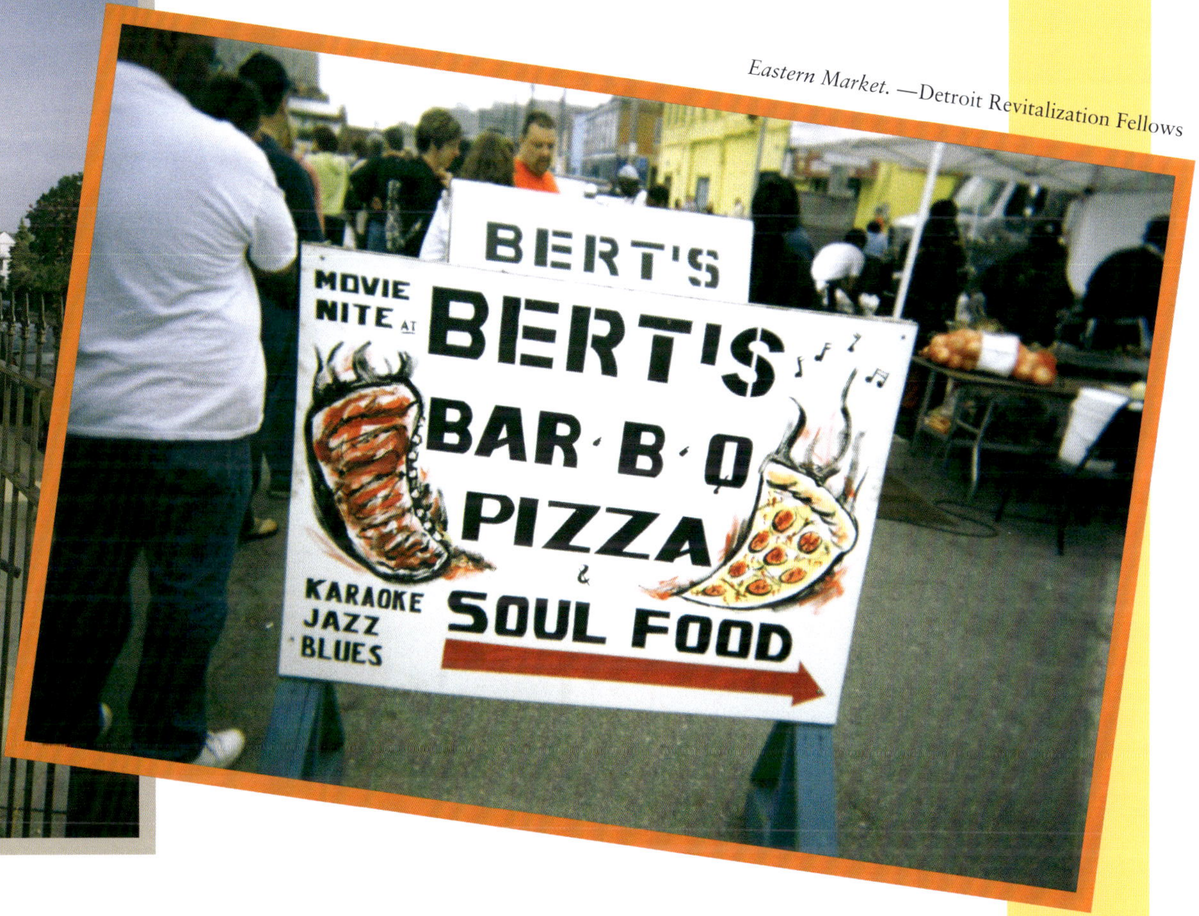

Eastern Market. —Detroit Revitalization Fellows

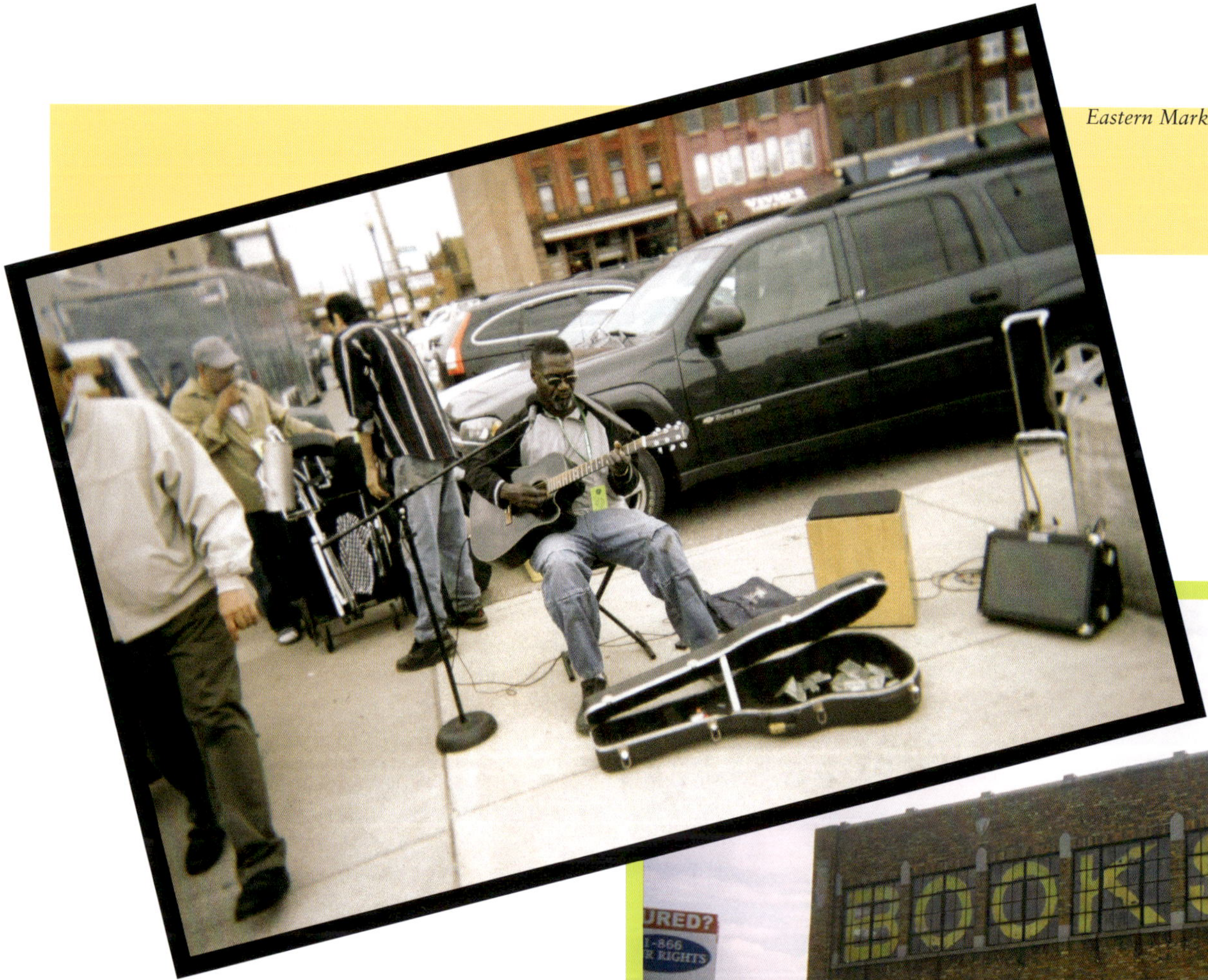

Eastern Market music entertainment. —Detroit Revitalization Fellows

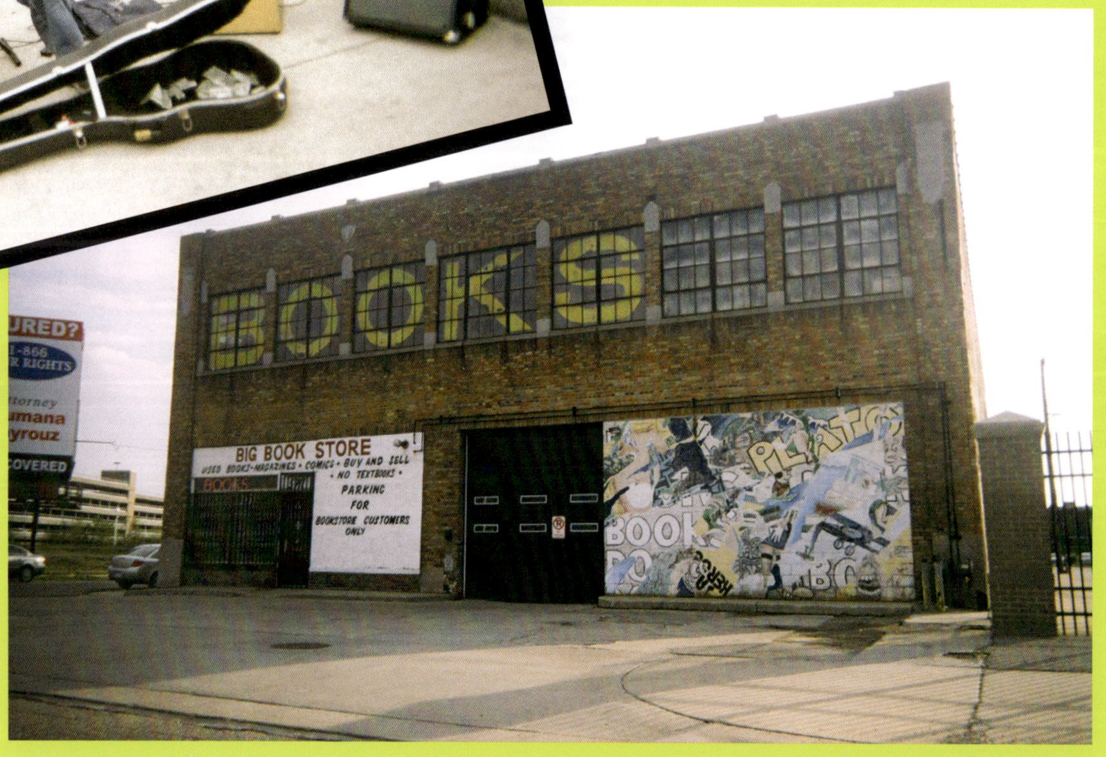

Big Book Store.
—Detroit Revitalization Fellows

WDET'S CROSSING THE LINES

Leader: Rob St. Mary

Participants: 8

www.wdet.org

CROSSING THE LINES is an exploration of what unites and divides us as people and as a region. We sought to present a broad, connected view of metro Detroit through our group, which was comprised of participants from communities in both the city and the suburbs.

The members of the group were excited to show images and ideas that reflect their individual experiences in the region. The effort allowed WDET's larger community to share and suggest places to capture via wdet.org, allowing for a robust online discussion.

Reveal Your Detroit opened a door for WDET's listeners to engage with the *Crossing the Lines* project through a series of photos that showcase the diversity of our region.

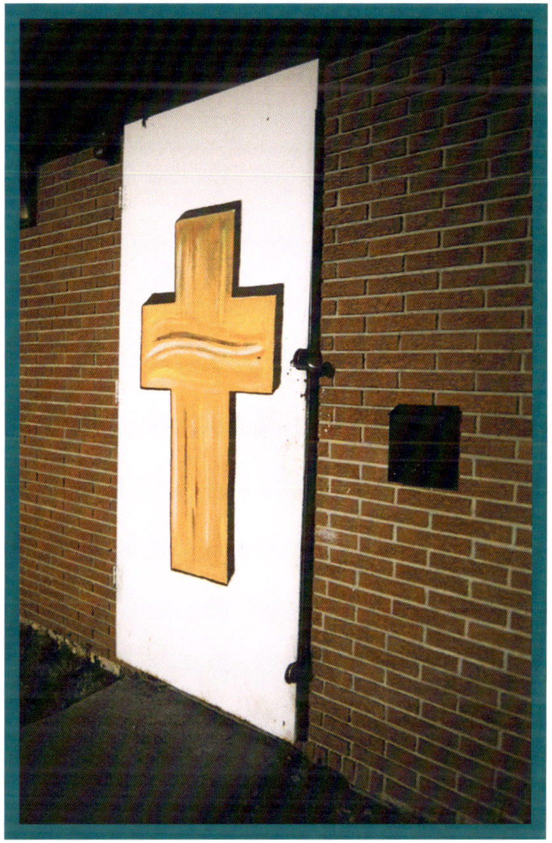

—WDET's *Crossing the Lines*

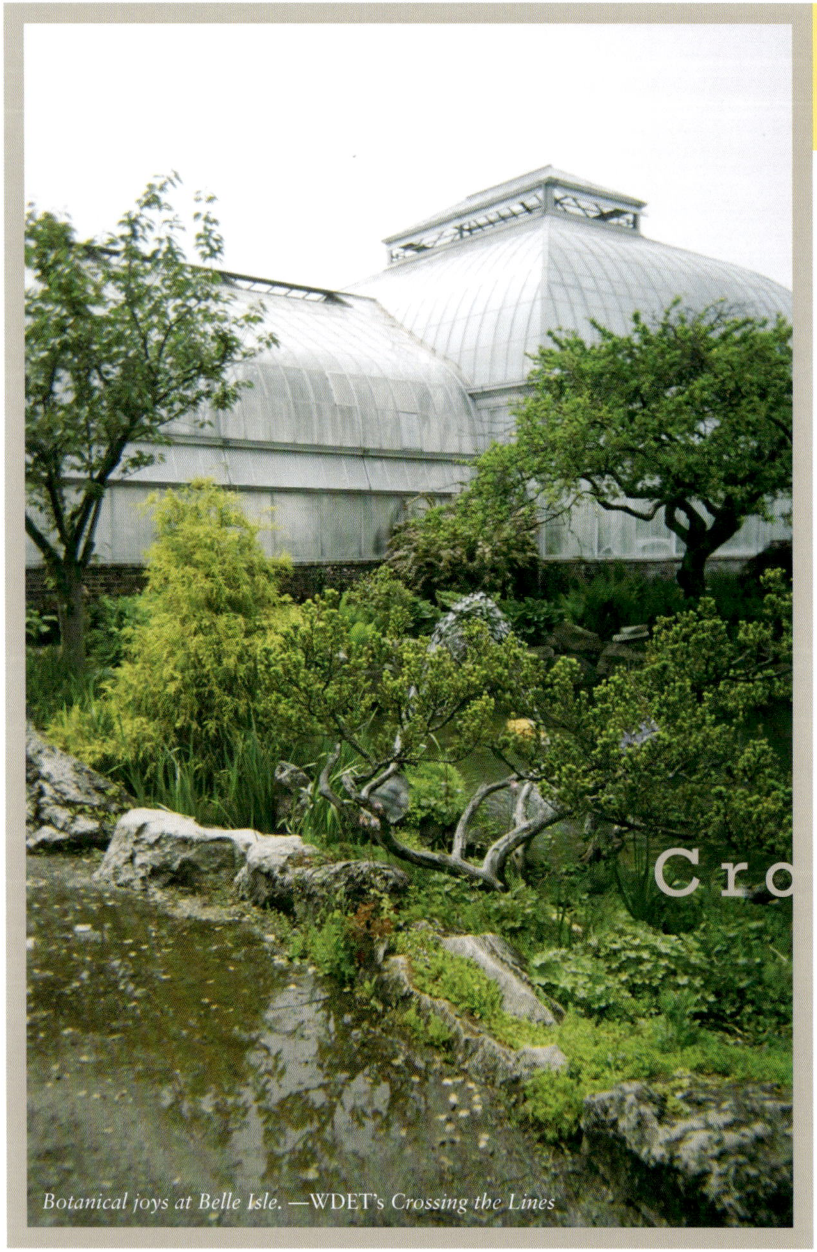

Botanical joys at Belle Isle. —WDET's *Crossing the Lines*

Rob St. Mary

leads the *Crossing the Lines* series for WDET, Detroit's public radio station. The DIA was excited when WDET accepted our invitation to partner as a way to engage their listeners and the *Crossing the Lines* series participants, a small but representative group of metro Detroit's diversity.

Rob's take on the Reveal Your Detroit project offered valable insights. He asked participants and listeners to take a broader perspective—to capture both personal images and to widen out a nd take pictures beyond our comfort zones in Detroit.

Rob accepted his own challenge head-on, capturing personal shots and distinctively Detroit takes. One in particular stood out as it relates to Detroit's housing challenges.

WDET

Crossing the Lines

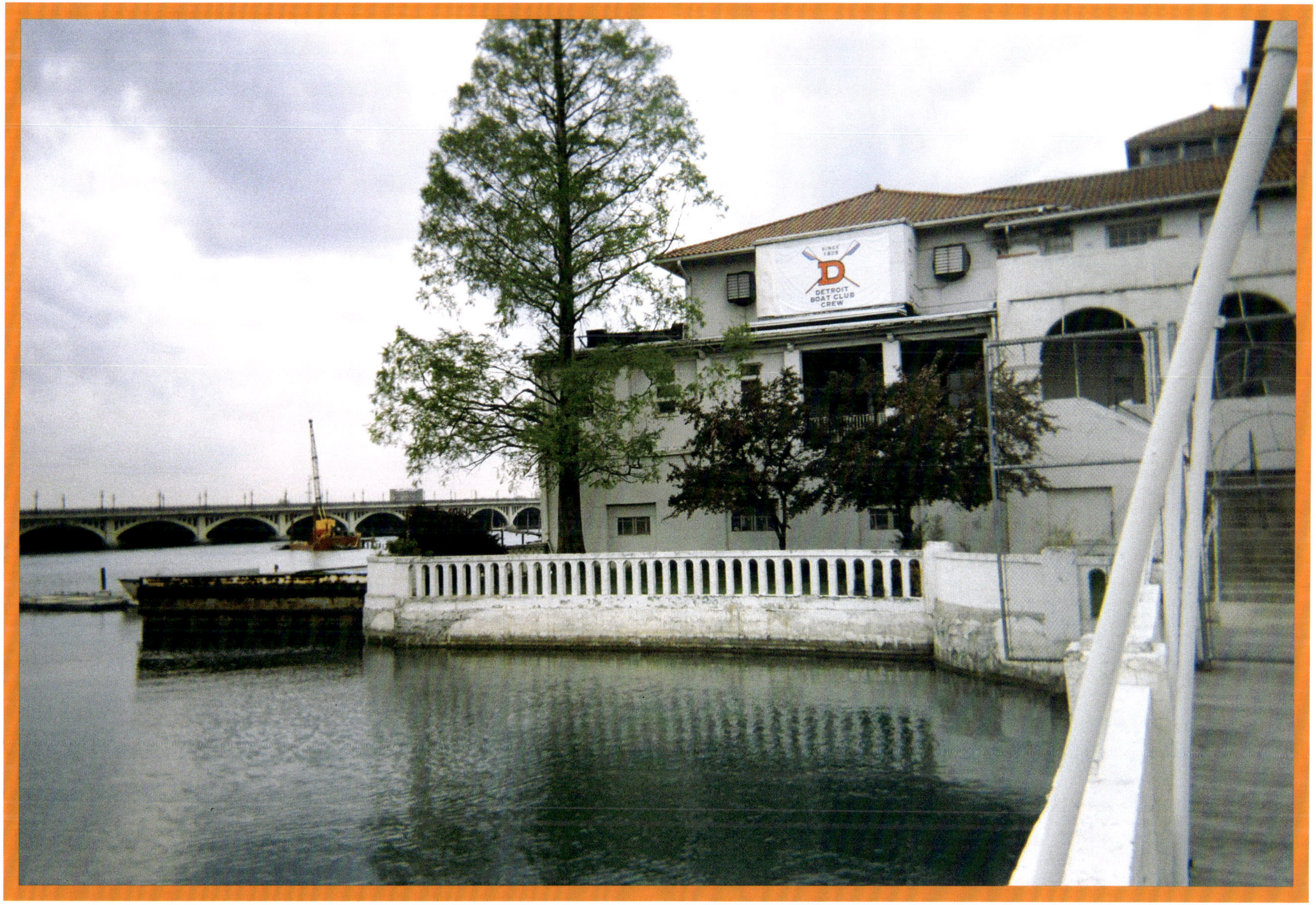

Detroit Boat Club on Belle Isle. —WDET's *Crossing the Lines*

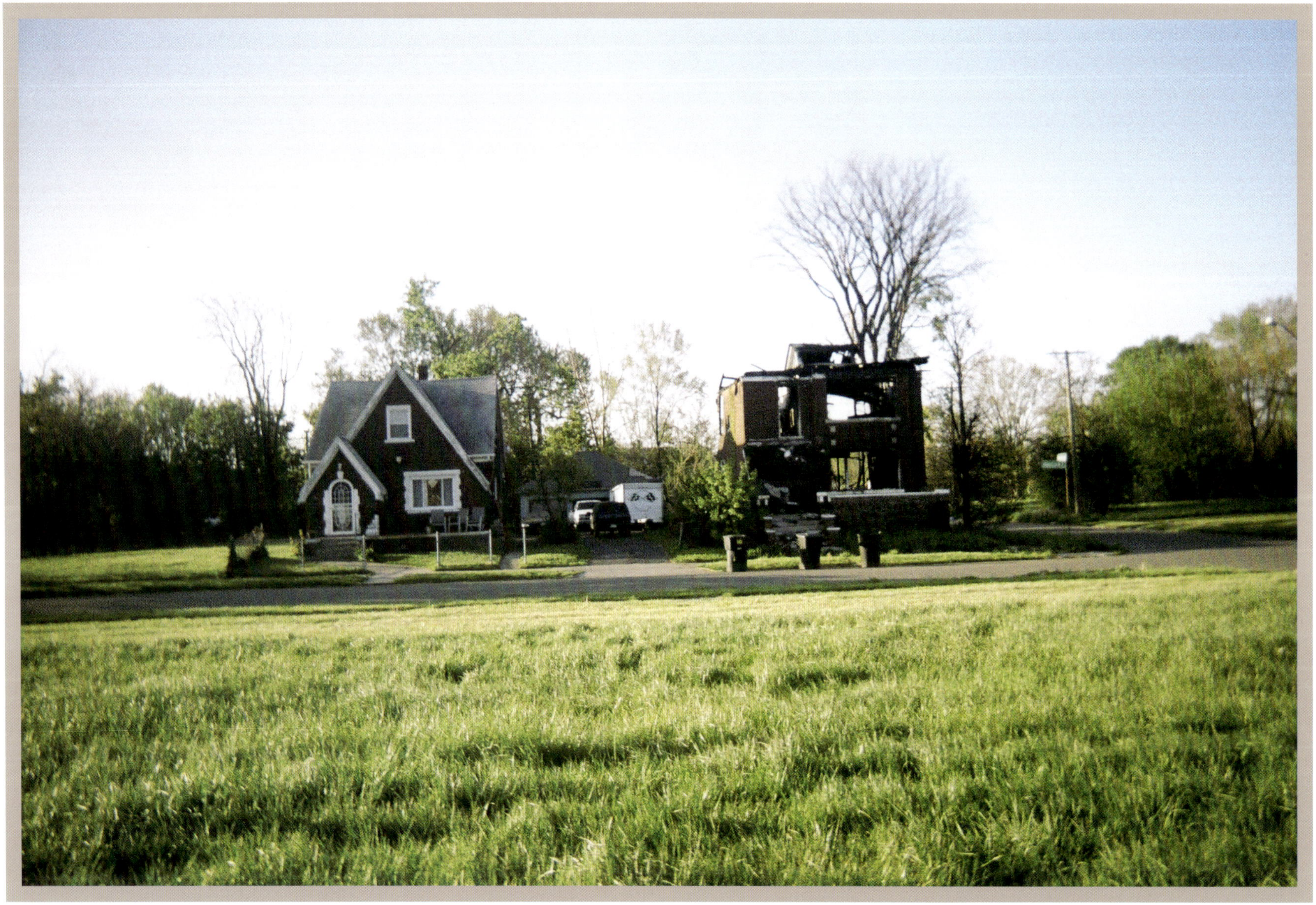

Two houses in a field. —WDET's Crossing the Lines

I took this shot while on my way to work one morning as I was driving past this big playfield. At the opposite end were these two houses that looked like mirror images of each other. Except one is very nicely kept up, while the other is obviously burned out and hadn't been torn down yet. It was just that dichotomy in the early morning sunlight and a big green field—it just spoke to me about Detroit and was a very interesting image.

ROB ST. MARY

—WDET's *Crossing the Lines*

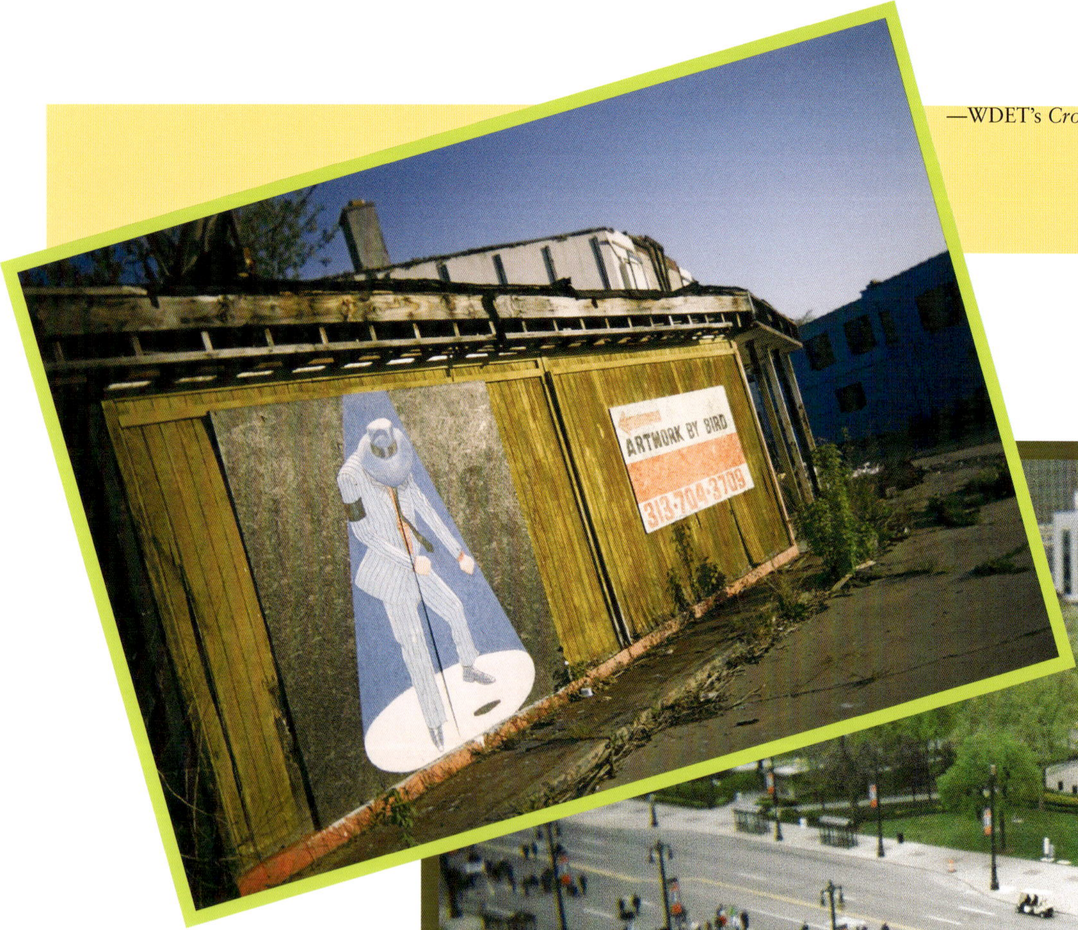

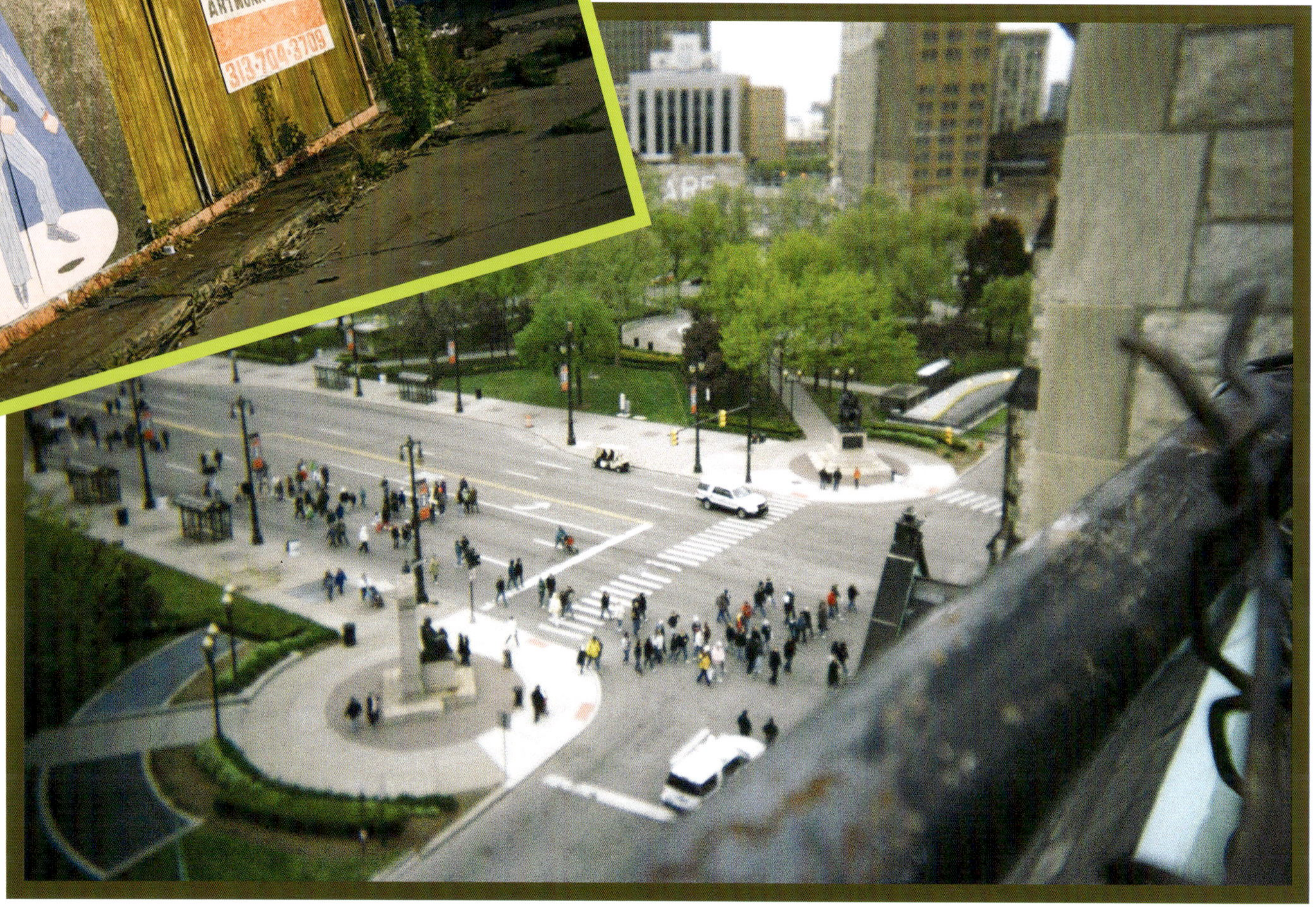

Cadillac Square downtown, captured from the People Mover stop.
—WDET's *Crossing the Lines*

YOUNG NATION: THE ALLEY PROJECT

Leader: Erik Howard

Participants: 10

www.youngnation.us

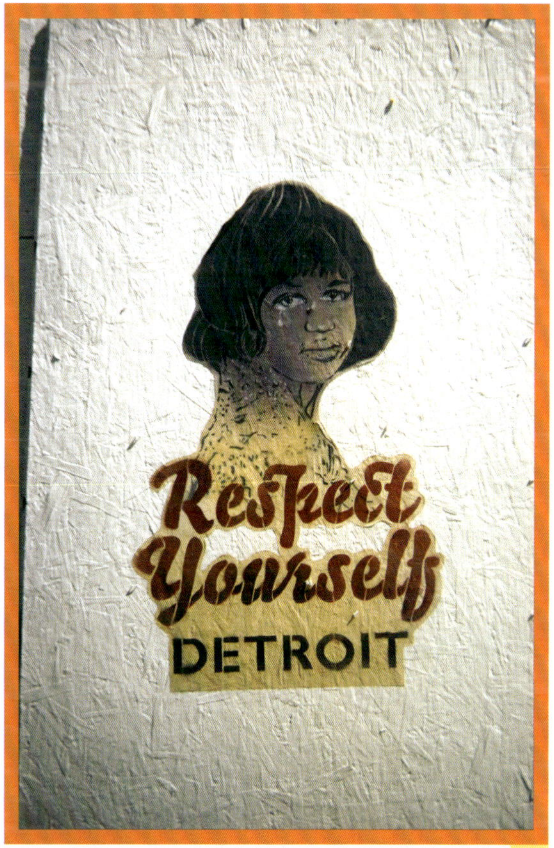

Truth. —Young Nation

YOUNG NATION employs cultural and educational initiatives to promote youth and community development. The Alley Project (TAP), an initiative of Young Nation, is an outdoor art environment where participants can view, create, and/or exhibit art in a space that promotes safety, creative expression, and relationship building. TAP is committed to reducing the legal and physical risks faced by young people involved or interested in street art.

Reveal Your Detroit enhanced our ability to support the mission of TAP. Through our connections with youth in the community we're able to activate their interests in street art as a door to the wider world of art. Youth from TAP participated in Reveal Your Detroit's tour and were able to submit images in a memorable experience that took them from The

Alley to the museum and back into their own communities to document and share as experts of their own experiences.

Reveal Your Detroit provided a voice for participants from TAP whose perspectives often go unheard by enabling them to create and share their own narrative about their community, their culture, and themselves.

Food trucks are hot. —Young Nation

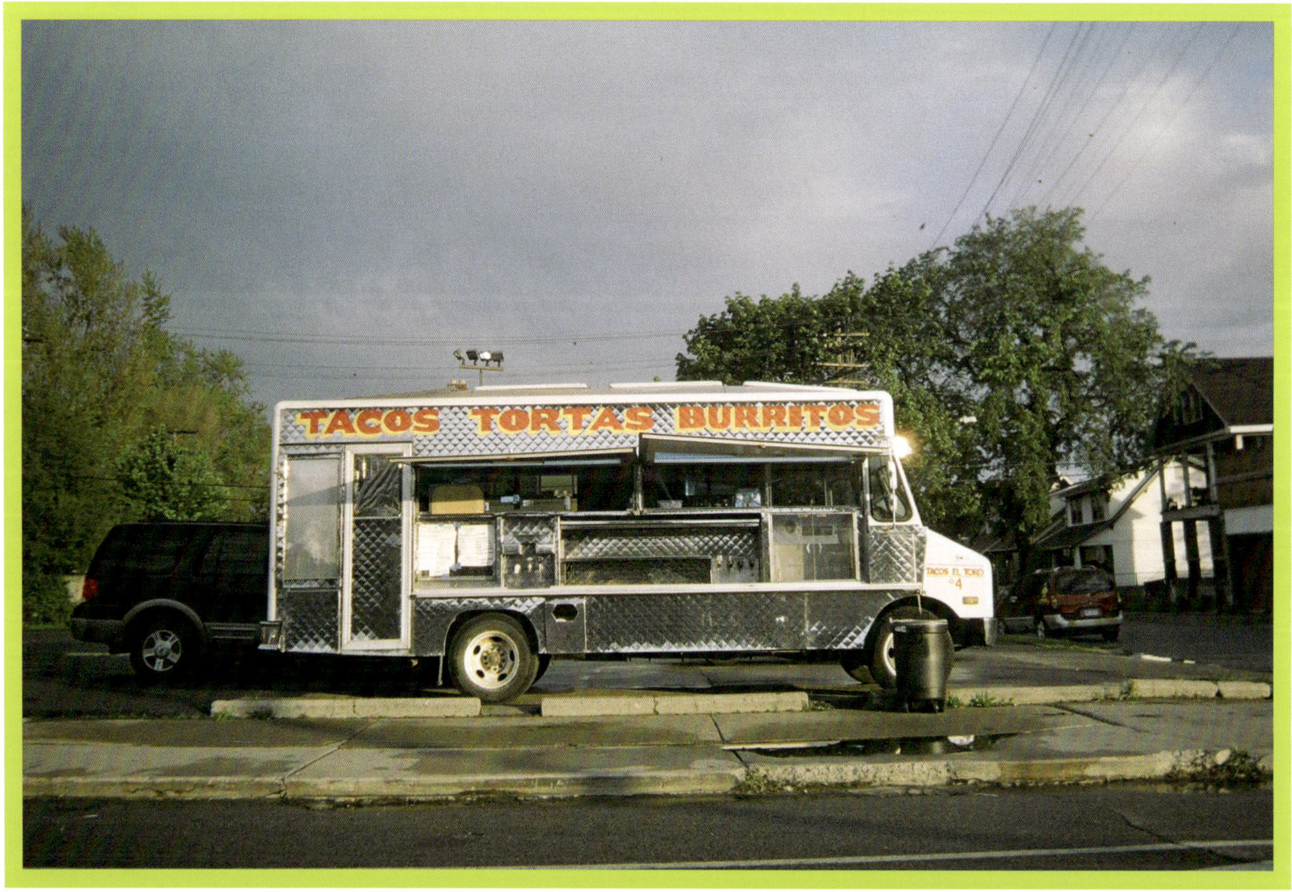

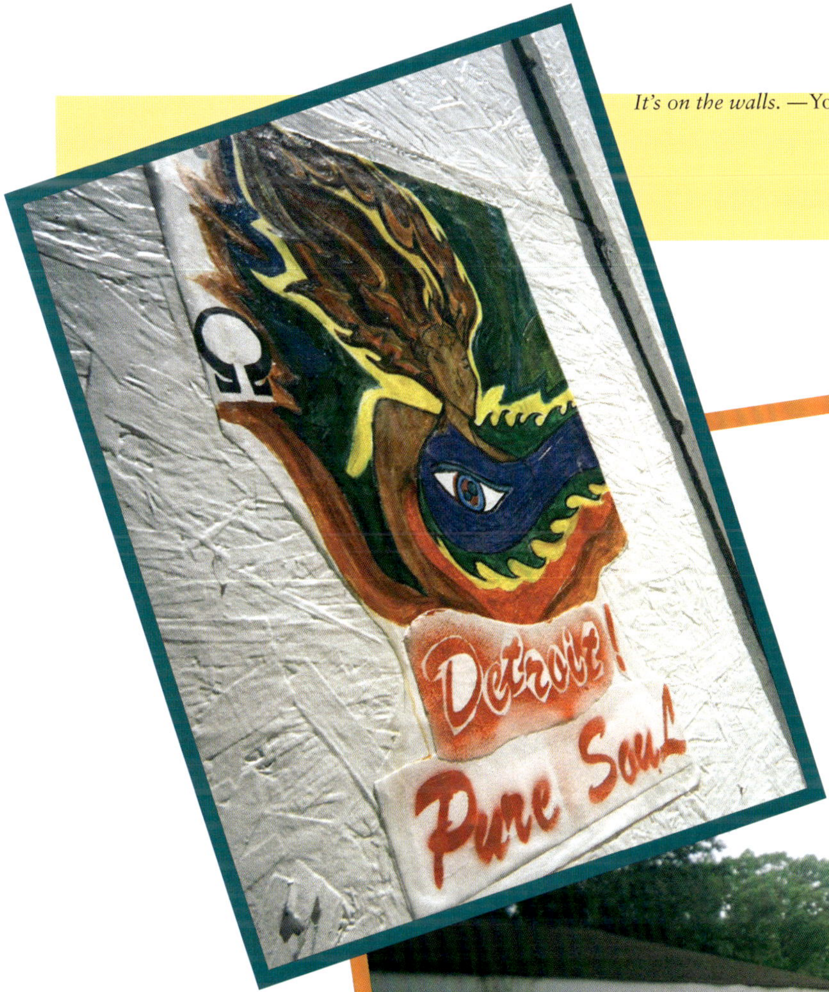

It's on the walls. —Young Nation

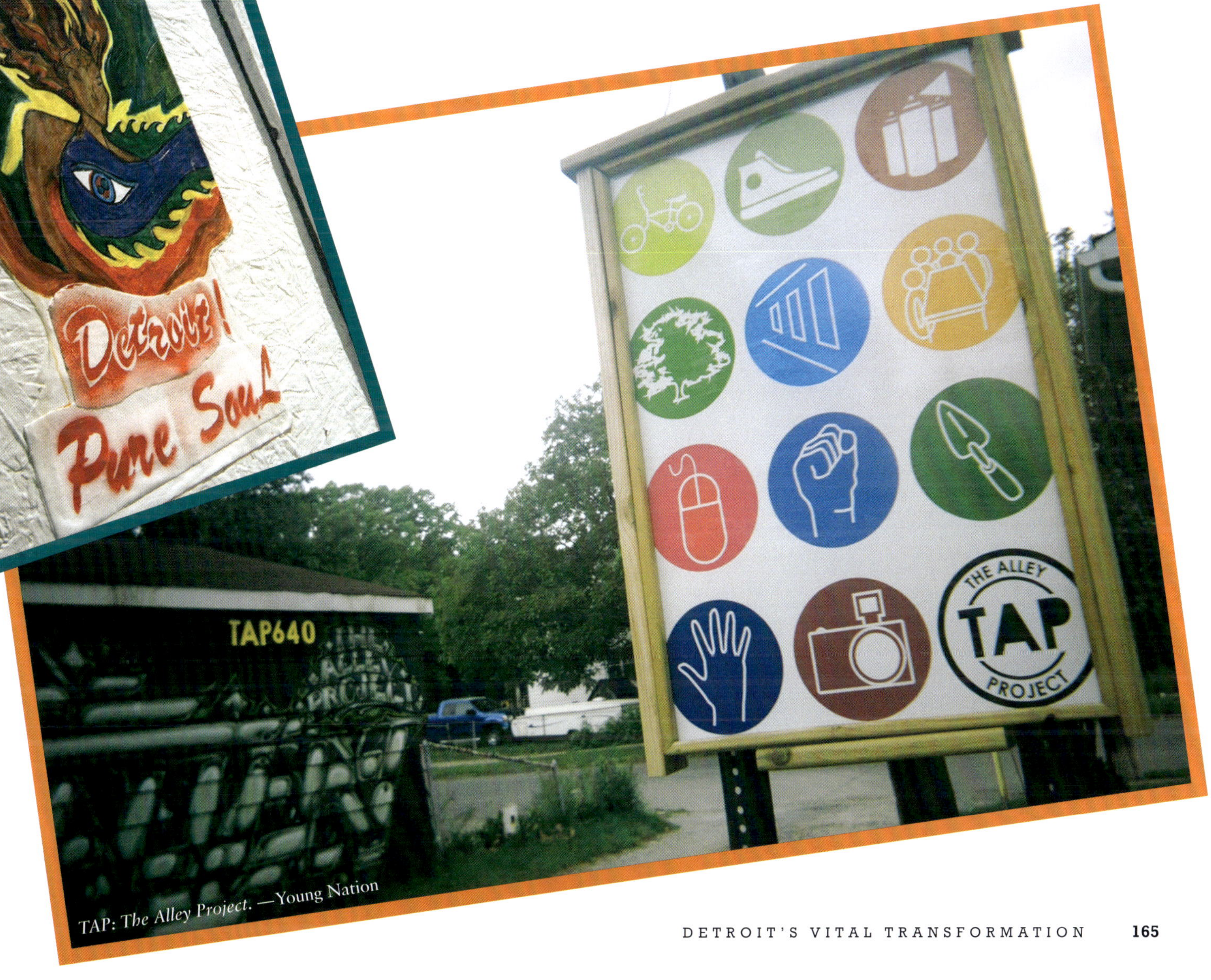

TAP: *The Alley Project.* —Young Nation

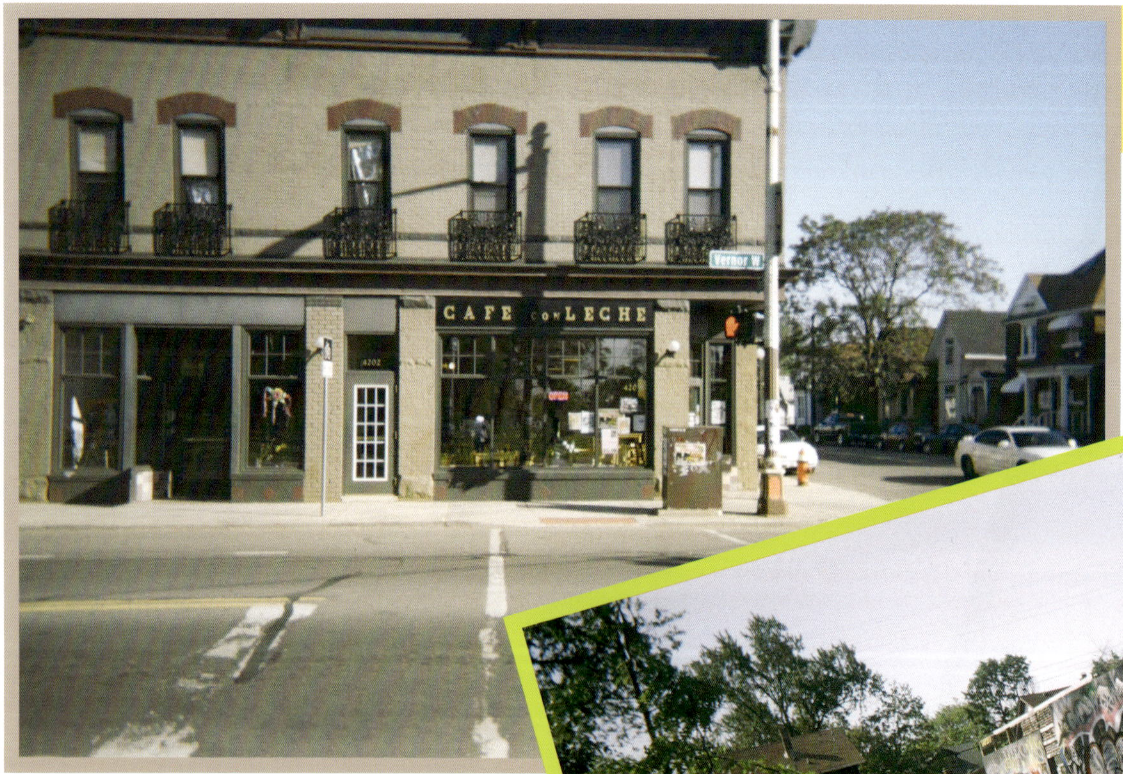

Café Con Leche. —Young Nation

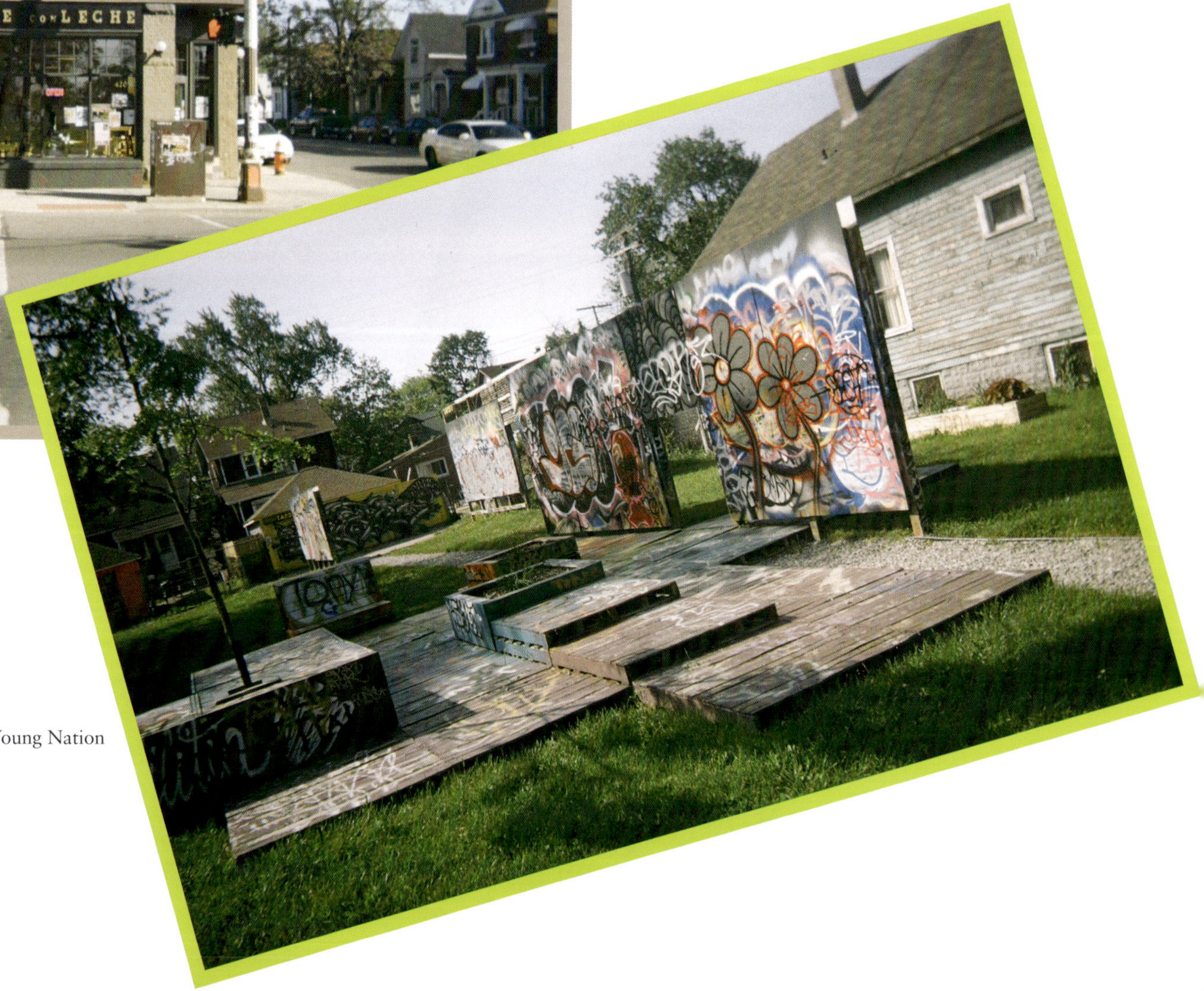

The Alley Project graffiti wall. —Young Nation

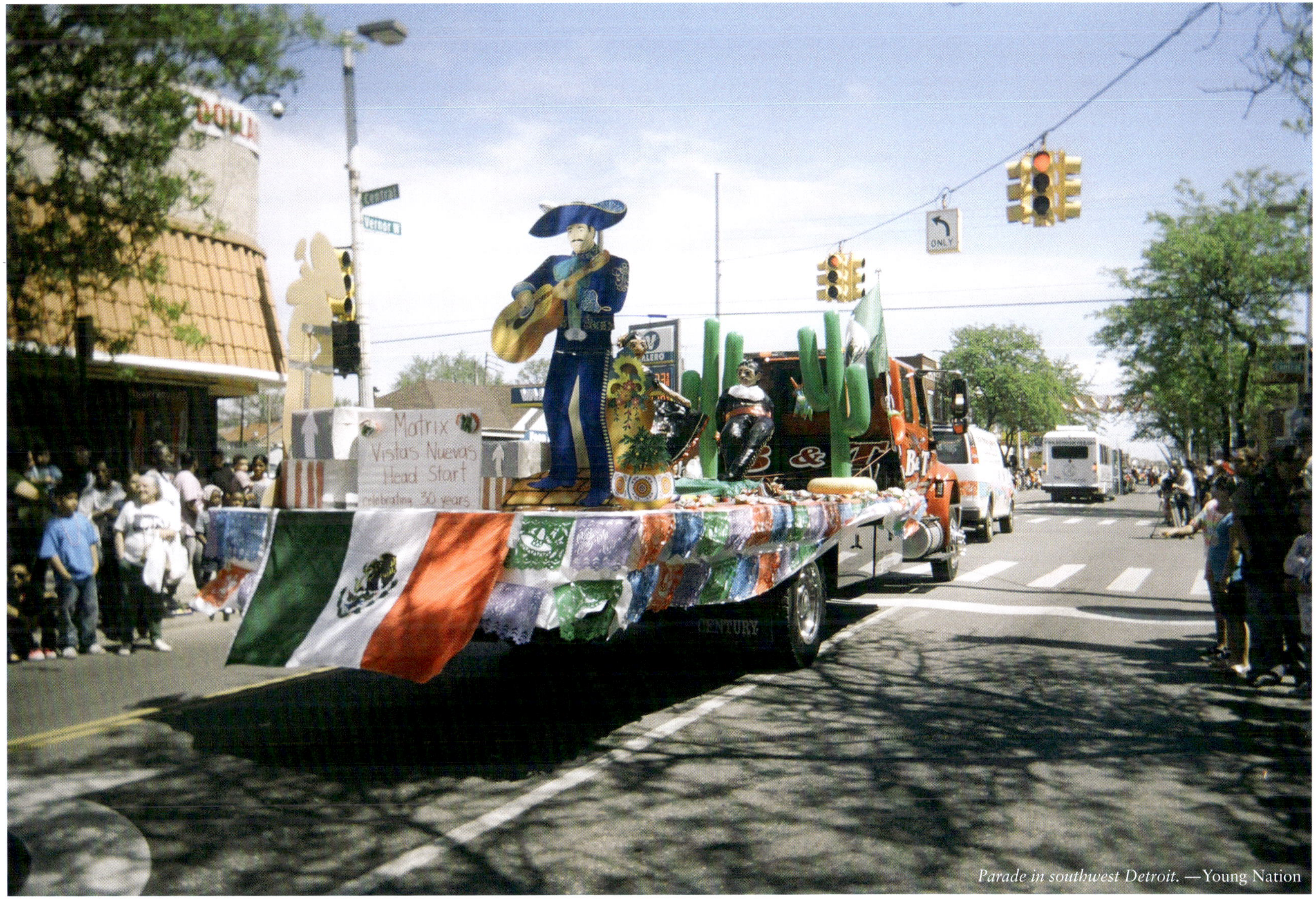

Parade in southwest Detroit. —Young Nation

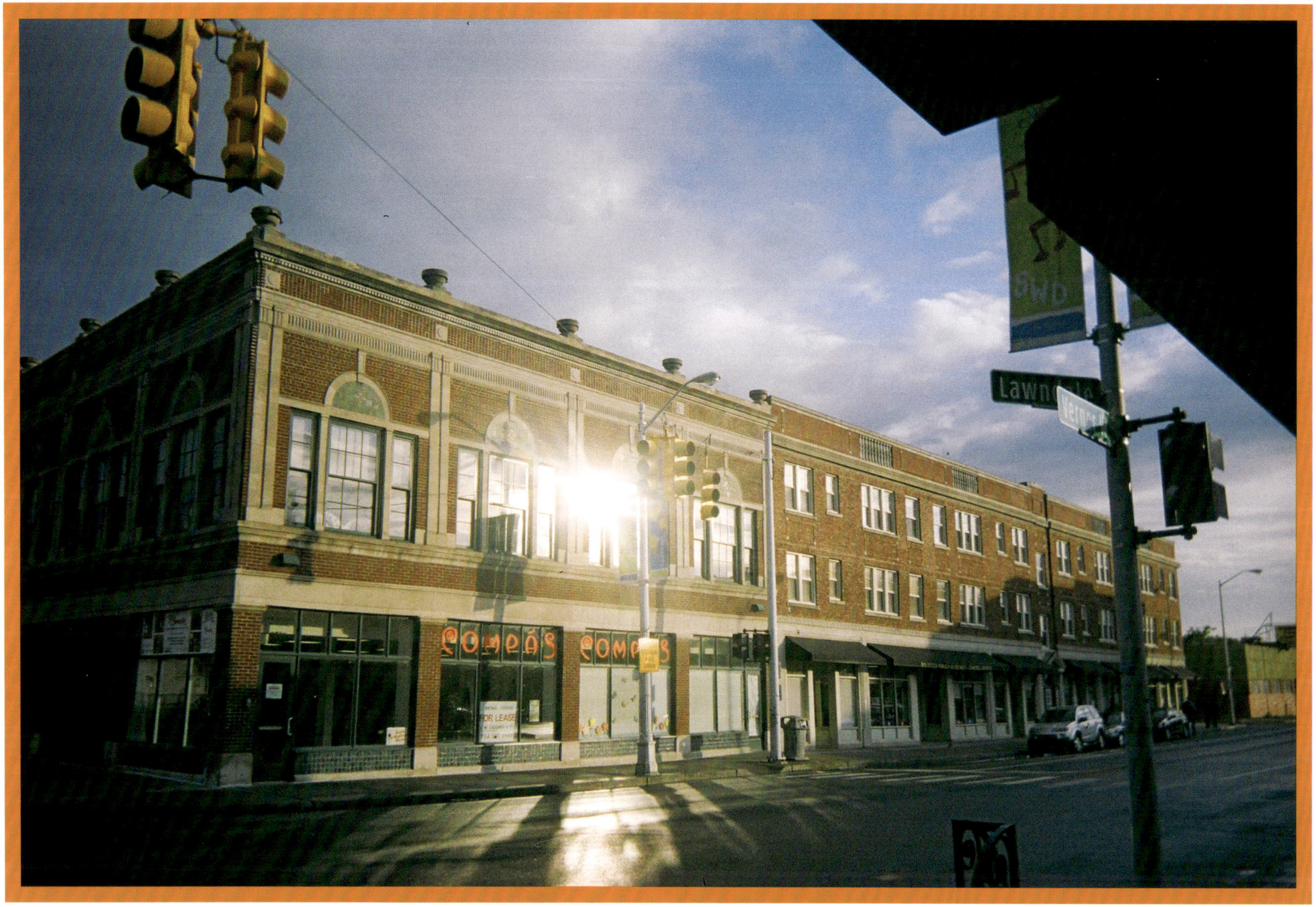

Morning sun off Vernor in southwest Detroit. —Young Nation

Low rider. —Young Nation

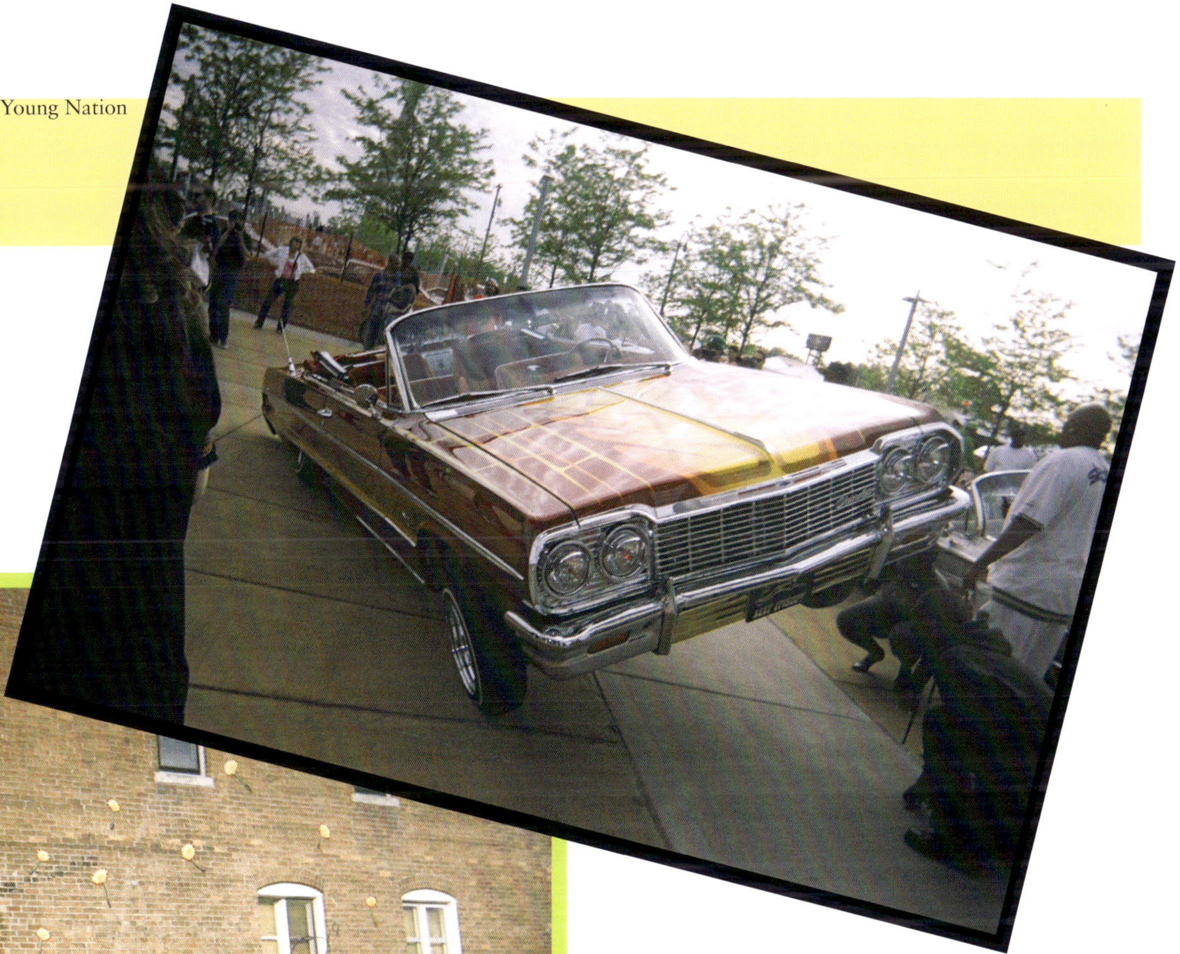

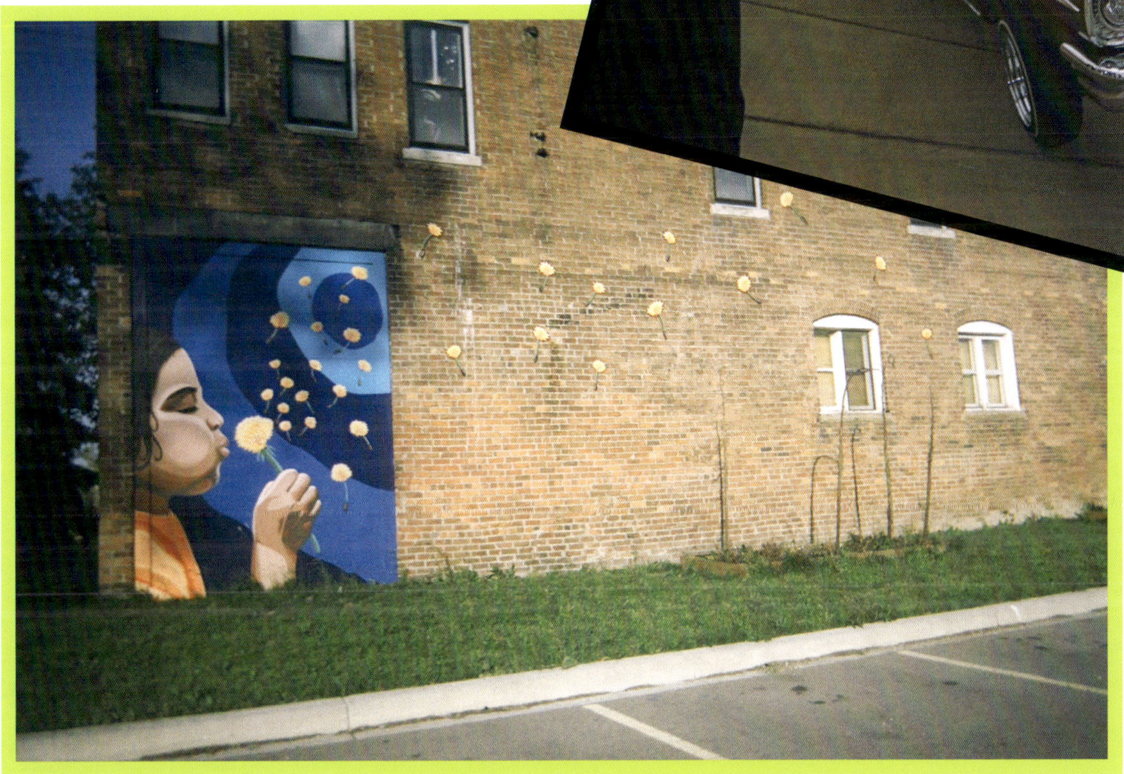

Make a wish. —Young Nation

BURNERS WITHOUT BORDERS DETROIT

Leader: Danielle Doxie Kaltz

Participants: 35

www.bwbdetroit.wordpress.com

THE BURNERS WITHOUT BORDERS DETROIT mission is to create random acts of kindness and service to Detroit's homeless one supply-filled backpack at a time.

We are grateful to have been involved in Reveal Your Detroit and hope readers will view homelessness in our city with a little more compassion.

MEET DANIELLE KALTZ, or Doxie as her friends know her. I'll always remember the day Doxie contacted me about her group, Burners Without Borders Detroit, a homeless outreach and advocacy group. Doxie wanted to take part in Reveal Your Detroit as a way to "give voice to the voiceless" through the DIA's cameras. At first Doxie was hesitant, worried that the idea posed too much of a risk, but we at the museum were eager to see what she would come up with and how the project would work with this unique audience, including opening the museum early one Saturday morning to provide her group a dignified visit to the *Detroit Revealed* show.

The results were really remarkable and well beyond our expectations. I asked Doxie to share her thoughts when we presented the highlights from the hundreds of images shared by Detroit's homeless community.

DOXIE KALTZ

Burners Without Borders Detroit

BURNERS WITHOUT BORDERS is derived from the Burning Man festival that meets every summer in Nevada's Black Rock Desert to celebrate shared values of radical self-expression and self-reliance. Burning Man honors the importance of art and employs the immediacy of experience.

Burners Without Borders (BWB) was born from the Burning Man principle of civic responsibility. Local chapters of BWB now exist in many parts of the world, each working toward healing social and civic issues. In Detroit, we concentrate on helping the homeless by creating random acts of kindness and service: giving away one supply-filled backpack at a time. Backpacks include items such as hats, gloves, socks, canned goods, can openers, juice, water, hand warmers, rain ponchos, and hygiene products, as well as blankets, shoes, and other helpful items.

We may not have the skill set to get people off the street, but we hope to make one night there a little easier.

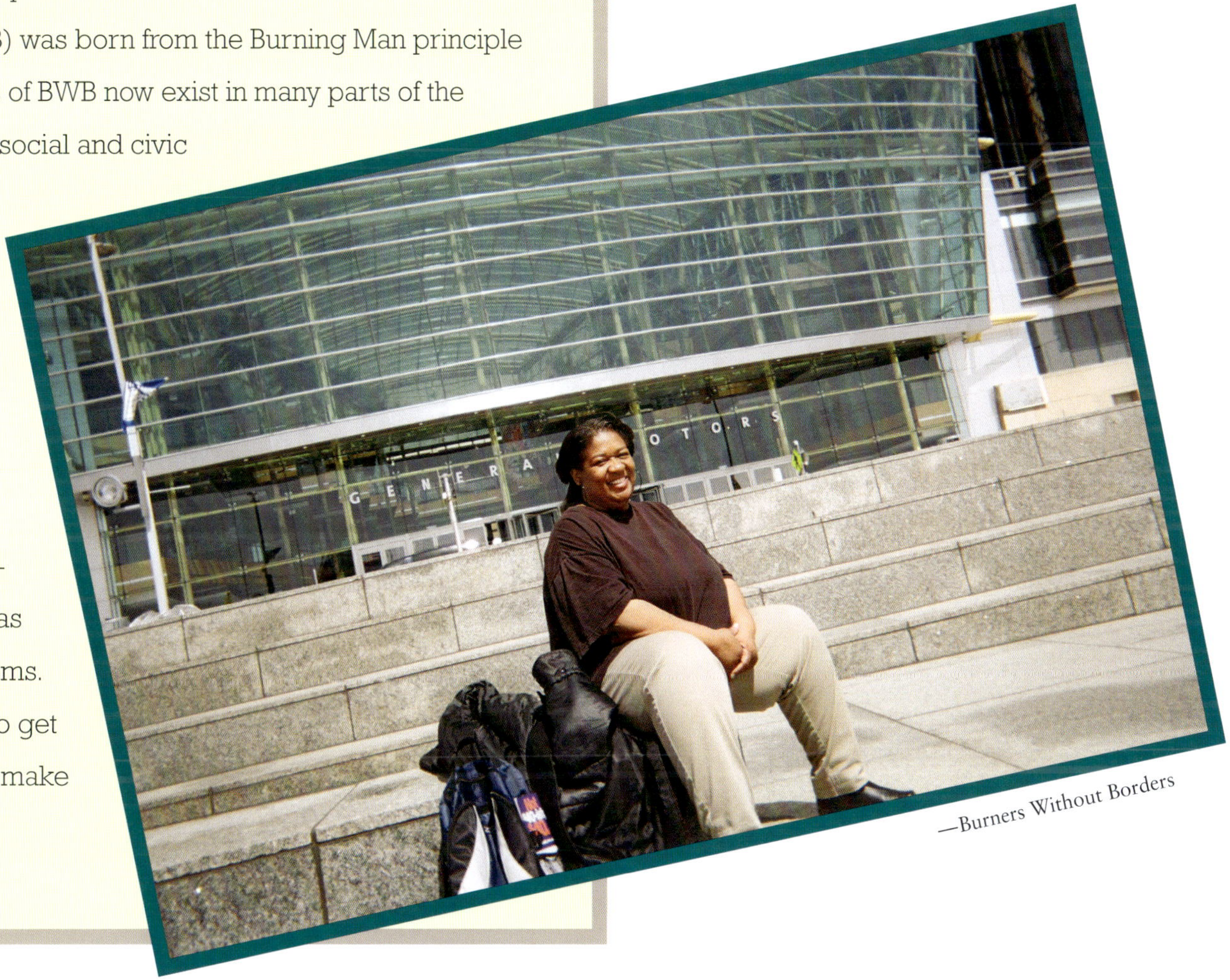

—Burners Without Borders

Burners Without Borders Detroit

—Burners Without Borders

As part of Reveal Your Detroit, BWB received thirty-five disposable cameras and gave them to homeless citizens—providing them with the chance to express their own stories and reach audiences typically unavailable to those who are housing challenged. As we approached the homeless, we explained how each participant could potentially "speak" to many people about their experience through the power of images and that sharing their lives could change how people treat and see their homeless neighbors.

Many times as we travel in our cars we do not see the homeless person asking for help at the corner; instead we make the choice to fiddle with our radio. When we walk into events or restaurants downtown we can quickly utter "No thanks" to someone asking for a quarter. Society sees homeless citizens as undesirables. We often think we are immune to homelessness, making it easier to stay distant and to not have to acknowledge them.

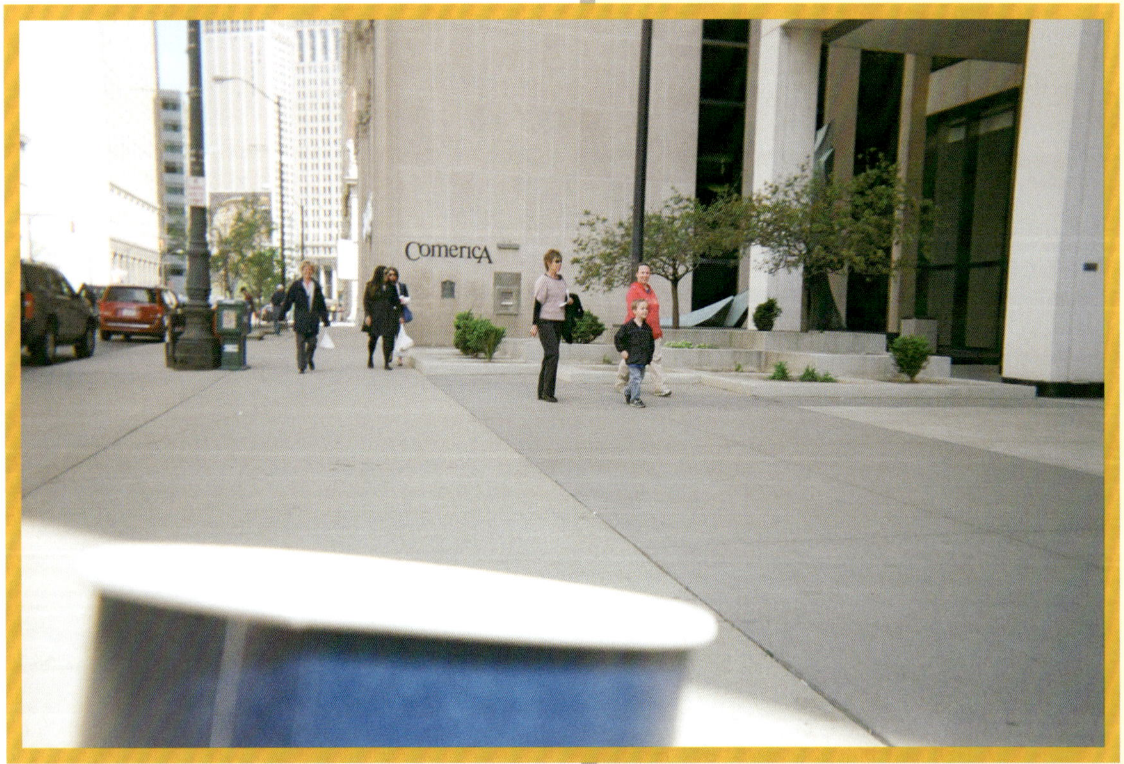

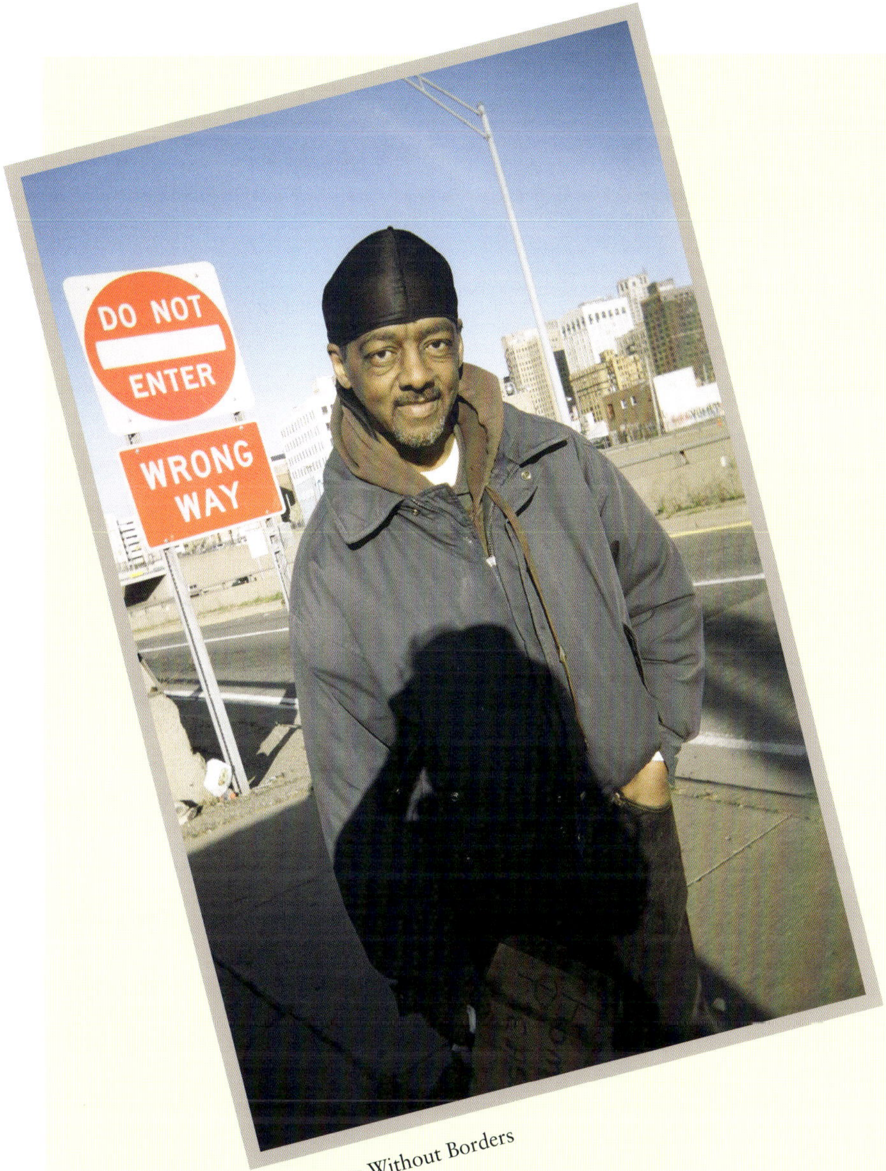

—Burners Without Borders

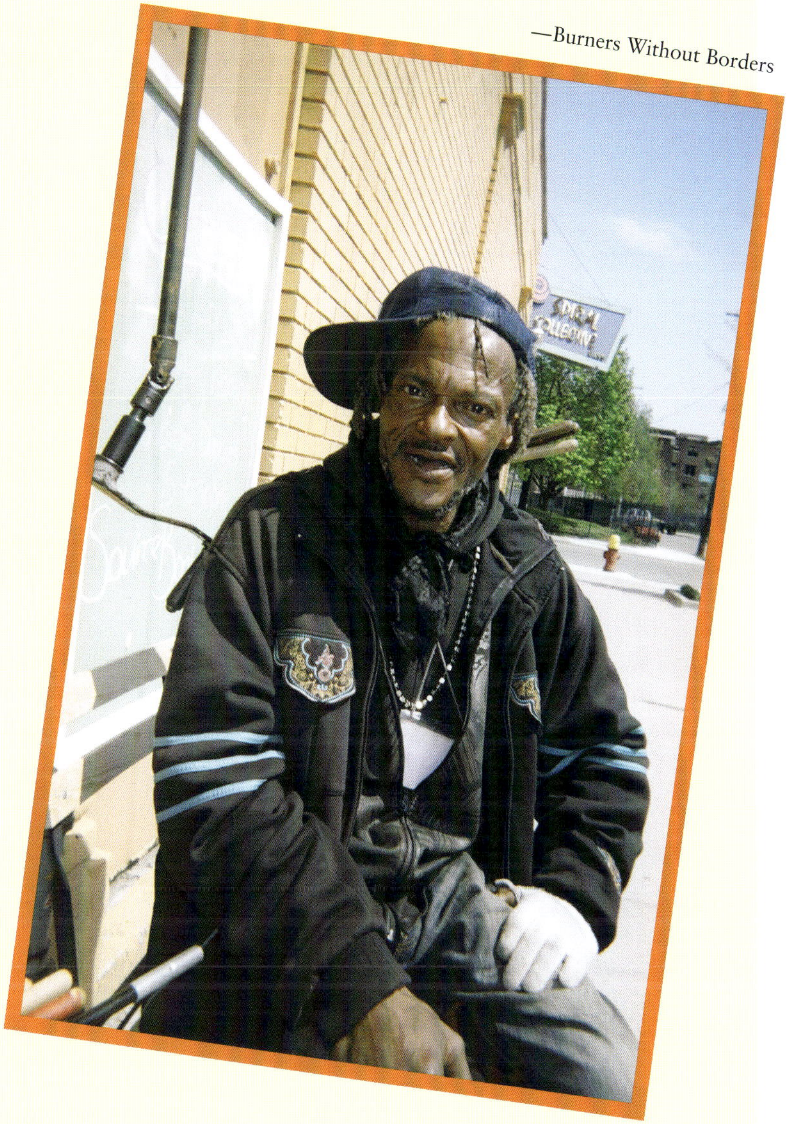

—Burners Without Borders

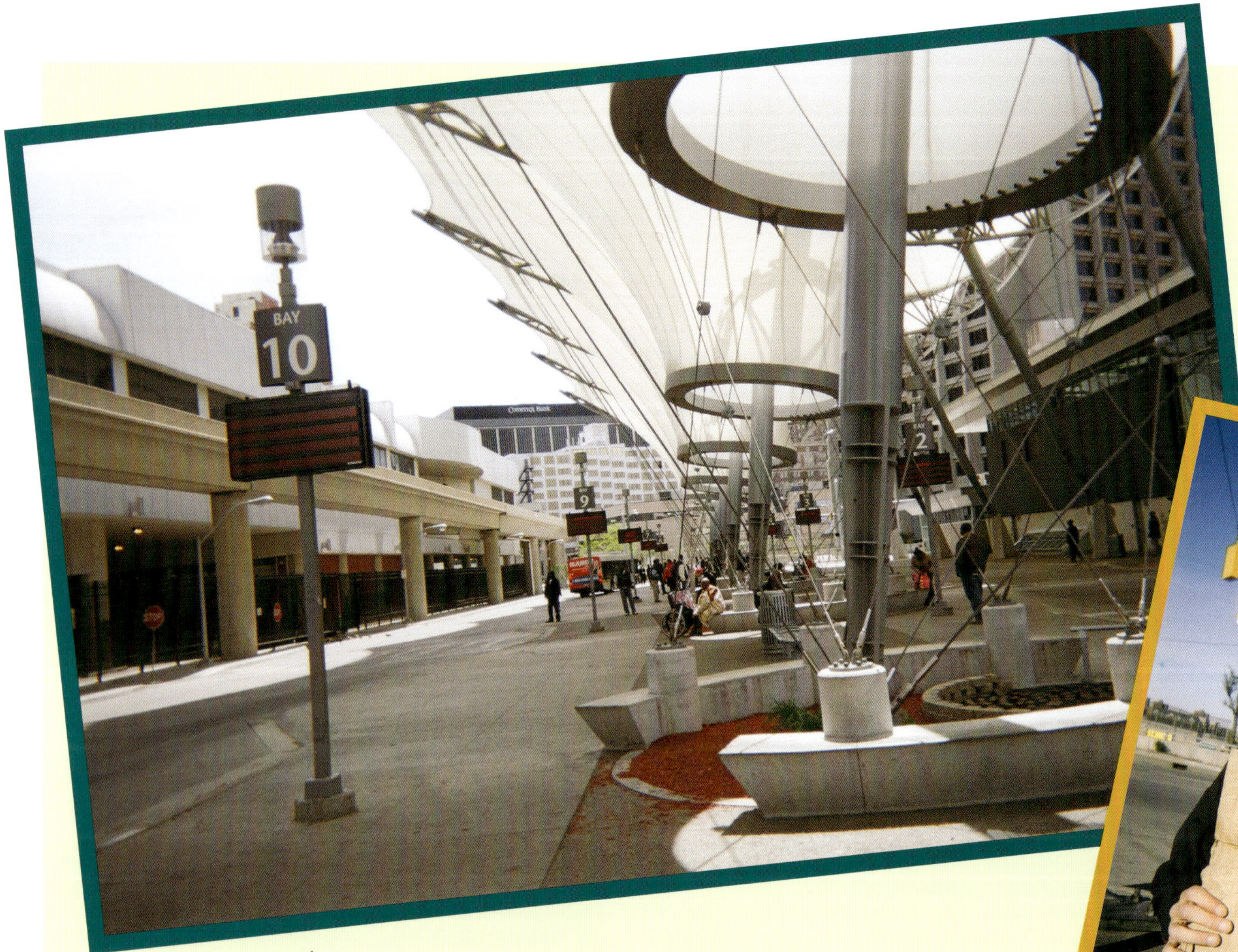

—Burners Without Borders

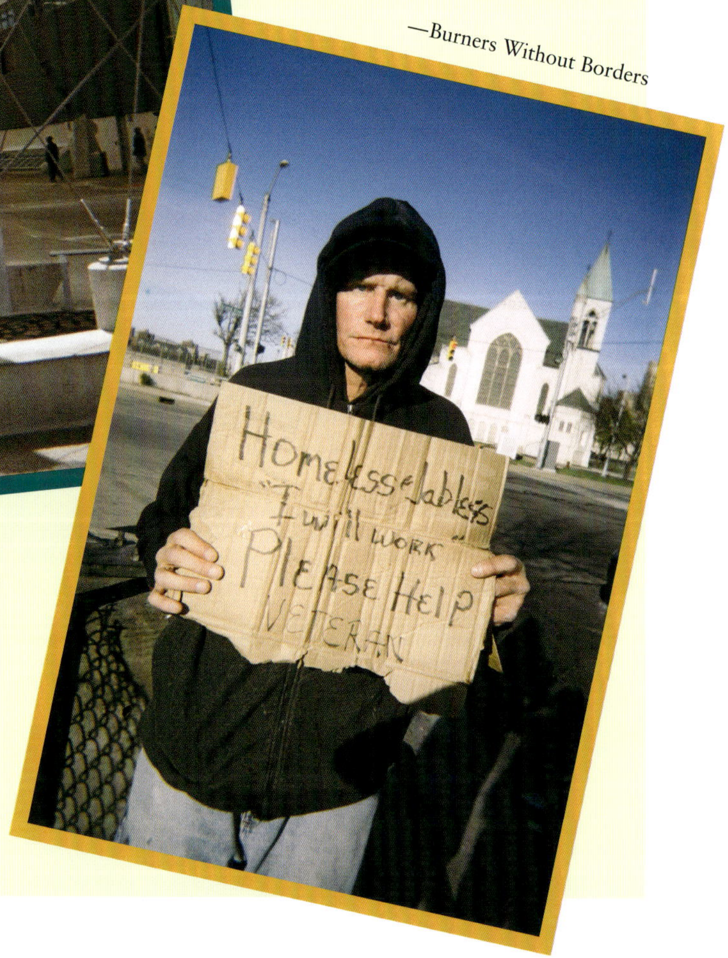

—Burners Without Borders

This was the mission of our project: if, as concerned and proactive citizens, we combine forces to volunteer, support, and assist others in need, we will succeed by building a stronger city and community by spreading hope to others.

Knowing that finding the same individual on the street twice would make retrieving the cameras very difficult, we decided to acquire envelopes, self-address them, and add postage so that each participant would be able to mail them back. We knew it might be a risky endeavor. Trusting homeless individuals to follow through was a valid concern. But we believed that the homeless would have an interest in telling their personal stories when given a chance. We had faith. Our goal was to get at least five cameras back and be happy with that.

Giving out the cameras required several rides through the streets. Many new volunteers came to help out on these trips and saw Reveal Your Detroit as a way to get personally involved with our mission.

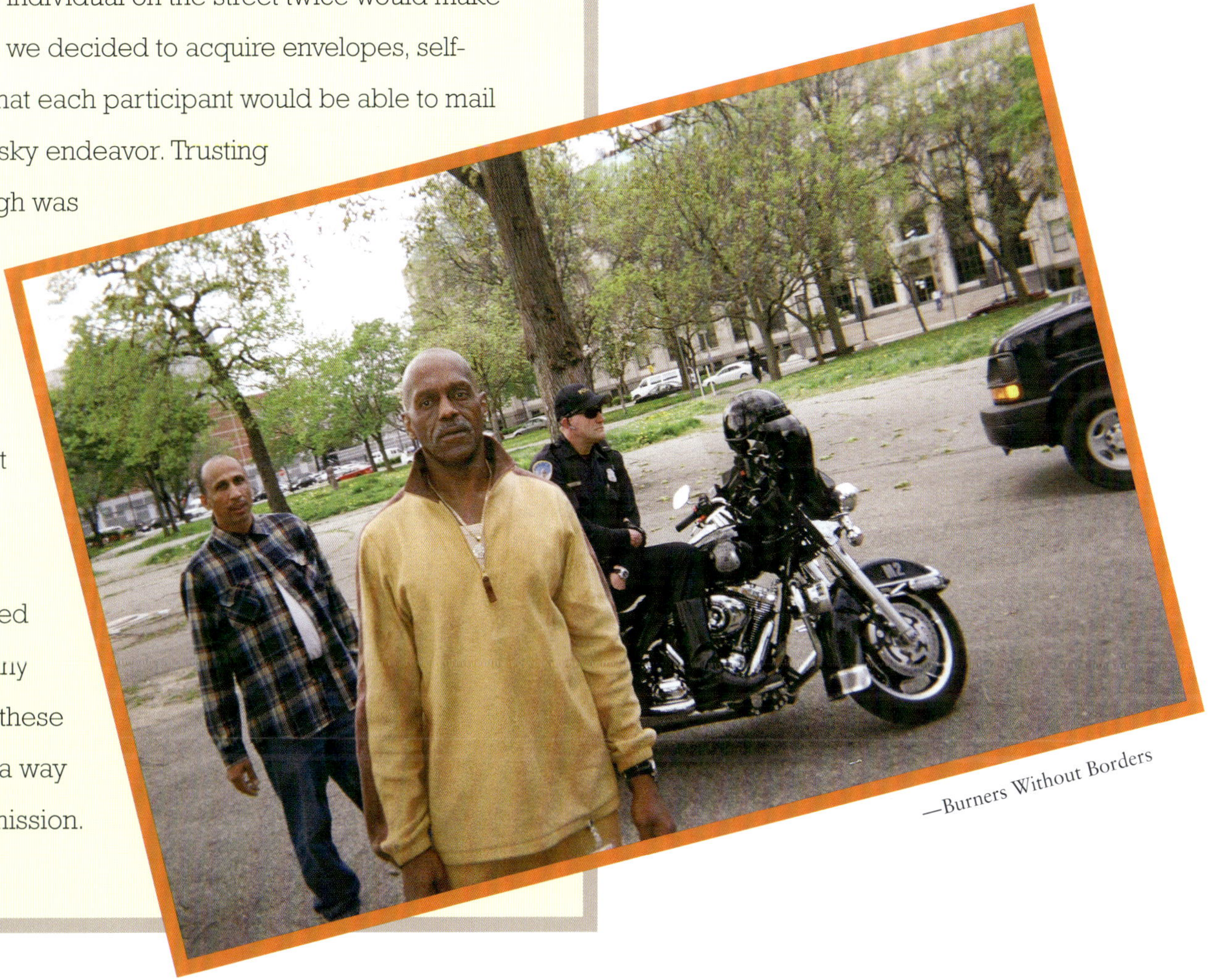

—Burners Without Borders

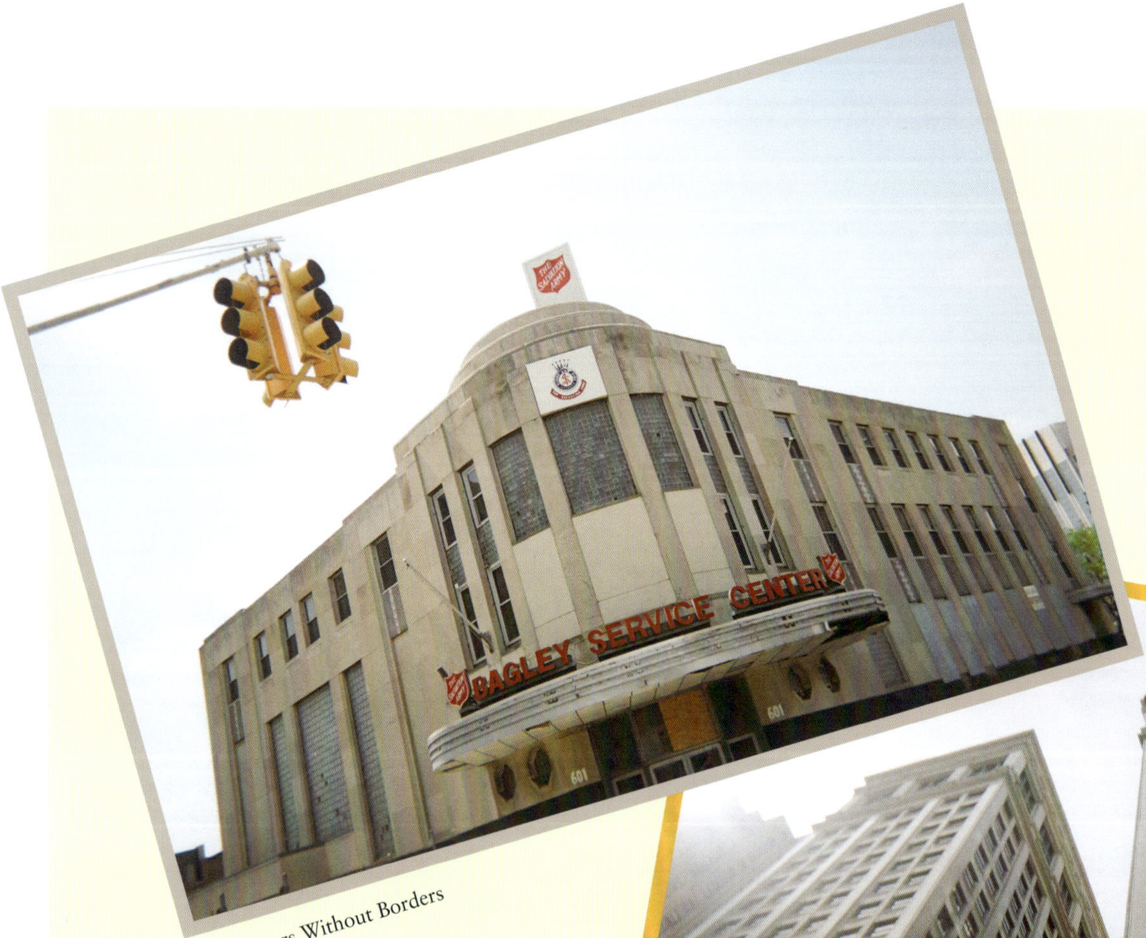

—Burners Without Borders

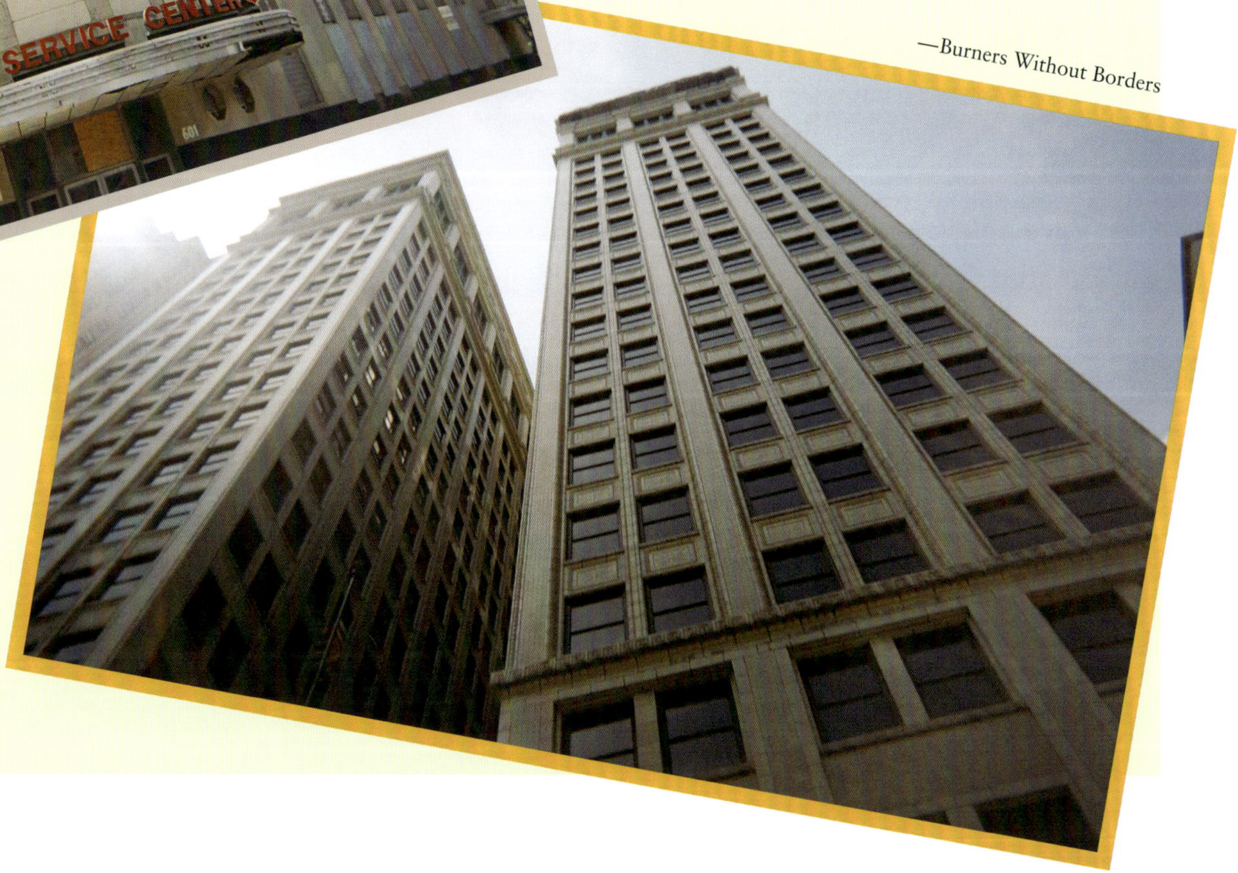

—Burners Without Borders

We also visited several soup kitchens and sent some cameras to a suburban church that works with people who have transitioned out of homelessness. Each time a camera was given to homeless individuals, we asked a few questions, such as their name, age, where they were from, and how long they had been on the streets.

Some folks had no interest in being involved, while others were shocked that we wanted to hear from them. One man told me that he would have the camera in the mail right away and that I could trust him because he was an honest man. I told him I believed him. His was one of the first cameras returned.

Each camera we received was like a Christmas present, confirming that people cared to have their voice heard by others. Of the thirty-five cameras, twenty-seven came back. Originally we were shocked by the number, but as that wore off we were left with a deep sense of honor from receiving the gifts of people who live moment to moment and day to day. Many street people took the time to collaborate, to be part of expressing their Detroit for everyone to see. We hope you enjoy the photos… but, most important, we hope you can understand the effort behind them and maybe view homelessness in our city with a little more compassion.

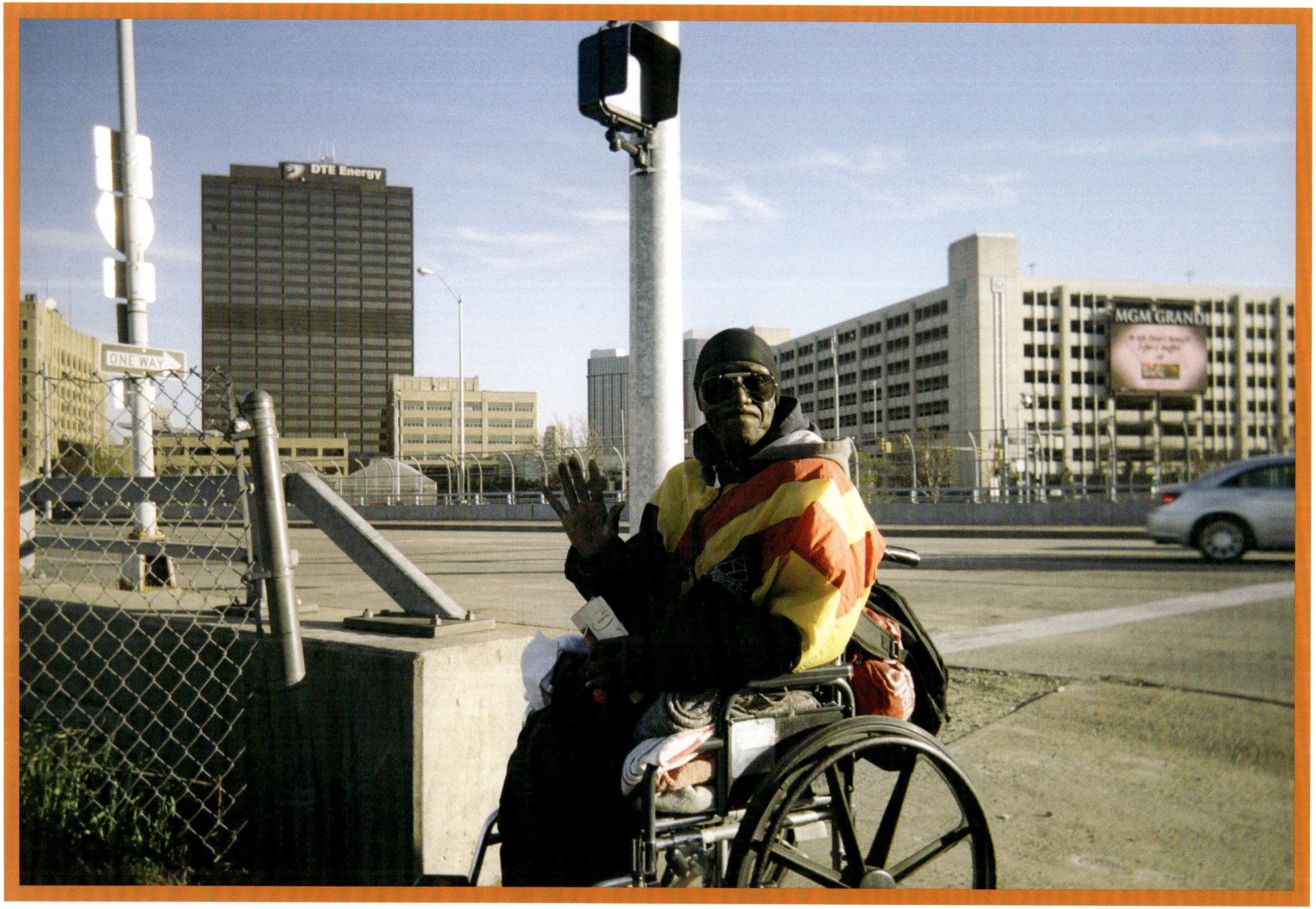

—Burners Without Borders

Doxie is a true community hustler. She is a passionate citizen, eager to make a difference in Detroit and to offer the homeless the dignity and respect we all deserve. We applaud her willingness to give the homeless a vehicle to share their perspective and their artistic voices through the Reveal Your Detroit project.

All of these profiles show how the museum's invitation to participate in a project like Reveal Your Detroit can provide a model for deep civic partnerships that connect community revitalization efforts to the arts. New momentum, energy, and dialogue can ensure that places like the DIA continue to develop the capacity for catalyzing the arts as a core revitalization tool for Detroit's long-term future. We just need to take it one step at a time.

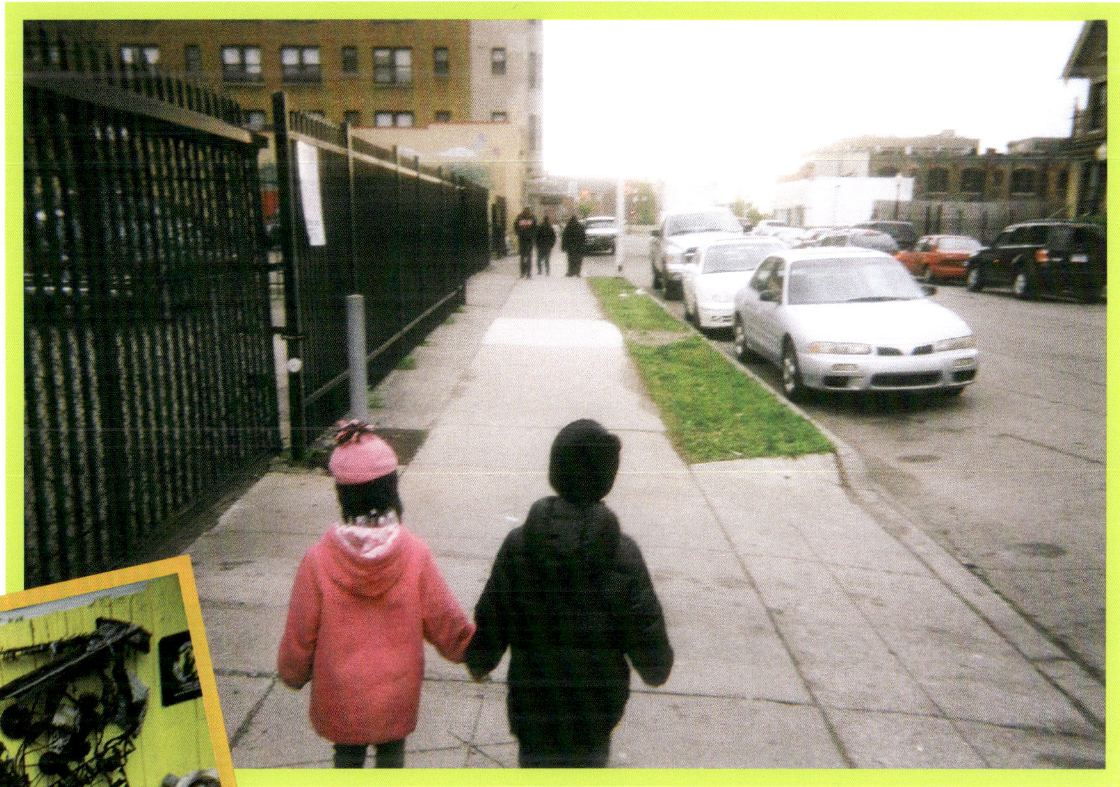

—Burners Without Borders

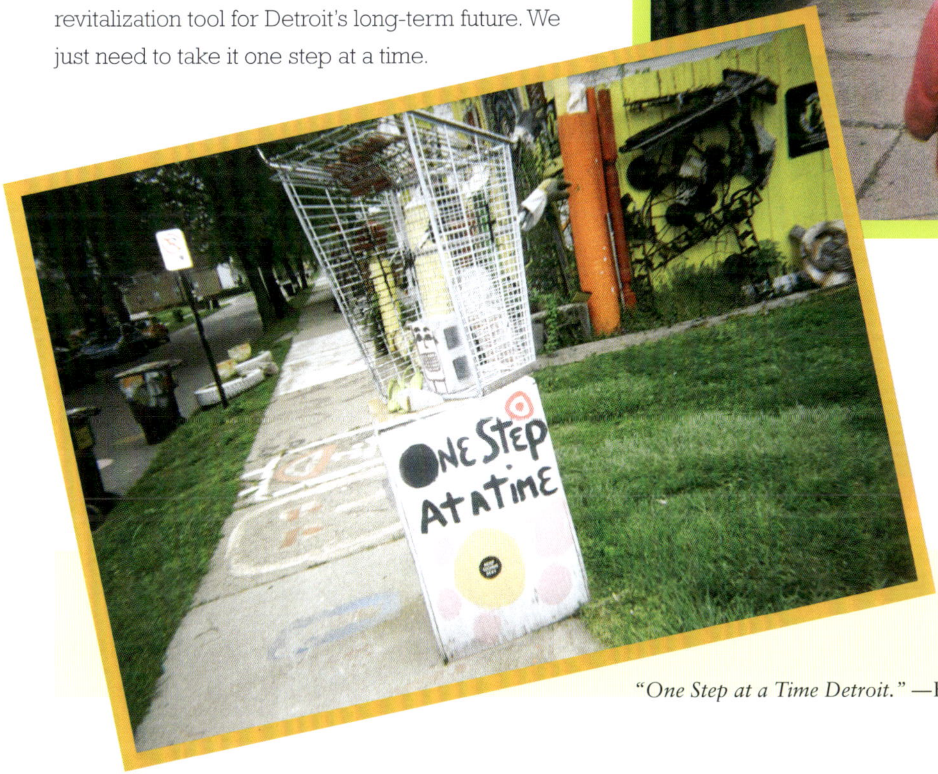

"One Step at a Time Detroit." —BE EXPOSED: DETROIT

Postscript

Reveal Your Detroit

WORDS ALLOW one conversation about Detroit. Images allow another.

It was only my second day on the job. Unclear and uncertain as to how to effectively link the DIA to local community revitalization efforts, it was then that I discovered that *Detroit Revealed: Photographs, 2000–2010* would be showing in the museum in just a few short months.

What a gift.

It was almost immediate—I designed a quick concept sketch to engage community-based organizations to offer a creative response to the *Detroit Revealed* exhibition. Over time, with DIA colleagues and the support of the Knight Foundation, we developed a community photography project to empower residents and local organizations to access the museum to execute their own engagement goals in new ways.

All told, over twelve thousand images were produced by Detroiters about the city they love. It was an unabashedly local and undeniably beautiful compilation.

I wrote the following words about Reveal Your Detroit when we started designing this project. They are as true today as they were then.

Home to countless identities, narratives, and perspectives, to claim Detroit is to claim oneself in this sea of diverse possibility.

How, then, has Detroit achieved the profound distinction as the epitome of American decay and unrelenting collapse, failure, and ruin?

Such narrative begs the question: is this the image Detroit residents carry about their city? For some, perhaps, but certainly not for most.

Detroit is a complex entity. To see Detroit through its citizens' eyes is to see Detroit's kaleidoscopic reality in powerful, even beautiful ways. Whether a city or regional resident, this truth emerges everywhere one dares to ask.

Detroit's narrative is central to our local identity. The prevailing "ruin" discourse overshadows the importance of empowering residents to own their own story. For Detroit's narrative to truly shift, we must conscientiously solicit the voice of Detroiters who are fully capable of imagining the city's next transformative era on their own.

In part, we must slow down the imagery and focus on particulars. To discern the contours of the whole, sometimes we must expose the minute details.

Words allow one conversation about Detroit. Images allow another.

Reveal Your Detroit is the DIA's chance to empower local residents by giving them artistic voice. We can learn together by what we share and reveal how we each carry this city in our mind's eye.

Together, let's give residents the chance to be the artists. Let's trust them to show us what they find beautiful about Detroit. Let's ask residents to reveal Detroit for themselves and give them a forum to display their images for all to see.

Detroit is in the eye of its beholders.

In my view, Detroit is passion personified in every person that takes part and believes in this place. Whether born here or not, this is our common bond.

My photographs? My Detroit? Very similar to that of everyone else—some intimate shots of my home and the places in this city that give my time here identity, texture, and purpose.

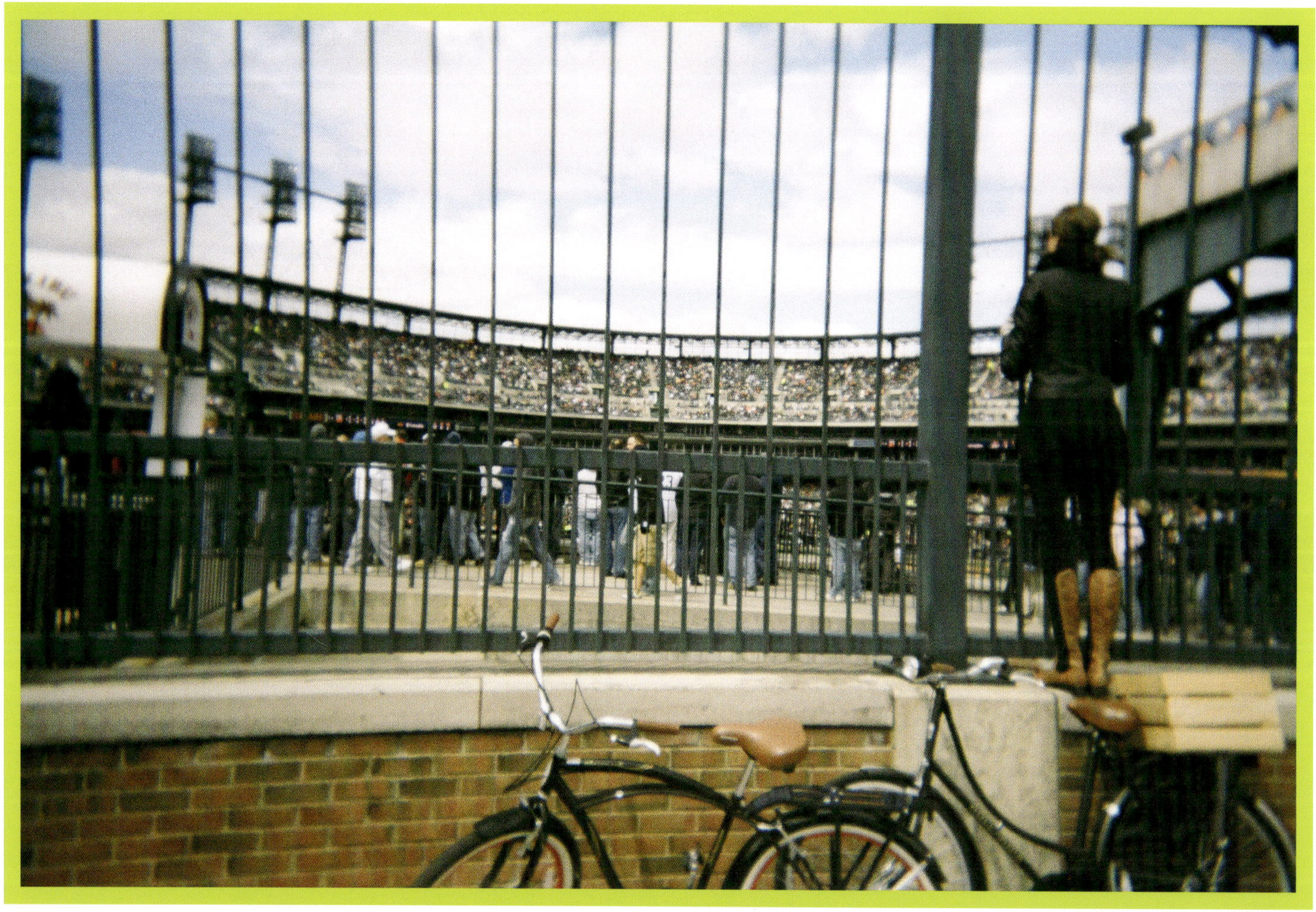

One of my first memories in Detroit was surprising the love of my life with Detroit Tigers fireworks from the right-field fence. This shot is of my wife looking on as we rode our bikes through downtown.

—Bradford Frost

This is the spot where I proposed to my wife in 2007 at the top of Midtown's Park Shelton Condominiums. It is also where we hosted what we like to call our "destination Detroit wedding" for our families—mine are from New England for the most part, and my wife's family hails from Virginia. —Bradford Frost

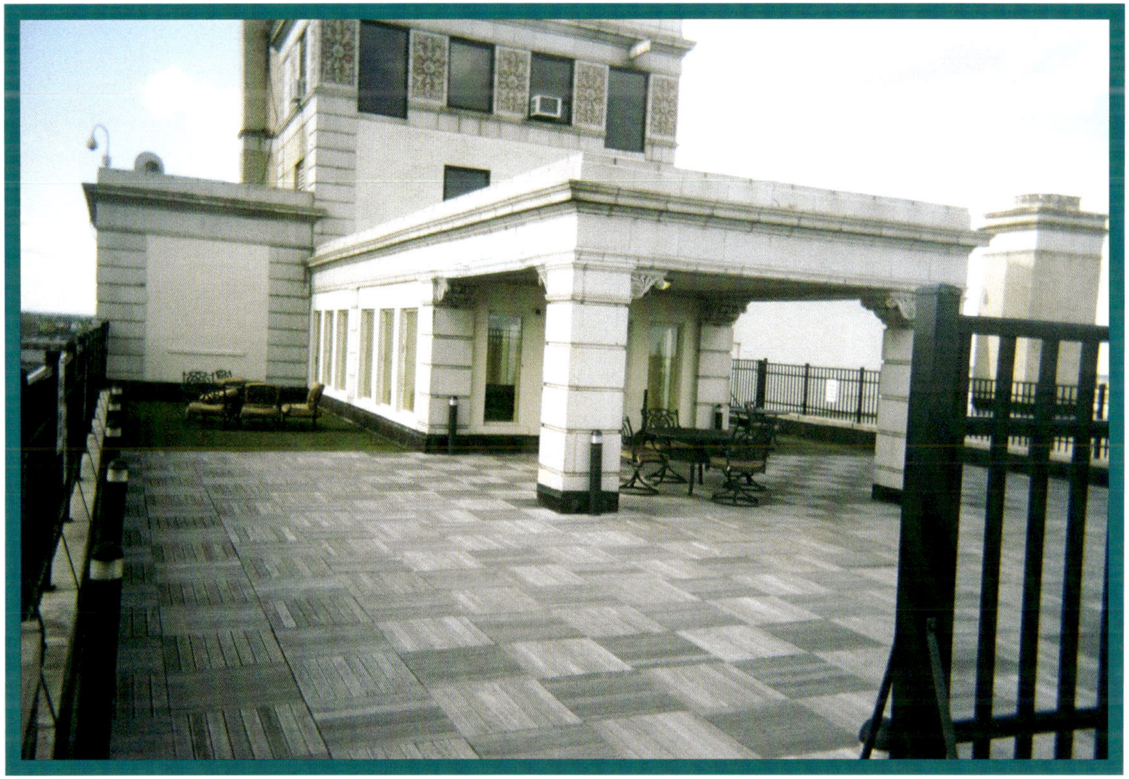

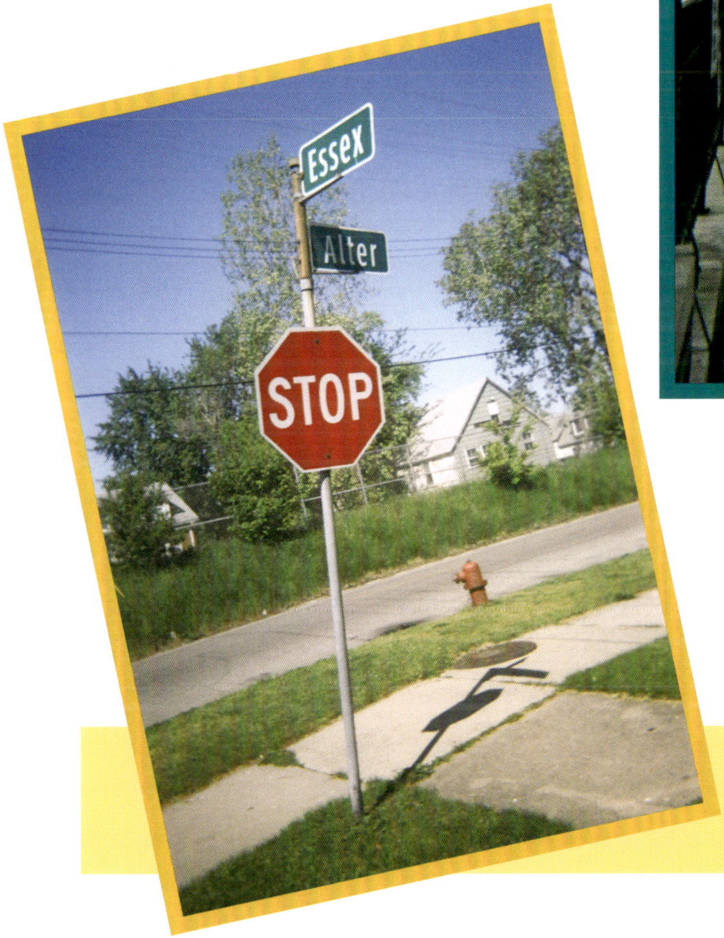

I grew up in the small town of Essex, Connecticut. When I first moved to Detroit, Alter Road took on a core symbolism for my study and work related to social justice; I even ended up writing my master's thesis on America's equal opportunity divide at Alter Road. I love taking the drive to this spot to show first-time visitors the stark contrasts across metro Detroit. Though my reasons for living in Detroit are as much about the city's enormous assets, this shot reminds me of why I first came here and why I'm passionate about the work I get to do in Detroit. —Bradford Frost

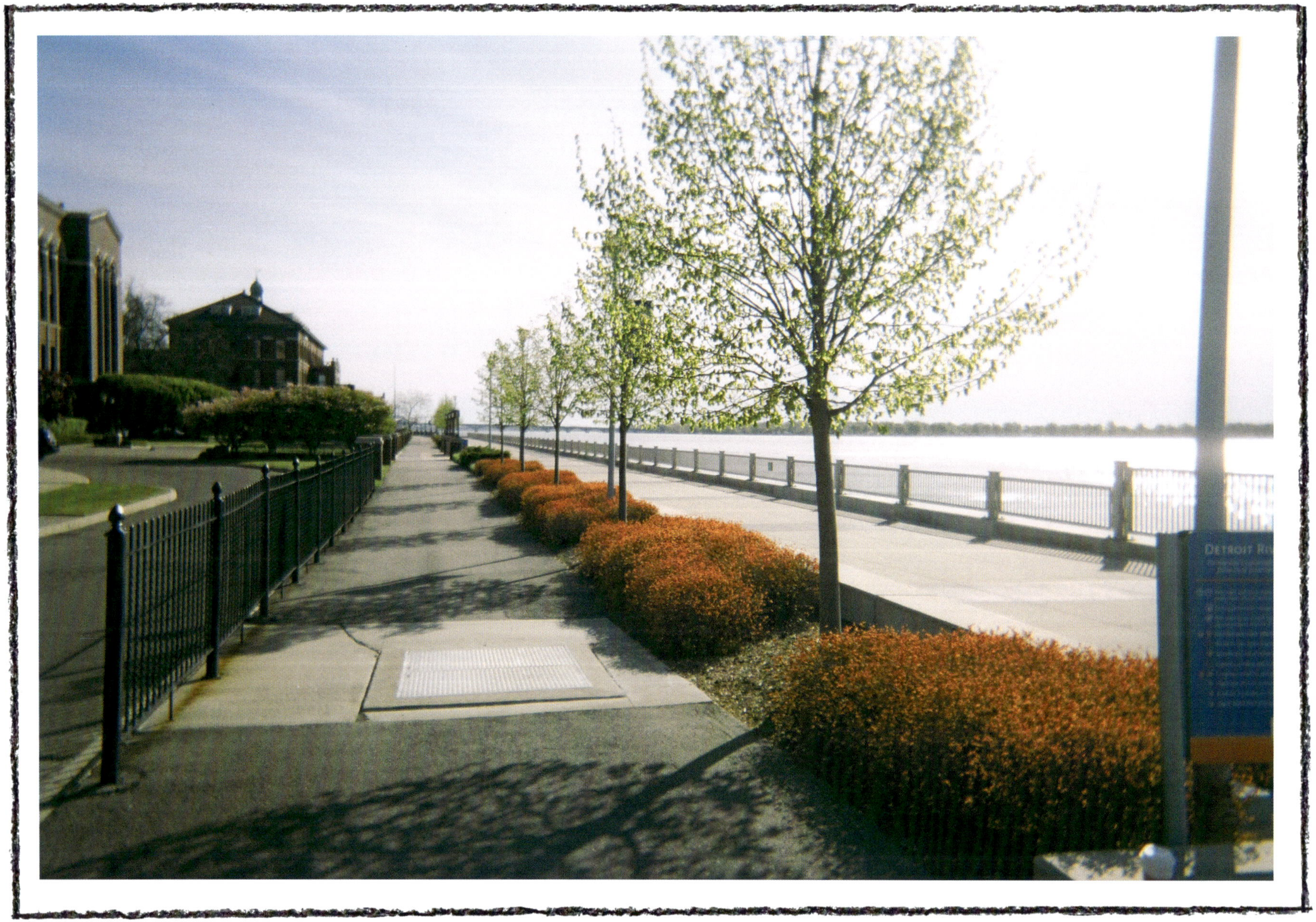

Reveal Your Detroit

These images make me feel connected to this place and truly remind me of what I love about Detroit.

Of course my pictures were far from flawless, as was true of many of the Reveal Your Detroit images. But the point was never to secure technically perfect photographs. The point was to uncover images that are meaningful because they honor the experiences of living here in Detroit. The point was always to reveal personal perspectives on our common canvas: the city.

Ultimately, how we see our city matters a great deal.

Is it a Detroit filled with challenges we can tackle? Will it be a place with possibilities for residents to fulfill their dreams, safe streets for children to play in, and vibrant neighborhoods in which to raise families in a distinct American city? Or is Detroit going to remain a place of dashed hopes and vacant chances for renewal?

For too long we've seen the Detroit that embodies the latter formulation. To look at the city and see its beauty in the nooks and crannies that these images depict is to see a dynamic Detroit tapestry. Detroit will never be all decline or all promise. But the measure of this city will largely fall on how we see it and what lens we focus on its 139-square-mile frame.

Reveal Your Detroit showed us how we all can contribute to that narrative. And it shows how regular citizens can influence the way others see this diverse landscape.

Whether you took part or not, you can still ask yourself: how would you Reveal Your Detroit?

I leave the last word to Glenn Corcoran, a photographer and civic leader with Focus: HOPE. Glenn's image reflects perfectly the idea that how we see and how we choose to frame Detroit matters tremendously.

In the end, that framing affects most how we choose to see ourselves, which will powerfully influence how others see Detroit.

With all its promise, how we see Detroit and what we do with those images will be essential to preserving the authentic city we adore, while we simultaneously strive to achieve Detroit's vital transformation.

Only by doing both can we ensure that Detroit will be a city where all of its residents' dreams can flourish for generations to come.

Opposite: *I live near the Detroit Riverwalk just east of Downtown and marvel at the promise of Detroit as it transforms before our eyes.* —Bradford Frost

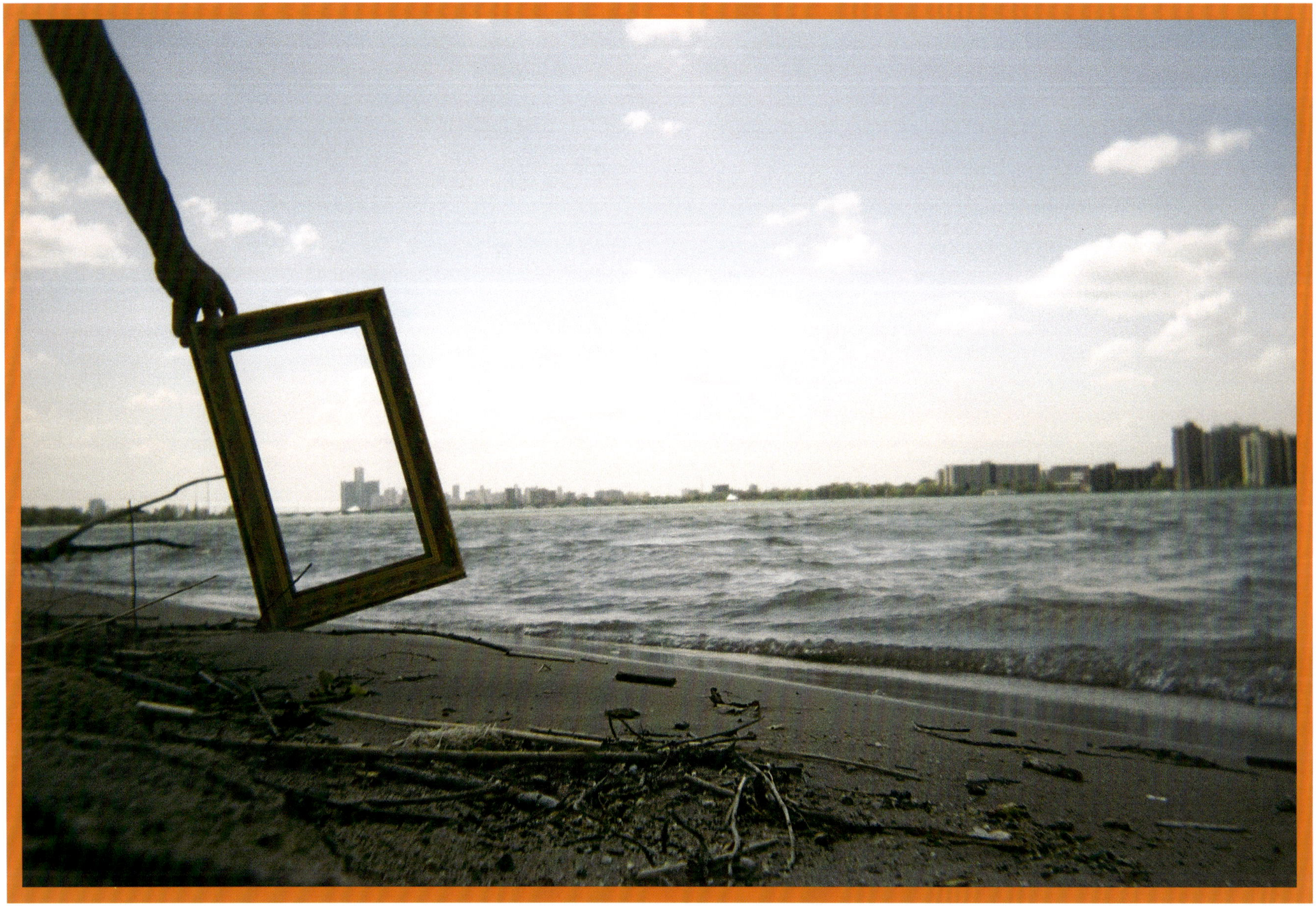

The framing of the downtown area from Belle Isle helps convey that Detroit is more than just the downtown perspective. Every national media image of Detroit shows the Detroit River and the Renaissance Center. With so much focus on downtown sometimes we forget the surrounding areas. I feel like the frame says, "Yes, it's Detroit, but there's so much more to see." As artists we have to get past the "ruin-porn" and dig deeper. I hope people will take a second and third look at Detroit.

GLENN CORCORAN

Contributors

This list captures all the names we collected of contributing photographers to the Reveal Your Detroit project. Because some groups gave cameras out after their visit without signing the participant list, it is naturally incomplete.

Apologies for any omissions or misspellings—they are unintentional.

Thanks one and all who contributed!

A. Flintoff
Aahner Washington
Abir Ali
Adrenna Richardson
Adrienne Eady
Ahmed Michael Beydan
Albert Jones
Alexis Mitchell
Alisha Opperman
Allyson McLean
Amber
Amber Sankofa
Amillon Thorpe-Mitchell
Amir McCaskie
Amir McCloud
Andre Spivey
Andrea Fleming
Andrea Perkins
Andrea Roelofs
Andree Tarrant
Andrew Webb
Angela Wilson
Ann Justice
Annette Vanover
Anred Spivey
Anthony Carmichael
Anthony Dicus
Antonio Harris
Antonio Peters
Aonor Washington
Arzane Neely
Arzenia William
Ashley Ardis
Ashley Greene
Asia Fields
Asia Mitchell
Asiana Hardwick
Aubrea Toone

Barbara Barefield
Barbara Jones
Barbara Stevenson
Beau Taylor
Betty McGraw
Bill Timmerman
Bonnie Odom-Brown
Bradford Frost
Breanna Shannon
Brenda Wesley
Briow Hunt
Brittany Moore
Briyon Hatcher
Bryce
Bryn Carter

C. J. Hynes
Caitel Woodberry
Caitlin Travis
Caleb Browner
Caleb Jackson
Camonique George
Candy Marshall

Carla Blount
Cedrick
Celeste Lane
Champagne Peterson
Chantal Simmons
Charlene Minatee
Charles Shannon
Charles Stokes
Charles Young
Cheryl Brown-Sankofa
Cheryl Moore
Chester Harris
China Zochran
Chris Ologol
Christina Ocasio
Christine Palffy
Christine Webb
Christopher H.
Claire Nelson
Clara Hardie
Claudia Meeks
Cora Whitehead
Cortez Shannon
Cortney Fletcher
Craig Peterson
Cuinn Woodberry

D. Jones
D'Aaron Hart
Dan Geoffrion
Dan Linna
Dana Frost
Dana Hart
Danielle Kaltz
Danielle Regier
Dara O'Byrne
Darius Smith
Darnell Moses
Darnell Thompson
Darryl Howard
Dave Marquardt
David Bell
David Harrison
David Legg
Davonna Jackson
Dawann Williams
Deangelo Bryant
Deangelo Johnson
DeAngelo Smith
Debbie Mclain
Deborah Kent
Deboratt LaViolette
Deialanique Readas
Deiondre Lynn
Doja Russ
Delana Pieodous
Demarius McCloud
Demetria Smith
Derick Blackmon
Derrick Bowden
Dewayne Wells
Dezmond Swanson
Diamond Mills
Dolores Braxton
Donald Waiters
Donna McDuffie
Dontai Mitchell
Dorothy Smith
Dorothy Tyler
Dorothy Yard
Douglas Brooks
Doxie Kaltz
Duane Wallace
Dway'nesha Burney

Earlander Taylor
Eddie Lee
Elizabeth Bailey
Elizabeth Garrett
Emily Doerr
Eric Anderson
Eric Canty
Erik Howard
Erin McDonald
Erma Leaphart

Fancis Nelson
Felicia Andrews
Francetta Cook
Fred Williams

Gabriel Daniels
Gabriela Santiago Romero
Gary Brister
Gary Torgenson
George Martin
Gilbert Sunghera
Gionni Crawford
Glenn
Grace Blakely
Greg Welch

Halima Cassells
Hassan Hassan
Henry Earle
Holly Clements

Ian Studders
Imani Maddox
Isaac Dilliard
Isaac Seymore

J. Johnson
Jack Sylvan
Jada Hatcher
Jaelin Chambers
Jahari Irvin
Jamar Thomas
James Allen Stephens
James Feagin
James Riggins
James Willer

Janae Hart
Janice Denson
Janice Harvey
Janice Murphy
Ja-Quan Handy
Jason Dixon
Jasonn Parnell
Jazmine Young
Jekki Johnson
Jenisis Moreland
Jennifer Shipp
Jeremy Maxwell Parish
Jessica Iwankowski
Jila Ellefson
Jillian Howard
Joan Moss
Joe Ann Williams
Joel Howrani Heeres
John
John Corcoran
John Owens
Jordan Cox
Jordan Williams
Joshua Jackson
Joshua Webb
josquice bain
Judith Barkey
Julia Ball
Julia Solis
Julian Kellman
Julie Baker
Justin Velez

Kaelin Austin
Kai Cassells
Kai Miller
Kamau Clark
Karen Moore
Karlee Derrick
Karole Balley
Katherine Biles
Kathleen Fry-Jones
Kathryn Barnett
Kathy Beltair
Kathy Marshall
Katie Craig
Kendell Spivey
Kenneth L. Wolfe
Kennis Wooten
Kenyara Bailey
Ke'Shauna Cylovet
Kevin Robinson
Kierra Irving
Kim Tandy
Kimberly Bani
Kimberly Biles
Kimberly Canty
Kimberly Etter
Kimberly Faison
Kimberly Hill
King Kold
Kofi Royal
Kyara Yarber

L. Blume
Larry Webber
Laura Breisch
Ledgra Johnson
Lee Gaddies
Leilani Jones
Lemonia DeClouette
Lettie Ann Miller
Linda Austin
Linda Bain
Linda Bowie
Linda Cassells
L'Kyia Hollie
Logan Brown
Lolita Haley
Luke William
Lytanga Yarber

Madhari Reddy
Maggie Taylor
Malik Manning
Malik Sankofa
Man W
Marcia Lee
Maresha Quirles
Margaret Weber
Maria Thomas
Mariyah Jackson
MarQuez Bell
Marshawda Roberson
Martees Smith
Marvin Nash
Mary Beth Baumeister
Mary Davis
Mary Mcleod
Mary Nelson
Matt Barkey
Matt Elliott
Matt Lewis
Matteo Passalacqua
Matthew Bode
Maya Stovall
Megan Puncy
Melissa Heil
Melissa Smiley
Mercedes Lucious
Michael Blount
Michael Forsyth
Michael Mayricio
Michele Busuito
Miguel Pope
Mindora Robinson
Minty Kelly James
Myra Lee

N. Blume
Natasha Barsukova
Neb. Neter Khnumenre

Neshea Richey
Nevin Gorden
Nicole Brown
Nicole Marem
Nick Jaskey
Noah King
Nollis Sanders
Nora Mandray
Nya Mays

Ona Moore
Ora Carter
Ora Ellis
Owiso Makuku

Parina Davis-Usher
Patricia Dockery
Patricia Johnson
Paula Harris
Peter Gillespie
Phillis Judkins
Priscilla McDonald

Quinn Omari Dickerson III
Quintez Henderson
Quintin Whitehead
Quinton Johnson

Rachel Moote
Rachel Perschetz
Raphael Hawkins
Rasheed Davis
Raymond T Chou
Raymoneley Daniels
Reggie Gaddler
Regina Ann Campbell
Reginald Spratling
Rena Bradley
Renee Kent
Renee Wallace
Rev. Barry Rudolph
Richard BeLue
Richard Ruffin
Ricotta Daniels
Rita B
Rita McKay
Rob D'Maria
Rob St. Mary
Robert
Robert Abrams
Robert Butts
Robyn Horton
Roland Leggett
Ron Hill
Ronald Cook
Ronald Mikulok
Rosey Zielke
Rosie Desantis
Rosie Sharp
Ruben Roldan

Sandra Butler
Sandra Yu
Sarah McGregor
Sarah Vang
Sarida Scott
Selena Houston
Seth Washington
Shane Bernardo
Shaun Rentie
Sherice Chambers
Sheryl Bolden
Shirley Lolles
Socomo Roldan
Spencer Olinek
Stan Mullins
Stephen Kirk
Steve Shaw
Steve Teer
Steven Bobalik
Steven Fuller
Susan Jackson
Susan Steinhauer
Suzanne Janik

Talise Yatara Reed
Tamiajoy Mitchell
Tammara Howard
Tasia Nelson
Tekeyla Byers
Texteoius Becker
Tierra Irving
Tiffany Gazic
Todd Stovall
Tom Habitz
Tom Neal
Tyler

Ulysses Newkirk

Valerie Soborek
Vassie Maxwell
Venessa Brandon
Virginia Monagne

Wakel Curtis
Wilbert Riser
Will Bowen
William
William Robinson
William Wilson
Willie Spivey
Willie Williams
Willis Talley

Yodet Mestin Johnson
Yvonne Dillaro
Yvonne Purifoy

Zalecia Conley
Zaria Wynn

Partner Organizations

Awesome News Taskforce

BE Culturally Exposed
BE EXPOSED: DETROIT
Beckham William Academy Elementary School
Burners Without Borders

Calvin East Presbyterian Church W.O.R.D. Literacy Program
Community Development Program, School of Architecture, University of Detroit Mercy
Creative Spirits

Declare Detroit
Dent Historical Society
Detroit Leisure League
Detroit Merit Academy
Detroit Mural Factory Gardens
Detroit Revitalization Fellows
Detroit Workers for Environmental Justice
Detroit Works Project Long Term Planning
Detroit Young Professionals

Fellowship Nonprofit Housing Corporation
Fender Bender
Focus: HOPE

Genesis Hope
Grandmont Rosedale Development Corporation
Grandmont 1

HERU Organization
Hostel Detroit

Imagine Detroit Together
Islandview Community

Lower Eastside Action Plan (LEAP)

Marygrove College Photography Class
McDougal Hunt Citizens District Council
Mt. Elliott Business & Community Association

North Rosedale Park Civic Association

Officers of the DIA
Our Life in the D

Pay It Forward Initiative
Ponyride Detroit
Rosedale Park Improvement Association

St. Paul AME Church

University Commons Organization
Vanguard CDC

WARM Training Center
WDET's Crossing the Lines
Westminster Kenilworth Association

Woodward Corridor Initiative

Young Nation: The Alley Project